the art of
awareness

the art of
awareness

a textbook on general semantics and epistemics

third edition

J. Samuel Bois

Wm. C. Brown Company Publishers
Dubuque, Iowa

contents

CHAPTER 15. THE HUMAN EQUIVALENT OF THE
                        COSMIC PROPULSIVE ENERGY, 248
   1. Love or Altruism as a Passion
   2. Conflict and Conflict-Fostering Practices
   3. Love as a Transforming Agent
   4. A New Human Being in the Making

Part VIII The Practice of Awareness, 269

CHAPTER 16. OUR MANY SELVES, 271
   1. Self-1, Self-2, Self-3 . . . Self-n
   2. Self-reflexiveness and Feedback
   3. Danger and Safety Indicators
   4. Further Development of Self-1, Self-2, Self-3 . . . Self-n

CHAPTER 17. PRACTICES IN SELF-DEVELOPMENT
                        AND SELF-RENEWAL, 289
   1. The Art of Listening
   2. Reading and Meditating
   3. Crisscross Reading
   4. Self-Training in Silencing Oneself
   5. From Abstraction to Abduction and Creative Innovation

Part IX Introduction to Participating, 313

CHAPTER 18. PARTICIPATING: FROM EXPERIENCES
                        TO A STAGE OF DEVELOPMENT, 315
   1. Distinction Between Stages of Experience and
      Stages of Development
   2. The Unifying Experience
   3. Some Qualifications Regarding Unifying Experiences
   4. Duality and Oneness
   5. Participating: As Experience and As Stage Five

CHAPTER 19. PRACTICES IN PARTICIPATING: COMMUNICATION
                        AS A CREATIVE EXPERIENCE, 336
   1. Communication and Empathy
   2. Three Levels of Communication
   3. From Communication-2 to Communication-3
   4. How to Communicate Effectively
   5. On Meeting Critical Situations
   6. Communion as an Art

illustrations

preface

Having studied and worked with Dr. Bois over the last twelve years, it was a great privilege for me to organize and contribute to his revision of *The Art of Awareness*. I wish to outline briefly for you the shape of the revision of the third edition and what new and useful material has been added.

One of the important tasks of revising *The Art of Awareness* was to introduce changes in terms and phrasing that are integral to the evolution of general semantics and epistemics as continually emerging processes. Changes such as these are meant to make our use of language more responsive to the needs of the emerging stages of human development. In this regard, some of the uses of static and mechanical terms and analogies of previous editions were found to be inadequate to the process under discussion. We have tried to change to a biological and human emphasis wherever this occurs. This is in keeping with the practices included in the chapter on "Mental Models."

The original construct of a human being as a semantic *reactor*, which is central to the structure of the whole book, has been changed to that of a semantic *transactor* to remove the connotation of traditional stimulus-response that might be evoked by the word "reaction" and to emphasize the participatory basis of all human exchanges.

These word changes are not arbitrary. Not only does the use of words reflect the ways in which we verbalize our experience, but it also influences the very way we relate ourselves and shape our experiences to allow the content of the worlds in which we live to manifest. In light of this, we have chosen to degenderize references to the human species and human individuals in general as much as possible. The habit of referring to "human" as "man" belongs to an obsolete past. Other changes will be called to your attention within the course of the text.

The outline of the book has been revised for a better grasp of its overall structure. The ten main section titles cover the primary subject areas, which are then discussed in various specifics. Summaries have been added at the end of each main section; the bibliography and suggested readings have been extensively updated.

Wherever possible, material of the two previous editions has been clarified or enhanced with new examples. While the revisions have been extensive, they have been integrated into the structure of the original text. These changes take into account the application of the text by thousands of users over the past ten years. This is in keeping with the original intention of creating a discipline that would remain open and fluid.

Initially, Dr. Bois stated that "this book gives information derived from the various human sciences to make possible a scientific awareness of what we live and how we function, individually, and in the world of humans at large. It also offers definite directives as to how to train oneself in a self-management which, it is hoped, makes us capable of surviving and progressing in a world undergoing a cultural mutation of worldwide proportions."

This revision adds another dimension, a further development of the *art* of awareness, as well as the science. In this direction, Dr. Bois and I created a deeper clarification of stages four and five of the Bois-Bachelard epistemological profile of the evolution of Western culture. Stage four, the stage of self-reflexive postulating, is now also called the creative process, while stage five is now called participating. In a section titled "Introduction to Participating," we relate this to the difference between unusual or "peak" experiences and to establishing new ways of human functioning.

In this same section, a major addition called "Practices in Participating" involves guidelines to creative communication. This is beyond communication as an exchange of information and involves the deeper aspects of human mutuality, cooperation, and convergence; this more appropriately is called communion as an art.

Also significant are new additions to Part VIII, "The Practice of Awareness." They include more indicators to heighten and clarify our awareness of our "inner" functioning; a further development of the construct of "our many selves"; new practices in training oneself in "silence" in order to actively participate in the greater ongoing not covered by symbols, language, and logics.

Dr. Bois also further clarifies some of the misunderstandings surrounding the field of general semantics by adding new material on epistemics. This is developed in the introduction and is titled "From General Semantics to Epistemics" and at the end of the book in a piece called "Transcending the Limitations of Non-Aristotelianism." The primary purposes of these additions are to develop a philosophical context that more fully acknowledges the notion of evolution in all human affairs and to make general semantics responsive to the needs of the current conceptual, value, and experiential revolution taking place in the twentieth century by not limiting its area of concern to communication skills and awareness of the use of language.

While *The Art of Awareness* has become a classic in the field of general semantics, it is becoming, at the same time, a forerunner of new developments. I see it as a handbook for individuals and groups who wish to take a deeper part in creating the world in which they live and in tuning their social, ecological, and life creations to the evolutionary thrust of our species. We are in a critical time when the values that underlie our institutions are visibly undergoing radical transformation. This calls for each person to be able to evaluate for themselves to a greater degree than ever before.

In this regard, I can only emphasize what Dr. Bois has already stated, that a light reading of this book is not encouraged. The reader is cautioned that many parts of this work will require more than just one reading and much meditating on what is read, as well as personal experimentation in order to receive its benefits.

Like Alfred Korzybski's *Science and Sanity*, I see *The Art of Awareness* as a landmark of its time. It certainly has been for me.

Gary David (Da'oud)

preface to the
second edition

In the introduction to the first edition I wrote: "Advances are made that run parallel to general semantics, or that go beyond its early formulations, and the discipline itself may become submerged in a flood of more daring initiatives."

Seven years have passed since this was written, and, if we take into account the constant acceleration of cultural changes, we may wonder if the time has not already come for something more than a mere reedition of this textbook. When we see the rash of best-sellers that broadcast the counter-culture, the greening of America, and the future shock, we should expect any time now, should we put aside the original views of Korzybski and their developments contained in the first edition of this textbook, or should we keep most of it as the necessary foundation of a solid structure in which the present sciences of man can establish their headquarters for a few generations?

I feel that this second alternative is the most practical. Of all the literature I have read in recent years, either in book form or in learned periodicals, none has dealt to my satisfaction with the inner workings of the new episteme-in-becoming, with the new general system of knowing-feeling-behaving that makes us view ourselves and our world in a perspective so far unforeseen.

Many writers are vivid in their descriptions of what is happening; many are eloquent in their announcement of what might happen. But I am still looking for a down-to-earth *how-to-do-it* text that tells the young generation how to enter the ranks of the parade of mankind on the march and become the relay team that will be capable of carrying on. Their own fate is at stake. They may think they have, as the saying goes, "discovered America," greening or drying up. They did not. Many individuals of previous generations, some well-known philosophers like Bergson and Whitehead, some statesmen like Jan Smuts, some scientific thinkers like Korzybski and Arthur F. Bentley, and a host of common folk have been aware of what was going on and what was likely to happen. Some of us are still here, very much alive, witnessing a young crowd that is just waking up, has a tendency to be dramatic about everything, and shows signs of getting emotionally involved. It might be good for them to know that some of us, way back when they were not yet born, had the same aspirations they now feel within their breasts. We had time to live with these puzzlements for many years, and we tried various formulations, some of which have proved helpful in our personal life and in our professional work. And that is the subject of this book.

The feedback I have received from the users of the book is most gratifying. This text withstands more than a casual reading or a quick cramming for an examination. Some have used it a second time for advanced studies, and they felt they had not exhausted the meaning buried in its depths. The reading references provided a well-orchestrated accompaniment to the main themes.

We have discovered, however, that both the instructors who teach from the book and the students who learn from it encounter difficulties that are traceable to their lack of familiarity with the overall sweep of our cultural history. It is not sufficient for them to know geographical and political history about kings, governments, wars, battles, and treaties of peace. They should have within reach and consult repeatedly such books as *An Intellectual and Cultural History of the Western World* by Harry Elmer Barnes, (Dover edition in three volumes, 1965), or the profusely illustrated *Great Ages of Man*, "A History of the World's Cultures," by the Editors of Time-Life Books, including at least four volumes of the *Nature Library* published by the same Time-Life Books: *Evolution, The Primates, Ecology,* and *Early Man.* For those who want more than that, the *History of Civilization*, of Will and Ariel Durant, in ten volumes, covers what it says it does, and with considerable erudition, until the time of the French Revolution.

Of the additions that make this second edition different from the first, two deserve special mention. One is inserted in Chapter 8, "The World in Which We Live"; it reproduces an article published in *Main Currents in Modern Thought*, (1970) under the title "Mankind as a Cosmic Phenomenon." The editor of *Main Currents* had summed it up in a subtitle: "Human solidarity is an evolutionary emergent to be discovered, experienced, taught."[1] An attempt is made to make of this discovery an enrichment of the picture we already have of the full space-time process of cosmic evolution.

The second addition of importance is in the last chapter entitled "A Growing and Expanding System." A new subtitle reads, "Epistemics, A Time-binding Emergent from General Semantics." In the June 1971 issue of ETC, the international review of General Semantics, which celebrated the fiftieth anniversary of the original publication of Korzybski's first book, *Manhood of Humanity,* in which he introduced his formulation of time-binding, the new science of up-to-date epistemology, often mentioned in the first edition of *The Art of Awareness*, was at last detached from the main stem of the Korzybskian system and presented as the new discipline of Epistemics. This new venture does not contradict any thesis proffered by Korzybski. Quite the contrary—it does away with the confusion so often experienced by people who see *general* semantics as a simple outgrowth of *plain* semantics, or as the art of effective communication. Now they can see as an original methodology that takes into account, not only linguistics, meta-linguistics, advanced theories of communication and their applications, but many other sciences of man, from paleontology to semantic ecology.

The *Art of Awareness* has given birth to many teaching programs that are distinct variations from the original. At the University of Southern California, Dr. William J. Williams has applied it to various aspects of public administrative theory and practice and authored a book entitled *General Semantics and The Social Sciences* (Philosophical Library, 1971) that broadens its scope to all the sciences of man. At the Western States College of Engineering, Inglewood, California, Professor David Muskat introduced a course that competes with the rigor of mathematical logic. At Queen's University, Kingston, Ontario, a teaching text, explicitly derived from the present volume and replete with practical exercises, was prepared by Donald Patrick of Montreal and is used for a course sponsored by the Institute of Canadian Bankers.

This second edition has the same objective as the first; it gives, against the background of our cultural history, an explanation of the changes we are going through and a set of directives as to how to make the most of the opportunities offered by these changes.

J. S. B.

---

[1]Reproduced by permission of *Main Currents*, which is gratefully acknowledged.

preface to the
first edition

The cultural movement called general semantics (GS) can be traced to the 1933 publication of a huge and abstruse volume, *Science and Sanity*, by Alfred Korzybski.[1] From this book, as from an overflowing spring, much writing originated that constitutes a definite class of self-help literature. It deals with the application of Korzybski's insights and formulations to various fields of human activity: word usage and communication (as in the works of the well-known authors, S. I. Hayakawa, Irving Lee, and Stuart Chase), psychological counseling (Wendell Johnson and Harry Weinberg), education (Catherine Minteer, and Weiss and Hoover), architecture and design (Newton), management skills (McCay), and even Wall Street operations (McGee).

While these and other authors were stressing the *practical* aspects of the new methodology, the mainstream of epistemological thought continued to flow and spread in a literature that concerned itself with the *theoretical* aspects of the change in ways of thinking that had been forced upon us by scientific advances and shifts in values. Most of the authors in this second area ignored general semantics, others criticized and ridiculed it without having studied it thoroughly, and only a few acknowledged its significance as one of the symptoms of our current cultural metamorphosis.

There is now, however, an abundant literature in this area, starting with Bergson, Blondel, Whitehead, and others. Recent authors include Percy W.

[1]Published by the International Non-Aristotelian Library Publishing Co. and distributed by the Institute of General Semantics (Lakeville, Conn.); 1st ed. 1933, 4th ed. 1958.

Bridgman, Karl Popper, Michael Polanyi, Ludwig von Bertalanffy, Gaston Bachelard, Louis Rougier, Floyd Allport, Gardner Murphy, Anatol Rapoport, Arthur F. Bentley, John Dewey, J. Z. Young, Benjamin Whorf, Harold Rugg, Laura Thompson, Oliver Reiser, among many. Most of these have written for their colleagues in the academic world about technical matters using technical terms not yet current in everyday speech. They have assumed the reader has a good background of information in contemporary sciences.

The present book belongs to neither the practical nor the theoretical group; it has something in common with both. It belongs to the general semantics family of publications, although it is not mainly concerned with practical applications; it deals with epistemological problems, although it is not directed to a sophisticated audience of scientists and philosophers. It treats the Korzybskian system as a system, by and for itself. It examines it as a system in evolution that was started by Korzybski one generation ago in the cultural climate of the time and that continues to develop today under fast-changing conditions.

I do not equate general semantics with other proposed theories and systems nor do I see it merely as a new science or technology, such as cybernetics. I postulate it as a *system* that, if properly developed, could assume in the future the role that Aristotelian epistemology and logic have played for centuries in the Western world.

Many thinkers recognize that a new set of general principles is necessary if we want to coordinate and utilize the findings of the new sciences of man.

> How are these insights to be brought together and synthesized? This is a task which I cannot claim to have performed here, but I have examined the problem long enough to believe that it cannot be done without some set of broad and informing principles such as is to be found in the general semantics of Alfred Korzybski.[2]

I agree with Professor Hayakawa, and I go one step further. I agree that such a synthesis cannot be achieved without some set of broad and informing principles, as are found in general semantics; but I also claim that the insights and formulations of Korzybski—if consistently developed in the self-correcting manner his system requires—are sufficient to bring about the desired synthesis. They form a matrix in which every advance in the sciences of man can find its place for many generations.

The present volume is the outcome of twenty years of experience in teaching general semantics, from the days when I was a visiting instructor at seminars conducted by Korzybski in 1947, 1948, and 1949. After his sudden death in March, 1950, I was the main lecturer at the first regular summer

---

[2]S. I. Hayakawa, *Language in Thought and Action*, rev. ed. (New York: Harcourt, Brace & World, 1964), p. x.

seminar held without him—at Great Barrington, Massachusetts. Later, I conducted advanced seminars at the Institute which Korzybski had founded, and, as a management consultant, I developed a course of training for business executives that was based on his methodology. For the last seven years I have been conducting adult-education workshops in general semantics in Beverly Hills, California. Three years ago we founded Viewpoints Institute, Inc., "a center for the study, practice, and development of general semantics," where workshops at the introductory, intermediate, and advanced levels are conducted throughout the academic year.

In 1961 I gave thirty half-hour talks on two radio stations owned by Pacifica Foundation: KPFK in Los Angeles and KPFA in San Francisco. The transcripts of these talks have been used as a text for the workshops conducted at Viewpoints and for the credit courses given for University Extension on three campuses of the University of California, at Los Angeles, San Diego, and Riverside. This book is a revision of these transcripts after four years of use with some fifteen hundred students, whose reactions and suggestions have been taken into account.

The book is intended for undergraduate and graduate courses in any discipline dealing with human behavior, such as psychology, sociology, anthropology, philosophy, education, political science, communications, literature. It also will serve a useful purpose in general background information required of students in such professional schools as medicine, architecture, engineering, education, business administration, and the ministry. It already has proved its value in courses, seminars, workshops, and discussion groups organized by local chapters of the International Society for General Semantics and by organizations that are devoted to adult education.

J. S. B.

acknowledgments

I would like to gratefully acknowledge the collaborative efforts of Dr. Gary David and Annie Muller who helped me in revising this edition of *The Art of Awareness*. It is gratifying for me to have two of my former students, teachers of general semantics and epistemics in their own right, contribute to this work.

Dr. David brought the whole manuscript together. He organized and integrated my revisions and additions into a new order, as well as contributed significant new material, especially in the sections titled "The Practice of Awareness" and "Introduction to Participating."

Mrs. Muller contributed many helpful suggestions, as well as unflagging support and assistance, as we worked together on the first draft of the manuscript.

For editorial assistance, I am indebted to Natalie Gould of Wm. C. Brown Company Publishers; her skill and experience were extremely helpful. I take this opportunity to give credit to the Wm. C. Brown Company as a forward looking publisher of academic works.

Special thanks to Verlin Heuton for important research and our conversations together. To Ethel Longstreet, my cofounder of Viewpoints Institute, who has helped me in developing this work over the years, my deepest appreciation. I would also like to acknowledge a grant from Viewpoints Institute, which made it possible for Dr. David to assist me in preparing this third edition.

J. S. B.

introduction

Epistemology Past and Present

The Art of Awareness describes a methodology or an operational discipline that relates to a practice inaugurated implicitly in the first periods of our cultural history. Socrates, Pythagoras, Aristotle, and other Greek philosophers would be described today as scientists and epistemologists. As scientists, they were concerned with the content of human knowledge, which developed into the various sciences of today. As epistemologists, they were concerned with the tools and the methods they used to discover the world that surrounded them and devising a technology of how to manage themselves and their activities in that world. Aristotle, as the creator of logic, was working in his role as an epistemologist. Busy with developing an awareness of what he was doing in his scientific work and how to improve his doing it, he devised the rules of sylogistic deductive thinking.

In the following generations, a series of people have continued Aristotle's work. To mention only a few, we may cite Descartes with his *Discours de la Methode,* Kant with his various *Critiques* and transcendental philosophy, John Stuart Mill with his work on the inductive process, Percy W. Bridgeman with his *Logic of Scientific Discovery,* and a host of others. One writer deserves a special mention in this list. He is William Frederick Ferrier, the Scottish philosopher, who, within a year or so of the *Origin of Species* by Darwin, came out with the newly coined term *epistemology,* then taken as the *Theory of Knowledge.* It was still described in this manner in the

1975 edition of *Britannica*. We thus come to Alfred Korzybski, the man who greatly influenced me as the author of this book. Korzybski was greatly helped and encouraged by two well-known scientists Cassius Jackson Keyser, mathematician and philosopher from Columbia University, and Arthur F. Bentley, political scientist and epistemologist.

Alfred Korzybski and General Semantics

General semantics dates back to 1921, when it was called Human Engineering, and its initiator, Alfred Korzybski, was a Polish veteran of the First World War. After the collapse of Russia, Korzybski served in various military capacities in Canada and the United States and eventually became a U.S. citizen; he died in 1950 at the age of seventy. His professional training had been in mathematics and engineering, and he felt that the time had come to apply to human affairs methods of thinking that were comparable to those that had made possible our spectacular advances in technology. Hence the term *Human* Engineering.

At the time, he was practically unknown to the American academic world. He had never published anything—in his native tongue or in the several languages that he knew well—but he felt a strong compulsion to broadcast an urgent message to the world, and he wrote the book he titled *Manhood of Humanity* (Dutton, 1921). For him, the First World War, which he described as a "wanton waste of life," marked the end of the childhood of humanity.

> This childhood, as any childhood, *has been characterized as devoid of any understanding of values*. It has been unduly long, but happily we are near the end of it, for humanity, shaken by this war, is coming to its senses and must soon enter manhood, a period of great achievements and rewards in the new and real sense of values dawning upon us.[1]

This new sense of values was to be developed by a more rigorous study of the laws of nature as they apply to human beings.

> I hope to show that, by mathematical philosophy, by rigorously scientific thinking, we can arrive at the true conception of what a human being really is, and, in thus discovering the characteristic nature of man, *we come to the secret and source of ethics*.[2]

As these statements indicate, Korzybski was not mainly concerned with words and their usage (as many people assume, because the term *semantics* is attached to his enterprise); he was concerned with values and human welfare. "It is the aim of this little book," he said, "to point the way to a new

---

[1]Korzybski, *Manhood of Humanity*, 2d ed. (Lakeville, Conn.: Non-Aristotelian Library Publishing Co. [distributed by the Institute of General Semantics], 1950), p. 27 (italics added).

[2]Korzybski, *Manhood of Humanity*, p. 17 (italics added).

science and art...of *directing the energies and capacities of human beings to the advancement of human weal.*"[3] His purpose was the development of scientific ethics as a technology of human welfare.

Defining man as a *time-binding* class of life, he used a mathematical analogy to differentiate plants as *chemistry-binders* (first dimension of life), animals as *space-binders* (second dimension of life), and men as *time-binders* (third dimension of life). By time-binding he meant "the capacity to summarize, digest, and appropriate the labors and experiences of the past...the capacity in virture of which man is at once the inheritor of bygone ages and the trustee of posterity."[4]

Manhood of Humanity went through four printings within two years, but this was not an earth-shaking event. Cassius Jackson Keyser, hailed it as "worthy of the serious attention of every serious student, whatever his field of study," but few persons gave it the attention it deserved. It almost became one of those esoteric books that reaches a limited public and is soon left forgotten on the shelf of some specialized section of a few libraries.

Korzybski was not the kind of man who would let his views be buried in the dust of library shelves. "He had faith in his message, and cherished the hope that he could stir the scientific world by his projects....He began to contact scores, if not hundreds, of well-known authors and scientists...and attracted many brilliant men to his ideas."[5]

In 1933, Korzybski published a second book, a huge volume, which was to become the sourcebook for many publications, seminars, and lectures on what is now called general semantics. He saw this second book as a continuation of his previous work.

> In the present volume I undertake the investigation of the mechanism of time-binding. The result of this inquiry turned out to be a non-Aristotelian system, the first to be formulated, as far as I know, and the first to express the very scientific tendency of our epoch.[6]

In the concluding remarks of this second book, we again see his concern for human welfare and for scientific ethics as the leading theme. There he lists, in a long column, the possible results of the non-Aristotelian epis-

[3]Korzybski, *Manhood of Humanity*, p. 1 (italics added).
[4]Korzybski, *Manhood of Humanity*, p. 59.
[5]A. A. Roback, *History of American Psychology* (New York: Library Publishers, 1952), p. 348.
[6]Korzybski, *Science and Sanity*, p. 555. This book has had four editions so far (1933, 1941, 1948, 1958), all published by the International Non-Aristotelian Library Publishing Company and distributed by the Institute of General Semantics, Lakeville, Connecticut. The page numbers of the body of the work are the same in all editions; the page numbers of the various prefaces, in Roman numerals, vary cumulatively from the first to the fourth edition. Permission to use quotations and illustrations from *Science and Sanity* and *Manhood of Humanity* was granted by the Korzybski estate, and is gratefully acknowledged.

temology, which he advocates, and, in a contrasting column, the tragic results of the Aristotelian standards of evaluation that dominate most of our
culture.[7]

By the title, *Science and Sanity,* Korzybski meant "the scientific
methods of 1933 as means of achieving sanity." He had to have the book
printed at his own expense, and the sale of it took years to acquire momentum, but it is now recognized as an epoch-making classic. In 1964, at the
occasion of its fortieth anniversary, *Saturday Review* asked twenty-seven his-
torians, economists, political analysts, educators, social scientists, and
philosophers to list "what books published in the last four decades most
significantly altered the direction of our society and may have a substantial
impact on public thought and action in the years ahead."[8] Of the 163 titles
mentioned, only twenty-four were rated higher than *Science and Sanity.*

In 1938, Korzybski founded the Institute of General Semantics. On the
letterhead, he stated that the purposes of the institute were "linguistic epis-
temologic scientific research and education," and he listed the names of
thirty scientists and professionals who had agreed to be honorary trustees.
This institute, still in existence in Lakeville, Connecticut, sponsors seminars
twice a year and publishes a yearbook that is distributed to the several
hundred members who support it with their contributions. In 1952, the institute organized a yearly Korzybski Memorial Lecture, which is held in
New York, where such well-known people as F. S. C. Northrop of Yale,
F. R. Roethlisberger and the late Clyde Kluckhohn of Harvard, Ashley
Montagu, the late Abraham Maslow, James Van Allen, Warren S. McCul-
lough, Henri Laborit, and others have paid homage to Alfred Korzybski.

In 1942, a group of general semanticists founded the International Society for General Semantics and in 1943 began the publication of a quarterly
called *ETC.: A Review of General Semantics* (Korzybski contributed many
papers to the early issues of *ETC.*). The articles published in the review are
not only from writers who profess to be general semanticists, or who acknowledge a specific indebtedness to Korzybski's influence; they include
contributions from people working in diverse fields of scientific, literary, or
artistic endeavor who are concerned with the cultural revolution of our time.
ETC. penetrates beyond the Iron Curtain, and its circulation of 7,500 copies
is one of the largest for magazines of that type.

When Korzybski died suddenly, in 1950, he had, according to Roback,

> . . .become an institution in himself. His successful teaching is attested by the
> fact that, all told, he had at his various seminars some two thousand mature and,
> in many instances, trained people from all parts of the country. He lived to
> preside at three congresses of general semantics, and if all he had accomplished

---

[7]Korzybski, *Science and Sanity,* p. 555.
[8]*Saturday Review,* 29 August 1964.

were only to stimulate the writing of several hundred papers on a large variety of topics, such as medicine, law, chemistry, politics, speech therapy, education, the use of words, marital conflicts, social work, all in relation to general semantics, . . .he would have merited a place in the history of psychology.[9]

Except for some rare articles in special publications, there are very few critical studies of Korzybski's views in the light of the developments that have taken place in the philosophy of science since the publication of the first edition of *Science and Sanity* forty-odd years ago. Advances are made that run parallel to general semantics, or that go beyond its early formulations, and the discipline itself may become submerged in a flood of more daring initiatives. And yet it is evident to whoever has studied it in depth that it is still the most comprehensive system available. It is like a matrix in which one can insert, in a logical order, the innovations in thinking and the findings of research that are coming to us from all directions. It is in keeping with the "new way of thinking" advocated by Albert Einstein, with the "conceptual revolution" of which Percy W. Bridgman spoke in his last book, *The Way Things Are,* and with the current search for a new look at what Teilhard de Chardin called *The Phenomenon of Man.*

Some critical readers are shocked by sweeping statements that appear here and there in *Science and Sanity,* and a few scientists and philosophers are not ready to accept Korzybski's claim that he was introducing, as he put it, a "new empirical science of man." A careful perusal of his work dispels such an impression; he was as much aware of his limitations as any of his most exacting critics.

In the present work, each statement is merely the best the author can make in 1933. Each statement is given definitely, but with the semantic limitation that is based on the information available to the author in 1933. . . .Some of the information may be incorrect, or wrongly interpreted. Such errors will come to light and be corrected in the future.[10]

The Art of Awareness is an example of the elaborations Korzybski was speaking of. Its Chapter 3, for instance, is the elaboration of two lines on page 23 of *Science and Sanity:* ". . .any psycho-logical occurrence has a number of aspects, an 'affective,' and an 'intellectual,' a physiological, a colloidal, and what not."

At the time the second edition of this volume was prepared, articles in popular magazines; books dealing with the application of Korzybskian method to such fields as psychotherapy, education, and management; the creation of an international society with its quarterly review *ETC.*; and the occasional nation-wide or local seminars and symposia, some held in outlying cities as Honolulu, Mexico City, had made the discipline generally known;

[9]A. A. Roback, *History of American Psychology*, p. 351.
[10]Korzybski, *Science and Sanity*, p. 142.

there were practically no educated persons, even in those days, who had not heard of Korzybski and his work. In the 7 June 1971 issue of *Time* magazine was an article on the current use of the word *media*, which ended by crying out: "Korzybski, where are you now that we need you?"

The introduction into the world of Academe was much slower. In 1954, Anatol Rapoport, the mathematical biologist, compared Korzybski and general semantics to another pioneer of our times, Sigmund Freud and psychoanalysis.

> Neither was Freud's approach to behavior and personality an empirical science. Freud's work contains many brilliant conjectures, fruitful generalizations, signposts for future workers; and, in the opinion of the writer, so does the work of Korzybski. . . . He has pointed the way toward the establishment of such a science. He was a precursor of an intellectual revolution which is just beginning and which promises to match that of the Renaissance. . . . He was a man of vision and an apostle. Such men are all too rare in our age of specialization.[11]

In 1952, when addressing the Korzybskian followers in a memorial lecture, Ashley Montagu had said:

> Before proceeding to the discussion of this brilliant conception of time-binding, I must say a few words about the dangers of making one's appearance too early. Intellectually, Korzybski was a prematurely born child. The views set out in *Manhood of Humanity* were from 25 to 30 years too early. While in 1921 Korzybski was occupied with science and its relation to ethics, with science and its relation to values, his contemporaries in the sciences and in philosophy were denying that science or philosophy could provide a sound scientific foundation for leading a good life. Scientists were inclined to an ivory-towerism and a hand-washing indifference to the consequences of their work. Thirty years later scientists are pretty generally agreed that they must take a more responsible view of their place in the world. Korzybski's warning has come home to roost, "if those who know why and how neglect to act," he wrote in 1921, "those who do not know will act, and the world will continue to flounder."

But Rapaport and Montagu were still lonely voices in the world in which they functioned. For instance, the American Academy of Arts and Sciences established in 1965 a *Commission on The Year 2,000*, for the purpose of providing the public with a "systematic anticipation, some form of thinking about the future." A group of forty-one scientists, all interested in the sciences of man, got together and exchanged their views on a long list of topics, fifteen in all, dealing with such things as governmental structure, intellectual institutions, population and age balance, location and husbandry of human talent, the use of leisure, and the state of the international system. They recognized that the socio-philosophical framework that had largely guided

---

[11]A. Rapoport, "What Is Semantics?" in *Language, Meaning and Maturity*, ed. S. I. Hayakawa (New York: Harper & Row, 1954), p. 17.

the organization of our society was outmoded and inadequate, and they stated that they were looking for a "bold new framework, a new philosophical view of man and society." Twenty-nine of them had already written books well received by our national intelligentsia. They were all well established in seats of advanced learning, and the mean age of the group was 49, ranging from 36 to 76. It indicated that all of them belonged to an elite of mature thinkers accepted as reliable guides of our population in matters of human survival and progress.

When I read the apparently verbatim reports of their deliberations in *Daedalus,* I was surprised to discover only one short statement, by the oldest member of the group, the late Lawrence Frank, that referred to the epistemological aspect of the present crisis. "We are now finding ourselves," he said, "baffled and frustrated in our attempts to cope with human problems because *we cling to the older deterministic linear formulations.*"[12] Anyone familiar with the now prevalent concern with philosophical issues and aware of the commissioners' wish for a "bold new framework," would expect that statement of a respected participant to arouse a keen interest and become the trigger of a lively discussion.

Nothing of the kind happened. The stream of speculations kept on flowing undisturbed, and nobody even appeared to notice that something of the highest significance had been said.

It is not because general semantics is a "cult," nor because of any learned objection raised against it by well-informed philosophers, it is simply because many teachers have not yet become aware of the cultural revolution we are going through. As Daniel Bell, chairman of the Commission, wrote: "We have not dealt with 'the future of culture,' perhaps the most unpredictable of the dimensions of human consciousness. . . .The new 'secular religions' and new cults—whether they be post-Christian moods of the theologians or the new hedonism of the young with its rites of pleasure and the pursuit of sensate involvement of psychedelic release—are radical changes in the nature of man's emotions and feelings and require explanation."[13]

From General Semantics to Epistemics

In Part X, titled "A Growing and Expanding System," a subtitle reads, "Epistemics, A Time-binding Emergent from General Semantics." In the June 1971 issue of *ETC.,* the international review of General Semantics, which celebrated the fiftieth anniversary of the original publication of Korzybski's first book, *Manhood of Humanity,* in which he introduced his for-

[12]Reprinted by permission of *Daedalus,* Journal of the American Academy of Arts and Sciences, Boston, Massachusetts. Summer, 1967, *Toward the Year 2000: Work in Progress* (italics added).

[13]Reprinted by permission of *Daedalus,* Journal of the American Academy of Arts and Sciences, Boston, Massachusetts. Summer, 1967, *Toward the Year 2000: Work in Progress.*

mulation of time-binding, the new science of up-to-date epistemology, often mentioned in the first edition of *The Art of Awareness,* was at last detached from the main stem of the Korzybskian system and presented as the new discipline of Epistemics. This new venture does not contradict any thesis proffered by Korzybski. Quite the contrary—it does away with the confusion so often experienced by people who see *general* semantics as a simple out-growth of *plain* semantics, or as the art of effective communication. Now they can see as an original methodology that takes into account, not only linguistics, meta-linguistics, advanced theories of communication, and their applications, but many other human sciences from paleontology to semantic ecology.

I have passed from General Semantics to Epistemics to make it clear that I take into account a theory that Korzybski barely mentions in *Science and Sanity.* That theory is evolution.

The word *evolution* comes twice in his big book, and once he speaks of the theory in very strong terms: "Without the theory of evolution, most of the natural sciences, medicine included, would be impossible."[14]

For a sweeping statement, this is surely one. If we accept that the sciences we are now developing are impossible without the theory of evolution, what of their further development, our understanding of their implications, and the applications of their findings? Are they possible without an explicit and frequent reference to the same central theory?

Personally I don't think so, and I have chosen to make my view explicit by adding to general semantics a characteristic that makes it an entirely different discipline. Epistemics is *structurally more* than general semantics. It is not general semantics plus a few special notions added to it; it is a new discipline, with its own postulates, theorems, and applications. (The implications of *structural more* are developed in chapter 9.)

Evolution means that we see ourselves on the move. We are undergoing a continuous transformation as creators of the significance and meaning that we give to our experience-as-a-whole. Our total environment is undergoing transformation as well. So are our institutions—political, economic, educational, religious. So is our place of abode, the planet Earth; so is the whole universe, of which we are—as far as we know—the self-reflexive element.

It takes time to assimilate that overriding notion, to get, as we say, the 'feel' of it. It is so new, so completely foreign to our well-established way of thinking, so overwhelming in its implications that a mere passing glance at it will not suffice. In my own case, it has taken me years of repeated meditations, reading books and articles that refer to it explicitly or implicitly, writing occasionally—for my own rereading—my own speculations about it, eventually to come to where I am now.

---

[14]Korzybski, *Science and Sanity,* p. 271.

Once you have this notion well established in the center of your think-ing-feeling self, the image you carry within you of yourself, of your fellow humans, and of the whole world is transformed to something you had never imagined before. You do not only see, as your friends of the hard sciences (viz. physics and chemistry), that the "stuff" of the universe is nothing but ceaseless activity, but you become conscious of the "stuff" of the universe, including yourself and all living things, as pure, constant activity *working itself in a definite direction.*

Its manifestations are most evident in certain well-recorded phenomena: the geological strata that tell of the evolution of the planet Earth, the paleontological fossils that reveal species of plants and animals that appeared at certain epochs and disappeared, the historical sequence of cultures and technologies with which we are all familiar. If we look well, it manifests itself in what we feel, what we do, what we plan, what we argue about, what we strive for or fight for, what we scheme and dream about. In recent years, it has become a new field of scientific activities, the field of futurism.

We are just beginning to become aware of that "formative tendency" (to use a term coined by the late Lancelot Whyte), of that vectorial push, within ourselves and around us in our human milieu. Some psychologists, few of them but some, like Rogers, Maslow, and others, have discovered a human tendency toward what they describe as self-actualization, toward becoming a fully functioning person. Some individuals may be doing it in inappropriate ways, but they are doing it according to recipes—magic or religious—long outdated; some rage because their deep unconscious desire is thwarted, and they blame the environment. But all are on the move, whether they realize it, understand it, cooperate with it, resist it, rebel against it, or not. It is indeed the human condition, an integral miniature of the cosmic condition.

In epistemics, we are investigating-learning-finding what is the most practical and least energy-wasting way of cooperating with that formative tendency. Right at the start, we quickly realized that we have to question the validity of all theories of human guidance, religious, moralistic, psychologi-cal, or empirical, that have held sway in some segment of our cultural world before this total change in overall orientation became imperative. You don't deal with human beings in inner transformation as you deal with an assumed "human nature" that has remained the same for centuries and will remain the same to the end of the world. If you want a simple analogy, look at a small growing tree in your garden and at the fence post near it. They belong to two different worlds and you do not treat them the same. Willy nilly, we have to abandon for good and forever all static notions, including the one that made you and me a chunk of matter, never changing much, and ani-mated by a soul identical with itself all through the years and after.

Indeed we are witnessing births of new forms of human life, and it may be more appropriate, from now on, to see these multiplying transformations as manifestations of rapid, intensive, and thoroughgoing evolution.

The present textbook, since its first appearance in 1966, has undergone a parallel series of mutations. It has to be so if we want to keep it a representative expression of what is going on in the world of living individuals and to provide definite suggestions as to how to manage our lives in a world constantly on the move.

I suggest that you keep this notion of evolution in the center of your experience as you read about "conceptual revolutions" and all of the formulations and methods that follow.

PART I

discontinuity in cultural evolution

Evolution is taken today as the general condition to which all theories, systems, and hypotheses have to conform if they are to be thinkable and workable. The development of human life introduced a new form of evolution to our planet. It is a more rapidly developing process than organic evolution. It is called societal or cultural. Just as the fossil records of the earth show the emergence of new evolutionary phases—physico-chemical, plant, animal, prehuman—our humanized world periodically undergoes transformations. We can call these "conceptual revolutions," but they indicate that, on a broader level, our very selves are changing and growing to new forms of existence.

Discontinuity in Western cultural development is a way of saying that the various stages that have historically emerged are not simply manifestations of additive increases. They are definite and differentiable periods in which things are not experienced, valued, symbolized, described, known, characterized, and used in the same manner as they were before. Each period can be seen as a phase in human development from our birth as a species to our anticipated adulthood.

the evolution of
conceptual revolutions

The term "conceptual revolution" was coined by the Nobel prize winning physicist and logician Percy W. Bridgeman a generation ago. At the time, it was a most appropriate formulation of a phenomenon that we were just beginning to single out as a distinct event in the world of happenings. A conceptual revolution involved the abandoning of well-established rules and procedures in mental work. In a wider context, that is, in the organization of human activities, it meant the eradication of long-standing conditioning from the brain and nervous system of individuals who were responsible for radically influencing the course of human evolution. In fact, it meant the destruction of generally accepted rules and procedures and replacing them with entirely new ones. Such happenings were new in a world where changes had been infrequent and sporadic, when generation after generation could pass without any major changes in the mode of living. But things are so different today that it seems a new term has become mandatory. The term that I suggest here and now is the term *evolution*, more in keeping with the relevant scientific mood of these current years.

In 1957, we heard for the first time the electronic bip-bip of the first Sputnik that the Russians had sent aloft to circle the planet Earth. Since then, we have had in rapid succession the various Explorers, Telstar, our first step on the Moon, the skylab in which three men lived for eighty-three days, the rendezvous of Apollo and Soyuz in 1975, and the beginning of an exploration of the planet Mars. Each of these happenings could be called a revolution, or better, a significant evolutionary emergence in advanced technology. In the field of mathematical thinking, we have had several generations of computers within a decade. In the field of human values, we have the passage from the friendly roommate of the same sex of the previous generation, to the heterosexual, intimate, life-sharing companion actually accepted on many college campuses, as well as in private residences. In the economic world, we have the multinational corporations that stretch their tentacles over and across national boundaries.

Thus, while we examine the "conceptual revolutions," I suggest that we see these discontinuities within a more inclusive context of human *evolution*. This may help to show that these "revolutions" did not just suddenly "happen" due to events and necessities of a particular time in history. The emergence of a structural innovation in living, while unprecedented, involves a long evolutionary preparation of many individual lives in transaction: individuals willing to risk the hazards of the "impossible" and the censure of those who resist fundamental change.

Conceptual Revolutions

Persons do not all respond in the same manner to what is said or done to them: some have more information, some have less; and this makes a great difference in the way they think, plan, and reach decisions. There is a difference that lies deeper still: persons behave differently relative to their way of looking at themselves and at the world.

In simple and obvious matters, understanding and agreement are relatively easy. "Two plus two is four," "the sun is bright," "rain is wet," "a dog is a dog and not a cat": these and similar statements are understood and accepted without discussion; but in most questions of human behavior there are differences in thinking, feeling, deciding, and planning. Tell a teenager that when he has reached adulthood he will regret having squandered his time; he will not believe you because he does not see the future as you do. In fact, he may see it as a rosy mist, full of magical opportunities, and not as an irreversible sequence of decisions and actions. Tell some southern senator that the Negroes did well to organize sit-ins and other demonstrations, and he will be impervious to your arguments. Tell a communist that the single-party system is undemocratic and he will show you—to his satisfaction if not to yours—that you are dead wrong.

Methods of thinking, feeling, planning, and deciding are not the same for persons who belong to different cultural groups; these methods also change, from generation to generation, within the same culture. There is a continuity, of course, a thread that can be seen running down through centuries. As heirs of the Judeo-Christian and Greco-Roman traditions, we have a common core of principles and values, but many of these have undergone transformations in the course of time.

The changes are most evident in the technical developments that have made our economic and political life vastly different from that of our ancestors, who gathered fruit and hunted game to survive, and different from that of the Greek citizen of a small city-state and that of the Roman member of a world empire. Between the incantations and potions of the medicine man and the laboratory procedures and surgical techniques of the modern physician, there is also a great difference. To these spectacular changes, so evident that we take them for granted, correspond other changes—less visible, perhaps, but no less important (and much *more* important, some will say)— in our ways of thinking about ourselves and about the world in which we live. For example, one of our contemporaries, who had much to do with the recent advances in physics, Albert Einstein, warned us that unleashing the energy of the atom calls for a radical change in our methods of thinking. And Kenneth Boulding, an economist-philosopher, said

> If the human race is to survive, it will have to change its ways of thinking more in the next twenty-five years than it has done in the last twenty-five thousand.[1]

The question is to find where we stand as individuals in this unrelenting advance toward more information about ourselves and the world and toward new and more adequate methods of handling that information in our daily life. In what domains are our methods of thinking-feeling-acting antiquated? In what domains are they equal to the new puzzling situations we have to face in our personal life and in matters of education, politics, and religion?

To find an answer to these questions, it may be useful to review the development of our methods of relating ourselves to ourselves and to the world in the course of the history of our Western civilization. We will find that they went through two revolutions and that we are in the midst of a third one. It is not within the scope of this book to cover adequately the development of *Homo sapiens* in other cultures, such as the Hindu, the Chinese, and all others known to anthropologists.

Revolutions

The word *revolution* usually brings to mind a political revolution; it makes us think of Cuba, Algeria, Zaire. It means a radical change in the form of government or a change of the ruling group by methods other than those provided by law. Some political revolutions were turning points in the his-

---

[1]Reprinted from "After Civilization, What?" by Kenneth Boulding with permission from the October 1962 issue of the *Bulletin of the Atomic Scientists*. Copyright 1962 by the Education Foundation for Nuclear Science, Inc.

tory of Western man; the American, the French, and the Russian revolutions are outstanding examples.

Revolution is also used to describe changes that have no military or political implications. The form of government is not changed, nor does the power to make laws pass from one group to another, and yet a radical change takes place in the life of the people. Insidiously or openly, some new source of social energy makes itself felt through the structure of the group involved; a transformation takes place that cannot be undone. After a revolution, things can never be what they were before.

Such was the Industrial Revolution of 150 years ago. The power of steam and of the machine did away with the artisans' guilds and created the new class of factory workers. It brought about movements of the population, changes in the laws, the appearance of what Marx called the "proletariat," and the emergence of labor unions. Another example is the appearance of the Model-T Ford, which brought the automobile down from the luxury class to the level of an ordinary tool of living for the plain citizen. As a consequence, roads had to be improved, highways had to be built, gas stations appeared at intersections, we saw more and more garage mechanics and fewer and fewer village blacksmiths, vacation travel took a different pattern, and the horse and buggy faded out of the picture.

Another example, less tangible but no less real and far-reaching, took place within the lifetime of some of us: the revolution of the personal income tax. It has made impossible such displays of ostentatious magnificence as Hearst's Casa Grande in St. Simeon; it has stimulated the creation of foundations and nonprofit institutions; it has reduced the differences between the standards of living of various socioeconomic classes; it has brought about a clear-cut distinction between wages and take-home pay. And no amount of wishful thinking will ever bring us back to pre-income-tax days.

Other revolutions are religious, such as the Protestant Reformation; others are artistic, such as the impressionist or the cubist; still others are educational, such as the current change in the teaching of mathematics in grade school.

How can we describe the common feature of all revolutions? I suggest the following statement: A *revolution is a radical and irreversible change in a fundamental element of our way of life.* We may compare it to a mutation in the genetic sequence of plant and animal species. We may speak of it as the appearance in the world of a new kind of existence.

Our brains, our hearts, and our habits of living have been going through such a revolution for the last fifty years. If our age deserves to be called an "age of anxiety," it is not because we have regressed, it is because we are going through a painful transition: we are waging within ourselves a life and death struggle that spells the doom of the past and the emergence of new forms.

The present conceptual revolution is the third of its type in Western history. The first one, which lasted about 300 years, from 650 to 350 B.C., was the age of the Greek philosophers. The second began around A.D. 1500 and ended around A.D. 1700; it was the late Renaissance and the birth of the scientific method. The third revolution began with our century, and is now in its most intensive phase.

Between these periods of conceptual revolutions were periods of relative stability. I call this stability *relative* because it did not prevent minor revolutions in the political, economic, or religious sectors of the life of our ancestors. Conceptual stability means that the basic understanding of human beings' relations with themselves and with the universe did not change appreciably.

The Greek Conceptual Revolution

The first period of relative conceptual stability extends from the appearance of *Homo sapiens* to the Greek philosophers. As far as we know our early ancestors had no conception of logic and science as we understand them today. Their interpretation of the world was animistic and mythological. They explained the operations of natural forces by supernatural agencies: everywhere there were gods.

An example of how people thought in those days is contained in the story of Cadmus, founder of Thebes, as recorded in the Encyclopaedia Britannica.

> Cadmus, son of Phoenix and brother of Europa. After his sister had been carried off by Zeus, he was sent to find her. Unsuccessful in his search, he came to Delphi to consult the oracle. Ordered to give up his quest and follow a cow, which would meet him, and build a town on the spot where she would lie down. The cow met him in Phocis and led him to Boeotia, where he founded the city of Thebes. Intending to sacrifice the cow, he sent some of his companions to a neighboring spring for water. They were slain by a dragon, which in turn was destroyed by Cadmus. By instructions from Athena, he sowed the dragon's teeth in the ground, and from them sprang a race of fierce armed men. These assisted him in building the city of Thebes. Because of the bloodshed, Cadmus had to do penance for eight years. Then the gods gave him to wife Harmonia, daughter of Ares and Aphrodite, by whom he had a son and four daughters. At the marriage all the gods were present. Cadmus and his wife eventually retired to Illyria, where they were changed into snakes.

The Greek philosophers, beginning with Thales of Miletus and including such well-known thinkers as Pythagoras, Democritus, Heraclitus, Socrates, Plato, and Aristotle, gave up these beliefs about the gods and their compelling whims. They looked for permanency and regularity in nature, and theorized about a common element in everything that existed: Heraclitus called it fire; Democritus spoke of the "atom"; Pythagoras thought of numbers; and Aristotle devised his explanation in terms of matter and form. They did not agree in their theories, but all held the revolutionary idea that there was such a thing as *the nature of things*, and that whatever existed remained identical with its natural self: a man was a man, and he could not originate from a dragon's tooth, nor could he be transformed into a snake.

On this principle of identity, there was no disagreement, and Aristotle used it as the basis of his system of logic. His was a tremendous achievement. He codified the newly discovered laws of the human mind, and, shortly after his death, his treatises on logic were called the *Organon*, which means the *Instrument* or *Tool for mental work*.

> Aristotle built the terminology of science and philosophy; we can hardly speak of any science today without employing terms which he invented: they lie like fossils in the strata of our speech: *faculty, mean, maxim . . . category, energy, actuality, motive, end, principle, form*—these indispensable coins of philosophic thought were minted in his mind.[2]

The second great achievement of the first revolution was the establishment of the rules of deductive logic. From the known nature of things revealed by common sense—that is, by observation unclouded by superstition—the scientists of the time derived conclusions according to the rules of strict logic. These conclusions were accepted as revelations of the hidden characteristics of phenomena.

From this brief analysis of the first conceptual revolution, we see that it involved four elements.

1. A radical change in the methods of thinking and valuing, which passed from mythology to philosophy, from superstition to reason, from divination to deduction.
2. Many talented workers and geniuses who made possible a spurt in the development of all the sciences of the time.
3. A codifier, or system-builder, who made explicit the methods of thinking that were characteristic of the age.
4. New terms in the general vocabulary.

The Revolution of Classical Science

The second conceptual revolution took place when people began to question the maxims of common sense. Instead of being satisfied with the nature of things as known, they wanted to find out how things interact with one another. The fundamental scientific process had to work in reverse: instead of going from assumed general principles to particular conclusions, it went from systematic observtions and careful experiments to general "laws

---

[2]Will Durant, *The Story of Philosophy* (Garden City, N.Y.: Doubleday, 1927), p. 66.

of nature." Induction took the lead over deduction; it was the birth of what we still call the scientific method.

At the time of the second revolution, many more geniuses and talented workers made their appearance. It was the age of Copernicus, Johann Kepler, Galileo, Harvey, Newton, Vesalius, Leibnitz, Descartes, Fermat, Spinoza, Leeuwenhoek, Mercator, and Francis Bacon.

The last named, Francis Bacon, was not the greatest of these—far from it. He proved to be blind to the significance of the achievements of some of his contemporaries, but he occupies a special position among them. The Royal Society of England, founded in 1662 as the first institution devoted to the advancement of science in our Western world, took him as the model for its members because in the second revolution Bacon played the part that Aristotle had played in the first: he formulated the methods of thinking that were characteristic of the period. One of his essays was called *Novum Organum* to emphasize the fact that it was of the same type as Aristotle's *Organon*. It was the new "tool chest" for scientific work.

Many new terms appeared and were added to those that had been coined by Aristotle. We find them not only in scientific treatises but also in everyday conversation, such terms as *factor, variable, attraction, repulsion, analysis, field of forces, dynamics, progress, evolution, interaction, vector, environment*, and many others.

The Revolution of Up-To-Date Science

A period of stability, almost of stagnation, followed for two hundred years. Then came the third conceptual revolution, which the editors of the *Autobiography of Science* describe in the following manner:

> "The future of physics is in the fifth decimal place." Such was the opinion seriously, and a little sadly, held by many distinguished classical physicists just before the turn of the twentieth century. The nineteenth century—the century of progress—they mourned because it had progressed so triumphantly that it had left them with nothing more exciting to do than calculate physical constants to the fifth decimal place. Then abruptly, everything changed. Within ten years the discoveries of Roentgen, Becquerel, Pierre and Marie Curie, Rutherford, Soddy, Max Planck, J. J. Thompson, Albert Einstein and others had completely revolutionized the older classical physics and opened entirely new worlds to conquer inside the atom and outside the solar system.[3]

As this was happening in physics, Freud was upsetting the young sciences of psychiatry and psychology. A host of altogether new disciplines were budding in the human sciences: neurology, sociology, anthropology,

---

[3]F. R. Moulton and J. J. Schifferes, *Autobiography of Science* (Garden City, N.Y.: Doubleday, 1950) p. 484.

psychometrics. For those who (like the author) have been looking for more than sixty years at the stage where the drama of our scientific revolution has taken place, the scene has been crowded with more geniuses and talented workers than it had ever been for a comparable period. Apart from the physicists already mentioned, there are many others, including those who engineered the A-bomb, the H-bomb, and the space technology of today. In the social sciences we have, apart from Freud and his dissident or faithful followers, such people as the Gestaltists, the transactional psychologists, the client-centered therapists, the personal construct clinicians, the transpersonal psychologists, the rational/emotive therapists, the anthropologists, and the metalinguists. In all disciplines, we have the philosopher-scientists: Russell, Whitehead, Bridgman, Bentley, Bachelard, Karl Popper, Mach and the Vienna Circle, Wiener, Shannon, von Bertalanffy, N. R. Hansen, Polanyi, Brillouin, among many.

Of all these there is one who, like Aristotle in the first revolution and like Francis Bacon in the second, took upon himself the task of explicitly formulating and arranging into a system the methods of thinking that make our epoch different from the previous ones. He did not limit himself to logic, deductive or inductive. He thought in terms of *psycho-logics,* of a science of thinking, not as an activity that stands by itself, but as a science of our evaluating processes—of how we react to persons, events, and symbols according to what they mean to us at the moment of impact. Alfred Korzybski was not, and never claimed to be, the greatest scientist of his age. He was concerned with the revision of the methods of thinking that were accepted and embedded in our language. He wanted to collect from the writings of his fellow scientists a new set of tools with which we could manage ourselves efficiently in a fast-changing world. He devised a few all-purpose tools of his own and invited his readers and students to experiment with them.

It is interesting to note that Korzybski did not claim that he was offering the world a complete system. His major work, *Science and Sanity,* published in 1933, is subtitled *An Introduction to Non-Aristotelian Systems and General Semantics.* In the first edition he announced that he had a volume in preparation, with *General Semantics* as the proposed title. We may assume that this was to be the formal treatise for which *Science and Sanity* could serve as an introduction, but Korzybski did not have the time nor the facilities to complete that second volume. What general semantics would have become had he completed and published that treatise nobody knows, and nobody can guess accurately. One thing is sure: he wanted his system to remain open, and he stated explicitly that he expected many "corrections and elaborations in the future."[4]

---

[4]Korzybski, *Science and Sanity* (Lakeville, Conn.: International Non-Aristotelian Library Publishing Company, 1933, 1941, 1948, 1958), p. 171.

The present *Art of Awareness* is an attempt to further develop an ever-evolving discipline, consistent with what Korzybski stated.

The present revolutionary period has the four characteristics of previous conceptual revolutions. It is crowded with geniuses and talented workers in the multiplying fields of science, and it has produced a bold pioneer who took it upon himself to devise an up-to-date methodology. The third characteristic, change in the methods of thinking, is not so easy to describe because the system has not yet been fully worked out. Already, a few terms are new and typify the new order of things. We have such words as *multiordinality, indeterminacy, process, multidimensionality, transaction, self-reflexiveness, semantic transaction, thinking models, noise and redundancy in communication*, and the introduction of the hyphen in such compound words as space-time, body-mind, and the like.

One of the problems is that most of the classical terms have already proved to be inadequate but have not yet been replaced by better ones. As early as 1926, A. N. Whitehead wrote that "The old foundations of scientific thought are becoming unintelligible. Time, space, matter, material, ether, electricity, mechanism, organism, configuration, structure, pattern, function, all require reinterpretation."[5]

The Present Conceptual Revolution

The revolution of up-to-date science has spread itself into every aspect of our lives. Many scholars and thinkers refer to this ongoing revolution in much broader terms than scientific. As the late Percy W. Bridgeman of Harvard said,

"the conceptual revolution forced by recent discoveries in the realm of relativity and quantum effects is not really a revolution in new realms of high velocities or the very small, but is properly a conceptual revolution on the macroscopic level of everyday life."[6]

S. I. Hayakawa, the well-known general semanticist and politician, calls it cultural; Anatol Rapoport, the mathematical biologist, calls it intellectual and compares it to the Renaissance and the birth of the scientific method; Peter F. Drucker, the economist and management consultant, speaks of our time as "an age of transition." Professor Lynn White, Jr., the historian, describes it as "a change in the very canons of our culture," a "general shift more fundamental than any since agriculture and herding displaced food-gathering and hunting as the habit of human existence."

[5]Alfred North Whitehead, *Science and the Modern World* (New York: Macmillan, 1926), p. 21.
[6]Percy W. Bridgman, *The Way Things Are* (Cambridge, Mass.: Harvard University Press, 1959), p. 8.

This leads me to make some definite suggestions on what we have covered so far, both in terms of meaning and in terms of how we can manage ourselves as we go through this revolution. Hopefully, this will set the stage for the models, methods, and new ways of thinking that I propose throughout the rest of the book.

What Does A Conceptual Revolution Mean?

1. A conceptual revolution does not simply mean new thoughts, new principles, new orientations; it means new patterns of brain work to establish sets of relations that have not been tested so far, to provide orientations in a life-space of many more dimensions than we now take into account.
2. It does not simply mean more knowledge of "human nature" as we have known it for centuries; it means a new way of contact and participation with the human phenomenon.
3. It does not simply mean an extension of logic, symbolic, metaphorical, or otherwise; it means asking ourselves whether refined logical consistency is not in the long run a self-defeating pursuit.
4. It does not simply mean constructing more elaborate mental models and feeding them to more complex electronic computers; it means asking ourselves if being sensitive to and managing human energies and values is not more important than building intricate models of war games, production games, distribution games, and other simulations of human situations.
5. It does not simply mean the improvement of our present political, economic, educational, and religious institutions; it means facing with an undisturbed mind possible changes in the very structure of these institutions and even questioning their relevance as they function today.
6. It does not mean a return to the "faith of our fathers"; it means the recognition of the need for a new faith, and the creation of such a faith.
7. It does not mean better communication and understanding, in the sense of more clarity and precision; it means a revamping of our best-established practices of communication to facilitate an unprecedented deeper human participation.

How do we manage ourselves through this revolution? I suggest a few guidelines in considering such a question. First of all, the question of "how" ultimately must be referred back to the questioner. By doing so, "how" becomes a question of each individual finding what he or she has become as a performer in the art of living and accepting to develop new attitudes and skills, rather than a question of figuring out what to do and how to do it. This involves the development of commitment that will hold when times are difficult beyond the conditions of the immediate environment. This is important in a cultural transition such as the present one. At times, discouragement, disappointment, and disillusionment can prevent us from going on.

"How" means becoming more keenly aware of our potentialities and responsibilities as participating members of the family of humankind, and not so much a question of learning more facts and theories. Many believe that more knowledge and power can "change the world." I disagree. I see it as gaining a fuller awareness of what each of us takes to be appropriate and necessary to fulfill her or his sense of purpose in the cosmic enterprise, free from self-images and role-playing of our cultural infancy. It becomes a matter of making the most of that limited part of the world that is within my field of influence: MY OWN SELF.

On a more general level, "how" is not a question of imposing on the rest of humankind our technology and our way of life, but one of long-range planning and making available to all inhabitants of this planet the most advanced mental and physical tools that may bring about abundance, peace, and self-actualization.

Those who feel themselves in the midst of a transformation to a new form of existence do not belong to any organized group that binds them together in a common religion, profession, pressure group, or political party. But they undoubtedly have something in common, not easily expressed in sharp formulations perhaps, but surely effective at the preconscious level. They share a common experience.

Summary

To summarize, we have examined the evolutionary development of the "conceptual revolutions" of Western culture, beginning with the age of the Greek philosophers from the seventh to the fourth centuries B.C.; the revolution of classical science, from the sixteenth to the eighteenth centuries; and the present scientific revolution, which was initiated around the beginning of the twentieth century. I have stated that these revolutions were more than "conceptual." They signaled a radical and irreversible change of fundamental orientation in our way of life. I relate this to the introduction of this book in which I sketched the history of epistemology and the emergence of the methodologies of General Semantics and Epistemics. We can now see them as growing out of the need to manage ourselves through a continually evolving and complexified human world, and developing guides to innovating—which means to take a hand in our own evolution.

This has brought a wider meaning to the word epistemology, and the epistemic methods that are developed from its up-to-date findings. We will develop this further in the next section.

CHAPTER 2

epistemology: classical and up-to-date

The general concern of general semantics and epistemics can be given in two words: *up-to-date epistemology*. Classical epistemology usually is described as "the branch of philosophy that investigates the origin, nature, methods, and limits of human knowing" (*American College Dictionary*). It is the science of our mental activities; and it deals with how we observe with our senses and how we introspect, how we think, how we doubt, how we attain certainty, how we accept the views of others, how we communicate our own views, how we differentiate facts from opinions, how we remember and forget, how we solve problems, how we invent and create. Such was the epistemology as introduced by Ferrier and accepted in scientific literature until recently.

Susanne Langer, in describing a new keynote that has been struck in philosophy in general, and in epistemology in particular, writes:

> To us whose intelligence is bound up with language, whose achievements are physical comforts, machines, medicines, great cities, and the means of their destruction, theory of knowledge means theory of communication, generalization, proof, in short: critque of science. But the limits of language are not the last limits of experience, and things inaccessible to language may have their own forms of conception, that is to say, their own symbolic devices. Such non-discursive forms, charged with logical possibilities of meaning, underlie the significance of music; and their recognition broadens our epistemology to the point of including not only the semantics of science, but a serious philosophy of art.[7]

[7]Susanne K. Langer, *Philosophy In a New Key* (New York: Mentor Books, 1951), p. 224.

14

The epistemology we are introducing here is much broader in scope. It is not simply the science of knowing, but the science of the totally functioning human being, acting and being acted upon within the culture in which he or she was reared. Michel Foucault, the contemporary French philosopher, greatly influenced me in making that change. This brings us to the following three terms and definition:

1. *Episteme*, or the general system of knowing-feeling-acting that was dominant in our culture at different times of history. The present one has emerged from previous epistemes that go back to our Judeo-Christian, Greco-Roman origins as a civilization. Each of us has an individual version of it in what I shall call later in this text, our *structured unconscious*. This can be described as the dynamic pattern of attitudes, habits, internalized values: modes of perceiving and thinking by which each person relates himself to the world of things and people, observes and judges their activities, and expresses himself to himself and to the world by what he thinks, says, and does.

2. *Epistemology*, or the science of *episteme*. It obtains information from a continuous survey of all the human sciences and arts, organizing their findings in a set of postulates and formulations that aims at being simple and teachable.

3. *Epistemics*, or the discipline derived from epistemology and that emerged from General Semantics. It views the whole of humankind and each individual as processes engaged within a process of evolution. It takes *Homo sapiens* as the only form of life that can influence the course of its own evolution. It has for its objective the knowledge and the practice of the skills of awareness and self-management as preparation for innovating in human participation.

In a sense, this is a new science and discipline. Or, better said, it is an attempt to translate into scientific terms and aesthetic practices the wisdom of the ages, including our own as the most advanced. Epistemics covers the whole range of human activities in the arts, in science, in politics, in religion, in administrative work and business transactions, in person-to-person encounters, in family life, in education—wherever and whenever humans are functioning.

It sounds like an ambitious program, and it is; but it is not proposed in a self-complacent or arrogant spirit. It is an endeavor to update and to make more teachable the wisdom and values of the brightest brains and the most dedicated souls of yesterday and today.

Strictly speaking, the practice of General Semantics and Epistemics cannot be classified as a science, but rather as a discipline, a set of skills that have to be acquired. We may compare it to medicine, which is a methodology, a study and practice of methods based on sciences that deal with the human body and its functioning—such sciences as anatomy, physiology, biochemistry. There was a time when medicine had to manage without stethoscopes, X rays, blood counts, electrocardiograms, or any of the instruments and techniques that are now routine in a well-appointed clinic. There was a time, further back, when gross anatomy and elementary physiology, as we know them today, were practically nonexistent. Before Vesalius and the sixteenth century, anatomy was much more guesswork than accurate science; and before Harvey, who lived in the same period, the circulation of the blood was a mystery. For centuries, medicine depended on commonsense observations, for which the great masters of antiquity, such as Hippocrates and Galenus, displayed an unusual capacity. To their observations they added speculation, or interpretation—in the light of the sciences of their time—of the symptoms that they had observed and classified.

What medicine was doing for the physical activities of human beings, classical epistemology was attempting to do for their mental activities. For generations—in fact, until recently—epistemology had to operate without the help of the recently developed human sciences. It depended on three sources of information: (1) introspection, or what the philosopher observed going on within himself; (2) observation, or the study of what other people said and did; and (3) speculation or theorizing, which amounted to making sense, in the light of the culture of the time, of what the scientist had observed within himself or in others. In short, epistemology was refined common sense, self-guided and self-controlled.

This classical epistemology gave us the rules of logic and rhetoric, or, to put it in modern terms, of sound thinking and effective communicating. These rules were applied in many fields of human endeavor: preaching, teaching, debating in legislative assemblies, stumping in electoral campaigns, pleading in courts of law, arguing with friends or with members of one's family, and rationalizing with others to explain away one's mistakes.

Up-to-date epistemology, like up-to-date medicine, is surrounded by an ever-increasing group of sciences. Each of these sciences brings to epistemology the harvest of its findings. As a consequence, epistemology must change and improve every year, sorting out what is of lasting value from what is just passing fancy in the sciences and the technologies that vie for attention. As medicine long ago gave up such practices as bloodletting, poultices, and drastic purges, so must epistemology give up thinking and communicating practices that have no other justification than immemorial usage. Debating, as we hear it on radio and television, is one of those practices that belong to the same age as the *purgare* and *repurgare*, which Molière ridiculed three hundred years ago.

General Semantics and Epistemics are attempts to organize, in a well-balanced system, the cumulative findings of the human sciences of our time and to derive from this system rules and procedures for self-management and mutual understanding. Instead of depending exclusively on introspection, observation, and speculation, as their predecessors had to, the epistemologists of today can tap the resources of many sciences.

Psychoanalysis has revealed that many of our thoughts, decisions, and actions are determined by unconscious drives and motives that work independently of logic. Psychology speaks of intelligences in the plural and not of intelligence in the singular; so it explains how a person who rates high in musical intelligence will not necessarily rate high in social intelligence, and how it happens that a person who writes books on how to be human fails to observe the most elementary rules of proper social behavior.

Sociology studies groups and their development; it shows how the mental activities of a person are influenced by the pressure of the groups to which she belongs and how these mental activities can be stimulated by interaction with fellow members. Cultural anthropology has discovered that cultures different from our own are not necessarily lower stages of human development, they are simply different; and some of them have potentialities that go beyond our most highly prized mental and emotional habits. Linguistics and metalinguistics show that thinking is directed, in great part, by the language we learned in childhood, and that logic itself is a code of mental etiquette that is ruled by local symbolic customs.

Neurology, which is mapping the topography of the brain, registers the electrical phenomena that take place in the cortical and the subcortical areas, and it links our old concepts of memory, imagination, and motivation with processes that nobody suspected before. Biochemistry uses drugs that produce hallucinations and tranquilizers that dull emotions; hormonal studies throw light on the stress syndrome; and muscular relaxation shows its direct influence on emotional flare-ups. Cybernetics and information theory introduce the new concepts of signal-noise ratio, redundancy, and feedback. Structural thinking leads us to the building of mental models, and it becomes even more dynamic and fruitful with the notion of consonance and dissonance of analogies.

Finally, there are theories one step removed from experimentation, engendered by the cross-fertilization of various disciplines: the General Systems Theory of von Bertalanffy and his associates; the cell assemblies and the phase sequences of Hebb; the hierarchy of empirical and theoretical systems suggested by Kenneth Boulding; the epistemological profile of Gaston Bachelard; the life-space postulate of Kurt Lewin; the holistic views of Jan Smuts and Kurt Goldstein; the Gestalt approach of Wertheimer, Koffka, and Köhler; the surveys of creative thinking by Hadamard, Ghiselin, and Sorokin; the motivation theories of Abraham Maslow.

From this multitude of sources, factual information and theories pregnant with possibilities pour into the study of the epistemologists who keep up with the times. Every year new tools and new procedures are invented with which they can survey, analyze, and interpret the behavior of human beings as individuals, acted upon by a culture and acting upon a culture—or as a sample of the time-binding class of life that Teilhard de Chardin calls the *noösphere*, the intelligent thin envelope of the planet that holds the earth under its grip and might destroy it if it so chooses.

The task that confronts us is to put some order in that wealth of information, to sort out the valid and the useful, and to devise methods of application that are practical, easily learned, and efficient.

New Technologies

Our predecessors derived the techniques of logic and rhetoric from old-style epistemology, and these need not be discarded altogether. They serve a purpose, just as the computations of pre-Copernican astronomers are still reasonably valid for establishing the calendar although they are not adequate for problems of space exploration.

Similarly, we need a new technology that is based on an up-to-date epistemology derived from the human sciences of today. It will take into account whatever is useful in logic (classical and symbolic) and rhetoric as common-sense communication, but it will be more comprehensive than its former counterpart. Humans are no longer seen merely as rational animals; we don't say with Descartes that our mind is the independent ruler over animal spirits.

Our reactions are subject to cultural pressures, to organismic conditions, to past conditionings, to anticipations of the future, and to environmental factors. The new technology must consider as many of these factors as it possibly can; it will be a technology of awareness and appropriate guidance, similar to the technology of the pilot who faces the instrument panel of his plane and maintains his flight on the proper course. It must tell us what is important to watch and what action should be taken to correct our own malfunctioning so as to counteract the buffeting of outside forces and to bring our performance to higher levels.

To label this new technology, some have suggested the term *Human Cybernetics*, an application of Norbert Wiener's epoch-making discipline, which he described as "control and communication in the Animal and the Machine." In the general semantics context, Human Cybernetics as a technology would mean the art of steering the whole person—mind, body, and activities, all immersed in a space-time environment—to obtain the most from one's personal resources. By the use of feedback controls, guidance systems are able to keep missiles set on their target even if it shifts its course to elude them. Similarly, we can speak of a personal guidance system, which is not automatic because it is human, but which is highly responsive and resilient. Its central feature is a guided and guiding awareness of self and of others as autonomous functioning units in a world of purposive clusters of energies.

Our awareness can be trained to consider our cultural and personal assumptions; our processes of abstracting at various levels; our techniques of listening and communicating; our motivations and our values; our purposes; the degrees of our emotional maturity; our body capacities, limitations, and habits; the physical, historical, and semantic aspect of our environment; the guiding power of our past experiences and conditionings; and the beckoning pull of the future as we anticipate it.

One of the most important elements of the culture we assimilated in our infancy is our mother tongue. It has become part of what we call our "second nature," which is a complex assemblage of conditionings and attitudes that form our structured unconscious. We see the world through the meshes of that human-made filter; we project on the world of phenomena the relations that we have learned to observe among the parts of speech; we interpret what is happening in terms of the logic of cause-effect that is embedded in our grammar.

Any person who is familiar with at least two languages knows that thinking in one language is not exactly the same as thinking in the other. My own mother tongue is French, and it still seems strange that, in English, a fly is a "he," when in French *la mouche* is so distinctly feminine. Butter*fly* is masculine in French, *le papillon,* and the shift from one gender to the opposite is altogether illogical; nevertheless, it sounds "natural" to a French ear. It seems as if the gender were there, in the outside world, to be discovered and recognized, when it is an arbitrary classification that was invented by some remote ancestor and has been observed religiously ever since.

There are many other differences, in nouns, in verbs, in tenses, in sentence structure. In English, we *are* many things: hungry, thirsty, right, or wrong (I *am hungry*). In French, one *has* hunger or thirst (j'*ai* faim, j'*ai* soif), and one *has*—with respect to what is being talked about at the moment—"reason" on his side (j'*ai* raison [I am right])—or something diametrically opposite to reason, for which there is no adequate English word, the French *tort.* In French, one *has* it (j'*ai* tort); in English, one *is in* it (I *am in* the wrong) or one *is* qualified by it (I *am* wrong).

When we say, in English, "I *have been here* for three hours," or "ten years," or "a number of years," a Frenchman would say, "Je *suis* (am) ici depuis trois heures," "dix ans," or "un nombre d'années." The French present indicative "je *suis*" may cover any length of time in the past; it asserts a continuity with the past, something like an existential identity. Not to be now what I have been until now is unthinkable, tantamount to saying that I am not. Circumstances may have changed *around* me, but all along I have seen myself as being—in each present moment—what I have been by nature, by inborn qualification, by right, by some existential quality that makes me what I am.

What difference does it make? The difference is a subtle one, and it is not easy to evaluate its practical consequences, but if you accept the postulate that it is "natural" for France to remain in an everlasting present that encompasses her glorious past, it becomes "natural" to think as de Gaulle did. You may argue that he lived "in the past," but what if your "past" was his "present"?

The moral is that I don't see the same things, don't observe the same events, when I change from my French to my English brain. I inherited my French brain from my mother tongue, and to be at home in English I had to be reborn culturally. Changing my language changes me as an observer. It changes my world at the same time.

When we take such differences into account and remind ourselves that their number is limitless, we are miles away from the old epistemology. In Lynn White's expression, "We are learning...to view mankind from vantage points other than the Acropolis."[8] It is, therefore, the purpose of this book to see the world from viewpoints more consistent with humankind on planet Earth at the present stage of evolution than with the condition of the ancient Greeks in the Mediterranean world.

We will study (among others) the following themes:

1. Logic—deductive or inductive, symbolic or classical—is superseded by psycho-logics. Mental activity no longer stands by itself, and it is not studied by itself. It is only one aspect of a greater whole, called semantic transaction, which is our main unit of discourse.

2. There is no one method of thinking that is common to all, and no laws of logic apply to all members of the human race. There are semantic states, now more and more frequently called *epistemes* by Foucault and others, that vary from culture to culture, or that change within a culture in the course of history.

3. Through our language—and the culture of which it is one aspect—we have developed a structured unconscious in us that involves a metaphysics—the metaphysics of subject and predicate, of substances and qualities, of agent and action.

---

[8]Lynn White, Jr., ed., *Frontiers of Knowledge in the Study of Man* (New York: Harper & Row, 1956), p. 313.

4. Our experiences are constructs of our own processes in transaction. Our contacts with the world "inside" and "outside" ourselves can be seen as so many acts of abstracting, and this process of abstracting proceeds at different levels. By being aware of the differences between these levels we can solve many paradoxes and facilitate agreement.

These are only a few samples. As we proceed through this book we will see that the list is much longer; in fact, it could be extended indefinitely.

semantic transaction

As a first step, we put aside the standard definition of *Homo sapiens*, such as, "rational animal," or any of its present-day equivalents, as for instance, "the naked ape." We see a human individual as a continuously transacting and expanding process that includes seven clusters of activities: (1) electrochemical; (2) sensory-motor; (3) feeling; (4) thinking; (5) environing (ecologically and psychosocially); (6) memory guided; and (7) anticipative of the future.

individuals as semantic transactors

If we examine the current literature that deals with the human phenomenon, we find that the term "man" or "human" is given many meanings. Korzybski, in his first book, *Manhood of Humanity*, speaks of the human species as a time-binder. He means the word "man" to cover, as he states explicitly, a certain "class of life." He differentiates that class of life from the plant class of life and from the animal class of life. It is a meaning quite close to this that we find in the book, *The Phenomenon of Man,* by Teilhard de Chardin. In fact, Teilhard has a small book published in French prior to his well-known popular volume, and this book was titled *Le Groupe Zoologique Humain.* When Alexis Carrel published his *Man The Unknown* in 1935, his meaning was less definite. Carrel could be interpreted to mean the individual or humankind as a whole.

In most cases, when a "definition" of "man" is given, the actual referent to the term is no more definite than in the title of Carrel's book. Quite often that "definition" implies a whole philosophy as in the small catechism I studied in my Catholic grade school. It read: "Man is a compound of a body and a soul, created by God to His image and likeness."

In this present handbook, I am trying to be more definite as to what I mean to talk about when I refer to the subject we are studying. I am not refering to "human" as a zoological group, and neither of humankind trudging along on the road of history. I refer strictly to individuals, whatever their age, sex, profession, or education; condition of health; cultural environment;

self-attitudes or attitudes toward the rest of the human race. There are billions of such individuals who lived or are actually breathing on the surface of the planet Earth; they are the definite reference of our discourse.

Also, I use the terms "human individuals" or "human beings" instead of "men" as much as possible. My intention is to explicitly include all members of the human family that do not fall within the limited category of "male," to which the masculine gender of *man* refers. The masculine gender so pervades our thinking and our use of our language that not only do we think of *Homo sapiens* as "he," but we even give a masculine gender to "God Himself." Emmeline Pankhurst, the London suffragette, undaunted by such presumptions, consoled one of her followers wounded in a demonstration by saying: "Don't worry, dear. God is with us, and *She* will take care of you."

Thus we can visualize the human race in space-time, moving about all over the earth through prehistoric times and recorded history—multitudes of individuals appearing and disappearing, milling about along the paths of history, all over the continents. Their crafts and their habits are changing as time goes on; their way of life differs from one place to another.

In this space-time multitude, I see groups and subgroups appearing and disappearing; families, tribes, associations, nations—growing at different rates, blending, and separating again.

With our referent for "human" established, and with the help of a mental model, we are ready to move into the "inner life" of ourselves as human individuals in continuous transaction.

Systems and Subsystems

Ludwig von Bertalanffy, a biologist, introduced a way of organizing our thinking that we could apply to our present work. He calls it a General Systems Theory. It could be translated in the following manner: Any phenomenon that we single down for observation and study could be seen as a "system," or as an assemblage of many elements interacting upon one another and acting upon the environment as a cohesive group. We can see systems in a hierarchical order, meaning that a system may contain many subsystems, and at the same time be itself contained in a larger container-system. In the present case, the individual is taken as an agglomeration of subsystems, as described in *Communication as Creative Experience*.

> The transacting organism is made of an intricate and inter-related network of systems:
> a. the nervous system, including the brain;
> b. the circulatory system;
> c. the chemical system (glands, hormones, metabolism, etc.);
> d. the habit system (sensory and motor activities: talking, listening, walking, gesticulating, taking notes, etc.);

e. the semantic system (preferred values, attitudinal sets, purposes, prejudices, etc.);

f. the linguistic and symbol system (mother tongue and acquired languages,
mathematical and professional modes of thinking, etc.)

These various systems may be considered one by one, but in the living
organism they are meshed with one another in a dynamic symbiosis that makes
them interdependent.[1]

It is important to note here that in this way of speaking of the individual as
made of subsystems, there is no division between body and soul. Habits and
modes of thinking are taken as systems, just like the circulatory system.

Of the various descriptions of the individual as a system made of subsystems, we chose one, casually suggested by Korzybski, as our main unit of
discourse. In conformity with the operational thinking that is now in fashion
in most sciences, we take as elements of that system, not physical objects
like muscles or brain nor old-style faculties as memory or imagination, but
activities. And so we describe the individuals as systems made of electrochemical, self-moving, feeling and purposing, thinking and deciding activities in ceaseless transactions with their space-time environments.

A Mental Model

We can look at scientific progress as an evolution of mental models
emerging in sequential order, each new one correcting and expanding the
one it replaces. The atom was first described as the smallest bit of matter
conceivable, homogeneous and unsplittable. Later, it was imagined as having tiny hooks that linked it to its neighbors. Nowadays a variety of models is
in use—the shell model, the liquid-drop model, the visual model—each
serving a different purpose for understanding and managing matter-energy.

In astronomy, the Ptolemaic model of the earth—at the center of trans-
parent concentric spheres—carried the sun, the planets, and the stars in
their daily revolution. Then we had the Copernican model, a static sun surrounded by seven planets that turned around it on the circumferences of
perfect circles. Later we had the Keplerian model of elliptical orbits with the
sun at one of the foci. Finally came the Newtonian model of gravitational
masses that moved according to definite laws and that integrated many
earthly phenomena with those of the planetary system. Today the Einstein-
ian model, capable of more accurate predictions than its predecesors, is so
abstract that it defies all graphic representation.

Something similar can be observed in the development of our mental
models of "man." We can compare the Ptolemaic model of the universe to

---

[1] J. Samuel Bois, *Communication as Creative Experience* (Los Angeles: Viewpoints Institute, 1968), p. 1.

the Aristotelian model of "man," both of which were acceptable in the same epoch of our cultural history. In its day, each served a useful purpose, replacing superstition with reason, divination with logic, mythology with philosophy, but each has outlived its usefulness. The Aristotelian model of "man" is just as inadequate for solving the problems of our generation as its coeval model, the Ptolemaic theory of the universe, is for guiding the policies and procedures of space exploration.

Our mental model of "man" is nothing but a formulation that dates back to the prelogical days of our civilization. "Man is a rational animal," said Aristotle, thus confirming the myth by giving it a place in his classification of the parts of the universe as it was known in his day. Since then we have taken it for granted that a human being is made of two elements, different in nature and in action: one is the mind and the other is the body; one is spirit and one is matter; one displays rationality and one displays animality. The interaction of these two elements, each belonging to a different order of existence, has remained for centuries one of the most baffling problems of our philosophy. The problem still lurks behind many commonsense dichotomies, materialism versus idealism, psychological versus physiological, and—in a derivative way—between the "two cultures," of which we have heard so much in recent years.

Korzybski was bold enough to announce a new human science, free from Aristotelian strictures and flexible enough to fit nonelementalistic systems. As said above, in his first book, *Manhood of Humanity*, he stated that the major problem of the day was to devise a new definition of *Homo sapiens*, free from the zoological and supernatural implications of the current definition. *"Man is a time-binding class of life,"* despite its originality and unquestioned value, was only a new classification of "man" as a "nature" among other "natures." It was well within the framework of Aristotelian thinking.

Later, in *Science and Sanity*, Korzybski became more operational, offering a picture of *Homo sapiens* in terms of human activities under various aspects. It is from this picture, delineated in verbal statements of Korzybski, that I constructed the visual model in Figure 3.1.

Korzybski referred to "man" as a semantic *reactor*, and his responses as semantic *reactions*. This was consistent with his view then of "man" facing an objective world. In my description, I have not only replaced the word "man" with "human individuals," but I have replaced *reactor* and *reaction* with *transactor* and *transaction*. This introduced the seed notions of epistemics that I described in another book:

> (The word) *transaction* has replaced the word *reaction* that Korzybski used. I continued using it without proper reflection. The word *reaction* reminds us of the Newtonian action and reaction, of the statement about actions and reactions shuttling back and forth. It fits with the standard psychological experiment

summarized in the two letters *SR* (stimulus response), as if the impact of a stimulus was the only determinant of the subject's activity. According to the *SR* formula, (humans) have to be set into motion, otherwise they won't budge. It is not so. We are always in activity. In fact, to use Kelly's phrase, *we are movement.* All that a stimulus can do is alter that movement, speed it up, slow it down, or give it another direction in a multidimensional life-space. When the human process relates itself to the relevant environment, a transaction takes place, not a simple reaction nor an interaction that leaves both of them unmodified in their inner structure. This transaction is viewed as a joint phenomenon that blends their energies for a while, and from which both emerge different from what they were prior to the encounter. Since the transaction is continuous, the changes in both the organism and the environment never stop. You may picture that continuity as a sequence of tiny units or quanta in order to examine

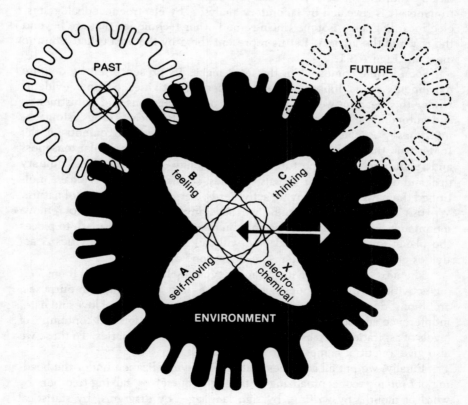

Figure 3.1. Individuals as semantic transactors. A semantic transaction has at least seven aspects or dimensions: (1) thinking; (2) feeling; (3) self-moving; (4) electrochemical; (5) environmental; (6) past; (7) future.

it, measure it, evaluate it, modify it; but all this fractionizing is the work of your discursive activity, which is always one step behind the actual transaction.[2]

The approach in Figure 3.1 is also operational: I do not attempt to define what a human being *is*, I describe what a human being *does*. Neither do I claim to cover exhaustively all human activities, I simply group—under a limited number of headings—the activities I consider most significant in the light of the sciences of today.

The first group is our *electrochemical* activities, from our embryonic immersion in the amniotic fluid to our eventual coagulation at death. It starts with the operations of DNA and RNA in the genes, and includes the metabolism of the cells, the firing of the neurons, the reactions to anesthetics and drugs, the effects of LSD, of the energizers and tranquilizers, the adaptation syndrome of Selye, the use of a supporting vital system for our astronauts. It is revealed by laboratory analyses, by electroenecephalograms, electrocardiograms, isotope tracings, and other techniques that are beyond the reach of the layman. Let us represent them by the area called X in the diagram, Figure 3.1.

Soon a time comes when the fetus makes its presence felt by definite movements of its limbs, and its *self-moving* activities become evident. Under this heading we can include sensory perceptions and adjustments, and autonomic movements of the vital organs: the heart, lungs, stomach, intestines, vascular system. We include the skilled movements of the tradesman, the machine operator, the athlete, the artist; muscular tenseness and relaxation, proper posture. We also include group activities: military drill and training, religious rituals, parades, sit-ins, and such. We have multiplied the power of our moving activities by harnessing the forces of nature. We use bulldozers and cranes, we have invented explosives to remove mountains, and we may soon be able, in one quick blow, to smash to pieces the planet on which we stand. We will call these moving activities A activities and will put the letter A in the second area.

The next group of activities is more typically human. We call them *feeling* activities, which includes not only drives and affects but also purposes, ambitions, desires, and responses to values. This is the area of love and hate, indifference and commitment, joy and sorrow, dedication and contempt, of levels of aspiration, of trust in friends, of frustrations, anxieties. To these we also give a neutral name: B activities.

Finally, we put all activities that involve symbolization under the heading of *thinking*: conceptualizing or talking to ourselves; talking to others by word of mouth, by writing, by sign language, by diagrams, by statistical curves to show trends, by gesticulation or facial expression; listening, read-

[2]J. Samuel Bois, *Epistemics: The Science-Art of Innovating* (San Francisco: International Society for General Semantics, 1972), pp. 42-43.

ing, asking questions, solving problems, planning, reaching decisions. We talk, listen, read, and write; we have newspapers, magazines, and books; we receive and send letters and telegrams; we have built schools, colleges, and universities; we have libraries and public monuments with inscriptions on them. Some people, elected or appointed by other people, go to great buildings where they speak, in turn, for hours and hours, and for weeks and months, about the affairs of their state, their nation, or the world. No animal species has anything that compares with this. Thinking, debating, planning, and communicating are human activities. Let us also give them a name that is noncommittal, and call them *C* activities.

These four clusters of activities overlap and interact. We see them not as distinct parts of an additive whole but as differentiated aspects—or dimensions—of an organismic process, within which they are interrelated and interdependent in a pattern of dynamic gradients. When we are given an anesthetic, we stop moving, feeling, and thinking. When we are emotionally excited, our muscular tonus changes, and our thoughts are stimulated or confused. Participating in a religious ritual, a sit-in demonstration, or an organized parade heightens feelings and gives direction to purposes. In other words, our approach to the observation of human beings is holistic: it ignores the old dichotomy of mind and body, spirit and matter.

Humans are not made of two parts, body and mind, that act one upon the other. We may be described as single, complex, integrated organisms whose activities may be described under at least four different aspects: *A*, *B*, *C*, and *X*. In general semantics, we call this complex transaction of the whole organism a *semantic* transaction; that is, a transaction that is determined by what the actual situation—the outside event, the word that is spoken, the thought that occurs, the hope that emerges—means to the individual at the moment.

This organism does not operate in a vacuum; it is influenced by an environment, transacts with it, and modifies it as it goes along. This environment has many aspects: physical, psychological, social, cultural, professional, racial, national. It is also indefinite at the edges, to the point that our semantic transactions are practically coextensive with our world awareness, clear or dim. We represent the environment by drawing a frame of wavy lines around the four overlapping ellipses.

Humans modify their environment and change it in an irreversible manner. Generations of human beings have transformed the North American continent of the Indians into the highly industrialized nations of the United States and Canada. The world in which we were born was the joint product of nature and the cumulative transactions of those who preceded us; the world that we shall pass on to the next generation will be in great part of our making. This participation involving the organism and the environment may be represented by a double-pointed arrow that links the very center of the cluster of ellipses to the environmental space.

Let us now introduce the time dimension into Figure 3.1. On the left side of the frame, let us draw a smaller frame that hides (in part) behind the central frame. In this receding frame, let us draw the four overlapping ellipses. This frame represents our past. In fact, we can imagine a long series of such frames, one for each year of our life. On the right side of the main frame, we can draw any number of similar frames—with *dotted* sinuous lines—to represent the future as we anticipate it. This past as we lived it, and this future as we anticipate it, are in a certain manner present in our semantic reaction of this moment. They operate in the "now" with their relative intensity, their tensions, and their direction. Many of our present reactions have been programmed into our system by the habits we have acquired in the past; they are oriented by what we expect or want our future to be. The individual may be seen as a space-time living totality that transacts with everything he or she has been, is, and anticipates being.

This, then, brings us to the description of the individual that I suggest should be substituted for the standard definition, "Man is a rational animal." It is a description, not a definition; it does not attempt to reveal the "real nature" of what a human being *is*; it simply tells what I think is important for whoever wants to deal with himself or herself and with others. *The individual may be described as a thinking, feeling, self-moving, electrochemical organism in continuous transaction with a space-time environment.*

This is a rather complex concept, but, with the help of the visual presentation, it is possible to encompass it. Physical scientists have achieved wonders because they see, behind the commonsense appearance of material objects, a complex structure of molecules, atoms, particles, and fields of energy. It is time that we begin to see, behind the commonsense appearance of individuals, complex space-time patterns of ceaseless activities.

It takes time to use, habitually and spontaneously, this complex picture as the foundation of our practical knowledge of ourselves and our fellow human beings. Our language does not help this new orientation; it is elementalistic. It assumes that thoughts, feelings, bodily movements, and biochemical exchanges within our tissues and endocrine glands are relatively independent phenomena. In what we are describing here, they are neither independent nor dependent in a cause-and-effect relation, they are *aspects* of *one* complex process. Instead of saying "I think," "I feel," "I move,"— which are elementalistic terms—I suggest that we say to ourselves "I transact." This means that my whole organism is engaged in a process with the momentum of its accumulated past, the drawing power of its anticipated future—depending on the environment in which it happens to be at the moment.

This transaction itself has a strong tendency to maintain a *status quo*.

It asserts the values I hold dear and confirms the ego-image that I have of myself. This is the exact spot where the practice of epistemics intervenes, correcting and reversing that strong tendency. It is in keeping with the *Philosophy of No* of Gaston Bachelard. It introduces the notions of participation and abduction, which are discussed in the more advanced practices toward the end of this text.

How will this eventually be said in one word—perhaps a brand new word—that will contain the whole complex formula? I don't know. In practice, I have often used the word transact, asking people who share my description of a human being "How do you *transact with* this or that?" instead of "What do you *think* of this?" or "How do you *feel* about that?"

The difference may appear slight at first, mere quibbling; but if one takes time to ponder over it he will quickly recognize that it is one of those differences that makes a great deal of difference. When we speak in terms of the transaction of the total organism we find it normal, for instance, that a lie detector should register physiological answers that are more reliable than the verbal answers.

Corollaries of the Model

From this diagram and description, taken as a theorem, we may draw several corollaries.

1. The larger frame—that of the present—is the center of gravity of the whole system. To shift that center to the past, in vain regrets or recollections, or to shift it to the future in wishful thinking, can create an unhealthy stagnation in one's living process.
2. Conversely, the past cannot be ignored nor the future left blank as when one has nothing to look forward to. In both cases, some trouble is bound to develop.
3. Within the framework of the present, the various aspects of our semantic transactions have a tendency to keep themselves in a steady state. A state of profitable equilibrium, which if maintained beyond its usefulness, may become stagnation or inertia, and thereby prevent needed development. An acquired equilibrium may have established itself and eventually become accepted as permanent. This is the case of a neurosis, and it resists changes as in the case of drug addiction and destructive emotional habits. The emergence of one steadying stage to a more complex one will be introduced later in the text as the practice of conscious participation.
4. The whole system itself—past, present, and future—tends to maintain a balance that is minimal for survival and maximal for self-actualization. A fully functioning person has a high degree of self-acceptance because he has learned to translate into a meaningful structure whatever has hap-

pened to him since the beginning, whatever is now within his reach, and whatever he is planning for the future.

5. No two persons experience an event, word, or person in exactly the same manner. In no case do the seven dimensions of their semantic transactions coincide in all respects. The wondrous thing is not that we disagree, but that we so often manage to get along passably well.

6. No response of one person ever repeats itself as an exact duplicate. As time flows, some change, slight or important, is likely to take place in one or several of the semantic variables. To be rigorously consistent may mean to be frozen to insensitivity, out of touch with oneself and with the on-going environment.

7. No transaction is exclusively intellectual, emotional, or physiological. We transact as a whole, whether we are conscious of it or not. This is what Korzybski meant when he spoke of psycho-logics as different from logic, the prefix *psycho* covering all nonintellectual components of the total transaction.

8. Solving a problem or making a decision is not merely a matter of logical analysis, of weighing the pros and cons, of thinking clearly and logically. It is a labor of the whole process, and it may be greatly helped by such conditions as freedom from undue haste and deeper and deeper relaxation, both physical and mental, which may appear to have little relation to the task at hand.

9. A conversation is not so much an exchange of objective information between two persons as the encounter of two semantic transactors of two human capsules in flight, each following its own orbit, with its mass, its momentum, its direction, and its capacity to withstand shocks. It may require advance technology and refined skills, as in the encounter of Apollo and Soyuz, which, starting from very different worlds, joined for over two days in common flight.

10. When several people gather together to work on a common interest or to discuss a theoretical issue, there is more than a matching of facts or a comparison of disembodied ideas. It could become a team wrestling match, where no rules are observed, or it could be a cooperative undertaking to live pleasantly together for a while, enriching one another by sharing diversified experiences.

11. The semantic character of our transactions does not depend on the dictionary meaning of the words we use or the "objective" nature of the event, it depends mostly on the meaning we attach to words, events, and persons, and how these meanings are related—positively or negatively—to the values we cherish, respect, or hold in contempt. This indicates that the "feeling" or *B* aspect of our semantic transactions is, more often than not, the determining factor in our behavior.

12. Finally, the world in which we live may be seen as a world of semantic transactions. What really counts, in this world of ours, is not so much what we see, hear, touch, weigh, and measure, it is how we transact with what our culture has singled out as natural things, man-made objects, and other humans. "What are the crude deliverances of sensible experience," asked Whitehead, "apart from the world of imaginative reconstruction which for each of us has the best claim to be called our real world?"[3]

Semantic States

When semantic transactions that have much in common gather together in space-time, they become semantic states. These semantic states may materialize into institutions, organizations, or cultural practices. I see religions as institutionalized semantic states with participants from various parts of the world and from many generations. I see nazism as a semantic state that grew among Germans after the Versailles Treaty, and that it was recognized in its inchoate stage by the sinister genius of Hitler and brought to maturity through his efforts. I see communism as a semantic state conceived by Karl Marx, nurtured by Lenin, and sovietized in Russia. Who will deny that these semantic states, and similar ones, were real forces in shaping world history?

With the semantic transaction model in mind, we see ideologies that split the world into opposite camps as something more than activities of thinking, for *ideology* implies differences in theories that are accepted as valid pictures of reality. With the present model, we see that ideologies are semantic systems in which the history of a nation, its acquired attitudes and habits, and its purposes, fears, and hopes for the future give dynamism and direction to the planning of its leaders and to the day-to-day activities of its common people.

Shortcomings of the Model

"The map does not represent all the territory," said Korzybski. This is true of all models, and this one is no exception. Its shortcomings are evident to whoever looks at it with a critical eye, and it is important to take them into account.

The figure and the sentence that describes it put the organism and the environment in undue contrast. It gives the impression that a more firmly structured unit, the organism, is within a less solidly organized milieu, the environment. This, we know, is not always true. We have witnessed cases

[3]Alfred North Whitehead, *The Aims of Education* (New York: Mentor Books [New American Library], 1949), p. 162.

where the environment crushed the individual, and we don't have to bring
in the story of Galileo to prove our point. Conversely, we know of cases
where the environment—physical, economic, cultural, or social—has
helped an individual make the most of his inborn capacities, or even go
beyond what could normally be expected.

This tendency to see the organism as a Gestalt against the environment
as a background is not due to a shortcoming that is specific to this model; it is
a mental set that we all have, without realizing it fully, and it is consistent
with our commonsense thinking about the world that surrounds us. We see
the world as made of sharply differentiated objects that stand within an
empty space and that move, or do not move, in a measurable time. We can
correct this commonsense view by viewing the diagram not as a picture of an
individual against a background, but as the fluid representation of a dynamic
system, of a space-time ongoing phenomenon of life-action, emerging from
the changing relationships among factors (activities A, B, C, X, the Past, the
Future as anticipated, and the Environment), which are themselves happen-
ings-in-flux.

The model is, at best, of the physical type, static in its graphic representation and made dynamic by a conscious effort of the imagination. It does not
show the conscious self-reflexiveness that makes self-observation, self-control, and self-management possible. It does not meet the requirements of
biological models, which would picture a human being as an open, self-maintaining, self-differentiating, and growing system. These various requirements will have to be met later, when we will devise models of all kinds
without worrying too much about their strict consistency among themselves,
and when we will place greater reliance on the complementary effect they
can produce when used with full awareness of their individual limitations.

We are still far from having a set of human mental models that are comparable to the pictures of the atom or the DNA molecule that are already
common in magazines and popular literature. It might help, as a start, to
consider all forms of human interaction—in politics, business, courts of law,
family life, love-making—semantic transactions. Most of the troubles we
have can be traced to the obsolete human mental models we persist in using.
The Ptolemaic model of the universe is obsolete, so is the Aristotelian model
of man; and Korzybski saw this more than fifty years ago.

> It requires no great wisdom, it needs only a little reflection, to see that, if we
> humans radically misconstrue the nature of man . . .we commit an error so fun-
> damental and farreaching as to produce every manner of confusion and disaster
> in individual life, in community life, and in the life of the race.[4]

[4]Korzybski, *Manhood of Humanity*, 2d ed. (Lakeville, Conn.: International Non-
Aristotelian Library, 1950), p. 2.

What Korzybski in this quotation calls the "nature of Man" is what we are attempting to present in an altogether different manner. Up-to-date science has given up the claim that it deals with the "nature" of anything. It deals with phenomena or clusters of activities, as Teilhard de Chardin says in the original French title of his well-known book, *Le Phenomene Humain*.

CHAPTER 4

the place and scope of non-aristotelian systems

Misunderstandings and Rectifications

It is one of the purposes of this third edition of *The Art of Awareness* to put an end to the misunderstandings surrounding the name General Semantics and, thus, the limiting of the discipline to linguistics and speech communication. I suggest for the discipline a new name that has no evident commonality with semantics in all its forms. As I've stated already, I call it Epistemics. This term was formally introduced in 1969. However, I deem it expedient to keep in this third edition, the sections in this chapter that were inserted in previous editions to dispel the misunderstandings. This will serve, at the same time, as an historical account of the gradual transformation of what Korzybski had labeled "a Non-Aristotelian System."

The term "general semantics" has created a great deal of trouble for those who promote the Korzybskian system and a great deal of confusion in the minds of people who have only a casual acquaintance with it. Of the two words, the second is the noun. and we expect the noun to tell us what the entire term "really" means. Semantics is semantics—"general," "special," "limited," or what-have-you—it is a *kind* of semantics. But all this is quite erroneous.

The dictionary says that semantics belongs to linguistics, that "it is the study of meanings and changes of meaning." General semantics would therefore seem to be a form of linguistics, dealing with words and communication skills, and we call it "general" because it probably deals with all kinds of communication media, not only with words. It probably covers other kinds of symbols and other kinds of techniques, such as diagrams, visual aids, and the like; it considers even mathematics as a language.

This interpretation is quite common. Thus in 1943 Raymond Moley wrote in his syndicated column: "Remember, those Administration boys are great believers in semantics, which is New Dealese for the art or science of picking words coated with the right kind of chocolate icing." In a more serious vein, some persons use semantics to mean the science and the art of avoiding verbal confusion, for example, Max Lerner in the *New York Post* in 1950: "By any Western standard of democracy, the Russian elections are a poor semantic joke. . . .The word democracy for the Russians does not mean what it means for us. When they call their elections 'democratic,' don't let the word fool you; it does not mean free elections as we have them here."

Several personal experiences illustrate the same point. Years ago, while giving a talk to the Montreal Personnel Association, I attempted to answer the ever-recurring question, "What is general semantics?" My explanations were apparently a bit confusing for my listeners, so in the question and discussion period, a good friend of mine—a psychologist who had turned journalist (and was very successful at it)—got up and took it upon himself to translate my rather confusing statements into plain, clear, commonsense language. Doing his best to excuse my esoteric approach and to assuage my feelings at the same time, he said (in effect):

> Scientists have a language all their own, and it is not always easy for the common man to follow them. As a journalist, it has been my role to translate scientific language into plain English, and I am sure that my good friend, the speaker of the evening, will not mind my translating what he just said. Semantics, as we all know, is the study of the meaning of words, and General Semantics is the study of the original, real, and pure meaning of words and symbols, so that they can be restored to their genuine value. Words could be compared to ships traveling the seas of communication. The job of the general semanticist is to scrape the hull of those ships, to remove the barnacles that have accumulated, and to restore the ships to their original, clean, smooth sailing shape. What is true of words is true of all symbols. Hence the term *general* semantics.

His statement was clear, very clear indeed. His intentions were good. He wanted to help me out, to clear away the fog of misunderstanding that he could see between my listeners and me. But he had done exactly the opposite of what I wanted of a helper. He had brushed aside all the differences I had suggested between semantics and general semantics. He had misled the audience in a most competent manner, by telling them that general semantics is just another kind of semantics, of word and symbol study, a bit broader than the commonly accepted branch of linguistics.

Another source of misunderstanding is that many of the books and publications that have made general semantics known to the public emphasize the linguistic aspect of Korzybski's system. They do not *explicitly* limit GS to what their titles imply, but they do little to correct the restricted view that the casual reader gets from such phrases as the following: "language habits in human affairs," "language in thought and action," "the tyranny of words," "words and what they do to you," "language, meaning, and maturity," "the use and misuse of language," "a quarterly concerned with the role of language and symbols in human behavior."

In many cases, the discipline has been accepted and taught in departments of speech and communication, as at the University of Denver; in departments of English as in the Illinois Institute of Technology; San Francisco State, in departments of education with emphasis on proper communication between teachers and students. There was even, in 1969, an annual meeting of general semanticists held as a symposium on communications, when a university professor from the other side of the Iron Curtain participated, thus giving to the communication aspect an international sanction. One of my own books, published by Viewpoints Institute, Los Angeles, in 1968, has a title that befoggles the issue even more. The title reads: *Communication as Creative Experience*.

In fact, semantics and general semantics hardly belong to the same order of things. Historically, they have nothing in common. In the preface to the third edition of his *Science and Sanity*, which appeared in 1948 (fifteen years after the original manuscript was completed), Korzybski wrote:

> My work was developed entirely independently of "semantics," "significs," "semiotic," "semasiology," etc., although I know today and respect the work of the corresponding investigators in those fields, who explicitly state that they do not deal with a theory of values. *Those works do not touch my field.* . . . The original manuscript did not contain the word "semantic" or "semantics."[5]

In the same preface, Korzybski calls his theory "a theory of values . . . for educational guidance and self-guidance." In earlier writings he had called it by various names, such as Humanology, Time-binding Theory, General Theory of Evaluation, and even Human Engineering. He quickly abandoned this last term when he realized that it had been preempted by psychologists and engineers who work on the adaptation of man to machine and of machine to man. We noted in our introduction that in his first book he described GS as an attempt to develop a scientific ethics, and Korzybski comes back to the same theme in the concluding remarks of *Science and Sanity* (pp. 555-557).

Finally, we have to take into account another statement of his, when he looked at his work from another angle and described it in a somewhat detached manner.

---

[5]Korzybski, *Science and Sanity*, 3d ed. (Lakeville, Conn.: International Non-Aristotelian Library, 1948), p. viii (italics added).

General Semantics turned out to be an empirical natural science of non-elementalistic evaluation, which takes into account the living individual, not divorcing him from his reactions altogether, nor from his neuro-linguistic and neuro-semantic environment, but allocating him in a *plenum* of some values, no matter what.[6]

Semantics and General Semantics

We may visualize the distinction between semantics and general semantics with the help of Figure 4.1. Here we have three men, each represented

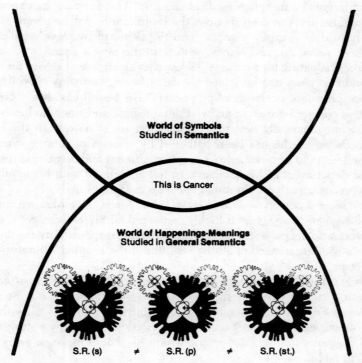

Figure 4.1. Semantics and General Semantics cover two different worlds. These worlds overlap to some extent, as shown in the statement, "This is cancer." The meaning of the word "cancer" may be found in a dictionary. The semantic response of the surgeon, S. R. (s), is different from the semantic response of the patient, S. R. (p), and different from the semantic response of the statistician, S. R. (st.). These are "happenings-meanings" not to be found in dictionaires or books. (Reproduced from a diagram by J. S. Bois, *Explorations in Awareness*, p. 47. Copyright, 1957. Harper & Row, with permission.)

[6]Korzybski, *Science and Sanity*, 3d ed., p. viii (italics added).

by a central frame that contains four overlapping ellipses and is flanked on each side by two receding similar frames, the one on the left representing their cumulative past and the one on the right representing their future as they anticipate it.

All three men happen to be in the same room in a hospital on a certain morning. From left to right we see, first, a surgeon, Dr. Jones; next a patient, named Jack; and the third man is Fred, a statistician who works for a research project conducted by the local university on the biochemical aspect of certain diseases.

Jack, who has been there for a few days, is under observation and has been undergoing a thorough medical checkup. This morning he expects the final diagnosis and the decision upon the treatment he will be given. He is in his early thirties, happily married, and the father of two lovely children—Bob, three years old, and Nancy, who is a little over a year.

After graduating from college, Jack was an electronic engineer for a large firm, and two years ago he joined the fast-growing company of which he is now vice-president in charge of production. His health has always been excellent; at college he was on many athletic teams, and since he has been at work he has practically never lost a day because of illness. In the last six months, however, he has been bothered by a series of strange symptoms that don't seem to be amenable to simple treatment and occasional rest. The medical department of his company, in full agreement with his family doctor, has recommended a thorough checkup in the hospital.

The second person we will observe is Dr. Jones, a well-known surgeon, about fifty years of age, who is highly respected for his knowledge, skill, and his devotion to his patients. He has accepted full responsibility for the case, and he is availing himself of all the facilities of the hospital laboratories and technicians.

Among the other persons who are present—Dr. Jones's assistant, the head nurse of the department, and others—we will single out Fred, the statistician. From what he was told, the present case may fall well within one of the categories the research team is interested in. He is now waiting for the official diagnosis that will determine where he should make an entry in his statistical table.

A final report from the pathological laboratory deals with a biopsy, a sample of the patient's tissue that was taken for examination under the microscope. The findings are very definite: it is cancer; and all interested parties are so informed. The surgeon knows, the patient is told, and the statistician is shown the original report.

How do these three people respond to the word *cancer* and to the happening it refers to? What does it mean to each of them—to the surgeon, to the patient, and to the statistician? We can safely assume that all understand what the word means in terms of its dictionary definition, but they surely do not respond in the same manner to what the word and the happening means in terms of their individual thinking, feeling, and planning.

The young executive, his career suddenly stopped short, and possibly ended, thinks of his wife, his children, his job, and his prospects. He may think of the treatment he must undergo, of the fight for life he has to undertake. His semantic response will probably be experienced at the feeling level, the level of *B* activities. The bright future he anticipated has been blotted out.

The response of Dr. Jones is different from that of his patient: it is mostly a matter of hard thinking, of reviewing his experience with similar cases, and of planning what can be done. He may think of discussing the case with some colleague who is a specialist, of checking a recent report in a medical journal. His response is, primarily: What should be done, when, and how?

For the statistician, this is simply one case among hundreds of others. He checks the proper square in a scatter diagram where the type of illness and the age group lines meet as coordinates, and he enters a reference number for the digest he will make of the dossier. Then he is on his way to the next room, where he is likely to find another patient whose data will also fit his sampling.

If we are concerned with the meaning of *cancer*, we are in the field of semantics, and we see that the differences in understanding it are not great: the surgeon, the patient, and the statistician agree on what it means. If we are concerned with their personal response to the word and what the situation means to each of them, we see great differences. The surgeon does not respond to the situation as the patient does, and the latter, in turn, does not respond in the same way as the statistician; much more than etymological and historical word meaning is involved.

Their thoughts, their feelings, their total organismic reactions, their experiences and memories, their views and expectations for the future, their hopes and their doubts, their professional statuses and their ambitions, their loves and their interests in life, their entire outlook on themselves and their personal values, all this is involved and gives either a tragic or a casual quality to what is said and to what occurs in that hospital room. This world of subjective turbulence is not the detached, objective world of the scientific study of words and symbols, it is not the world of simple semantics; it is the world of what I designate by a hyphenated double word, the world of *happenings-meanings*. It is not the world of what happens "objectively," but the bipolar world of what happens and of how one responds to and is affected by what happens; it is the world of self-awareness and self-management. This world of happenings-meanings is the field of General Semantics; it is that plenum of values within which we live and of which Korzybski spoke in the passage quoted in the previous section.

Our purpose is to become aware of our transactions under their various aspects, to learn how to manage them with as little wear and tear as possible, to learn how to make the most of them for our personal growth and for smoother and more productive transactions with our fellow human beings in our family, our profession, and in public life. Of course, a well-informed and judicious use of words and symbols has its place in such an undertaking, but it is evident that linguistics, etymology, good grammar, and communication skills are not all. We need the information that the sciences of man can offer, and we have to integrate their findings in a balanced program. Semantics deals with words and their generally accepted meaning; general semantics deals with the meaning we find or put in whatever we do and whatever happens to us.

The task is more easily stated than performed. To get the feel of the general semantics orientation, we have to overcome our well-established habits of elementalistic thinking. Korzybski was most insistent on this, and I agree with him wholeheartedly. The philosophy of Jan Smuts' holism and the clinical evidence of Kurt Goldstein—to mention only two distant and very different authors—confirm these views.

What does it mean, exactly? It means that we have to learn not to dissociate thinking from feeling or from bodily phenomena. When we try to make sense of a perplexing situation, we are not juggling disembodied ideas that are either true or false or right or wrong. We are tossed about by our semantic responses, alive, sensitive, dynamic, and responsive to space-time pressures, of which we are not always conscious. To master a delicate situation is a laborious process that may wear us out if we don't know how to manage it under the seven aspects of the semantic transaction diagram (Figure 3.1).

The complexity is compounded when two or more persons engage in the study of a practical or theoretical issue. They do not simply fit together the pieces of a jigsaw puzzle, each of which has a predetermined place that will be recognized by all once it is found; they crowd together, in a "fenced-in" area, a diverse group of semantic responses, each with its acquired momentum and direction, its set habits, and its more-or-less conscious purposes. These responses push one another, momentarily clash or join, rearrange themselves in groups and subgroups, help their allies and fight their opponents, stop the struggle in a compromise, or leave the scene hurt and mangled by a battle where no quarter was given nor received. Unless we are aware of what occurs in such an encounter, we cannot deal adequately with the situation.

We have a ringside seat for such encounters when we listen to certain debates on the radio or look at certain discussion programs on TV. Sometimes they are advertised in advance, and highly recommended, because they will be exciting (it seems that "exciting" is one of the qualities that make a debate worthwhile). The participants are known to hold diametrically op-posite views, and they are recognized as able debaters. It will be a verbal fight, but something like a boxing match as well, and in such a game seman-tics, as the art of manipulating words for offense and defense, may indeed make a winner.

General semantics is not a training for fighting in debates, it is a method for joint creative work. The purpose is not to beat or win over an opponent, it is to work together in order to find a solution that will be better than either of the participants could have invented by himself. This calls for the skill of talking effectively, but also for the more difficult skill of listening well.

We can imagine our brain as a radio set on which we can both receive and send, which also works as a combination set, containing a library of records that can be put on automatically. An untrained listener tries to do all three operations at once: while listening to the speaker, he puts on one of his records and plays what he has already registered in his past experience on the subject that is being discussed. If the incoming program does not har-monize with his own record, we know which one will "make sense" to him.

He may also, while pretending to listen, rehearse his answers and objec-tions as he waits impatiently for the other fellow to stop—rehearse on his "brain set" the broadcast he plans to give in his turn. If we observe ourselves closely, we may see that these three activities often go on simultaneously in our brain. We listen to a speaker, we listen to our own pet ideas, and we tell ourselves what we are going to say as a rejoinder.

I was once studying this observation with a group of executives who were training in general semantics and I asked them the following question: "From your own experience in business conversations, which would you rather do: listen to the other fellow or speak your own mind? Which is harder, more unpleasant, less satisfactory?" The general answer was: "Of course, listening is harder. You have to listen to so many stupid things these days"!

Of course, the *other* fellow does not make sense very often, but when we broadcast our own wisdom what a wonderful message it sounds—to us! If we could drown out those stupid incoming programs once and for all, what a sensible place this world would be! And we rush to a course on public speak-ing to master the techniques of putting our ideas across. There will then be one, or two, or a dozen more "expensive" broadcasting sets in our organiza-tion, and fewer and fewer receiving sets.

The debater does not stop here, he practices how *not* to listen to the valid arguments of his adversary; he is given his side of the question, or he is chosen to defend what is already his side, and his first task is *not to* accept the version of the other side. He marshals arguments, rehearses his own broadcast while his opponent is speaking, gets up his own story in words as sizzling as he can make them—and the audience admires the side that can jam the other broadcasting station most effectively and that shouts its own program with more kilowatts of verbal noise. Is this training for communication—or is it training for misunderstanding?

I do not claim that all persons who confuse general semantics and semantics are limiting themselves to the skill of debating as I have just described it. I also admit that it is most useful to know the shortcomings and the possibilities of the spoken and the written word—in fact, a good deal of training in general semantics is devoted to this—but we must start with a clear statement of what general semantics is *not*. It is definitely *not* the science or art of picking words coated with the right kind of chocolate icing, as Raymond Moley said.

Logic and Psycho-logics

In their attempt to make general semantics fit within the generally accepted classification of the sciences, some people see it as a new form of logic. The term *non-Aristotelian system,* which Korzybski often used in describing it, lends itself to such an interpretation. Many questions come to mind: Is it a refined form of symbolic logic, or an extension of Boolean algebra? Is it related to cybernetics? Since Korzybski speaks with enthusiasm of mathematics and calls it "a language similar in structure to the world in which we live,"[7] is not his system an attempt to introduce mathematical rigor into the conduct of human affairs? Is general semantics intended to do for the social sciences what mathematics has done for the physical sciences?

These questions reveal one of the most deeply hidden assumptions of our culture, for they imply that to progress as a human being is to devise and practice more sophisticated thinking skills. After all, is it not thinking that makes man different from his animal cousins? And, as a consequence, is not every human advance an advance in methods of thinking?

It is, and it is not. Thinking is *one* aspect of human activities, but it is only *one of many*. It involves special disciplines, and mathematical logic is one. It is one of those highly specialized techniques that are of very little use in simple life situations. It is a refinement of classical Aristotelian logic, a chest of mental tools reserved to specialists. General semantics is less specialized than this; in a sense, it is a *denial* of logic as an adequate method of self-management.

The word *think* refers to an activity that was classified centuries ago, at the time when our ancestors still believed that the four basic elements of the universe were air, fire, water, and earth. It seems that everybody knows what thinking is and what it is not. Long before Mr. Watson of IBM made it a slogan in his firm, it was taken as the supreme characteristic of man. Au-

[7]Korzybski, *Science and Sanity,* p. 247.

guste Rodin's statue, *The Thinker,* shows a man sitting with his muscles tense and working hard with his brain to solve some abstruse problem. Electronic engineers have built machines that do complex thinking by electricity, quickly and accurately.

The more we consider thinking in this manner, the farther we are from general semantics. Let us put aside Mr. Watson's slogan, Rodin's statue, the cybernetics of Norbert Wiener, the metaphorical thinking of Synectics as applied to problem solving, symbolic logic, and Boolean albegra; and let us stop looking at thinking as a distinct entity, dissected out of man alive and struggling, and kept functioning all by itself like a tissue culture in a flask of nutrient fluid.

When you and I think, a great deal more than "pure" thinking goes on within us. Our past has much to do with our thinking, and our anticipation of the future influences our thoughts. In fact, to say that we are thinking is to speak of only one aspect of our semantic transactions, and it is not always the most important aspect. It is occasionally subservient to other aspects: we rationalize to justify our past decisions, to give vent to our feelings, to make ourselves acceptable to our social environment, or to obey some unconscious urge that we cannot perceive.

There is also a chemical aspect to our semantic transactions: LSD and tranquilizers affect our thinking, as well as does the nutritional content of the food we eat. There is an electrical aspect as well: an electroshock will destroy stubborn thinking patterns; and through various biofeedback techniques we can also learn to influence our brain wave patterns, thus changing the electrical "weather" in which our thinking activities take place.

Symbolic logic—and all less sophisticated techniques of guided reasoning—deal with only one aspect of our multifaceted semantic reactions whereas general semantics attempts to take all aspects into account, concurrently and interrelatedly. An expert in symbolic logic is like an expert in a particular sport, but a well-trained semanticist is a well-rounded "psychological athlete." The latter's model is not Rodin's *Thinker* in its tense attitude and not the electronic robot that flashes answers in fractions of a second; his ambition is to keep himself in dynamic balance within himself and with his environment, aware of his past and realistic about his future, actualizing himself and his world as he proceeds from commitment to commitment.

This calls for new skills and techniques. At the thinking level, it takes into account phenomena that standard logic did not bother with; and it introduces terms and practices that are entirely new.

We have already dealt with one of these terms, *semantic transaction,* which we take as fundamental. Other chapters of this textbook will deal with

[8]Morris R. Cohen and Ernest Nagel, *An Introduction to Logic and Scientific Method* (New York: Harcourt, Brace & World, 1943), p. iv.

such questions as abstraction, circularity, and multiordinality; additive thinking will be corrected by the structural more. We shall go into model-building, and we shall introduce an epistemological scale for measuring the relative obsolescence of the components of our key notions.

Treatises on logic, elementary or advanced, do not use these terms or their equivalents; they leave it to psychology to study systematically how the mind works. "Logic, as the science of the weight of evidence in all fields, cannot be identified with the special science of psychology," says a standard textbook on logic.[8]

Contrary to this view, Korzybski puts psychology and logic together: he speaks of psycho-logical analysis, of psycho-logical occurrences; and these occurrences are our semantic transactions. We may study them at two levels: (1) the nonverbal level, which includes our unspeakable feelings, emotions, purposes, needs, and which is by far the most important; and (2) the verbal level, which includes what our grammar lists as parts of speech, and their arrangement according to the rules of syntax. Korzybski considers this verbal level as "auxiliary, sometimes useful, but at the present often harmful, because of the disregard of semantic reactions."[9]

Logic is often considered an absolute, an ideal form of human activity that has a value of itself, independent of time and space. This fits well with the Aristotelian view of man, who is taken to be essentially the same at any age, under any condition, and at any time of history.

Psycho-logics is not an absolute. It views each person as an individual, different from everyone else—in age, in bodily condition, in experience, in habits, in purposes—and as having a different physical and cultural environment and occupying a different place in time and space. What all individuals have in common is not so evident as was imagined in previous philosophies; in fact, man is still very much "the unknown," as Alexis Carrel put it several years ago. In our provincialism, we took humans as we knew them—that is, Western humans, who grew within the Greco-Roman culture and in the Judeo-Christian tradition—as the typical model of humankind. All outsiders were atypical; they were underdeveloped or spoiled patterns of true humanity. Their logic, because it did not jibe with our own, was considered imperfect and inconsistent, if not completely wrong.

Psycho-logics is an empirical science of individuals as they actually exist and function. It sees each and every human being as a historical product, time-bound and time-binding. A person's past history, including physical and cultural ancestry, is part of his or her uniqueness, and it is with this unique living individual that we must deal—not with an abstract human nature that should be the same for everybody, and that should in all cases conform to the rules of some absolute, unerring logic.

[9]Korzybski, *Science and Sanity,* p. 24.

Has any area of human endeavor reached that rock-bottom form of invariant human logic? Perhaps mathematics; but, for our day-to-day guidance, we have to understand that this hypothetical core of essential human logic is buried deep in thinking patterns that are not reducible one to the other any more than blood types can be mixed or substituted for one another. Absolute logic is a metaphysical discipline that assumes that we know "human nature." Psycho-logics, on the other hand, is an attempt to create, test, and improve a mental model that can be used to observe any specimen of the class *Homo sapiens,* to make sense of what one does, and to predict, within a range of probable error, what one is likely to do in particular situations.

In this science, our unit of discourse is not thinking as a separate activity—nor feeling, nor sensation, nor any of the generally accepted bits of human behavior—it is behavior as a whole, taken under its aspect of meaningful value. This behavior is cut into lumps or units of experience; and the cutting and the lumping is not done once and for all, it may vary depending on purpose. I like the way Dr. David Krech, of the University of California (Berkeley), puts it: "We must conceive of our fundamental unit of experience (or behavior) as a motivational-perceptual-cognitive unit—no matter how trivial or momentary, or how important and enduring that experience might be."[10]

In simple language, this means that the most significant "chunks" of behavior, the basic "molecules" of our lives, are like bundles of perceivings, feelings, strivings, thinkings, and understandings that cohere by some strange force that binds them in a package. These bundles may extend in time. They may last a few seconds, as when one bursts into laughter at a good joke; they may last for hours or days, as when one worries over a personal problem.

Now let us try to form some idea of the special force that holds these units together and packs the bits of experience that they contain into a tight bundle like atoms packed into a molecule. What makes a behavior unit different from another that appears just as short or just as long, just as simple or just as complex? According to Korzybski, the force that binds together the atoms of these molecular units of behavior is their meaning to the individual. They form a unit according to what they mean to us at the moment we experience them.

John Dewey, the famous philosopher and educator, once said that "a stimulus becomes a stimulus in virtue of what the organism is already preoccupied with." In other words, our responses to what happens, to what we encounter in life, to what is said to us, to what stirs within us, is not deter-

---

[10]David Krech, "Dynamic Systems as Open Neurological Systems," *General Systems,* ed. von Bertalanffy and Rapoport (Ann Arbor: Braun-Blumfield, 1956), p. 150.

mined so much by the cold "objective" facts, words, or events as by what we are concerned with at the moment of impact—by what the impact itself causes to emerge from within us. Our responses depend—in intensity, quality, duration, and relative importance—on what the total experience means to us. The meaning of an experience is not something that is added to an otherwise neutral experience, it is what causes the experience to be what it is.

The experience, then, is shot through with meaning, and this is what Korzybski expresses when he calls it semantic. According to this view, our human world is not so much a world of things, constructions, laws, and institutions as it is a world of human activities and of their meanings, a world of semantic transactions. Psycho-logics is the science of these transactions.

In psycho-logics, we take our semantic transactions as our working units of discourse. We see them as complex processes that are made of an unlimited number of subprocesses, interrelated and interdependent. Our means of observation and description are limited to the consideration of seven main clusters of these subprocesses, one of which we call *thinking*. It covers what we say to ourselves or to others with reference to what is going on within ourselves while we transact with our space-time environment. It is a resultant of the whole semantic process, and it gives it a structure and a direction.

If we look for an analogy to help us grasp the dynamic complexity of this semantic mind-body-environment process, we may use a tree that is in full activity. Whether our thinking is plain common sense or refined symbolic logic, we can compare it to the "greening" of the leaves of the tree. The greening is a function of the total metabolism of the tree, and it is a necessary component of the whole process. If the whole process is in harmonious balance with itself and with its space-time environment, the greening of the leaves will be healthy, and it will fulfill its potential development. We can also observe this in an orchard: the bushes and the trees bloom and bear fruit if the conditions are right; if any of the conditions varies above or below an optimum range, there is trouble, and this trouble will show in any of the many aspects of the behavior of the tree.

We went away for a couple of weeks one summer, after instructing the boy who was left in charge of watering our garden to water this new bush every other day, to water these trees once a week, and not to bother with those other bushes—they can wait until we are back. The boy did exactly as he had been told, following our detailed instructions to the letter. But the weather did not follow the course we had expected; it was beastly hot for days and days in succession.

The Royal Jasmine on the archway to the patio, the young camellia near the compost pit, and the persimmon tree in the orchard were the worst affected. Their leaves were wilting a bit when we came back and they were listless and old-looking in the burning sun. Their greening aspect was not good, revealing a disturbance in the soil, in the air, within the plant itself, or within the whole plant-soil-air system. It was most evident at the greening level, but it was not exclusively—or mainly—a greening problem.

So is it with the thinking aspect of our semantic transactions: we do what we expect should be done, and suddenly we find that our thinking is inappropriate and ineffective. It loses its healthy vitality, like the leaves of our jasmine, our camellia, and our persimmon tree. Is it exclusively a *thinking* problem?

Here is the case of a wife who recognized that her thinking and that of her husband went awry.

> The main feeling that we both carried with us is fear. Our separate reactions to this emotion are almost diametrically opposed: I freeze all feelings to protect myself, and Fred fights verbally. All our married life we have each interpreted the other's behavior as anger, when it was really fear, and thus a vicious circle has been set up.

What theorem of symbolic logic applies in this case? It is evident that their thinking turns round and round in a vicious circle. The thinking aspect of their semantic transactions has a neurotic character, just as the greening aspect of our trees had a sickly appearance when we came back from our trip.

In both cases, we look for the condition that is within our control and that might alter the situation. For the jasmine, I used a rooter and a chemical fertilizer; for the persimmon tree, only a thorough soaking was needed. The young camellia was in a critical condition, but we eventually saved it. In the case of my correspondent, it is probable that the couple is doing more "thinking" than is good for them; simple relaxation and sharing experiences at the silent level may be indicated.

Symbolic logic works at the level where the thinking disturbance occurs; it deals with thinking as with a relatively independent mechanism that either works or fails to work. We adjust our thinking as we adjust the timing in our car. The psycho-logics of general semantics may or may not intervene at the level where the disturbance has occurred: it deals with the whole organism-in-a-particular-environment-at-a-particular-time. It is not so much concerned with consistency in thinking as with appropriate semantic growth and effectiveness.

By appropriate semantic growth, I mean the healthy state of a person who develops and participates within the optimum range for his age, his education, his past experience, his anticipated future, and the possibilities of the environment in which he happens to be. "When I was a child, I spoke like a child, I thought like a child, I reasoned like a child," wrote the apostle Paul. The logic of the child is different from the logic of the adolescent. When the gonads become active at puberty, the biochemical changes in the organism also cause the face of the world to change. The boy and the girl are not "kids" any more; they think like teenagers, they speak like teenagers, they reason like teenagers. When one becomes a parent, responsible for the life, welfare, and future of children, one assumes a new kind of psycho-logics. He or she thinks like a parent, speaks like a parent, reasons like a parent.

When, for example, I withdrew from active professional work, my whole world became different from what it had been before. I began thinking, speaking, and reasoning like a man who does not struggle any more, who does not compete any more, who looks at the game from the bleachers and not from his former position in the field. What keeps me in a state of appropriate semantic growth today is different from what I needed for my effective development years ago.

The skill of the psychotherapist is a constant application of that all-encompassing psycho-logics. Psycho-logics is behind the art of the educator, the efficient executive, and all leaders. They are "at one" with the total situation; they think, they speak, they reason as befits the occasion.

In logic, one strives to be consistent with his premises; in psycho-logics, we strive to keep in touch with the situation as it develops.

To summarize what has so far been covered in this chapter, we introduced, as a first step, a mental model that describes the human individual as a thinking, feeling, self-moving, electrochemical process in continual transaction with a space-time environment. Historically earlier mental models attempted to define what man *is*. The model of a human individual as a Semantic Transactor postulates what an individual *does*; that is, an operational description based on what is considered significant in the light of a survey of today's human sciences.

This model eliminates the split between mind and body as two parts that act upon one another. Our transactions are *semantic*, or what-my-experience-means-to-me at a moment. These transactions are seen as dynamic units of significance that bind our electrochemical exchanges, our perceivings, movements, feelings, strivings, thinkings, and understandings into a valueful whole.

The construct of semantic transaction is fundamental to the beginning of a new understanding of ourselves; it allows whoever uses it to make use of the suggestions of general semantics and epistemics as a means of self-guidance in a time of accelerating change.

In the following section, we will begin an in-depth examination of the various activities within a semantic transaction in order to bring about a differentiated awareness of our functioning-as-a-whole. Differentiate does not mean "separate" here. One of my purposes is to show the integral participation within a whole, evolving individual. Thus, any separation of these activities is a matter of verbal dissection only.

the neurological aspects of semantic transactions

One of the standard experiments that students of psychology have to perform in the laboratory is to measure individual differences in reaction time. Reaction time means the time, measured in fractions of a second, that it takes for a person to press a telegraphy key after he is given a visual signal to do so. It is the time that it takes the nerve impulse to travel from the retina of the eye, through the brain, the spinal column, and along the arm to the finger tip that actuates the telegraphy key.

There are individual differences: some are slow at this, some are fast; but all take a certain amount of time to react. In no case is pressing the key simultaneous with the signal flash. Everyone has a reaction time that is relatively long or short, but that is measurable in fairly large fractions of a second. It is assumed that this simple reaction time experiment measures the rock-bottom individual speed of the nerve impulse in its undelayed flow along the reflex arc, from the eye to the finger.

In a second experiment of choice reaction time, the subjects have to decide which key to press—in a set of four—to indicate the color of the signal they are responding to (of four possibilities): red, green, yellow, or white. This involves a certain amount of rudimentary thinking, at least enough to differentiate colors and to react accordingly. The nerve impulse has to follow a more complex path and find its proper direction among a network of nerve cells. In all cases, the choice reaction time of an individual is longer than his simple reaction time. Thinking and choosing, even of the most rudimentary kind, is not an instantaneous affair.

The Dimensions of Nervous Activities

Perceiving, reacting, thinking, choosing, learning, remembering, feeling, planning, evaluating are processes that have observable dimensions in time-space. They have a beginning, somewhere, somehow; they follow a certain course on a network of nerve fibers; they repeat themselves in cycles, or they string along as chain reactions that spread all over the organism or die out for lack of proper stimulation.

It is obvious that certain organismic processes take time. We know that digestion and assimilation take time and distribute themselves in space; from the moment we put solid or liquid food in our mouth to the moment when that food becomes part of our tissues and organs, a great many physical and chemical transformations take place. We know that breathing is also a time process; the oxygen of the air enters our nose, penetrates our lungs, fixates itself on red corpuscles, travels down our body where it is needed, and it changes place with carbon dioxide that travels back in venous blood to the lungs and out into the air. In fact, all body activities are time-space processes, and many of them can be observed directly.

But when it comes to what we still call "mental" activities—according to the old distinction between body and mind, flesh and soul, matter and spirit—we are easily led to think that they can be instantaneous processes. As activities of the spirit, they are assumed to be spiritual and somewhat independent of matter, space, and time. We obey, unconsciously, an assumption that we seldom reexamine or criticize, and this assumption—of the immateriality of our thinking and feeling processes—is at the bottom of many misunderstandings and unhealthy practices in communication, education, and self-management. It leads us to geometrize our mental processes as phenomena taking place in pure abstract space. In up-to-date science, our thinking about such phenomena is less simplistic.

Mental activities are not independent of organismic activities; thinking has a physical aspect, just like digestion or respiration. The main difference is that instead of going slowly along a series of visible organs, such as the mouth, the stomach, the intestines, the blood, or the lungs, mental activity goes along a series of microscopic nerve cells at a speed that has to be measured in fractions of a second. This, however, does not change the basic nature of the process: it is not a spiritual happening, independent of matter, it is not straight like the path of an arrow, and it is not instantaneous, but dependent of variable timing. It follows a course that new methods of investigation can detect, at least in its main characteristics.

The organs through which our mental activities are processed—as our metabolic activities are processed through the stomach, the intestines, the digestive glands, and the circulatory system—are nerve cells, billions of them, that connect every part of our organism with every other part. There are differences among nerve cells, but all may be described as made of three essential parts: (1) a cell body with (2) dendrites on the receiving side and (3) an axon on the transmitting side. The nerve impulse is a wave of electrochemical energy that enters through the dendrites and goes out through the axon. Nerve cells are interconnected and form a most complicated network: one cell may receive impulses from many cells, and it may, in turn, fire nervous impulses to a whole group of sister cells.

Today, thanks to the progress that has been made with computers, we speak of the activities of groups of nerve cells as programming. For instance, it is assumed that in the motor area of the brain, there is a programming of the three individual letters *m-a-n* when I write the word *man*. This directs the movements of the hand and finger muscles as they trace the letters, seeing that *m* has three legs and *n* only two; and that *a* requires the tracing to turn around the loop and not to go up in the longer stem of the letter *d*.

This is the way we acquire skills; and, with time, the operation becomes easier, faster, and smooth-flowing. These growing series of such cell-assemblies are called phase sequences. The disturbance in a phase sequence can be demonstrated as not only a thinking happening, but at the same time a physical, often unpleasant, disruption of an acquired habit. You may find those cell-assemblies and phase sequences under other names in the literature. Some may speak of reverberatory circuits, and new terms may be invented and put into circulation as time goes on. The important thing for the lay person is to have some idea of the phenomenon and thus recognize allusions that are made to it.

The study of the nervous system, from the brain to the outer and inner organs of our body, is one of the most fascinating fields in the modern human sciences. As is true of all contemporary sciences, it is in a state of constant flux and rapid progress; only specialists can keep up with its findings and theories.

But some individuals in these fields of study help to bring the new visions of the world we live in to the general public in nontechnical, even poetic, language. One of these is Dr. Lewis Thomas, a physician and medical researcher. For instance, in his excellent little book *The Lives of a Cell* he writes:

> A good case can be made for our nonexistence as entities. We are not made up, as we had always supposed, of successively enriched packets of our own parts. We are shared, rented, occupied. At the interior of our cells, driving them, providing the oxidative energy that sends us out for the improvement of each shining day, are the mitochondria, and in a strict sense they are not ours. They turn out to be little separate creatures...they have maintained themselves and their ways, replicating in their own fashion, privately, with their own DNA and RNA quite different from ours...Without them we would not move a muscle, drum a finger, think a thought.

. . .But what of the other little animals, similarly established in my cells, sorting and balancing me, clustering me together? My centrioles, basal bodies, and probably a good many other more obscure tiny beings at work inside my cells, each with its own special genome, are as foreign, and as essential, as aphids in anthills. My cells are no longer the pure entities I was raised with; they are ecosystems more complex than Jamaica Bay.[11]

It is possible, however, for those of us who are not specialists to grasp a certain body of knowledge, which seems to be well-established, that we can use for our own guidance. This knowledge corresponds to today's almost universal knowledge about bodily health: the existence of microbes; the importance of vitamins and minerals in our diet; the need to count calories in case of overweight. We do not claim to replace medical experts when we consider these factors in matters of personal or public health; similarly, one does not claim to be a neurologist when studying a few simple facts about the functioning of the nervous system. This knowledge brings down to earth the discussion of many problems of human behavior that are so often described in such mentalistic terms as neuroses, complexes, fixations, repressions, abreactions, misunderstandings, resistences, habits, personality traits, mental blocks. It clears up the mist of abstruse theories that hide the simple mechanisms of organic functioning, and it makes "mental" health a matter of teachable skills in self-management.

We have already mentioned, in discussing reaction time, that no human activity, mental or otherwise, is instantaneous. We shall now discuss the three main neurological aspects of our semantic transactions: their speed, rhythm, and pattern. Let us remind ourselves once more that, when we speak of semantic transactions, we avoid the old distinction between mental and physical activities. Semantic transactions have at least seven aspects, and probably many more; they can be observed under their thinking, feeling, self-moving, electrochemical, environmental, historical, and purposive aspects—separately or in combination. At this moment, we are concerned mostly with their electrochemical, their self-moving, and their thinking aspects.

Let us first consider the speed of the nerve impulses along the nerve fibers and across the synapses—or jumps—from one cell to the next. Because nerve impulses travel at an average speed of 155 miles per hour, or 225 feet per second, we may feel that, even if a person is six foot tall, a speed of 225 feet per second will cover one's whole nervous network in practically no time at all. But 225 feet per second is an average speed on a single, continuous nerve fiber. It includes much slower rates (in some cases), and it does not cover choice reactions, problem-solving, or changes in dynamic patterns—all of which multiply the time required for a reaction to complete itself. Even in the simple case of direct transmission of a physiological message, however, the time element should be taken into account. For instance, the speed of the nerve impulses does not approach the speed at which a voice travels from a broadcasting station to a receiving set.

The following analogy is a vivid example of the time dimension in a simple semantic reaction.

> In earlier times, the rapidity with which an impulse was conducted along a nerve fiber was considered the quintessence of speed, hence the expression: "quick as thought." This idea has been superseded, however, by the accomplishments of modern technology; an airplane flies faster, not to mention the achievements of the telephone, the telegraph, and the radio.

> If a giant were stretched out over the earth so that his feet lay in the water at the southern tip of South America at Cape Horn, while his head lay in Alaska, the bite of a shark that had attacked him on Monday morning would first be perceived by his brain on Wednesday evening. And should he now wish to withdraw his foot "rapidly" from the water, his desire would avail him little, for it would take until the end of the week before the volitional impulse would have reached his foot. After having withdrawn his foot, he would still have a feeling on Sunday, Monday, and Tuesday that his foot was in the water and was bitten, for it would take so long before he would receive the news that the foot had been drawn up on the dry land.[12]

None of us has the size of that giant, of course; but we shall see later on—when we discuss patterns of nerve impulses and how difficult it is to change them—that the slowness of transmission is an important factor.

To the slowness of transmission we must add the slowness of fixation. A neural pattern takes time to impress itself on the brain and to become a permanent "taping" on our electrochemical network.

> There may be (this is still hypothetical) a difference in the amount of time taken (that is, the amount of activity that has to reverberate around the brain) between the time a message comes in and the time it has fixed a memory. We have been able to measure this time as something like fifteen minutes. A blow on the head can give a lasting amnesia for the preceding minutes; an animal given an electroshock each time after running a maze shows no progressive learning if the shock occurs within fifteen minutes after the experience. The failure is not due to damage by the shock, because if it is given four hours after the maze running, learning is perfectly good.[13]

What was "hypothetical" at the time of the first edition of *The Art of Awareness* is now generally accepted. In other words, a statement covering information or an opinion with which we are unfamiliar takes on the average fifteen minutes to be "heard." It is only after that time that its assimilation begins.

[12]Fritz Kahn, *Man in Structure and Function* (New York: Knopf, 1943), p. 471.
[13]R. W. Gerard, "Panel Four: The Evolution of Mind," in *Issues in Evolution*, ed. Sol Tax and C. Callender (Chicago: University of Chicago Press, 1960), p. 202.

The second aspect of the nerve impulse is its rhythm. Who today has not heard of brain waves, those sinuous lines on paper that indicate the variations of electrical potential, even during sleep? These sinuous lines change shape when the subject awakes, starts thinking hard, is given certain drugs, and when certain local tumors or disturbances are present. The brain cells function like the instruments in a symphonic orchestra: they stop and go, they play loudly or softly; the needle that registers the overall rhythm in biofeedback gives a very inadequate picture of what is actually going on. To enrich that picture, we have to take into account the pattern aspect of our neurological functioning.

If we go deeper into this phenomenon, we will find that each nerve cell has a refractory period that alternates with a responsive period; its chemical exchanges cannot go constantly in one direction, they have to slow down and go into reverse (refractory period) if the proper metabolic balance is to be maintained—just as the larger organs of our body have their own rhythm of activity and rest, absorption and elimination.

Take habitual handwriting, for instance; it is a personal pattern of movements that are traced down on paper and are easily recognizable, at least by handwriting experts. These movements are controlled by a set of nerve cells in the brain that fire one another in a definite sequence. This sequence has become habitual for these cells and for the arm and the hand muscles that they control.

If we want to find out by an actual experiment how hard it is to break that pattern, we can write at our normal speed, and for half a minute, the following sentence: *The Declaration of Independence was signed in 1776.* Don't stop; keep writing it again and again until the half-minute is over; then turn the sheet over so that you will not be guided in the next phase of the experiment by what you have written. Now write the same sentence for another half-minute, omitting every other letter as you write and linking whatever letters are left that belong to the same word—also doing your best to keep your normal handwriting style. If you count the number of letters written in the first phase and compare it to the number written in the second, you will see that your output was reduced to 20 or 25 percent of its normal rate, and that your handwriting in the second phase was hesitant, perhaps childlike, and contained errors.

What happened? The speed of your nerve impulses was slowed down, and their pattern was interfered with. They had to come to a stop at each jump from one letter to the next—from one cell assembly to the next, as the experts would say—and a new connection had to be established over the gap created by the omission of a letter. A similar disconnecting and reconnecting of nerve cells and groups of nerve cells takes place whenever we have to modify our train of thought on any central issue in our life, such as our relations with our spouse, family, our professional work, our status in the community.

If, to the relatively minor motor disturbance that took place during this writing experiment, we add the fact that something similar must be happening at the deeper level of the autonomic systems where our feelings have their own neural patterns, we realize that thinking and feeling are not simply matters of the soul, or the spirit, or what-have-you; they are, as well, a physical function of our organism. They are actual disturbances of the chemistry of the body, because the synaptic jump from one nerve cell to another is both an electrical and a chemical process. It is no wonder that the accumulation of such disturbances in very delicate parts of the organism eventually brings about all sorts of physical derangements; headaches, bad digestion, loss of sleep, stomach ulcers, heart seizures.

Apart from their limited speed, their rhythm, and their patterns, our nerve impulses have another characteristic of which we have to be aware. When we think of our nervous system, we may take it for granted that our nerve cells are at rest most of the time, waiting for a stimulus to stir them into action. We already know that their action will follow certain patterns, most of which are determined by our cultural and personal experiences. But even between spurts of activity, they are not at rest and neutral. An authority in these matters, the late Karl S. Lashley, a psychologist, said in 1951:

> Neurological theory has been dominated by the belief that the neurons of the central nervous system are in an inactive or resting state for the greater part of the time; that they are linked in relatively isolated conditioned reflex arcs and that they are activated only when the particular reactions for which they are specifically associated are called out. Such a view is incompatible with the widespread effects of stimulation...and also with recent evidence from electrical recordings of nervous activity. It is now practically certain that all the cells of the cerebrospinal axis are being continually bombarded by nerve impulses from various sources and are firing regularly, probably even during sleep. The cortex must be regarded as a great network of reverberatory circuits, constantly active. A new stimulus, reaching such a system, does not excite an isolated path but must produce widespread changes in the pattern of excitation throughout a whole system of already interacting neurons.[14]

To get the full meaning of this sober quotation from a scientist, let us use our imagination. As I narrate an experience of mine, revive in your own memory a similar personal experience.

I remember a day in New York, when I was in the corridors that connect the subway to the lobby of the Pennsylvania Station. It was during the traffic rush, when a turbulent flow of humanity was pouring out of the subway and

[14]K. S. Lashley, "The Problem of Serial Order in Behavior," in *Cerebral Mechanisms in Behavior*, ed. Lloyd A. Jeffress (New York: Wiley, 1951), p. 130.

racing madly for the commuter trains. They did not have to look for the direction signs on the corners, they knew where they had to go; and they went headlong, without a glance to the right or left. I, a stranger, coming in the opposite direction, wanted to find my way to the Statler Hotel across the street, or to some outlet to the surface. I would walk a bit, then stop, look around to orient myself, and glance above the crowd to read the signs. I eventually made it, after having been jostled about for many unpleasant minutes and after having lost my way more than once.

All brains are active, some more, some less; and their nerve impulses are like the crowd of commuters at the rush hour. Nerve impulses race head-long to their familiar conclusions, their long-range purposes, and their im-mediate objectives; and to introduce a countercurrent in that flow is like trying to stop the crowd that races blindly from the subway to the commuter trains. When we realize that this is the way things go on in the human brain, we understand how artificial are the measured steps of formal logic, which assumes not a crowd pouring through in a mad rush but a team of ballet dancers ready to follow a well-prepared choreographic design.

Professor Lashley had a different analogy, almost poetical, to illustrate the relative stability of brain patterns.

> I can best illustrate this conception of nervous action by picturing the brain as the surface of a lake. The prevailing breeze carries small ripples in its direction, the basic polarity of the system. Varying gusts set up crossing systems of waves, which do not destroy the first ripples, but modify their forms....A tossing log with its own period of submersion sends out periodic bursts of ripples, a tem-poral rhythm. The bow wave of a speeding boat momentarily sweeps over the surface, seems to obliterate the smaller waves yet leaves them unchanged by its passing...[15]

The prevailing breeze, which eventually wins over disturbances caused by contrary gusts of wind, tossing logs, and speeding boats, is the general orien-tation of a person's method of thinking and guiding values.

Sir Charles Sherrington, the famous British physiologist and writer, used a simile that has become a classic. "The brain appears as an enchanted loom where millions of flashing shuttles [the nerve impulses] weave a dissolv-ing pattern, always a meaningful pattern, though never an abiding one; a shifting harmony of subpatterns."[16]

None of these three analogies exactly represents what goes on in our nervous system, but all help correct the old-standing errors that fail to give thinking its time dimension, its biochemical features, and its dynamic pat-

[15]Lashley, "The Problem of Serial Order in Behavior," p. 133.
[16]Charles Sherrington, *Man on His Nature* (Garden City, N.Y.: Anchor Books [Double-day], 1953), p. 184.

terns. The conclusion we can draw from the previous considerations are many, and they apply to mental hygiene that is understood not as a technique to ward off neurosis and psychosis but as a technique of self-management, self-development, and self-training for a more sensible and more productive life. Here, at random, are a few of these conclusions.

1. We need not feel stupid if we cannot understand—let alone accept—a new idea or theory. It takes time to disconnect our habitual nerve cell patterns and reconnect them in a different order.
2. We need not strive too much for speed in mental activities. To get speed, we have to keep the same patterns of thought; and if we do so, we renounce all possibility of being original and creative.
3. It serves no useful purpose to complete the thought of another when he speaks to us or when we read the first part of his statement. If we do, we may have switched to our own patterns of thought, which were aroused by what he began saying, and we may miss the point he is trying to make.
4. It is an illusion to expect to change people quickly by a clever demonstration or a logical argument. Many people are like sailing ships: they obey the breeze that prevails in their cultural, professional, or social environment; they are not powered with the critical sense that is necessary for bucking the waves.
5. The interval between "understanding" what we read or hear and "internalizing" it—to the point that it becomes an integral part of our thinking-feeling orientation—takes at least fifteen minutes, or perhaps much longer. It is therefore a sound practice to stop occasionally and meditate on what we read or hear that sounds different, challenging, or questionable.

These conclusions give us a striking example of the difference between what was taught as effective communication two or three generations ago and what is now accepted as scientific practice. In my undergraduate years in the first decade of the present century, I was taught that to practice effective rhetoric was first to convince my opponent by an appeal to reason, and second to persuade him by an appeal to his feelings to achieve my own aim. The feelings to be stirred in him were those of his personal self-interests and those of whatever group to which he belonged: family, profession, or nation. It was, in fact, reinforcing selfishness and self-centeredness on both sides, his and mine. Today, I propose altruism as a passion. I am aware that without such a radically different orientation the whole human family may be heading for its doom. This brings us to the importance that affect or "feeling" has in the direction of our growth as individuals and in the development of our institutions.

Affects as Integrators and Reflectors of Valuing

We often contrast thinking with feeling, and values that are taken to be subjective with principles that are viewed as objective. We sometimes speak of the brain versus the heart, and we claim that the brain should rule—and some philosophers advocate the primacy of the intellect. An international business enterprise takes the magic word THINK as the epitome of practical wisdom; and a common expression is "Use your brain!"

We are dealing here with one of the most firmly rooted assumptions of our culture, with one of those "of course" verities that no one questions in earnest, which is implied in the mental picture that is suggested by our standard definition of a human being as a *rational animal*. If humans are distinct from animals because they are endowed with reason, must they not then assert superiority by using reason? Whoever sides for feeling against thinking, for the heart against brain, must be trying to justify some weakness or is indulging in mushy sentimentality.

The higher we go in praiseworthy performance, the tighter we must keep, we assume, our feelings in check, and we must make greater use of our reasoning powers. When we climb the pinnacle of human endeavor in scientific achievement, we are expected to have purified ourselves of all subjectivity; we deal with a universe of cold, colorless, translucid objectivity, from which all human passions have been exorcised. We weigh, and measure, and feed these data into our logical computer, and the answer comes out with a tag that tells us the relative respectability of the prediction.

The dream of Laplace is on the verge of becoming a reality; "An intelligence that knows at a moment of time and embraces in one formula the largest bodies and the lightest atoms would possess complete scientific knowledge of the universe." We have not quite reached that stage, but we are heading for it. Give us a few more years, and the human brain—aided by superelectronic gadgets—will be like the God of the unenlightened believers; it will know all, perceive all, control all. The dream of the medieval metaphysician will come true; we shall reach the supreme level of what they called "first principles," "eternal verities," "ontological absolutes." Of course, we have changed the names, now we speak of "invariants under transformation." It may sound better; but, if we are honest, we have to admit that we share one basic belief with Aristotle, Aquinas, Kant, and the rest of them: we regard "thinking" as the supreme human achievement.

While Korzybski stressed the need for "cortico-thalamic" integration, he does not seem entirely free from these assumptions. People interpret many passages of *Science and Sanity* as meaning that we must look forward to a late-model messiah, a *Homo mathematicus*, who will be a superexpert in symbolic logic and high-order abstractions. He will know how to translate into firm and unchanging categories the shifting dynamics of sensation and emotion.

The value is chiefly in the fact that such higher abstractions represent a perfected kind of memory, which can be recalled exactly in the form as it was originally produced. . . .Thus critical analysis, and therefore, progress, becomes possible. Compare this perfected memory, which may last indefinitely unchanged, with memories of "emotions" which, whether dim or clear, are always distorted. We see that the first are reliable, that the others are not.

Another most important characteristic of the higher-order abstractions is that, although of neural origin, they may be preserved and used over and over again in extra-neural forms, as recorded in books and otherwise. This fact is never fully appreciated from a neurological point of view. Neural products are stored up or preserved in extra-neural form, and they can be put back in the nervous system *as active neural process.*[17]

A library is a repository of the products of the brains of previous generations. These products keep alive, even in their dried-up state, and they will grow again if planted in the minds of today—just as the seeds that were kept for centuries in the tombs of Egyptian mummies sprouted and bore fruit when sown in fertile soil.

But this, perhaps, is not the only explanation of human dominance and progress. Some scientists are not so definite about the supremacy of the brain as is the lay person or the devotee of superlogic. These scientists, in fact, seem to feel quite differently about the whole thing.

Science can no longer hope to survive as an island of positive facts, around which the rest of man's intellectual heritage sinks to the status of subjective emotionalism. It must claim that some emotions are right; and if it can make good such a claim, it will not only save itself but sustain by its example the whole system of cultural life of which it forms part. . . .I want to show that scientific passions are no mere psychological by-products, but have a logical function which contributes an indispensable element to science.[18]

This brings us back to the beginning. Since the assumption is that "brain" and "heart" are exclusive of each other but have to live together, which has the deciding vote in a tie? This is an old and out-of-date question. Instead of using the terms brain and heart, let us use two terms sometimes used in the neurosciences: the cortex and the thalamus. And instead of "opposing" them, we will begin to look at them functionally in terms of self-development. The cortex is the new brain, as opposed to the thalamic region (or old brain). The new brain is more fully developed in humans than in other animals, a sure sign of our higher complexity. The cortex is the outward layer of the brain mass, folded in convolutions that form a surface of rounded ridges and deep grooves. The thalamus and its neighboring ganglia are somewhere

---

[17]Korzybski, *Science and Sanity*, p. 291.
[18]Michael Polanyi, *Personal Knowledge* (Chicago: University of Chicago Press, 1958), p. 134.

in the center of the brain mass, where the spinal column joins the cerebrum proper.

These two regions are interconnected, of course, but their functions are different. The cortex has centers of sensation and movement that are linked to one another by a complex criss-crossing of associative fibers. The cerebral cortex is further differentiated into two halves or hemispheres that communicate by means of a mass of fibers called the corpus callosum. The left hemisphere controls the right side of the body, including the right side of the visual and auditory functions. The right hemisphere controls the left side of the body. For most people, the hemispheres tend to specialize in function, with the left side appearing to predominate. For some left-handed people, the brain organization is reversed.

It was previously believed that the cortex was the region associated with rationality and logical thinking and that it functioned as a whole. For over one hundred years, neuro-anatomists and neurophysicists have known that verbal functions mainly involve the left hemisphere; only recently has it been demonstrated that the right hemisphere is responsible for spatial abilities. This research eventually led to the present acceptance of the cortex as processing in two different modes. One mode, the left side, processes analytically, rationally, logically, verbally, and mathematically, and is linear and sequential in operation. The other mode, the right side, processes tacitly—its verbal articulation is quite limited—spatially, and can integrate many inputs simultaneously. It operates in a holistic, relational manner and is usually referred to as intuition.

Of course, it must be remembered that all of these distinctions are not so clear-cut in the actual functioning of the whole person.

The thalamic region, which involves the limbic system, is the center of affective reactions. It has a great deal to do with our emotions, our blood pressure, and our autonomic nervous system generally.

When Korzybski wrote his big book in the early thirties, he saw the cortex as the regulator—although some of the authors he quotes are not so definite. For instance, Henri Piéron says:

> The thalamus, which in the lower vertebrates deprived of the cortex ensure the general reactions of the organism and the elementary mental functions, possesses an affective excitability in relation with the profound biological tendencies of the organism; among the higher mammals, indeed, it seems to preserve this role of affective regulation, whose importance in the behavior of the organism and mental life is so often misunderstood.[19]

Many present-day theories for managing our emotions are little more than the old "use your brain," put in different words and accompanied by modern-sounding techniques. Many are advances beyond "When excited,

[19]Korzybski, *Science and Sanity*, p. 188.

count to ten," such as the General Semantics recipe of "Delay your reactions." The trouble is that there are times when counting to ten and "using your brain" do not work, and one eventually discovers that the thalamus keeps running the show. Our most sophisticated logic is still at the service of our feelings; or our logic fails to influence our feelings. We understand and accept—intellectually—a new idea, but we do not apply it to our behavior. We protest that we want the truth and nothing but the truth, when, on closer examination, we must admit that we want to have it our way and no other. In the meetings at the United Nations, viewpoints are different because feelings, ambitions, fears, and purposes are different. All contestants appeal to some form of logic, giving implicit adhesion to a "League of Sound Logic," and it makes the cold war a permanent institution. They do not yet know how to bring about a League of Human Solidarity that would make peace the only acceptable form of international life.

There are times, however, when our acceptance of a new idea goes much deeper. It actually makes a difference in our life. We *feel* for it. We feel different about certain things, certain persons, certain ways of behaving. We no longer have the "heart" for certain things that we evaluated highly, or at least accepted willingly; we are ready to do things that previously meant very little to us.

Such changes involve an affective element. Something has happened within us that is not purely and exclusively intellectual, that reaches to the vital parts of our inner self. This can occur in psychotherapy, in a general semantics seminar, in any insightful experience. Is this new integration of our thoughts and behavior mostly a question of logic at the psychological level? At the neurological level, is it mostly a cortical activity dominated by left hemisphere functions?

Although I have learned that it is not always safe to take the latest pronouncements of neurologists as the final and deciding dogmas in such matters, it is interesting to note that recently they have repeatedly stated that the integrative center may very well be in those subcortical areas that Korzybski called the thalamic region. They speak of the reticular formation and of the centrencephalic system or organization. Listen to Dr. Wilder Penfield as he addressed his colleagues at the close of the International Symposium on the Reticular Formation of the Brain (at Ford Hospital, Detroit) in March, 1957.

> Neurosurgeons have been forced into the realization that the very existence of consciousness depended upon the integrity of subcortical mechanisms rather than cortical ones....For a long time I have been thinking of the "old brain"...as the place where the organization mechanisms were to be found—the mechanisms that made the cortical functions possible, the mechanisms without which conscious processes and voluntary action could not exist....I proposed the term "centrencephalic system"...to describe the coordinating and

organizing fiber and cell connections. . . .The phrase "centrencephalic organization" was intended as *a protest against the supposition that has satisfied some neurologists and physiologists for too long, namely that cortical association and cortico-cortical interplay was sufficient to explain the integrated behavior of a conscious man.*[20]

Elsewhere, Dr. Penfield writes:

The human cortex is made up of numerous functional areas, each of which has its most important connections with areas of gray matter in the brain stem, including the thalamus. Thus, each functional area in the more recently evolved cortex makes possible the elaboration of the function of a portion of the older brain. Expressed in another way, the subcortical areas of gray matter, by means of their projection fibers, serve to coordinate and to utilize the functional activities of cortical areas and to integrate that activity with the rest of the brain. Transcortical association fiber tracts are of importance, no doubt, but certainly of less essential importance than *subcortical integration.*[21]

Translated into layman's language, this means that our "logic" and "intuition" or cortical activity is an elaboration of the basic drives, feelings, and purposes that fire the nerve cells of our thalamic region. When a change takes place at the affective level, the thinking orientation follows, and not vice versa. The integration is not due to the cortex regulating the thalamus by means of high-order abstractions, but to the thalamus giving all activities a unified meaning that involves value and purpose.

So much for the neurological interpretation—but what of the psychological aspect? Is the theory that gives primacy to the intellect the only acceptable theory? I am convinced that it is not.

The *B* aspect of our semantic transactions has an importance of its own. Our contacts with our environment are always colored with feeling-tones; they are pleasant or unpleasant, boring or interesting, threatening or encouraging, dull or lively—with degrees between these extremes, of course. We are not insensitive machines that register occurrences without evaluating them. Our brain is not a radar screen that is unaware of the significance of what it perceives. Our reactions are affective reactions; our mood gives a color, an intensity, and a direction to our cortical processes whether rational or intuitional. It determines, in part, what we plan and what we do.

In many instances the mood is prior to the reaction. We abstract from our environment what we feel will serve our purposes. Our motivation facilitates certain modes of behavior and inhibits others. We do well and re-

[20]Herbert Jaspers et al., eds., *Reticular Formation of The Brain* (Boston: Little, Brown, 1958), p. 740 (italics added).

[21]Wilder Penfield and Lamar Roberts, *Speech and Brain-Mechanisms.* (Princeton, N.J.: Princeton University Press, 1959), p. 205.

peatedly what is gratifying to us. And we derive new energy from a sense of achievement.

A strong drive to reach a certain goal is occasionally described as dedication, but when such a drive goes *against* our plans we may call it fanaticism. Dedication—or fanaticism—is what Hitler stirred up in the Germans before World War II; it is what many observers recognize as the driving force behind the Russian advances in science and technology; it is what accounts for the achievements of the Chinese people; it is what some persons claim we lack in our Western democracies. We see it in the individual who is "all wrapped up" in his profession, be it painting, baseball, science, or bullfighting. When we say "It means so much to me!" we are expressing the affective aspect of our semantic transactions.

We usually put feelings in two contrasting groups. Some are evaluated as positive and constructive: they increase our alertness, our efficiency, and our *joie de vivre*. Some are evaluated as negative and disruptive: they sap our energy, dull our wits, impair our very health. On the positive side, we make such differentiations as mutual appreciation and trust, acceptance of self and of others, cooperation, readiness to compromise, willingness to give credit to the other person, sense of humor, empathy, love, and so on. On the negative side, we differentiate such emotions and moods as hostility, guilt, self-defensiveness and self-disparagement, criticism of others, suspicion, jealousy, worry, cynicism, tension, fear, resentment, hate, and the like.

The point is that we cannot dissociate efficiency from positive feelings. Whether we are aware of it or not, the human organism works as a whole; there is constant and immediate interaction between the various aspects of our semantic transactions. It is very difficult to be "below par" at the feeling level and remain creative at the thinking level, energetic at the muscular level, and healthy and vigorous at the electrochemical level. Positive feelings do more than release our energies and ensure whatever productivity we can achieve, they actually increase these energies and bring them to a level that they otherwise could never reach. If educated, they impart a refined sensitivity for what is important and what is not, for what is of lasting value and what won't stand the test of time.

Feeling is therefore an indispensable element of creativity, as is clearly evident when we observe great scientists at work. They have described themselves as animated by what Johann Kepler called his "sacred fury" and what Michael Polanyi describes as "intellectual passions."

These passions involve a deep sense of, and belief in, the universal appropriateness of one's personal experience. They are selective, heuristic, and persuasive. Selective, they choose what they feel is important and interesting; heuristic, they guess in advance what they are going to discover; persuasive, they want all people to share a new outlook on the world.

The discoveries of science have been achieved by the passionately sustained efforts of succeeding generations of great men, who overwhelmed the whole of modern humanity by the power of their convictions.[22]

Korzybski was also aware of the fact that all creative work starts, continues, and completes itself within an affective state.

We can only speak legitimately of "meanings" in the plural. Perhaps, we can speak of the meanings of meanings, although I suspect that the latter would represent the un-speakable first-order effect, the affective, personal raw material, out of which ordinary meanings are built.

The above explains structurally why most of our "thinking" is to such a large extent "wishful" and is so strongly colored by affective factors. Creative scientists know very well, from observation of themselves, that all creative work starts as a "feeling," "inclination," "suspicion," "intuition," "hunch," or some other un-speakable affective state, which, only at a later date, after a sort of nursing, takes the shape of a verbal expression, worked out later in a rationalized, coherent, linguistic scheme called a theory. In mathematics we have some astonishing examples of intuitively proclaimed theorems which, at a later date, have been proven to be true, although the original proof was false.[23]

It is easy to see the parallel (at the psychological level) between these statements and the statements of the neurologists when the latter assert that the centrencephalic system integrates the activities of the cortex around our drives, feelings, values, and purposes. A further distinction needs to be made here. When we say that the cortical processes elaborate the "old brain" activities, we now see that the elaboration can happen in two different modes. We can utilize both functional modes provided we have the proper training. Robert Ornstein of the Langley-Porter Neuropsychiatric Institute lists various names given to these two modes: intellectual-sensuous; active-receptive; explicit-tacit; sequential-simultaneous; focal-diffuse; time-space; verbal-spatial; analytic-gestalt.[24]

Ornstein, whose laboratory investigations in split-brain research have involved literally thousands of normal, uninjured people has this to say:

I propose, then, two complimentary principles in human mentation: an ordered sequencer which underlies language and "rational" mentation, and a simultaneous processor employed for coordination of movement in space, for artistic creativity and reception, for the tonal aspect of music, and for other functions which I subsume under intuition, a faculty of holistic perception . . . a simultaneous mode of experience. Both . . . modes have their proper levels of functioning and interaction. Most of us have been educated and have developed sequential

[22]Polanyi, *Personal Knowledge,* p. 171.
[23]Korzybski, *Science and Sanity*, p. 22.
[24]Robert E. Ornstein, *The Psychology of Consciousness* (San Francisco: W. H. Freeman Co., 1972), p. 67.

abilities (readin', 'ritin' and 'rithmetic) at the expense of the fluid and simultane-ous. Many, well-trained verbally, say they cannot "understand" art; the rationalist opposes the "mystic," partly because we attribute only our verbal-analytic abilities to our "mind" while often denying "mental" status to the intui-tive. We may compliment a painter or photographer's "eye," a craftman's "touch," an artist for an apt "gut" feeling—and rarely for the powers of their mind.[25]

Yes, I agree that the "intuitional" half of the cortex has been neglected in our training and education. And each person interested in self-develop-ment and innovating would do well to be equally at home in both modes, as scientist-artist in fusion. I also want to strongly emphasize that the area of human values and purposes as reflected in or through the affective system is the primary factor in the integrating action of the brainstem. The latter is postulated here as "the indispensible substratum of consciousness", in the words of Wilder Penfield, and lies outside the cerebral cortex. This cen-trencephalic system is regarded as the functionally "highest level" of integra-tion in the brain.

The development of our use of this center I see as essential to the future of humankind. There are those who have created and introduced in the human mass the values entire populations have lived by for centuries. They are such people as Buddha, Jesus, Ghandi, and the like. To become a center of such irradiation of human values is a skill that can be learned and practiced.

If we look at science as an organized cultural activity, we will also see it as an exchange of trust between neighbors who are working in adjacent fields, none of whom has any organizational control over the entire enter-prise. The scientific consensus is

> a joint appraisal of an intellectual domain, of which each consenting participant can properly understand and judge only one small portion. . . . Its operation is based on the "transitiveness" of neighboring appraisals—much as a marching column is kept in step by each man's keeping in step with those close to him.[26]

An appraisal is an evaluation. It is the subjective answer to such ques-tions as—Is it true or false?, Is it good or bad?, Is it acceptable or not?, and Is it useful or not? The transmission of an appraisal is an act of confidence in one's own judgment: we feel that our view is worth being communicated. Its acceptance is an act of trust in the transmitter. In the case of scientists, we may call it enlightened trust, but it seems quite clear that the assent has a strong element of implicit belief, which takes us far away from the "primacy of the intellect" of certain philosophers. Not that we should despise intellec-tual capacities and achievements, far from it; but we want them to stay where they belong, at the service of "humanness." Cortical activities make

---

[25]Robert E. Ornstein, *The Mind Field* (New York: Grossman, 1976), p. 30.
[26]Polanyi, *Personal Knowledge*, p. 217.

possible a finer discrimination of the means and methods of being truly human in a world where the stranger of today may become our immediate neighbor overnight.

It is their humanness, much more than their superior intelligence, that made creative scientists what they were. Korzybski recognized this when he wrote that "the greatest men of science have always had wide human aims and interests. From the *non-elementalistic* point of view, they probably became productive *because of that broad human urge.*"[27]

A similar view has been held by many essayists and philosophers; for example, Count Hermann Keyserling, who in his *South American Meditations* made statements that anticipated the findings of Penfield, the neurologist.

> The prejudice that everything must needs follow the laws of reason and intellect has obscured the true meaning of their own inner experience for most moderns.
>
> It is to feeling, not to reason, that the idea of humanity, as everybody involuntarily understands it, applies. Not the stupid man, but the man devoid of feeling has always been called "inhuman." As a matter of fact, all progress in the sphere of humanity, such as the abolishment of slavery, the recognition of fundamental rights belonging to all men, laws more accordant with justice, etc., has its origin in growing sympathy.[28]

Keyserling goes even further. Instead of thinking of the order of the universe as the result of a superlogic that transcends human capacity, he sees it as an order of a different type.

> The structure of the universe as a whole is entirely different from what corresponds to the demands of the intellect. . . . With man, natural ties between those nearest each other precede all that we call "order." These ties endure even through states which for Reason would mean absolute disorder. . . . This is the sole reason why there are recoveries after wars and revolutions and economic crises. This explains why the ways in which these recoveries take place always differ widely from those prophesied by scientists.[29]

Summary

In this brief discussion we have outlined the neurological aspects of our sensory-motor and affective activities. It was shown how "time" plays a primary role in our awareness of self-moving and perceptual activities and that the affective system gives our semantic transactions their direction. The

---

[27]Korzybski, *Science and Sanity*, p. 728.

[28]Hermann Keyserling, *South American Meditations* (New York: Harper & Row, 1932), pp. 251, 256.

[29]Keyserling, *South American Meditations*, p. 246.

neurological basis for this lies in the findings of brain research, which shows the integrative function of the higher brainstem. Changes in behavior must be effected here before there is a change in thinking, and not vice versa.

We now pass to the "thinking" or *C* activities in order to show the importance of the construct of abstracting in the shaping of our experience.

abstracting

We relate ourselves intelligently to the surrounding world that we know only in part; and from the parts that we know, we attempt to construct a world that makes sense to us.

To "abstract" means to leave out certain features of a situation, to register only those that are relevant to our needs, our purposes, or our habits. We do this "silently" and verbally, and between these two levels there is no common measure. Our mental constructs are not pictures of an "objective reality," but schemes of how we can participate in our life experiences and situations as aspects of an ongoing cosmic process.

the process of abstracting

Korzybski often said that the main aim of his work was to bring about self-realization through a *general consciousness of abstracting.*[1] One of his best-known commentators, Wendell Johnson, describes the process of abstracting "as a natural process...that provides a basis for human progress, for personal cultural adjustment."[2] Practically, all books that deal with general semantics and its applications have a reproduction or a special version of the Structural Differential (Figure 3.1), a diagram that has become the equivalent of a trademark for the entire discipline.[3] Two hundred pages of *Science and Sanity* are devoted to abstracting and training in abstracting.

Early in the book, Korzybski says of the Structural Differential:

This diagram, indeed, involves all the psychophysiological factors necessary for the transition from the old semantic reactions to the new, and it gives in a way a *structural summary* of the whole non-Aristotelian system.[4]

[1]Korzybski, *Manhood of Humanity,* 2d ed. (Lakeville, Conn.: International Non-Aristotelian Library, 1950), p. li.

[2]Wendell Johnson, *People in Quandaries* (New York: Harper & Row, 1946), p. 167.

[3]For versions of the Structural Differential, *see* J. S. Bois, *Explorations in Awareness* (New York: Harper & Row, 1957), p. 124; S. I. Hayakawa, *Language in Thought and Action*, 2d ed. (New York: Harcourt, Brace & World, 1964), p. 179; T. M. Weiss and K. H. Hoover, *Scientific Foundations of Education* (Dubuque, Ia.: Wm. C. Brown Company Publishers, 1960), p. 13.

[4]Korzybski, *Science and Sanity* (Lakeville Conn.: International Non-Aristotelian Library, 1933, 1941, 1948, 1958), p. 13.

Korzybski describes his invention, the Structural Differential, in the following words. (*See* Fig. 6.1.)

> For the event we have a parabola in relief (E), broken off to indicate its limitless extension. The disk (O_h) symbolizes the human object; the disk (O_a) represents the animal object. The label (L) represents the higher abstraction called a name (with its meaning given by a definition). The lines (A_1, A_2, A_3) in the relief diagram are hanging strings which are tied to pegs. They indicate the process of abstracting. The free hanging strings (B_2) indicate the most important characteristics *left out*, neglected, or forgotten in the abstracting. The Structural Differentials are provided with a number of separate labels [L_1, L_2 ... L_n] attached to pegs. These are hung, one to the other, in a series, and the last one may be attached by a long

Figure 6.1. The structural differential.

peg to the event, to indicate that the characteristics of the event represent the highest abstractions we have produced at each date.[5]

In our own discussion of the process of abstracting, we do not comment on what Korzybski called the *animal object,* and very few commentators insist on it. It seems that the distinction made by the author of *Science and Sanity* is now taken for granted and has passed into the stock of our cultural acquisitions. It is interesting to note, however, that the Differential illustrates how the animal starts with the object, without relating it to the whole event, of which it has no mental model.

In the present treatise we do not present consciousness of abstracting as the most important notion of the whole program, and we do not take the Structural Differential as the summary of the whole system. Awareness of our total organismic functioning is our main theme, and the diagram that pictures man as a semantic transactor (Figure 3.1) becomes central; however, we hold that a thorough understanding of the process of abstracting is necessary.

We Pick and Choose What We Observe

Abstraction and *abstracting* belong to our everyday language, and it is necessary that we divest these terms of their popular connotations if we want to use them as technical words in an epistemological system. The *American College Dictionary,* for instance, gives four definitions of *abstract* as an adjective, five as a noun, and four as a verb. As a noun, it may mean "summary, essence, idea conceived apart from some material basis, ideal," and in the phrase *in the abstract*—it means "without reference to special circumstances or particular applications." As a verb, it denotes actions that are associated with the nouns. The other term, *abstraction,* covers two rather undesirable mental conditions, "reverie" and "absentmindedness," and it is discussed at length in its relations to the fine arts.

Abstract, abstracting, and *abstraction*—as used in general semantics— are not identical with the dictionary's categories. In the new discipline, they are both more simple and more comprehensive. Many of the words used in serious discussions of scientific subjects have become unintelligible—in the sense that they lead to misunderstandings if we content ourselves with the current dictionary definition. In each science and in each school of science, they assume meanings that have to be explained if we want to make sense of what is to follow. From these new special meanings, a new "average meaning" often emerges that is current in scientific circles but unknown to the lay person. The terms we are now studying, *abstracting* and *abstraction,* are striking examples.

[5]Korzybski, *Science and Sanity,* p. 399. The diagram for Figure 3.1 is from p. 471 of the same volume. Both are reproduced with permission from the Korzybski estate.

Once we have rid our minds of the dictionary definitions of these terms, including our personal variations, we can start building—piece by piece— the mental model that fits the present purpose. It is quite simple, after all, and it will include many of the popular meanings.

When we observe something, that is, when we see, hear, taste, touch, or otherwise sense what is going on within ourselves or without, we can give our attention to only one or to very few elements at a time. By "at a time" we mean a very short fraction of a second. (After all, we are in the scientific age, and today, in ballistics and in other technologies, we must consider intervals as short as a few thousandths of a second.) Our nervous system takes time to operate, and what appears continuous at the level of gross observation is discontinuous and quantum-like at the level of scientific measurement. Training may increase the speed of scanning and the size of units that we can register in a flash, but it does not do away with the quantum-like nature of all perceptions. To use a simple analogy, our brain is not like a film that registers an entire scene simultaneously, it is more like a blank sheet on which we sketch—rapidly or slowly—the features of the situation, the person, or the object that we are observing. These details are taken in some order of preference, conscious or unconscious, but they are taken one at a time.

This is what is meant when we say that we "abstract." We pick and choose the elements that we assemble to form the picture of a limited totality, object, person, or scene. From what is happening—from the universe of processes that flow incessantly, and of which we ourselves are a moving part—we abstract, collect, and put together some of the features that are within the range of our attention to form a consistent whole. We do not abstract all the features that we can perceive, we select those that we are interested in, those that we are in the habit of paying attention to, or those that suit our purpose at the moment; and we ignore the rest. For instance, as you read this page many sounds impinge on your eardrums; some are faint, perhaps, but if you stop and pay attention, you will hear them distinctly. Prior to my suggestion, you did not abstract them; now you do.

The parabola in Figure 6.1 represents the limitless number of point-events that constitute every situation, or the totality of the cosmic event at the moment we are considering. We can say that it is the symbolic picture of *what is going on* at all known levels of existence, from atomic elements to galactic spirals racing away from one another. With the four initials of this phrase, we create the word *WIGO* (What Is Going On), and it is from this WIGO that we abstract whatever falls within the range of our sensory organs. The features that we thus abstract are represented by the strings that stretch from the parabola to the circle below. Korzybski called this circle the *object*, but now we call it *first-order experience*—or we describe it as *what we are paying attention to, what we are busy with, what we are concerned with*.

So far, we have spoken of features that almost everybody can abstract, but there are persons whose sensory system is either less or more sensitive than the average, and whose range of abstractions will vary accordingly. If a person is tone-deaf, he will never abstract certain musical themes; if he is color-blind, he will miss certain shades; if he has lost the sense of smell, he will not be impressed by the most bewitching concoctions of the art of perfumery. What we cannot abstract because of sensory defects simply does not exist for us as individuals. on the other hand, a musician with refined sense of pitch or a winetaster with a refined sense of taste will notice differences that do not exist for the average person.

Some aspects of situations, events, persons, and objects are beyond the range of human perception and can be detected only with the aid of instruments. If we do not have the proper instruments, we cannot abstract them. By using a certain instrument and by calibrating it in a definite manner, we can select the features that we are going to take in. For instance, when we listen to a radio station, we know that other radio waves are also spreading through our living room, but we did not tune our set to receive them. For some reason or other, or by mere happenstance, we are abstracting from a complex tangle of radio messages the one that our set is receiving. Many other things are going on, within us and around us, that can be detected—or abstracted—only by the use of proper instruments. In ordinary life, we cannot take them into account unless we infer their presence from scientific information.

Finally, there are features of situations or characteristics of objects that none of us can abstract directly or with the help of instruments. Yet we know about them, and we have good reason to believe that they are real. In fact, they are the most powerful sources of energy known to man. We are speaking here of atoms, nuclei, and particles that nobody has ever seen, but their effects can be observed and measured. Before they were discovered by scientists, very few thinkers suspected their presence. The list is increasing every day; and their potential number and variety is beyond all imagination.

Therefore, when we say that we abstract, we mean that of the different point-events that fill the flow of what is going on, we can come in conscious contact with only a few of the most simple ones. I perceive some of the things that are within the range of my senses unaided or made more powerful by means of instruments, but I do not pay attention to everything that happens within that range at any moment.

My contacts with the world are limited in a variety of ways. My span of attention is limited, and, of the infinite number of features of the total situation, I can take in only a few at a time. These are pictured by the lines that link first-order experience to WIGO. There are other features that I could take into account, but I neglect them either because they do not suit my present purposes or because something distracts me from them. They are represented by the lines that hang from the parabola without reaching the circle of first-order experience.

Finally, there is a limitless number of features of the total cosmic event that are altogether beyond the reach of my senses, working alone or aided with instruments. These are represented by the very large number of holes in the parabola to which no lines are attached. It is the limitless world of *et cetera* (ETC.), the world that lies outside the field of my awareness. We abstract only a tiny portion of what is going on. We are like someone trying to find their way at night in a dense forest, having only a small flashlight to direct their steps, and discovering—one at a time—very small areas of the forest they are groping through.

This simile misses an important aspect of the situation, however, for it assumes more stability than there is. The forest may be a jungle, the night may be very dark, the flashlight may emit only a thin shaft of illumination, but we see the forest as relatively unchanging—and we see ourselves as having a relative permanence. All this is true at the level of gross observation, but the underlying reality is quite different. Both the world that surrounds us and our own organism undergo subtle changes from moment to moment, and the relationship between the observer and the observed constantly varies. There is no real permanency anywhere but in our delusional static picture of what is going on in the world and in us. Our acts of abstracting are passing pointed contacts between two moving "realities," or ongoings, the world and ourselves, and the relation between them is an undetermined variable.

This is not easy to accept; it may sound highly theoretical and utterly impractical, and so far from the commonsense view of the world that one may feel we can ignore it. In fact, we ignore it most of the time. In the world of thinking and of evaulating human situations, we are still at the age when medicine limited itself to common sense, when it did not even suspect the circulation of the blood, existence of bacteria, vitamins, and hormones. We are still at the stage when physics spoke of atoms as round balls with hooks on them. In those days, the views that are now accepted in medicine and in physics would have sounded highly theoretical and contrary to practical sense. But our new views even influence policies in public health and sanitation, and—when it comes to atomic physics—they loom large in our discussion of world affairs. A conceptual revolution, such as we are experiencing, means that we have to replace commonsense notions by ideas that are bound to appear strange and farfetched for a while; we must probe much deeper into what is going on and revise our views of what is "evident" and "obvious."

Being conscious of abstracting means that we now know that what we observe, what we are concerned with, what we take into account is only a small fraction of all that is going on. We abstract—that is, we select from among the characteristics of the total ongoing world of processes—what lies within our capacity to observe with our unaided senses or with instruments. The immensity of the characteristics that we ignore, or that we cannot reach, is described in general semantics as the limitless world of ETC., the world that we don't know, that we don't perceive, that we deliberately neglect, that we may not even suspect exists—and that may have a direct influence on what is happening to us.

The first step of abstracting takes us from what is going on to what we take into account, or, as Korzybski would have said, from the event to the object of our attention, from E to O_h in the diagram (Figure 6.1).

The second step of abstracting takes us from what we are concerned with to what we say about it, either to ourselves or to others—from first-order experience to description of experience, from the unspoken level of reflexes, feelings, and organismic reactions to the level of words and symbols. In the first step we saw that there is no common measure between the total cosmic event and the present object of our attention. In the second step we see that there is no common measure between an actual experience and the description of that experience. Who will say that making love and talking about making love are identical? From the experience, we pick and choose the features that we consider relevant, and we utter words that are generally accepted as descriptive of these features. The words we use are not the experience we have: what we say of our feelings is not what we actually feel, but only a report of what we feel.

In the second abstracting step, as in the first, there is a reduction, a simplification, a fractionation, a translation; and a great deal is left out at each step. What is left out is lumped together at every step into an ETC., the dimensions of which are indefinite. In Figure 6.1 the strings (B_2) that hang from the disk and are unattached to the first label represent those characteristics of the first-order experience that are not covered by the verbal description of that experience. The choice of the features that we include in the description may be due to a variety of factors: the limitations of our vocabulary, the relative importance—in our personal judgment—of the details to be mentioned, the limit of time allowed for a description.

When we described the two abstracting steps that we have already studied (there are many others, as we shall see later), we had to use a personal pronoun. We said: The first abstracting jump is from what is going on to what *I* experience (what *I* am concerned with, what *I* see, touch, taste, etc.). For the second step we said: it is from what *I* experience to what *I* say about it. In both cases, the personal pronoun is used; a choice was made of what to take into account and what to leave out. The choice is made by a person; it is subjective; and it cannot be otherwise.

This choice will vary from individual to individual. Whenever I say *I*, I speak only for myself; when another says *I*, he speaks only for himself. I am a semantic transactor, and, as such, I am different from you; by the same token, you are different from me. From the semantic transaction diagram that we discussed earlier, we see that in our past, our present, and our anticipated future we are very different from each other. We are different in age, in education, in experience, in habits, in interests, in environment, in ambitions, and in purposes. My abstractions are filtered through a series of psychological meshes that are made of the elements I have just enumerated and of many more; your abstractions are filtered through a different set of meshes; and therefore our abstracting processes are different from each other. Suppose we participate in the same event: we see the same motion picture, or meet the same celebrity, or see the same accident, or hear the same speaker. Your experience will be different from mine, and our descriptions of it—if they are descriptive at all—will be more different still.

Shall we ask which of us is right and which is wrong—or look for a so-called "objective" report? Of course not. If we understand what happens in the process of abstracting, we realize that these "commonsense" questions do not make sense at all. Experience and verbal report are filtered through different semantic transactors, and no two of these are identical in their space-time makeup.

To give up the delusional search for absolute objectivity is not as simple as might appear; it calls for more revolutionary changes in our habits of thinking and speaking than most of us are ready to make. If we begin practicing such a change in a consistent manner, our friends may begin to wonder what is "the matter" with us. We may have to explain, and our explanation may be taken as a rationalization, a defense, an escape, an excuse; something that will reflect on us in an unfavorable manner.

When I wrote *Explorations in Awareness*, I made it a point to state clearly that I was not speaking in the name of objective science but was simply describing my own experiences, and I quoted a friend, Professor Elton Carter, who had written something that, I felt, justified my attitude. He had said: "Did you know that, in all our talking, we are always in a sense talking about ourselves, no matter what else we believe we are talking about?" I liked his statement because it suited my semantic transactions, but some reviewers of the book felt differently. For the few who approved what they called my courage in using the pronoun *I*, there were many who warned the prospective readers that the book was mostly "autobiographical," which, in the context, meant something like "not of general interest."

What else could it be? The only semantic filter that one possesses is oneself; and whatever one sees, learns, explains, or talks about is an abstraction that emerges from that process. Why not be candid about it?

I was singularly comforted when I discovered, later, that at least one prominent scientist shared my views, the late Percy W. Bridgman, the famous physicist from Harvard, wrote:

> My feeling of the desirability of giving my analysis in the first person has been with me for a long time, and I have in the past not infrequently used first person reports and have argued to justify it. This argument, and related arguments, I feel have to

a large extent been misunderstood, and criticisms of my writings have frequently accused me of solipsism. These criticisms have always puzzled me. However, it is only recently that I have come to appreciate that the use of the first person, which is all that I am urging, need involve no commitment whatever to a solipsistic "ego" or "self," the implied existence of which is what I suppose has principally disturbed the critics. My use of the first person has the neutrality of grammar. That it can have such neutrality I regard as an important observation.[6]

The neutrality of grammar, of which Bridgman speaks, matches the detached study of our process of abstracting. No two of us see the world in the same manner. To paraphrase the great diplomat Talleyrand: "If it goes without saying, it goes better if we say it explicitly and face the consequences."

If we apply this to the present study of general semantics, we accept the fact that no two authors present the system in exactly the same manner. The point is not to decide who teaches "true" general semantics but for each of us to find which version gives us the most satisfactory results when we honestly experiment with it.

Orders of Abstraction

We have already studied the first step in abstracting, from the cosmic event to the object of our attention. The second step is from the object of our attention to our description of it. This short study has made us aware of the fact that what is actually going on within us and around us—to the limits of the universe—is so complex and so immense that we can grasp only a tiny portion of it at a time, and that this tiny portion is made of smaller bits that we select one by one. When it comes to describing that first-order experience, we have to use words, each word corresponding to an element of that experience. As we string words one after another in writing or in speaking, we stretch—as if on a line—the pieces of a picture that is always a step behind what it is expected to represent.

Korzybski described the process of abstracting by using the analogy of a "map" and a "territory," and he often repeated two statements, which he called the premises of his system. *The map is not the territory,* and *the map does not represent all the territory.* What did he mean by "map" and "territory"?

In the first step of abstraction, the "territory" is what is actually going on; it is the total cosmic event at one time, which is represented by the parabola in the Structural Differential (Figure 6.1). The "map" is what we abstract from it; it is the imprint that our transaction with a fraction of the universe of processes makes on our psychophysiological organism. We have already called it our first-order experience, which is represented by the disk or circle

[6]Percy W. Bridgman, *The Way Things Are* (Cambridge, Mass.: Harvard University Press, 1959), p. 4.

in the diagram. This map, this live picture of a portion of the ongoing world of processes, is not of the same order of existence as the territory, as the world of processes itself. It is something different, something brought into existence by our own activity. It is a distinct happening, which emerges from that transaction between "subject" and "object" world; it is a human event that creates and manifests a new cosmic event. Korzybski calls this human event the map. He reminds us that it is not the territory, not the cosmic event in its totality, but only an abstraction from it.

This transaction between our semantic self and the "objective" world is now taken as a territory in its turn, as an event that has a certain type of existence of its own. We map this new territory when we draw a picture of it. The picture may be a word picture, a sketch, a pantomime—or any form of representation. This picture or map is not the territory it represents, nor does it represent all the details of the territory. It is an abstraction from it, a translation of its features into a different medium, as when one draws the ocean, the shoreline, the plains, and the mountains on a piece of paper and says "This is California." No quibbling is possible here: we know that the map is not the territory, and we know that a geographical map, being a flat reproduction of a curved surface, distorts the territory to some extent. A map is a reduction and an approximation.

In the same way, each level of abstraction may be taken as either a map of what it is abstracted from or as a territory in reference to what can be abstracted from it. At each step there is a transformation. A more advanced stage of abstraction is not an extract, like the juice squeezed from an orange; it does not contain any elements that were in the territory. The component parts of the territory are *transformed* into elements of a different order of existence, and it is these new and different elements that constitute the map. It is not a matter of more of the same elements in the territory and fewer of them in the map, it is a matter of *radically different* elements, features, or characteristics. In word maps, the relation between the first-order experience (the circle in the diagram) and its description (the labels) is very arbitrary,[7] and Korzybski sums this up in a statement that sounds like a paradox: "Whatever you say it is, it is not." This could be translated, "Your describing it is not your experiencing it."

The string of labels that hang from the disk in Figure 6.1 represents the various names and statements that can be used to describe, interpret, evaluate, and generalize our first-order experiences. These labels could be grouped under three headings, beginning with those that are closest to the

[7]The abstraction ladder diagram in Hayakawa's *Language in Thought and Action* (p. 179) fails to emphasize these differences between the process and the object and between the object and the words. The characteristics, represented by small geometrical figures, appear to remain of the same kind all the way up, and the text speaks of "characteristics left out" as if it were a matter of subtraction.

circle: (a) description, (b) interpretation, and (c) conclusion or generalization. This classification is not absolute, and these activities may overlap (as we shall see later); but it is a working device that puts a certain order in our study of the differences among the names and statements that may be used in speaking of first-order experiences. For this purpose, we introduce Figure 6.2, a slightly modified drawing of the Structural Differential.

In this new diagram, the description is spread over three levels: D_1, D_2, and D_n. (Three is not an absolute number here; there could be fewer or more levels of description). Level D_1 is the most explicit, the most "specific" as we

Figure 6.2. The structural differential. Original terms and new descriptive statements.

say in popular parlance. Levels D_2 and D_n are said to be of a *higher order of abstraction;* they describe the experience with fewer details, though in some cases they may be sufficiently explicit. Next to description comes interpretation, at a higher level of abstraction. Finally, we reach a conclusion for what to do as a consequence of the experience, or we make a generalization that puts the experience, interpreted and evaluated, in a class with similar ones that are already filed in our memory.

Here is an example of a description that belongs to a higher order of abstraction than would appear at first sight. Suppose we agree that "Both the United States and Canada have a democratic form of government." This statement is sufficiently descriptive if we simply mean to compare these two countries to, say, Cuba or Saudi Arabia. But if we want to be more explicit, and compare the first-order experiences of a lawmaker—or even of the ordinary citizen-voter—in the two countries, we have to bring our description to a lower level. We have to speak of the check-and-balance system in this country as different from the parliamentary system in Canada, and of the registration of party members here and of the absence of such registration there. High-order descriptions, of the D_n type, may be deceptive; they oversimplify and do away with differences that make a difference. If we confuse them with low-order descriptions, we run the risk of misunderstanding. If, in the present case, I take it for granted that the words *democratic government* are rigorously descriptive, of the D_1 type, I may draw unwarranted conclusions from the statement.

Here is another example, which starts at a high-order description and comes down to a lower one. If I say "I bought a new automobile last fall," I give very little information about the car I am now driving. *Automobile* is a very general term, a term of high order, not at all specific. If I say "It is a sedan," you begin to see a more definite picture; I have limited the field by eliminating sports cars, convertibles, and station wagons. If I also say "It's a Ford," I come one step lower on the abstraction ladder and I limit the field even more.

Another way of evaluating how high we are in abstraction is to figure out how much guessing a statement will require of a person who wants to have an accurate picture of the situation it describes. The more guessing, the more distant is the description from first-order experience. If I say, for instance, "we have a wonderful pet in our house," I am not telling you much. You may ask "What kind of pet?" By this question you invite me to come down a few rungs on the ladder of abstraction. If I answer "It's a dog," your guessing will not have to cover such possibilities as cat, turtle, parakeet, canary, or what have you. If I say "It's a big dog," chihuahuas are eliminated, of course.

The main trouble is that we often confuse the orders of abstraction, and we take our guessing as a reliable way of supplementing our information. What we actually do when we guess is to confuse our past experiences with the present one. We really abstract from two distinct sources: (1) from the present situation that lies open to our observation, and (2) from an unsorted stock of memories, interpretations, and prejudices that have accumulated within us in the course of life. From this mixture, we form opinions and utter statements that we take for reports of facts, when they are mostly fancies of our imagination.

Suppose you wanted to tell someone about the following incident. You were walking through an office and you saw a girl sitting at a stenographer's desk just outside Mr. Brown's office. Her face was unfamiliar; she was holding a magazine open in her hands; and there was a pile of papers on both corners of her desk.

A D_1 statement about this situation could run like this. "There was a girl sitting at the stenographer's desk outside of Brown's office, holding a magazine open in her hands." This statement contains no guessing; it describes without comments; it could easily be checked; and it leaves very little room for disagreement. It is couched in low-abstraction report language.

This statement may sound just as factual. "Mr. Brown's new stenographer was reading a magazine as I passed by her desk." This may appear to be a description, but it is not; it contains some guesses. First of all, you guessed that the girl is "Mr. Brown's new stenographer": she could be just waiting to see Brown, or she could be a friend of Brown's stenographer, and so forth; and second, you guessed that she was "reading" the magazine. Both of these guesses might be correct, but we are not at this point concerned with the truth or falsity of the statements, we are concerned with their guess content. Generally speaking, the more guess content, the greater the likelihood that one is in error. If we happen to be right, it is a matter of coincidence; it is not derived from an awareness of the abstraction process as it is meant here.

Another statement, which might include even more guess content, is: "Brown's stenographer is letting her work pile up on her." We would be guessing not only that the girl is Brown's stenographer but assuming that holding the magazine is not part of her work, that the papers on the desk are part of her work, that these papers are unfinished work. This is an inferential statement: it draws much more from our accumulated stock of memories, interpretations, and prejudices than from a reliable abstracting of what we see.

We can go even farther from the evidence at hand and say: "The efficiency in Brown's department is dropping." Or we may find that the present situation is "proof" of some set of our ideas that we take as a basic principle of acquired wisdom. We might say: "People don't work the way they used to." This level of generalities is so high in abstraction that its meaning has disappeared in the clouds.

There may also be a great amount of guess content in a question. Our son comes home for the weekend, and he occasionally uses some of the tools I have back of the workbench in the garage. Once he left my good hammer in his car and went away with it. I searched for it all week, and when he came back I told him in no uncertain terms to leave my tools where they belong. Two weeks later I again missed my good hammer. When he came home I asked him: "What did you do with my good hammer this time?" My question included the guess—quite reasonable, it seemed to me at the time—that he had mislaid or taken away the hammer. As it happened, he had nothing to do with this—in fact, had I not guessed as I did, I could have found the tool early in the week. I should have started with a statement—to myself—that would have been strictly descriptive and devoid of guessing; "I do not see my hammer in its usual place. Let us find out who used it last, when, and where." This would probably have led me to where I had left the hammer a few days before.

When we ask a question, we are often responsible for the level at which the answer will come. If we invite an interpretation, at a high level of abstraction, we should not expect a description that is close to a first-order experience.

In four lines of *The Elephant Child*, Rudyard Kipling listed the six standard question words:[8]

I keep six honest serving-men,
They taught me all I knew;
Their names are What and Why and When
And How and Where and Who.

Of these six questions, four are definitely of a low order of abstraction; they ask for a descriptive answer and leave very little room for interpretation or fantasy: *who, what, when,* and *where.* One of the six, the ubiquitous *why*, asks for an interpretation; and *how* could be placed almost anywhere between these extremes.

When we ask "Why did you do this or that?" we are obviously not looking for a neutral statement of fact. We are, in effect, saying "Give me your interpretation of what happened"; and we have no right to be surprised if the interpretation appears to be biased in favor of the one who gives it. This is the result of abstractions that are processed through one's own semantic transactions. Do we expect another to be self-destructive? If our own interpretation does not agree with the one we are given, we should not accuse the answerer of lying, of being self-defensive, of avoiding responsibility; if we do, we are indulging our own interpretations—which may be just as groundless as the one we were given. Both persons are up in the air, out of contact with reality, and tossed against each other in a full-blown hurricane of emotional conflict. *Why* is a dangerous question, unless both of us are ready to take the risk of

[8]Rudyard Kipling, "The Elephant's Child" in *Kipling—A Selection of His Stories and Poems*, ed. John Beecroft (New York: Doubleday, 1956), p. 383.

digging into our motivation, and this is not easy. Most of our statements and actions are the result of many contributory antecedents, some of which are quite evident and some of which are buried in our habits and in our subconscious. Asking *why* is asking for a theory, and no theory—even the most respected in today's science—is an exhaustive explanation of what happens.

Another common practice that goes against the principles we are now studying is asking, at the start of a meeting—as is often done in business— "What do you think of this plan?" Here, again, we are asking for an answer of a high order of abstraction, assuming without reason that all participants have the same facts on which they can base their conclusions. This is not a *what* question in the strict sense. It amounts to saying: Give us your interpretation of what you know of the situation under study. It really comes to a *why* question. It means: Give us the reasons why you reached whatever conclusions you did in the case at hand. This sharp division between data reporting and opinion giving was emphasized once at the annual meeting of executives of a firm with offices all over the country and outside. They were put in two rows, one for data reporters and one for opinion givers, sitting in front of a huge blackboard on which the answers were inscribed in verbal or diagrammatic form. At least one data giver and one opinion giver came from each and every center of operation. First data were asked for and no opinions were allowed to be inserted in the answers. If an opinion giver felt he had an important fact to include in the deliberations, he had to move bodily into the reactors' row and describe the fact without any comment or evaluation. Then he was allowed to go back to the row to which he belonged from the beginning. Once the members were satisfied that as many data as were considered necessary had been put on the board, the opinion givers came on the scene and were invited to give their views on the basis of these data. The results were spectacular. Instead of having to spend three full days in deliberating as expected, they were through at the end of one day and a half. There had been practically no arguing, no speech making, no hard feelings expressed.

In brief, consciousness of abstracting brings about an awareness of the fact that thinking is a multilevel affair: our statements may travel close to the ground of first-order experience or they may soar to the stratosphere of almost limitless generalizations. Thought traffic is more like air traffic than like ground traffic. If two theories go in opposite directions or at an angle with each other, they do not have to come into collision; they may well be at different levels of abstraction, and they can pursue their courses without interference with each other. If, on the other hand, we keep to the practice of flat thinking and want no disturbing theories, we have to keep our ideas, theories, and doctrines moving along parallel lines, all in one direction, which for us is the only right direction. We become followers of a leader or assume that everyone should follow our own advice.

Paradoxes, contradictions, and dilemmas are often plain delusions because we take our thinking as movement on a flat surface. In any book on classical logic the opposition of statements—or propositions, as they call them—is described in terms of contradictories, contraries, subcontraries, and subalterns, which implies a comparison on a level of abstraction that is assumed to be one and the same for all of them. Or, to put it differently, we may say that in Aristotelian logic—and in popular common sense that is guided by it—the vertical aspect, the high and low levels of our statements are not taken into account. There is no ladder of abstraction in this Aristotelian world. An original thinker of our generation, Rudolph Jordan, says:

> In the realm of more advanced philosophy, most logic is satisfied with two dimensions, so that lines of thought can be related and drawn on paper. . . .Three-dimensional thought in philosophy is new and without precedent and cannot be found in textbooks. It must be thought and explored anew.[9]

We have said that we are going through a conceptual revolution, and the passage from two-dimensional to multidimensional thinking is part of the present revolution. We no longer content ourselves with syllogistic steps from premises to conclusions, we use mental models of ever-increasing degrees of complexity. Our whole world of thought becomes a complex structure in which consciousness of abstracting in a hierarchy of orders, from first-order experiences to all-embracing generalizations, is a must for whoever wants to keep his sanity.

Circularity

> You insist that you are seeing the black-and-white page of this book, do you not? You're not. You have a brain-centered television set, and the light is bouncing off the page. The resultant comes back through your optical system and is scanned and actually goes back into the brain, and you are seeing the page in your brain. You are not seeing the page in front of you. We have gotten used to the idea that we see outside of ourselves, but we just don't do so. It only takes about a billionth of a second for the light to bounce off the page and get in the brain to be scanned, so the child is fooled into thinking that he is seeing outside of himself. And we are misinforming ourselves in discounting the lag and assuming that we see it "over there."[10]

The above statement by Buckminster Fuller can serve as introduction to circularity in the abstracting process, and the role we have given to perception in our contacts with the world. But since perception is only

[9]Rudolph Jordan, *The New Perspective* (Chicago: University of Chicago Press, 1951), p. 23.

[10]Buckminster Fuller, *Synergetics* (New York: Macmillan, 1975), p. 440.

one activity within a whole semantic transaction, let's examine what happens in the journey of light through the humanized brain.

"Seeing is believing" is one of the popular sayings that is seldom re-examined. It is usually, but not always, true; it is part of our accepted theory of perception, and we use it as a reliable principle not only in common observation but also in scientific work. What we see with our own eyes has an acknowledged character of objectivity and stands in opposition to pure imagination. What normal people see is really there, and what they don't see does not exist. When an alcoholic in delirium tremens sees pink elephants, we know that he suffers from hallucinations because normal people do not see them. The alcoholic sees what his disturbed condition causes him to believe is there, but a healthy individual has no such belief.

By using such instruments as microscopes and telescopes we increase our capacity to see, and we extend our knowledge of the world in the realm of the very small and in the realm of the very distant. We can see microbes in a microscope and double stars in a telescope. The electron microscope lays bare before the scientist a whole world in which we believe, and with good reasons. What may appear on a radarscope may well decide the fate of the world some day.

Seeing with our own eyes has, indeed, a tremendous influence on what we do, and we have the word *evidence* to express our age-long belief in the validity of visual perception. Its etymology stems from the two Latin words, *ex*, meaning "out of," and *videre*, meaning "to see," which, when combined, imply that evidence is what grows out of the act of seeing. The word is a condensation of the aphorism "seeing is believing." The same could be said of other sensory activities, such as hearing with our own ears, touching with our own hands, tasting with our own tongue, smelling with our own nose.

When I studied Aristotelian philosophy in my college days, I learned that "our senses, within the limits of their proper objects, are valid criteria of truth." General semantics, which is a non-Aristotelian system, agrees that our sensory perceptions have some value, but it insists that perceptions are gross approximations; in more cases than we ordinarily suspect, they may be a source of error. These errors multiply in a fantastic manner when we fail to pay attention to orders of abstraction and when we confuse interpretation with first-order experience. A time often comes when we see not what is actually there but what we believe is there, because our cultural unconscious causes us to believe that it is there. In such a case, believing is tantamount to seeing.

To make more sense in all this, we have to come back to our fundamental description of ourselves as semantic transactors. Our activities of thinking, feeling, moving, and sensing are not separate activities, relatively independent from one another; they are different aspects of a single organismic phenomenon, which we call semantic transaction. When I say that I see, I am describing one aspect of a complex totality and am neglecting the others that are there all along—and just as real, and in some cases just as important. I see with my eyes, true; but I see also with my feelings, my past habits, my belonging to a cultural environment that I have internalized and that is now part of myself as a transactor. If I fail to see what you see, you may call it a visual illusion, but this does not change my perception at the moment. I may agree that it is an illusion, but it will not prevent my seeing it as I do. To change my vision I would have to reeducate my whole semantic transaction, correct past habits embedded deep in my nervous system, renounce some of my past, and contradict the culture or the subculture I have appropriated. I am a space-time process that reacts as a whole, not a loose assemblage of parts that can be replaced or adjusted one by one.

We can illustrate this by inserting between the parabola of the Structural Differential and the circle that stands for first-order experience a diagram of the semantic transactor that was given in Chapter 3. In fact, we can imagine such a diagram between any two consecutive orders of abstraction (Figure 6.3).[11] A member of the New York bar, in an article entitled "The Unreality of Accident Litigation: A Plea for a New Approach," put it this way: "What an individual perceives is the result of his personality, his environment, and his history filtered through his experiences.[12]

Hundreds of experiments have established the appropriateness of this proposition. A psychologist employed seven assistants and one genuine subject in an experiment in which all were asked to judge the length of a straight line that they were shown on a screen. The seven assistants, who were the first to speak and to report what they saw, had been instructed to report, unanimously, an evidently incorrect length. The eighth member of the group, the naïve subject, did not know that his companions had received such an instruction, and he was under the impression that what they reported was really what they saw, and in one third of the experiments he reported the same incorrect length that they had. The pressure of the environment had influenced his semantic transaction and had distorted his vision. When one of the assistants, under the direction of the experimenter, started reporting the correct length, it relieved the pressure of the environment, and the perception of the uninformed subject improved accordingly. This indicates that the environment, which we tend to see outside the subject, is really a component element of his semantic transactions. It plays a part in our thinking, our feeling, and in our sensory activities.

[11]You will notice, in addition, that the position of the differential is reversed. This may make it easier to visualize the "high" and "low" order implications of the diagram. Wendell Johnson in his book, *People In Quandries,* has a similarly positioned diagram.

[12]James Marshall, "The Unreality...," *American Bar Association Journal* (August 1964), p. 714.

Generalization,
Conclusions

Abstracting
through ST
filter

Interpretation

Abstracting
through ST
filter

Description

Abstracting
through ST
filter

First-order Experience

Abstracting
through ST
filter

WIGO

Figure 6.3. A new version of the structural differential.
1. WIGO—the cosmic event, shown as made of a limitless number of "infinities" of lower order.
2. First-order experience includes limited number of "infinities" of a lower order (parabolas).
3. The abstracting process shown as a filtering through the sieve of semantic transactions.
4. Circularity not expressed by returning arrow, but implied in ST filtering.

Our organismic activities interact among themselves—or, better, the variation of one aspect often means the variation of another aspect. The following list of statements is based on reports of psychological experiments.

1. Bodily needs, which I called electrochemical activities, tend to determine what is perceived. Subjects who were deprived of food for varying lengths of time saw articles of food depicted in blurred drawings much more frequently than did subjects who had just eaten a meal.
2. Reward or punishment associated with the perceiving of objects tends to determine what is perceived. In other words, feeling and anticipation guide perceiving.
3. The values that a subject holds dear make him more perceptive of words that are related to these values. Again, a matter of feeling.
4. The value that the individual attaches to objects tends to determine his estimation of their size. Whatever is important to the subject, positively or negatively, is likely to "loom larger" in his perception.
5. The personality of an individual predisposes him to see things in a manner that is consistent with his personality makeup.
6. Words that are disturbing or threatening to a person are not easily perceived, and they provoke a physiological reaction that may be unknown to the subject but are easily detected by his skin's galvanic response (lie-detector).

You may say that these statements cover more ground than what we usually mean by believing. Do they really? So many beliefs are implicit in our attitudes, our accepted values, our personal preferences! They are even hidden in the habits we have acquired and in the language we have learned to speak. Because our language is a subject-predicate language and describes the world as made of things and qualities and agents and actions, we say "It rains," asserting that something is there that does the raining, when the pronoun *it* refers to nothing at all. This is almost like believing in ghosts.

The trouble is that there are times when we believe that what is going on is what we have learned to say is going on. It works fairly well in simple cases, but it often creates unnecessary problems. The hidden implications of what we say cause us to look for things that may not be there; and Poincaré gave an example that has become classical. In the days when very few chemical elements were known, scientists tried to isolate the element "heat." What was involved in their looking for heat as a chemical element, comparable to sulfur, oxygen, or mercury? I suggest that the strongest factor involved its having a name that belonged grammatically (and therefore logically) to the same class as elements, the class of nouns or substantives. By implication, substantives refer to substances (or elements), and, consequently, the scientists were looking for the "substance" heat (or *phlogis-*

ton). There was none. Back of that substantive was a process, not a permanent element like sulfur, oxygen, or mercury.

The influence of past habits on our perception has been demonstrated in a series of spectacular experiments that were originally devised by the late Adelbert Ames, Jr., of Hanover, N.H. His apparatus are now at Princeton University, and they have been reproduced in many laboratories. One of them, the trapezoidal window, has become a well-known demonstration that is widely used in courses for adult education. It was discussed and illustrated in *Life* magazine, and its use was demonstrated in a motion picture (Figure 6.4).

Trapezoidal Window   **Rectangular Window**

Figure 6.4. Ames' perceptual experiment with trapezoidal window.

This apparatus consists of a window frame made of a thin sheet of aluminum 14 inches in horizontal length and 12½ inches in height at one end and 9 inches at the other. It stands on a rod, soldered at the midpoint of its length, and it is made to rotate in a clockwise direction by a small electric motor to which the rod is connected. When viewed at a distance of more than 22 feet, the window, though actually rotating, appears to oscillate back and forth. A small red cube, attached to a vertical side, appears to move in a circular fashion, and, in part of its course, seems to leave the frame and float through the air, passing in front of the window and finally returning to the original point of attachment. Once the observers have looked at the window and have seen it oscillating, they are invited to come near and to see for themselves that it is actually rotating. But when they go back to the original distance, they see it oscillating again—although they know that it does not oscillate. The red cube still appears to detach itself from the window and to turn around it—although they know that it is wired to the window. They know that they are victims of a delusion, but they cannot correct their false perception.

What makes them see the window oscillating when they know it is rotating, and see the cube floating in the air when they know it is attached to the frame?

The answer is that a long training, of which they never were conscious, has caused their vision to be influenced by the laws of perspective. When we look at a row of telephone posts along the road, the farther away they are the shorter they appear. Long means near, short means distant. In the case of Ames's window, the difference between the long and the short vertical sides is exaggerated so that the distance between them appears longer than normal. When the long side turns away from the observer, it remains apparently taller than the short side that is coming forward. As a consequence, the long side does not appear to recede, it seems to remain close to the observer, and this causes the window to appear to oscillate—the long side being always in the front and the short side being always in the back.

When we see that, of two telephone posts along the road, the shorter is farther away, we are not simply seeing, we are interpreting what we see. The retina of our eyes is like a photographic film that registers what is out there, without interpreting it in the least. But the retina, alone, does not account for our perception; it is connected with the visual area of the brain in which the interpretation takes place. This interpretation has become automatic in the course of years; we have learned to believe it as the true picture of reality. When we think we see (as we say) with our own eyes, we are actually projecting upon the world the picture of it that we have unconsciously created in our own brain as we learned to interpret the retinal image. Our belief in the reliability of this interpretation is stronger than any information that goes against it. After observing that the window rotates, we still see it oscillate, as our interpretation dictates. We have learned to see in a certain way, and we keep seeing that way despite all evidence to the contrary.

I had a personal experience with Ames's trapezoidal window that gave me a "counterdemonstration" of this law of perception. With a New York associate, I was demonstrating it to fourteen executives of an industrial designing company. To our great surprise, most of them—twelve out of fourteen, if I remember rightly—saw the window rotating from the very start, and only two saw it oscillating. We were startled with this result, and we checked carefully on the distance, the illumination, and other conditions of the experiment. But the twelve men kept seeing it as rotating. I was ready to give up, to declare the demonstration unsuccessful when one of the senior partners said:

> No, it's not a failure; quite the contrary! It proves your point better than you expected. Didn't you say that this would show that we see the way we have

learned to see, and therefore that our seeing depends on our training? Check on those who were not taken in by the illusion. They are all industrial designers. They were trained not only to detect visual illusions but also to create them. The two who do not have that training react as the average person does. They are salesmen.

He was right. Later, I checked with a member of the Princeton laboratory, where the original Ames material is kept, and they told me that their experience had been similar. Designers, architects, and people trained in the visual arts do not all react to the trapezoidal window as the average person does. We learn to see as we learn anything else, and different learning brings about different seeing.

We take it for granted that the outside world is actually what our experience has proved it to be. We believe implicitly in our mental picture of the world, and our new experiences conform to our preestablished picture. Our assumptions, our preconceived notions—particularly those that served us well in the past—act as a filter for our abstracting processes.

It seems that such a filter is a necessary part of our functional makeup. Without it, without that second nature that we have acquired as we grew up, we would see only patches of color. We could not distinguish shapes and forms; we would not be able to identify objects by sight.

This was brought to light in recent years when eye surgeons succeeded in giving sight to people who had been born with congenital cataract. After being operated upon and provided with the proper glasses, these persons have normal vision, as far as their retina goes. When they first open their eyes to the world they report only a spinning mass of lights and colors. They are unable to pick out, by sight, objects that they knew by touch, and it takes time for their brain to learn the rules of seeing, which have become second nature for others. If they are to make use of their eyes, they will have to train their brain. When shown a patch of color that is placed on a larger patch, they will quickly see that there is a difference between the smaller patch and its surroundings, but they will not see the shapes of the patches.

Such a patient, when shown a blue square, said that it was blue and round, and also described a triangle as round. When the angles were pointed out to him, he said: "Ah, yes, I understand now, one can *see* how they *feel.*" For many weeks after beginning to see, he could only with great difficulty distinguish between the simplest shapes, such as a triangle and a square. If such a person is asked how he does it, he may say: "Of course, if I look carefully I see that there are three sharp turns at the edge of one patch of light and four on the other." But he may ask: "What on earth do you mean by saying that it would be useful to know this? The difference is only slight and it takes me a long time to work it out." Two days later he will be unable to say which is a triangle and which is a square; it takes at least a month to learn to recognize some objects by sight. What these people lack is the store of rules for seeing that is lodged in the brain, rules that are usually learned by long years of exploration with the eyes during childhood.

People who are born blind have their own ways of perceiving, of using their sense of touch; they are content with these ways and can not see the point of trying to find others. "And why not?" you may say; "why must anyone seek new ways of acting?" The answer is that, in the long run, our survival and our progress depend on making new experiments, on inventing new ways of seeing, new ways of thinking, and new ways of persons and situations.[13]

Circularity does not always work to our detriment. The well-trained and experienced professional knows what to look for in a situation that is very confusing to the layman. The professional abstracts details that are significant and quickly makes sense of what is puzzling to his client. On the other hand, the professional may rely too much on his experience and content himself with a cursory examination of the case. If it is useful to recognize similarities that make classifications possible, it is equally important to watch for differences that make a difference.

Circularity also operates in a person who has a few pet ideas, for which he seeks confirmation in almost everything he observes. The extreme case is the paranoiac, who interprets the most innocuous events as machinations of his assumed persecutors. The milder cases are those of people who "prove" their pet theories by giving what they call "examples" of what they claim is true. The mechanism that operates in their case is obvious: instead of going step by step from the parabola (WIGO), through a genuine experience (the circle), and through the stages of description and interpretation, they swing around from their preestablished conclusions and generalities back to the parabola, abstracting from the total event whatever aspects fit their convictions, attitudes, and purposes (see arrow pointing upwards in Figure 6.2). This is circularity in its naked form. A person who is not aware that such a mechanism might be at work within himself is impervious to any logical counterdemonstration.

Types of Abstracting

The term *abstracting* covers a wide range of processes, some of which can be observed in the lower forms of life. For instance, if we put a seed and a small rock side by side in well-prepared soil, we will soon notice differences in their behavior. The rock will remain visibly identical with itself and appear to be inactive and practically unchanged; the seed will wake up, as it

[13]This is precisely the place where a science-art of innovating, or the field of epistemics, concerns itself: to meet the human need to survive, evolve and renew ourselves in a conscious way, and from a more organized basis in order to minimize the risks involved.

were, burst open its shell, stretch roots downward, and push a stem upwards. It will seek, pick, and choose in its environment, and will ingest—in definite proportions, and according to a definite timetable—the chemicals, the moisture, the air, and the sunlight that are necessary for its survival and its growth into a plant or a tree. It does this abstracting according to an action pattern that is programmed in its genes; it transforms the elements that it abstracts into its own substance. If these elements are not within its reach, the plant cannot pursue the transactions that are vital to its existence; and it withers and dies. Animals can move about; they can seek, in space, what they have to abstract and transform in order to survive and develop. The cattle in the field do not depend on rain or irrigation to provide them with moisture, they walk to the stream or the water trough; but if they are fenced in, out of reach of the elements that they need, animals also starve and die. In a sense, abstracting may be seen as an aspect of living, as partaking selectively of the environment in order to survive and to grow.

Humans share with plants and animals that abstracting capacity, need, and function. By neglecting the usual distinction between mind and body, we may include under the term *semantic* those transactions that do not ostensibly go beyond the physiological level. The first time I read a particular statement of Dr. George K. Zipf, I was a bit startled, even shocked; today I find it quite acceptable.

> The fact that we administer pills to cure certain diseases and words to cure others (mental diseases), and use either for some, does not mean that there is a dichotomy between mind and body. In all cases we are evoking selected kinds of responses by administering selected kinds of stimuli. To the upper "cultural" level of organization we talk with "words," to the lower and more determinate levels we talk with aspirin pills. But it is still talk, though we use the terms of conventional cultured language for the one and the terms of the more invariant language of physics-chemistry for the other. Opium that is food for some organisms is narcotic for us because it has that meaning in terms of our semantic system.[14]

It is accepted that we can produce a physiological reaction with *chemical* means, as well as with *mechanical* means such as puncture, friction, pressure; *physical* means such as light, heat, magnetism, sound, rays, electrical currents; and with *biological* means such as microbes, sperm, parasites. Now it has been generally established that means involving words or visualizations could be used interchangebly, and, at times, together with the above means to produce a desired reaction at the physiological level. Two examples are Dr. Carl Symington in his treatment of cancer patients, and Luther Burbank in his production of cacti without spines.

[14]George K. Zipf, *Human Behavior and the Principle of Least Effort* (Reading, Mass.: Addison-Wesley, 1949), p. 200.

But we also abstract characteristics from our environment that we are more ready to consider as typically human. From the moment we are born—and perhaps earlier; who knows?—we unconsciously abstract from the environment vital elements that we internalize and transform into our growing self. We take in the love or the rejection of our mothers, the relaxed attitudes or the tenseness of those who handle us, the comfort or the discomfort of the place we are in, the noise of the city or the calm of the country. We become what we abstract, transform, and assimilate.[15]

We are now concerned with the abstractions of the adult that are mostly "intellectual," with the C aspects of our semantic transactions (*see* p. 30). To use Korzybski's analogy, we are studying the various kinds of "maps" that we make of the "territories" we are dealing with when we transact with our environment. This "environment" may be inside as well as outside our physical organism. The founder of general semantics speaks of only two classes of abstracting; in an earlier volume, I gave a tentative list of five,[16] now I present a list of four in a different order and two under different names.[17]

The first kind of abstracting is *evaluative* (I called it *normative* years ago, but now I find it a poor label). Our first interpretation of the world about us is mostly a matter of sensing and feeling. We take the feel of our reactions as the adequate map of objective reality. Things are good or bad, pleasant or threatening, attractive or repulsive. We do not suspect that the qualities we ascribe to things, persons, and situations are abstractions that come not from them alone but also from our previous experiences with them and from our cultural assumptions about them. A standard experiment, made popular by the American Genetic Association, brings this out very vividly. Small bits of paper, treated with an entirely harmless chemical, phenylthiocarbamide, are distributed to subjects. On the average, seven people out of ten, on chewing a bit of that paper, will detect a definite taste: most of them will find it bitter; a negligible percentage may find it sour, or salty, or even sweet; and three out of ten will taste nothing. When the subjects report their experience, they will say "It is bitter" or "It is tasteless"—as if the bitterness or the tastelessness were a quality that resided in the paper. But such a quality cannot be there as an objective fact, since different people, because of their genetic constitution, get a different taste from it. Clearly, this is a case where our language of subject and predicate, things and qualities, fails to describe the phenomenon. It is not the treated paper that is bitter or tasteless, it is

---

[15]This "becoming what we abstract, transform, and assimilate" is powerfully described in Walt Whitman's poem "There Was a Child Went Forth," in *The Poetry and Prose of Walt Whitman*, edited by Louis Untermeyer (New York: Simon and Schuster, 1949), pp. 346-48.

[16]J. Samuel Bois, *Explorations in Awareness*, p. 135.

[17]These types of abstraction, when put in the order suggested, give us an advance outline of the major scale of human development described later on in this volume.

our tasting that creates the sensation. It is our first-order experience that deserves the label of bitter, not the paper itself. The statement "It is bitter" is false to fact, and the metaphysics derived from it is also false.

This observation applies to all our evaluative statements. We say that things are beautiful or ugly, good or bad, and threatening or attractive when, in fact, we are abstracting these qualities not from the objective reality outside us but from our personal interaction with it. From these low-order abstractions, which emerge from subjective experience, we climb the ladder of abstraction in confidence and place, at the top, our general notions of beauty, goodness, attractiveness, truth. We build a hierarchy of values that we eventually accept as the absolute rules of taste, even of morality. We make idols of our evaluative generalities.

I used to call the second type of abstracting *nominalistic*—an awkward term that smacks of the epistemological quarrels of the Middle Ages—but I now prefer the more simple label *classifying* abstracting. This abstracting is the type that is most commonly discussed in seminars on General Semantics. Professor F. S. C. Northrop of Yale, in his Korzybski Memorial Lecture in 1954, belabored the expositors of the discipline who limit themselves to insisting on the value of the Cow_1, Cow_2, Cow_3 device. The fact is that this classifying abstraction is not inconsistent with Aristotelian thinking.

To put some order in the facts we have gathered, we classify them according to the features we think they have in common; and we decide—rather, our language has decided for us—what label will apply to each group of them. When a child meets something new to him, he asks "What is it?" meaning "With what shall I file this away in my mind?" We answer by naming the thing: "It's a dog...a snake...a bulldozer...a machine," or what not. When we do this we abstract, according to the language we speak, the features that this object has in common with other objects of the same accepted class. If we are very specific, we use descriptive terms and remain at a low level of abstraction; we say, for instance, "I am attending UCLA Medical School." We may also give a general answer, and stay at a high level of abstraction, because we feel that under the circumstances it is sufficient to say "I am attending a University" or "I am in college." The higher we are on the abstraction ladder, the less we describe the individual university and the more we can generalize about schools.

A special type of classifying abstracting may be named *objective* abstracting. In *classifying* abstracting we have classes that include subclasses; for instance, the class "animal" includes dogs, cats, cows, horses, elephants, and the class "dog," in turn, includes various subclasses or breeds, such as bulldogs, chihuahuas, terriers, police dogs. The "container" class is of a higher order than its subclasses. In objective abstracting we have containers *and* contents, but the containers are not simply logical classes, they are *ac-*

tual groups that are made up of *actual* units—as a family is made of individual members, a book is made of individual chapters.

In a sense, all terms of objective abstracting can be considered as of a low order of abstraction: a book has a title that differentiates it from all other books, a family has a name that makes it unique. But when we compare the family as a whole to its members taken individually, or the book as a whole to its chapters taken one by one, we are at two different levels of objective abstraction. "Family" is higher than "family member" in abstraction, and "book" is higher than "chapter." Each term of the pairs belongs to a different order of existence: what is true of the family is not necessarily true of each member, and what is true of a member is not necessarily true of the family as a whole. The same is true of the book and its chapters: we cannot judge a book by one of its chapters. A book made of chapters that do not fit together is a poor book, although each chapter, taken one by one, might be a very good essay. Book and chapter do not belong to the same order of things.

Relational abstracting, our third type, is the typical human achievement when we function according to what is now called the "scientific manner." Many people, including outstanding scientists and lay people consider it as the supreme achievement of the human brain. The cultural mutation we are now going through may be seen as the painful process of disentangling ourselves from the snares of this all-pervading system.

Here we do not simply invent classes so that we can file our information in some arbitrary order; we "discover" how the elements of a situation are actually related to one another, and we express these relations in a mathematical formula, in a mental model, or in a telling analogy. What we abstract is not concrete, not material, not something that we can see, weigh, or touch; yet it is claimed to be more real than anything that is tangible: it has been referred to as "invariant under transformation," and of late the word paradigm has become more popular. It is not only information, it is structural knowledge; that is, we relate our experiences, thus creating knowledge. Then we relate these bits of knowledge to one another and make of them a structure of some kind. This we call science. Then we may go one step further and scientize about that structuring itself; this is the field of epistemology.

Every scientific advance is an achievement in relational abstracting. A simple formula, such as $a^2 = b^2 + c^2$, which states the unvarying relations among the three sides of a right-angle triangle in Euclidian geometry, is the result of relational abstracting. Einstein's $E = mc^2$ is another one, one that towers at the top of a pyramid of phenomena, some of which are still to be discovered. Mendeleev's periodic table, and Freud's trilogy of the superego, the ego, and the id, Korzybski's analogy of the map and the territory, and my own diagram of the human individual as a semantic transactor, these and similar formulas are types of relational abstracting. They are human-made guesses and approximations of the order that we assume is somewhere, somehow, behind the phenomena of nature.

The fourth type of abstracting is *self-reflexive*, and it is a human achievement that deserves more attention than is usually given to it (we shall discuss it in greater detail when we study multiordinality). We are not simply aware of our existence, we are aware of our awareness. We can think about our thinking, talk about our talking, worry about our worrying, and can go up and up on the ladder of self-observation until we reach the philosophical summits—or, in reverse order, the depths of morbid introspection. We are not simply turning in circles, we are spiraling up to wisdom or down to complete personal misery. It could be seen as a second-generation abstracting, or abstracting of the abstracting process itself, introducing a science of sciences and inviting a new kind of human functioning. This is the field in which we are now working.

Every time I am in a situation, the situation acquires a structure, assumes a degree of tension and direction, that is due to my presence. It is impossible for me to witness the situation "in itself," as we say; it is always the situation-with-me-as-a-component-participant. Being aware of my awareness brings the situation-with-me-as-a-component-participant to a third order of existence, and so on indefinitely, until the discrimination between my two roles, that of participant and that of observer, becomes so tenuous as to be imperceptible. The blending of me and the outside world gives birth to a compound that is not one element plus the other taken additively, but is of a new order of existence, with characteristics and properties that did not exist before. If I see myself as an element of a compound, and my awareness is that of an element within a compound, not of an element "really" detached from the compound, then I become an element that has the specific capacity of detaching itself from the compound to which it belongs without ceasing to belong to it. This is what we refer to when we speak of self-reflexive awareness. It differentiates us from our animal cousins.

We cannot get out of the human individual-world compound laterally, that is by moving to the side of it on the same plane of existence, so to speak. We have to jump to a higher order of dimensionality. To use a three dimensional model: we cannot get out of the box that our very presence creates unless we actually "create" a fourth dimension by observing our observing, thinking our thinking, evaluating our evaluating in recurring cycles of higher and higher dimensions of finer and finer amplitude, the span of which can never be reduced to zero. Self-reflexiveness means more than just "thinking."

As we will show later in discussing Self-1, Self-2, Self-3 . . . Self-n, observing our behavior in wide-awake self-reflexiveness is useful not only in preventing trouble and waste of energy, but it has proved to be a powerful means of discovering hidden assumptions and unearthing behavior patterns within ourselves in ways we seldom suspect.

It can also be considered an art as well as a science, the art of soaring above my first-order experience in a self-reflexiveness that transacts with the experience-as-a-whole and not with the experience as analyzed by verbal means. This is when myself-as-observer becomes myself-as-participant in the shaping of the environment of values that gives my living experiences a direction and out of which emerges the content of my world.

If we want to use the formulation of abstracting and of orders of abstraction to guide ourselves, we must train ourselves to differentiate between levels of knowing and to see them as levels of existence—as Harry Weinberg puts it so well in his book of that title.[18] Our thinking thus assumes a vertical dimension as crisscrossing traffic keeps moving without interference in multilevel highway interchanges.

To summarize the types of abstracting: Evaluative abstraction reminds me that I am always in the picture, with my hidden assumptions and prejudices, when I speak of "honesty," "goodness," "beauty," and the like.

The rules of classifying abstraction forbid me to generalize about teachers from my knowledge of a few teachers that I have met: this would be confusing the higher order with the lower order. In objective abstraction I am reminded that the whole, as a whole, is different from the sum of its parts taken as distinct units; therefore I am not surprised if five mature men happen to behave like immature children when they are put together in a committee.

Relational abstraction gives me the pure theory that guides my practice, although it has never happened that all the conclusions drawn from a theory have agreed with the observable facts.

When I am tempted to place blame on "the outside world" for all my troubles, self-reflexive abstracting can allow me to see my existence as a condition that I create by my own activity. I can use this creative ability for the benefit or to the detriment of myself, my species, and my whole environment.

[18]Weinberg, *Levels of Knowing and Existence* (New York: Harper & Row, 1960).

CHAPTER 7

orders of abstraction and multiordinality

Abstraction is an activity of all living forms. From the seed that, after it is put in the soil, breaks open its shell, selects and absorbs chemicals, breathes the air, and fills itself with the energy of the sun's rays, we saw this phenomenon of abstracting, assimilation, and transformation become more complex and far-reaching until, in conscious *Homo sapiens,* we reach the apex of the living segment of our planetary world.

Like the seed that returns to the soil from which it grew, human abstractors take their place in the cultural environment from which they emerged. They break open the shell of their unspoken first-order experience, they seek avidly, and they select—from the traditional and recorded experiences of those who proceded them—the nutritive elements that will make them grow into conscious specimens of humanity.

The seed reproduces the plant or the tree from which it came, but it does not change the pattern of development it has inherited with the genes of its species. Most people are like the seed: they reproduce without improving the cultural pattern they inherited from their parents and teachers. But once in a while a cultural mutation takes place; the patterns of abstraction, assimilation, and integration undergo a transformation. A new kind of *Homo sapiens* emerges, who makes and discovers itself as the creator of a new order of things.

We have said that such a mutation is now taking place in many individuals of our generation, and we called it a conceptual revolution. It does not seem to be a case of biological evolution: nothing spectacular seems to be happening in our bones, our muscles, our nervous system, or our sensory organs; the change is within our awareness mostly at the level of our thinking activities. Of these activities, abstracting is one of the most important. We have it in common with all forms of life, but in us it has a very distinctive characteristic.

In all other living things, abstracting seems to be a dumb process,[19] unspoken and unrecorded. Neither the tree nor the animal conceptualizes what it does as it reacts to its environment. A chimpanzee or a child may manage to develop skills in terms of things immediately sensed, or remembered as sensed. For them, abstraction stops at the level of first-order experience; it does not reach the level of description, of translation into words and propositions, into symbols and formulas. Lynn White, Jr., said that

> We are beginning to see that the distinctive thing about the human species is that we are a symbolmaking animal, *homo signifex*, and that without this function we could never have become sapiens. We have not only the capacity to make symbols; we are under the necessity to create them in order to cope humanly with our experience.[20]

Once they have been made by us, these symbols become a tool: they multiply our power of thinking, but at the same time they limit our capacities to their own range of significance. The art of *Homo sapiens*, the symbol-user, increases and directs—within definite channels—the wisdom of *Homo sapiens* the philosopher. By making better thinking models, we become better thinkers. If certain problems still are baffling, it is because we have not yet devised the proper symbols for observing and managing them. The inventor of symbols and symbol systems is the person who blazes the trail of our advance. The mathematician has been doing it with spectacular success for the natural sciences, and it is the task of the epistemologist to do it for the human sciences.

This brings us back to abstracting. Because it is a most important activity, it follows that any invention that will increase our awareness of this process and improve our skill in managing it is a major achievement in our cultural evolution. One of these epoch-making inventions was formulated by Alfred Korzybski in 1925.

> All the most humanly important and interesting terms are multiordinal, and no one can evade the use of such terms. Multiordinality is inherent in the structure of "human knowledge." This multiordinal mechanism gives the key to many seemingly insoluble contradictions, and explains why we have scarcely progressed at all in the solution of many human affairs.[21]

---

[19]As we are learning more about dolphins and whales, our assumptions in this regard are being seriously questioned, at least in aural forms of abstracting.

[20]Lynn White, Jr., *Frontiers of Knowledge in the Study of Man* (New York: Harper & Row, 1956), p. 305.

[21]Korzybski, *Science and Sanity*, p. 74.

What do we mean by multiordinality? When is a word used in a multiordinal manner? Is it simply when the same word means different things to different people? Not at all.

Most words have many meanings in the dictionary; statistics show that, on the average, every word of the English language has from two to three accepted meanings. Moreover, it is well-known that the same dictionary meaning of a word may trigger different reactions in different people who hear it or read it at the same time. We mentioned this when we described the reactions of the surgeon, the patient, and the statistician to a statement about cancer (p. 41).

Multiordinality deals with orders of abstraction. A word is multiordinal when, without any change in its dictionary meaning, it is used in the same sentence—or the same context—to refer to different orders of abstraction. Multiordinality belongs to the vertical aspect of our thinking.

When we move to higher orders in the process of abstracting, we pass, for instance, from the proper name "Mickey" to the breed name "spaniel," then to the more general names "dog," and "animal." There is no confusion here. To each order corresponds a different word. In objective abstracting, we also give an example where no confusion is likely to occur: individual, family, community, state, nation, and so on.

The trouble begins when we have to use the same term in many different orders. Then we may well pass from a lower to a higher order and vice-versa, without realizing that we are sliding back and forth from the particular to the general. Since a great many of the words that we use are of this type, no wonder that misunderstandings are frequent. Let us start with a simple example.

In the army, the term "unit" applies to formations of different sizes: a unit is part of a larger unit, which in turn is part of a still larger unit. Fortunately, there are specific terms for each type of unit: platoon, company, battalion, brigade, division, and so forth. However, it remains that we can make statements that will sound paradoxical if taken literally. A captain commanding a company could say to his lieutenant colonel, "My unit is in your unit"; and the lieutenant colonel could say to his brigadier general, "My unit is in your unit." In these two statements, we have the term "unit" at three different orders of abstraction: company, battalion, and brigade. A peculiar feature becomes evident: the lowest unit is contained in the next higher, and this middle one is both the container of the lower and part of the contents of the next higher one. This feature is common to all multiordinal terms: they refer to containers and contents at the same time. The problem is to determine which is which.

This term "unit" is also used in other contexts. We speak of units of distance, of time, and of money. In science we may take as our *unit of discourse* a limited field within a broader field. The psychologist studies the individual as a *unit*; the sociologist studies the group as a *unit*; the anthropologist studies the culture as a *unit*.

So we see that *unit* can be applied to army units (platoon, company, battalion, brigade, division), to units of time (second, minute, hour, day), to units of money (cent, nickel, dime, quarter, dollar, "grand"), to units of discourse in science (gene, chromosome, cell, organ, organism, or individual, group, culture). I say that the term "unit" is multimeaning and multiordinal. By "multimeaning," I want to describe the fact that this term is used in many areas (army, time, distance), and by "multiordinal" I want to describe the fact that in each area the term may be used at any lower or higher order of abstraction.

This can be visualized by spreading the various uses of the word in a two-dimensional array, as in the following table:

UNIT$_1^n$	UNIT$_2^n$	UNIT$_3^n$	UNIT$_4^n$	UNIT$_5^n$	UNIT$_6^n$
"	"	"	"	"	"
"	"	"	"	"	"
"	"	"	"	"	"
UNIT$_1^4$ (brigade)	UNIT$_1^4$ (day)	"	"	"	"
UNIT$_1^3$ (battalion)	UNIT$_2^3$ (hour)	UNIT$_3^3$ (yard)	"	"	"
UNIT$_1^2$ (company)	UNIT$_2^2$ (minute)	UNIT$_3^2$ (foot)	UNIT$_4^2$ (nickel)	"	"
UNIT$_1^1$ (platoon)	UNIT$_2^1$ (second)	UNIT$_3^1$ (inch)	UNIT$_4^1$ (cent)	UNIT$_5^1$ (gene)	"
UNIT$_1^n$ (army)	UNIT$_2^n$ (time)	UNIT$_3^n$ (distance)	UNIT$_4^n$ (money)	UNIT$_5^n$ (biology)	UNIT$_6^n$ (anything)

From left to right we have the multimeaning aspects, which go from 1 to any number $(_n)$. From the bottom up, we have the multiordinal aspects which go also from ^{1} (low order) to any order you wish $(^n)$. No two units in this array have the same two indexes. They are all different. By giving the two indexes to the unit you choose to talk about, you pinpoint it with accuracy; thus you avoid confusion.

If you want to take another dimension into account, say the date, you may picture to yourself a tridimensional system of coordinates and use three indexes instead of two. Again, you avoid confusion; with the three indexes you can pinpoint with accuracy the particular unit to which you refer.[22]

But, what of the word "unit" itself, the word common to all points in the array, the word that could be written with zeros as indexes: "unit$_0^0$"? What does it mean, all by itself? Does it mean something as definite as those numbered units that spread all over the table? Of course not. Does it mean nothing? Of course not. It must mean something that makes it different from other multiordinal terms. We know, however vaguely, that "unit" is not quite the same as "fact," "reality," "situation," and other terms of that very confusing class of multiordinals.

How shall we describe that vague "something" that "unit" means, vague but

[22]Korzybski takes care of multidimensionality, including multimeaningness and multiordinality as well as any number of precision indicators, when he proposes chain-indexing. *See* Korzybski. *Science and Sanity,* pp. XVIII, 167-169.

different from the other "something" that "fact" means? This is no easy task. It brings us to the rock bottom of human thinking, abstracting, consciousness, awareness, or whatever you want to call it.

Yes, you will find the word "unit" in the dictionary. I have a college edition of the Winston here. Let us see what it says. "Unit: one person or thing of a number which make up a group." Fine! Now, let us look at the first word used in the definition, the word "one." The dictionary says: "One: being a single unit, being, or object." So, there you are! "Unit" means "one," and "one" means "unit"! If this is not turning in circles, I don't know what is!

The scientists have done their best to tackle this problem. They give all sorts of names to that strange, hard-to-describe phenomenon, by which we know what we mean, yet don't know how to define the term that we use. They speak of "conceptual organization," of "conceptual structure," of "patternment," of "core of analogy," of "paradigm," and what not. That "structure" or "patternment" is something that you feel somewhere, somehow, inside you and that you may express by a generalized tension, a movement, or a gesture, as, for instance, when you hold up your index finger to describe "unit."

Now, if you want to get the feel of our limitations as regards precise meanings, take any multiordinal word that you please, and bring it to its rock-bottom signification. You will find it a very sobering experience. You will discover that the clear mind of which we like to boast is not so clear when we go down to its depths.[23]

So, one of the characteristics of multiordinal terms is that they cannot be easily defined in general terms. Compare the word *fact*, which is multiordinal most of the time, to such other words as *chair* or *courage*. Chair refers to something fairly definite; we can point to a piece of furniture and say "This is a chair"; we can draw a picture of it. Courage does not refer to a tangible object, but it can be defined pretty sharply. The *American College Dictionary* calls it "the quality of mind that enables one to encounter difficulties and dangers with firmness or without fear." We can give examples of courage in action, and show that its opposite is cowardice. In the end, our listener will have a reliable picture of what we mean. In this case, as with the chair, we can live up to the prescription of classical logic: "Define your terms."

The word *fact* is altogether different. A sharp definition will not help; indeed, it is practically impossible. If we take the word to have a clear-cut meaning, we will be disappointed. We will run into paradoxes and misunderstandings without end.

"Peter loves Mary." This is a fact, but Peter has just bawled Mary out, perhaps cursed or even beaten her; and this too, is a fact. Does it cancel out the first fact? If we take the two facts as belonging to the same level of

---

[23]J. Samuel Bois, *Explorations in Awareness*, (New York, Harper & Row, 1957), pp. 149-152.

abstraction, it does: loving Mary and cursing her stand in opposition. In strict logic, Peter cannot claim to love her if he curses her at the same time.

This strict logic, however, does not always correspond to what is actually happening. Peter may justly claim that he still loves Mary in spite of the fact that he is cursing her. And Mary may resent the bad treatment she receives, and love Peter at the same time. Shall we account for the apparent contradiction by some complicated psychological theory about the ambivalence of feelings?

We could—we could say that love and hate may coexist in Peter and in Mary at the same time; but we don't have to accept this theory as the only theory. The multiordinal formulation is much more simple.

The fact that Peter loves Mary is at a higher order of objective abstraction than the fact that he is actually fighting with her. The two facts don't contradict each other, they are superposed on each other. The higher-order fact is a broader objective reality that encompasses a multitude of lower-order facts, of which the present fighting is only one, lost among all the rest. This is like the reports from the stock exchange: it is a fact, let us say, that the stocks went down today, but it is also a fact—of a different order—that the trend has been upward for the last three months. One fact is the container: "Peter loves Mary" or "The stocks are going up"; the other fact is the contents: "Peter curses Mary" or "The stocks are going down." Multiordinality, being a methodical formulation that can apply to any science, is preferable to an *ad hoc* explanation that is created in a particular science for every ambiguous case—as is done in psychology with the theory of ambivalence of love and hate.

If we realize that a characteristic of multiordinal terms is that they can be both containers and contents, we quickly realize that these terms are legion. Take the word *problem* as an example. A mother brings her son, Johnny, to a consulting psychologist because Johnny does poorly at school. The consultant finds that Johnny lacks the necessary motivation because he feels insecure in a home where his father and mother occasionally threaten each other with separation or divorce. This problem of the father and mother, in turn, is due to the fact that theirs is a mixed marriage, she being Jewish and he being of German-Lutheran parentage—and both remain in close contact with their respective families. Where is the *real* problem?

It is everywhere at the same time, at all levels. The practical question is not to determine *what* or *where* is *the* problem, it is to decide at what level the elusive situation can be tackled under the circumstances. If the family squabbles cannot be stopped, Johnny will have to make up for his parents' lack of common sense. If the cultural and religious prejudices cannot be ironed out, the chances of the family's survival as a functioning unit are slim. The solution of the problem at a lower level has to take into account the continuation of the problem at a higher level. On the other hand, a solution at a higher level—in this case, the problem of the cultural and religious differences—automatically reduces the tension at the lower levels.

Management, a word that is frequently used in business circles, is ambiguous and multiordinal; in the chain of command, a person may be managed and managing at the same time. I remember some specialists in human relations who wanted to arrive at a precise definition of management, and who spent a whole afternoon in the library of a company going through books, professional magazines, and monographs that gave management definitions, then compared these definitions to arrive at the core, the essence, of what management is. At the end of the afternoon they were more confused and frustrated than ever. They had hoped to find a good definition, or to make one themselves, but they had to abandon the attempt. They could not agree among themselves, although all knew what they were talking about and what they were looking for.

Had they known that such an elusive word is multiordinal, and therefore undefinable in the usual logical manner of genus and difference, they would have saved time and energy. They would have determined the level of management they were concerned with, in what division, at what time, and for what purpose. The old prescription, "Define your terms," does not apply to multiordinal terms, and, because multiordinal terms are so numerous and so frequently used, this prescription is now recognized as one of the most burdensome and useless legacies of Aristotelian logic. It is one of many sententious statements that we keep repeating without ever stopping to question their value, as if they had sprung up—immutable—from the wisdom of the ages.

Instead of being subservient to an obsolete tradition, let us pinpoint, as sharply as we can, what we are talking about. Let us not ask ourselves "What is a fact? What is management? What is the problem?"—let us be soundly operational and answer the simple questions *who, what, when, where,* and *how.* Let us determine at what level of abstraction—and consequently at what level of existence—we think we can best deal with the situation.

Multiordinality can also be described by means of a diagram, as in Figure 7.1. First, we draw a horizontal line to represent the level of first-order experience, the down-to-earth level of contact with what is going on. On the center of this line we draw a small arch, with its two sides resting on the line, and within this arch we write the figure *1.* This is the first stage of abstraction, the first descriptive use of the term we employ in a multiordinal manner. In the case of the child mentioned above, it is the problem of Johnny as an individual.

Next we draw a larger arch, resting on the same line and enveloping the first arch. This is level two. In the same case, it is the problem of the father and mother talking of separation or divorce in front of Johnny. It is more

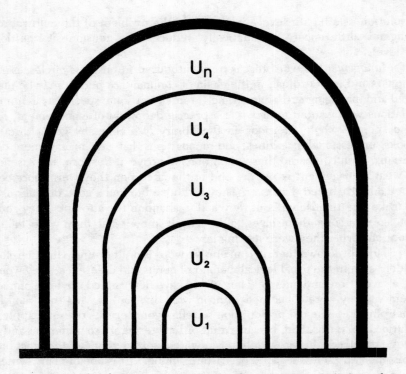

Figure 7.1. Multiordinality, or units of lower order within units of a higher order.

comprehensive than Johnny's individual problem; it includes it. Problem 2 includes problem 1. It is higher in objective abstraction, but it also touches the ground of first-order experience. The ends of arch 2 reach the same baseline as those of arch 1.

We can draw any number of arches, each new one superposed to the previous ones. Each new arch represents a higher level of abstraction, so that the highest of all is at the same time both a first-order experience (touching the ground in a sense) and a high-order generalization (holding all the lower ones within its framework).

This multiordinal diagram lends itself to a limitless variety of applications. It gives us a visual picture of theories within theories, of decisions within decisions, and systems within systems where the highest of all has the overall control—like the board of directors of a holding company. It shows that a "theoretical" principle, which is couched in general terms and apparently out of touch with day to day practices, is really a down-to-earth measure that holds within its grip the behavior of those who have accepted it, or have been forced to accept.

As a consequence, the study of such general principles (often hidden as commonsense assumptions) becomes one of the most important activities of people who want to be practical. It does away with the common belief of the opposition between theory and practice.

Summary

In this chapter, I have emphasized the importance of consciousness of abstracting as a way of making our "thinking" multidimensional, thus avoiding the collisions of "two-dimensional" logic that hinder human transactions.

We saw that a human experience is a multileveled affair: that our 'silent' personal experience of what is going on (WIGO) emerges through the structure of our semantic state at the moment. We do not simply perceive as a camera perceives what it is focused on. With the aid of various diagrams, we took that a step further by saying that our verbalized constructs are higher in order and not at all commensurate with our 'silent' lower orders of abstraction. Each order emerges through a semantic transaction involving attitudes, feelings, purposes, habits, electrochemical conditions, anticipations of the future, and pressures of the past. This is called *circularity*.

Not only *what* we abstract is important, but *how* we abstract is important as well. I described four primary types of abstracting.

Finally, I described the multiordinality of terms and situations, and that activities of a higher order give a definite pattern to activities of a lower order, from dominant values to specific preferences, from mental set to 'silent' experiencing, from long-range purposes to the choice of means we deem appropriate.

A Sufi tale described by Idries Shah sums multiordinality up in another way.

> A wise man, the wonder of his age, taught his disciples from a seemingly inexhaustible store of wisdom.
>
> He attributed all his knowledge to a thick tome which was kept in a place of honour in his room.
>
> The sage would allow nobody to open the volume.
>
> When he died, those who had surrounded him, regarding themselves as his heirs, ran to open the book, anxious to possess what it contained.
>
> They were surprised, confused and disappointed when they found that there was writing on only one page.
>
> They became even more bewildered, and then annoyed, when they tried to penetrate the meaning of the phrase which met their eyes.
>
> It was: "When you realize the difference between the container and the content, you will have knowledge."[24]

[24]Idries Shah, *The Book of the Book* (London: Octagon Press, 1969) p. 9.

Awareness of the abstracting process as an aspect of human functioning is a first step in realizing that the unspoken, 'silent' level is "where things happen," whether we talk of them or not; where they eventually burst into some unexpected manifestation way beyond what our discursive capacity could have forseen. I see that our acceptance of this is critical in shaping a new human condition, whether on the personal level or on the level of our species.

The shaping of our world is the work of countless generations of human experience being passed on and transformed. This is what Korzybski called time-binding. We are going to look at this next to show that our actions, which are guided by mental constructs, may bring about irreversible changes that our children will have to live with.

PART IV

time-binding

The capacity to experience ourselves and our world today is the cumulative result of the work of bygone generations, each of which has enriched itself from the knowledge, the technology, and experience of all those that preceded it. This phenomenon of cultural accumulation is called time-binding, the specific human characteristic.

the world in which we live

We have described the individual as "a thinking, feeling, self-moving, electrochemical organism in continuous transaction with a space-time environment" (p. 27). And now is the time to take a fresh view of our environment. By environment, we do not mean only the physical place where a people live and function; we mean—together with this—the entire aggregate of conditions, institutions, and traditions that surround each person and penetrate to the very core of their self.

Our primitive predecessors were without the cultural environment that we now take for granted. Cassius Jackson Keyser invites us to look at their condition as it must have been.

Long ages ago there appeared upon this planet—no matter how—the first specimens of our human kind. What was their condition? It requires some meditation and some exercise of imagination to realize keenly what it must have been. Of knowledge, in the sense in which we humans now use the term, they had none—no science, no philosophy, no art, no religion; they did not know what they were nor where they were; they knew nothing of the past, for they had no history, not even tradition; they could not foretell the future, for they had no knowledge of natural law; they had no capital—no material or spiritual wealth—no inheritance, that is, from the time and toil of bygone generations; they were without tools, without precedents, without guiding maxims, without speech, without any light of human experience; their ignorance, as we understand the term, was almost absolute. And yet, compared with the beasts, they were miracles of genius, for they contrived to do the most wonderful of all things

that have happened on our globe—they *initiated*, I mean, the creative movement which their remote descendants call Civilization.[1]

In contrast to this, let us also look at Pitirim A. Sorokin's rapid survey of
the cultural world in which our generation is living.

> Man has created a new realm of reality in the cosmos known to us. Besides the
> two basic classes of reality—inorganic and organic phenomena—which existed
> on this planet before the emergence of man, he has built a third basic class of
> phenomena: the superorganic or cultural. . . . At the present time this cultural
> realm consists of: (1) an infinitely rich *ideological* universe of *meanings* unified
> into systems of language, science, technology, religion, philosophy, law, ethics,
> literature, painting, sculpture, architecture, music, drama, economic, political
> and social theories, and so on; (2) the totality of so-called "material culture,"
> representing "an incarnation and objectification" of all these meanings in
> biophysical media, beginning with the simplest tools and ending with the most
> complex machinery and gadgets, books, paintings, sculptures, buildings, high-
> ways and airways, villages and cities, and so forth; (3) the totality of individuals
> as *socio-cultural persons* ("kings," "farmers," "criminals," "saints," "husbands,"
> "wives," "prostitutes," "citizens," "debtors," "masters," "slaves," "French-
> men," "Americans," "Catholics," "Socialists," etc.) and of *socio-cultural groups*
> (political, scientific, religious, economic, occupational, national, artistic, etc.);
> and (4) the totality of *overt actions, ceremonies, rituals, proceedings,* in which
> the individuals and groups actualize, realize, and practice this or that set of
> meanings. The total superorganic universe made of the above . . . cultural
> phenomena has become the most powerful environment that immediately en-
> velops, conditions, determines, and molds every individual and group in its own
> image.[2]

Years ago I devised a diagram to express visually what Keyser describes
as the condition of prehistoric people devoid of any means but their bodily
senses, in contrast to the people of today who, say Sorokin, can use to their
advantage—or to their disadvantage—the tools, the institutions, and the
knowledges of civilization. This diagram, entitled *The Worlds in Which We
Live*, is reproduced here as Figure 8.1. It is made of four concentric circles
situated in an indefinite blank space that represents the unknown. Between
the first human beings and this unknown there was nothing but raw perceptions, wild imagination, fears, and a felt need for survival. Circle one was
immediately surrounded by the unknown (area five). Gradually, instruments
of perception and action together with methods of thinking-feeling-behaving
were invented, and they developed theories and doctrines to fixate in tradi-

---

[1]Cassius Jackson Keyser, "Korzybski's Concept of Man," in A. Korzybski, *Manhood of
Humanity*, 2d ed. (Lakeville, Conn.: International Non-Aristotelian Library Publishing Co.,
1950), p. 295.

[2]Pitirim A. Sorokin, "Integralism Is My Philosophy," in *This Is My Philosophy*. ed. Whit
Burnett (London: Allen & Unwin, 1958), pp. 182-83.

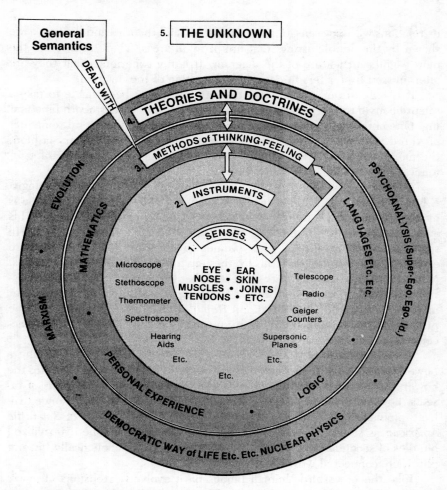

Figure 8.1. The worlds in which we live (Copyright, 1948, J. S. A. Bois).

tion and in symbolic forms the fruits of their accumulated experiences. By doing so they established between themselves and the unknown sort of a buffer zone in which they can live and manage their existence to some extent. Each circle represents ever growing extensions of human life that merged with the environment in unprecedented ways. The environment became more and more humanized—not an additive more, but a structural more.

This buffer zone has a tightly woven system of communication and organization, which gives it a definite structure. This articulated system is in circle three, *methods of thinking-feeling*—to which I now add *acting*—and its relations with raw sensations, instruments, and theories and doctrines are shown by the double arrows that link it to all areas. These arrows are the more significant feature of the diagram. It is my experience that they are often missed by readers in cursory examination of the diagram.

It is only in our day and age that attempts have been made to take a scientific inventory of that system and to devise rules of its smooth functioning. One of the most successful of these attempts was the general semantics of Alfred Korzybski. From it has emerged, in normal evolutionary fashion, the modern science of up-to-date epistemology and the discipline of epistemics, the science-art of innovating.[3]

Among the few others working in this area of concern is anthropologist Edward T. Hall. The title of his book *Beyond Culture*[4] indicates that he is moving beyond well-established investigation in his field. In it, Hall gives his own version of what I called *The Worlds in Which We Live* (Fig. 8.1). He speaks of the bowerbird of New Guinea to illustrate how extensions are evolved and become integral to the environmental life of a species. Nineteenth century naturalists suggested that the bowerbird should be classified as different from other birds as *Homo sapiens* is different from all other mammals. What the bowerbird and *Homo sapiens* have in common is the practice of elaborating their extensions, and, in the process, greatly accelerating their own evolution.

The bowerbird gets its name from the male's practice of building a bower or enclosure of grass and twigs to attract the female. He decorates the bower with various brightly colored objects, shells, shiny skeletons of insects, flowers, pebbles, seeds. The result is an "extension" of his once brilliant plumage. Hall quotes Thomas Gilliard from an issue of *Scientific American* as stating, ". . .these objects have in effect become externalized bundles of secondary sexual characteristics that are psychologically but not physically connected with the males."[5]

Like the bowerbird, human beings have evolved extensions of every aspect of their semantic transactions. They externalize their functioning in various ways, which I will describe in greater detail later; they then internalize their own web of inventions to the point where the extensions are undifferentiated from, or take the place of, the original human process. Hall calls this phenomenon "extension transference." One example is "thinking" becoming identified with language, and its built-in logic. Hall mentions James Joyce's *Finnegan's Wake* as portraying in writing the workings of the verbal parts of the brain.

---

[3]Bois, J. Samuel, "Epistemics: A Time-binding Emergent from General Semantics," in *ETC., A Review of General Semantics* 28, no. 2 (June 1971): 177-189.

[4]Edward T. Hall, *Beyond Culture*, (New York: Anchor Press/Doubleday, 1976), p. 33.

[5]Edward T. Hall, *Beyond Culture*, p. 33.

Another example is the difficulty in differentiating "self" from culture. The explosion of therapies and Eastern religious practices will attest to this latter extension transference. "Who am I?" seems to be the question at the forefront of many people's concerns.

In speaking of culture as an extension of human activity, Hall states:

> It is the characteristic of all extension systems to be treated as distinct and separate from the user and to take on an identity of their own. Religions, philosophies, literature, and art illustrate this. After a time, the extended system accretes to itself a past and a history as well as a body of knowledge and skills that can be learned. Such systems can be studied and appreciated as entities in themselves. Culture is the prime example.[6]

The ability to use our environment in this way both protects us and offers the opportunity and advantage of innovation without having to wait for the internal process of biological evolution, which seems to go according to its own slower time dimension. At the same time, our ignorance of the process of extending ourselves and developing a new kind of evolution, that is, our ignorance of the acculturation and time-binding process, threatens our very existence as a species.

> The study of man is a study of his extensions. It is now possible to actually see evolution taking place, an evolution that occurs outside the organism and at a greatly accelerated pace when compared to intrinsic evolution. Man has dominated the earth because his extensions have evolved so fast that there is nothing to stand in their way. The risk, of course, is that by enormously multiplying his power, man is in the position of being able to destroy his own biotrope—that part of the environment that contains within it the basic elements for satisfying human needs.[7]

We are now going to go deeper into this new environment, starting with Korzybski's formulation of time-binding.

Homo sapiens, the Time-binding Class of Life

The creation of a superorganic universe was taken by Korzybski as the specific characteristic of *Homo sapiens,* and it led him to propose a new definition of man: "I define HUMANITY," he wrote, "to be the TIME-BINDING CLASS OF LIFE."[8]

What did Korzybski mean by "time-binding"? According to the dictionary, "to bind" means, among other things, *"to cause to cohere,"* or to bring things together and to make out of them a compound that becomes a new

---

[6]Edward T. Hall, *Beyond Culture,* p. 33.

[7]Edward T. Hall, *Beyond Culture,* p. 33.

[8]Korzybski, *Manhood of Humanity,* 2d ed. (Lakeville, Conn.: International Non-Aristotelian Library, 1950), p. 60.

thing, a new unit, of which the original elements, previously differentiated, are blended and homogenized, thereby reaching a new level of energy, a new order of existence. A simple example would be that of concrete, which is made by mixing together three elements: cement, water, and sand. Once properly blended and "left standing," this compound hardens to a point that none of its elements, taken singly, could ever reach. The end result of such a binding operation is, structurally, more than a mere addition of its elements. Korzybski believed the capacity to bind together elements of a very different nature is the characteristic of all forms of life.

The lowest form of life is that of plants; they are binders of chemicals. Side by side in our garden are rose bushes, chrysanthemums, rosemaries, irises, and other plants. Out of the common soil, each chooses the minerals and the amount of water that are necessary for its growth. Each picks them in definite proportions, transforms them into tissues that are different in softness or hardness, and into leaves, flowers, and seeds that are barely comparable to one another. Stones are not able to do this, nor, left to itself, does the soil bind its chemicals together in such a fashion. Therefore "chemistry-binders" is a good description of what plants are and do; it puts them in a class by themselves, which applies equally to the least conspicuous moss and to the most majestic tree.

The next higher form of life is the animal. It has the chemistry-binding capacity of plants, of course; it chooses its own food, ingests, assimilates, and transforms it into its own tissues and organs. But, besides doing this, it is capable of moving in space, of roaming about to reach for food that is not available where it stands, of going for water without waiting for rain or irrigation to quench its thirst, of gathering materials from its surroundings to build a nest or a storehouse. Animals are not only chemistry-binders, they are space-binders; binders of elements scattered in space.

We now come to humans. They of course are capable of doing what plants do as chemistry-binders and what animals do as space-binders, but they are not limited to these activities of plants and animals. They have a characteristic that is distinctly human, that neither plants nor animals can share with them. Humans are time-binders; they select, gather together, and combine into something new the various elements that belong to different periods of time. They combine them, transform them, and make out of them something that did not exist before. They can repeat this operation as often as they wish, each time creating a modification, an enlargement, a complexification of the world in which they live. Time-binding means producing civilization, inventing farming to replace hunting and fruit-gathering, technology to replace the use of raw materials, central government to replace smaller and insufficient political units, printing to replace handwriting, steam and electrical power to replace manual labor, the telegraph and telephone to replace couriers, radio and television to multiply the presence of artists and speakers. Time, in this context, does not refer so much to calendar time as to the number of productive past generations whose products are parts or necessary conditions of what is done in the present.

> We have observed that each generation of (say) beavers and bees begins where the preceding one began and ends where it ended; that is a law for animals, for mere space-binders there is no advancement, no time-binding—a beaver dam is a beaver dam—a honey comb is a honey comb. We know that, in sharp contrast therewith, man invents, discovers, creates. We know that inventions lead to new inventions, discoveries to new discoveries, creations to new creations; we know that, by such progress breeding, the children of knowledge and art and wisdom not only produce their kind in larger and larger families but engender new and higher kinds endlessly; we know that this time-binding process, by which *past time* is embodied as a co-factor of toil in enduring achievements thus survives the dead and works as living capital. . ., is the secret and process of civilization-building. [9]

For many years I was misled in my thinking by the word "time" in the expression "time-binding." I understood that, in the long run, progress would be manifested as time went on. I could see that our advance was like the accumulation of compound interest, but I knew very well that our rate of advance in the last fifty years—at least in the physical sciences and in the corresponding technology—was twice as great as it had been in the previous fifty years. I also saw distinctive spurts of advance at certain dates, as it were, where people pooled their creative resources.

I knew, for instance, that, when Einstein wrote his famous letter to President Roosevelt, there was enough knowledge about the atom scattered over the world to make the creation of the atom bomb possible, and that the time for achieving this was shortened when scientists got together and worked intensively as a team. I also knew that Japan in the last century and Russia after the 1917 revolution had shortened the time necessary for them to catch up with our technology. I therefore felt that the Korzybskian formula needed some addition and should consider another factor of progress. At the time, I thought this other factor was the interaction of scientists who work together on a particular project.

But if we take "time" as a plural, meaning the frequency with which humans have decided to go through the three steps of time-binding (1) questioning the value of what they know or do, (2) inventing something new that holds promise of being an improvement, and (3) criticizing that invention by the test of experiment, time then becomes not the absolute number of generations as recorded in history but the number of generations or groups that are ready and willing not to be simply replicas of the past. If, within a calendar generation, a group of people is ready and willing to reexamine its

---

[9]Keyser, "Korzybski's Concept of Man," in *Manhood of Humanity*, p. 316.

achievements and to repeat the act of creation, we may have two or more time-binding generations within a span of twenty-five or thirty-five years. If, on the other hand, several consecutive generations content themselves with uncritically repeating the theories and the practices of their predecessors, we may have only one generation of time-binders within a long period of history. Progress is not an additive affair, it goes by cycles that increase their outputs in geometrical progression. The shorter the interval between cycles, the faster the total advance within a definite period of years. We don't know how fast the new nations will reach a level of development that is comparable to ours. Complete dedication to creating a new order of things may advance them far ahead of us.

Instead of the algebraic formula of time-binding (which still appeals to me because of its precise design[10]) we could use an alternative formulation and say that *the capacity to invent is the characteristic of Homo sapiens*. This means that a fully functioning human being sees tradition not as something to preserve in a static form but as something to exploit, something like the humus formed by fallen leaves, which facilitates the growth of new crops.

It is hard to concede that the results achieved by the human capacity to invent can be measured by the *a priori* formula that Korzybski suggests. For instance, when he says that if each generation doubles the progress of the preceding one, the progress made by the tenth generation would be 1,024 times the progress made by the first (and the total gain of the ten generations would be 2,046 times the progress made by the first) he is evidently playing with numbers—and enjoying the exercise. As he muses over his "discovery," he becomes enthusiastic, and, he bursts into sweeping statements.

Humans are, unlike animals, naturally qualified not only to progress, but to progress more and more rapidly, with an always *accelerating acceleration*, as the generations pass.

This great fact is to be at once the basis, the regulator and guide in the science and art of Human Engineering. Whatever squares with that law of time-binding human energy is right and makes for human weal; whatever contravenes it is wrong and makes for human woe.

And so I repeat that the world will have uninterrupted, peaceful progress when and only when the so-called social "sciences"—the life-regulating "sciences" of ethics, law, philosophy, economics, religion, politics, and government—are technologized; when and only when they are made genuinely scientific in spirit and method; for then and only then will they advance, like the natural, mathematical and technological sciences, in conformity with the fundamental law of the time-binding nature of man; then and then only, by the equal pace of progress in all cardinal matters, the equilibrium of social institutions will remain stable and social cataclysms cease.[11]

[10]Korzybski, *Manhood of Humanity*, pp. 90-91.
[11]Korzybski, *Manhood of Humanity*, p. 92.

This quotation is peppered with terms and statements that make it easy for self-satisfied critics to ridicule Korzybski and his followers. Some people want science to behave like a sedate matron who moves majestically with measured steps. They deny the legend of Archimedes, running naked through the streets of Syracuse and shouting "Eureka!" They forget Johann Kepler's "sacred fury." But living science is still a very human experience, running the gamut of human emotions, from excitement and enthusiasm to self-doubt and criticism. What Korzybski "saw"—in a unifying or peak experience—has been verified and measured by researchers.

A survey made at the beginning of this century by Ludwig Darmstaedter[12] shows that the number of discoveries and inventions in the Western world has doubled every fifty years since the scientific revolution of the seventeenth century. A more recent study, by Professor Pierre Auger—published by UNESCO in 1961—is a survey of current topics of scientific research in the fundamental sciences (mathematics, physics, chemistry, biology), earth and space sciences, medical sciences, food and agricultural sciences, fuel and power research, and industrial research. The book lists over 200 national and international organizations and almost 300 individuals who were consulted during the preparation of the report. The growth of scientific activities follows an exponential curve, just as Korzybski had stated *a priori* in the early twenties. According to Auger, the volume of scientific work increases twofold every ten years. Other forms of human activities are, of course, also increasing, but at a far slower rate. The doubling time of activities not directly related to science is forty years. (There are, however, indications of a slowing down in the rate of growth of science.[13])

When a new idea or a new system of thought appears, it has a tendency to spread over wider and wider areas, to gain converts in larger and larger numbers. Witness the appearance and growth of Christianity and Islam, the spread of revolutions for the freedom of the individual started by the American Revolution, the emergence of Marxism and international communism in the last hundred years. This tendency to gain adherents in ever-increasing numbers, and by whatever means, is not a manifestation of time-binding energy; it is an increase in volume—as happened to the dinosaurs. It is not an improvement in vitality and in capacity for eventual survival; it is the transformation of a revolution into a tradition.

But there is a second tendency, which is a true manifestation of time-binding energy. It is the tendency to keep reexamining a new system of thought in the light of its own development, to keep stirring revolutionary

---

[12]Ludwig Darmstaedter, Handbuch zur Geschicte des Naturwissenschaften und der Technik (Berlin: Verlag von Jullus Springer; 1908.) Passim.

[13]Joseph Rothblat, "International Science—A Review," *Bulletin of Atomic Scientists* (March, 1962), p. 40. It must be noted that the term "science" here means the physical sciences and biology; the "social sciences" were not covered.

thinking so that it won't jell into tradition. This second characteristic is the one that holds promise for the far-reaching future. If we accept time-binding as a characteristic of human growth, this continuing attempt at self-renewal becomes a normal expression of humankind in action, a feature that differentiates us from lower forms of life. Clinging to tradition, whether it is centuries old or of more recent vintage, is the very negation of that distinctive human trait, and brings human life one step down, to the level of animal life, where generations after generations keep repeating the same patterns of activity. We thus copy animals in our nervous systems, as Korzybski so often deplored.

From this we see that there are two criteria for evaluating change. One criterion is that of numbers: how many people join the new political creed, the new school of thought, the new religion? The second criterion is: how much time-binding vitality is apparent in this cultural change? Does it favor its own renewal by facilitating corrections and elaborations in preference to conformity and respect for tradition? In human affairs, we often go by the first criterion, the criterion of numbers. In technology we go by the second criterion, the criterion of "renewalness," invention, and creativity.

Nobody is afraid to daydream publicly in matters of technology, to plan—at whatever cost it might entail—for a future world that will dwarf the present one. In a one-page advertisement in an issue of the *Scientific American*, an aircraft company displays eleven models of space vehicles. Apart from the now conventional rockets, there are three nuclear spaceships—one of which is intended to travel to Venus and Mars—two vehicles for traveling on the surface of the moon, one craft designed to collect lunar ore specimens, another craft to load this ore in containers that will be rocketed back to earth, a space observatory that will be sent aloft in sections and assembled in orbit, and a supply-and-escape vehicle that will shuttle back and forth between space stations and the earth.

We are ready to spend billions of dollars and thousands of hours of human labor to bring this about, but let a social scientist dream of a human world different from our world of misery and cold war as Gardner Murphy attempted to do in a very modest way in his book, *Human Potentialities*, and the traditional advocates of common sense express their learned doubts in the name of what human nature *really* is. Their view of "human nature" comes from the old definition of *Homo sapiens* as an animal whose basic nature has a thin coating of reason, a definition that makes no more sense than would a definition of an animal as "a plant with the capacity to move about in space." Such a definition would convey a mental model that would fit neither plant nor animal. Similarly, when we define a human being as an animal endowed with reason, without including that essential characteristic of time-binding creativity, we have a mental model that fits neither animal nor human. Keyser insists on the importance of differentiating humans from animals:

> Though we humans are not a species of animal, we are *natural* beings: it is as natural for humans to bind time as it is natural for fish to swim, for birds to fly, for plants to live after the manner of plants. It is as natural for man to make things achieved the means of greater achievements as it is natural for animals *not* to do so.

> This fact is fundamental. Another one, also fundamental, is this: the time-binding faculty—the characteristic of humanity—is not an effect of civilization but its cause; it is not civilized energy, it is the energy that *civilizes;* it is not a product of wealth, whether material or spiritual wealth, but...the creator of wealth, both material and spiritual.[14]

Adequate mental models are a necessity. Before we had a mental model of electricity we could not deal with that form of energy, we could not control it, we could not manage it, we could not generate it. Now it is inserted in practically all of our daily activities, but generations ago it belonged to the category of mysteries. It was thunder and lightning, the dreaded "acts of God." It could burn, kill, and destroy without human recourse against its devastations. Now it is our helpmate, keeping our houses bright at night; acting as a courier to transmit our messages by telephone, telegraph, radio, and television; heating our houses in the winter and cooling them in the summer; keeping our food fresh in freezers and refrigerators; performing routine brain functions in electronic computers; working for the treatment of diseases in hospitals; and advancing our knowledge of nature in research laboratories.

Before all this could be done, we had to discover electrical energy and invent a way of managing it, and I see a parallel in the discovery of the cosmic energy that has its locus in humankind. Time-binding energy has been mostly destructive; it seems to accumulate as electricity accumulates in storm clouds, and it bursts out in revolutions, wars, and social cataclysms. It appears where we do not want or expect it. It works itself into a frenzy before we find time to shut it off, and explodes and plays havoc in our well-established institutions. Its power has increased as it has brought within its grasp other forms of energy, from the tensile strength of the bow, to the explosive force of gunpowder, to the power of atomic fusion. "War," as Keyser said, "is a bloody demonstration of human ignorance of human nature."[15]

More than fifty years have elapsed since our new concept of *Homo sapiens* was offered to the Western world, and during those fifty years we had a second world war. In fact, war has become a permanent institution under

[14]Keyser, "Korzybski's Concept of Man," in *Manhood of Humanity*, p. 315.
[15]Keyser, "Korzybski's Concept of Man," in *Manhood of Humanity*, p. 315.

the name "cold war." The two men who had the vision of humanity as a time-binder, Keyser and Korzybski, have passed away, and some of their hopes and previsions have not materialized.

Were both men completely mistaken? I don't think so.

That special form of cosmic energy—that they "discovered" and called time-binding energy—still operates in *Homo sapiens,* the latest product to emerge from the long and slow-moving process of evolution. It throbs in the ever-increasing mass of nervous matter that spreads like a network over the inorganic and organic substance of the nonhuman world, that holds it in its grip and that gradually transforms it into a huge artifact.

Knowing about this phenomenon, participating in it with full awareness, and steering it intelligently is an all-important task at this critical moment of history. George Gaylord Simpson, the paleontologist, referred to it when he wrote:

> [Man] happens to represent the highest form of matter and energy that has ever appeared. Recognition of this kinship with the rest of the universe is necessary for understanding him, but *his essential nature is defined by qualities found nowhere else*. . . .It is part of this unique status that *in man a new form of evolution begins*, overlying and *largely dominating* the old organic evolution, which nevertheless also continues in him.[16]

The World as We Make It

All forms of life are energy-binders. They bring to a higher order of existence the energies that surround them; they form islands of order in the sea of entropy where the nonliving world disintegrates into chaos.

The human species is the most complex developing process on our planet, the most resourceful of all energy-binders. Humans do not simply exploit their surroundings to ensure their own survival and that of their species (like the animals and the birds), they transform them according to their purposes and their whims, creating personal needs that demand satisfactions that nature, unaided, can not provide. They make the world to their own image.

A group of promoters who have decided to build a retirement community go over the accumulated records on the climate of various states and sections of states. They want a place where there is no winter, no fog or smog, where it is generally cool at night, bright and warm during the day, away but not too far away from big urban centers. Eventually, they choose a valley, devoted to dry farming, halfway between the lowlands of the California coast and the high ranges of the Rockies. Then they use the knowledge,

---

[16]George Gaylord Simpson, *The Meaning of Evolution* (New Haven, Conn.: Yale University Press, 1949), p. 344 (italics added).

tools, and equipment that the technology of town-building has accumulated. They survey the land and cut it into building lots strung along curving streets and wide boulevards; they have bulldozers, earth-moving machines, excavators, a concrete mixing plant and a fleet of delivery trucks, piles of lumber, and a swarm of workers from all construction trades.

The whole valley becomes noisy and active; and the central part of the town begins to take shape: a townhall, a swimming pool, a golf course, an open-air theater, a row of hobby workshops, a shopping center, a hotel with a cocktail lounge, a fine dining room, and a sales office with an enticing plan of the prospective community, all come into being within a few months. In a year or two, there is a bustling new town, with service clubs, churches, a social life, and budding traditions. The quiet farmland has become a new world, created after a pattern that *Homo sapiens*, the time-binder, has materialized in a permanent structure.

What has been made within a short time and on a small scale in such a retirement community is a miniature of what has been going on for generations around the planet. Our nation was built in somewhat this way, from the debarkation of the colonists in an almost empty land to the vast complex of states, cities, transportation systems, and political superstructures of governments and institutions that make our country. So was built the Western world, to which we belong culturally; and so is being built the planetary community of humankind, which we can make a place of comfort and joy, or misery and death.

Instead of the vacant valley let us imagine the multidimensional world of processes that stretches, without limit, in time and space. In this world of undifferentiated continuity, *Homo sapiens* appears and immediately begins to survey it, to cut it into parcels of various sizes, using the genetic instruments given by nature: senses and limbs for perceptions and action and a brain for classification and ordering. What the senses cannot detect is ignored at first; what cannot be structured in an acceptable order in the brain is mysterious, or supernatural. As experience is accumulated from generation to generation, there is an increase in the range, the efficiency, and the power of the senses and limbs. Vision is extended with microscopes, telescopes, electron microscopes; there is an extension of hearing and communication with telegraph, telephone, radio, radar, television; touch sensitivity is expressed with seismographs and ocilloscopes; to the senses of taste and smell are added the techniques of chemical analysis; power is added to the limbs with levers, machines, and engines of all sorts; instruments are invented that measure distance, weight, and pressure; means of locomotion are devised. Along with all this, methods of thinking are developed that make it possible for the brain to classify perceptions—old and new, as well as human actions—simple or multiplied in power. Means of integrating perceptions and actions in a structure that makes sense are devised; and from this organized world ventures into the unknown are made, gradually annexing parts of it to the expanding human domain.

When we, as individuals, appeared on the scene in this twentieth century of the Christian era, we did not inherit the earth as it was when our first *Homo sapiens* ancestors found it, we were born into it as participants in the accumulated wealth of methods of thinking, of instruments and techniques developed by the race. We accepted the world as it is parceled into chunks of reality by the language that our ancestors invented to classify and order their experiences.

If our senses were calibrated to perceive what we now discover with the aid of microscopes, we would live in a world of microbes, cells, viruses, and crystal lattices instead of a world of full-size plants, animals, and things. If our senses and limbs were calibrated to grasp the whole planetary system, much as we hold a cluster of grapes, the worst earthly cataclysms would require very delicate instruments to be detected. We simply register the forms of cosmic energy that lie within the range of our perceptual capacities, and we relate ourselves to them according to whatever system of relations we can conceive. It is within that range, structured, organized, and manipulated by the succeeding generations of humankind, to which we belong, that we have our being and experience. As a whole, we do not yet know how to participate outside of this world of perceptions and action. At our present stage of development, "outside" is for us nothing but the unknown. It is from that world of the unknown that we emerged when we were conceived, and it is to the same world of the unknown that we shall return when we disintegrate at death.

To what extent is this world in which we live a result of human activities? We don't know exactly. Today the trend is toward a fuller acceptance of our human share in making the world in which we live. When we speak of humanity's share here, we do not limit the meaning of "human being" to the individual born and reared in our time, we mean human being as a member of a distinct species, different from animal cousins. We also mean human being as a member of a culture, different from members of other cultural groups while similar to members of his or her own. Finally, we mean human being as an individual, distinct and unique within a particular cultural group.

I am all of this at the same time, as if I were made of many concentric shells that have grown within an outer shell, until the center of my personal ego takes shape within the inherited environment—physiological, mental, affective, spiritual—that is an integral part of my total self. I can see myself as a cumulative cluster of experiences, structured in a unique manner, that exists nowhere else in space-time, that never existed before, and that will never be duplicated exactly at any other time in the totality of the ongoing cosmos. In a sense, I can say that I constitute a miniature world of my own, a world that I could destroy if I wanted to, a world that I can possibly modify and transform by my own initiative and decision to a degree that is probably beyond what I have learned to believe.

We are apt to hesitate in accepting the idea that we are actually making the world in which we live. The statement sounds paradoxical; we appeal to our personal experience, and many instances come to mind when things did not happen the way we wanted them. The evident conclusion that imposes itself upon us is that we *do not* make our world. Even when one can say that he or she is the master of his or her own soul, each must recognize that an individual is not the master of circumstances, of the environment in which one lives. The very opposite is quite evident: I must adapt myself to the world in which I happen to be; I cannot adapt the world to my personal plans and wishes.

Quite true. This is plain common sense, and if we remain at the level of common sense, no refutation is possible. No commonsense refutation was possible when, generations ago, some of our ancestors refused to accept the idea that at the antipodes men were standing upside down. The fact was that the "upside-down" of common experience did not apply in this case, but this was not as evident in those days as it is now. Similarly, the statement "We make the world in which we live" goes against our commonsense experience if by "we" we mean only ourself and the individuals we know. But if "we" means the whole of humankind, viewed in space-time since the appearance of our species, the statement begins to make sense.

Yes, the world as a newborn child finds it is of human origin to a greater extent than we commonly realize, and the young *Homo sapiens* of today needs that humanized world to survive. That child has exchanged the brute capacity that its first ancestor had to emerge from the animal world for the accumulated culture that generations of time-binders have made a natural endowment of the race. Experience has shown that "wild children," found occasionally among the beasts, cannot, within the short span of their individual lives, recapitulate the century-long experience of the race, but children reared in a human milieu do so easily. These are thus incorporated in the "we" who have made and continue making the world in which we live. They are born and reared in a world richer than the lithosphere of rocks and mountains and the biosphere of plants and animals; they are full-fledged members of the *noösphere*, as Teilhard de Chardin calls the humanized planet.[17]

If the proverbial visitor from Mars came circling our planet now, there would be many differences from what an earlier Martian would have found two generations ago. The night side of the earth, formerly pitch dark except

[17]Pierre Teilhard de Chardin, *The Future of Man* (New York: Harper & Row, 1964), pp. 155-184.

for the days when the moon shone, is now speckled with bright spots made by the lights of hundreds of cities. In the formerly empty space that surrounds the earth for a few hundred miles, a swarm of satellites appear that did not exist before. And, according to a Martian scientist, the Earth would be too old to engender a new satellite out of her now hardened body. These new earthly phenomena are not the results of changes produced by the planet as lithosphere, hydrosphere, or biosphere, they are born of the activities of the earth-human complex. They are due to our human intervention in a world that we alone can modify, remake, or destroy, according to our whims. "Man takes a positive hand in creation," wrote a perceptive genius of our generation, Frank Lloyd Wright, "when he puts a building upon the earth beneath the sun."

This acceptance of humankind's role in creating the world in which we live is beginning to echo in other fields as well. Conventional economics, for instance, deals primarily with a determined rather than a designed world. But Eugen Loebel, one time First Deputy Minister of Foreign Trade and Director of the State Bank in Czechoslovakia and now Professor of Economics and Political Science at Vassar College, writes of a new economics that he calls *Humanomics*. He insists on an economy *by* and *for* human beings, based on the realization that economic "laws" and trends are human creations:

> Whether technology turns against man or serves man, and whether we have unemployment and inflation or full employment and stable prices, are not contingent upon the form of ownership nor on the subjective quality of the economic factors. This is a startling fact to recognize, because implicit in this awareness is the understanding that man can create his economic system and can choose his alternatives.

> Economy and society are a creation of man, the result of his creative genius. . . . Knowing this we must not be satisfied any longer with economic laws which supposedly govern us. We must realize that we have the ability to design our world, to make it serve us.

> Thus, the question of whether our society and economy are our creations or part of a determined universe is not a mere search for truth. It is far more a philosophy which will guide our action. If we accept the philosophy of determinism, then our society will be governed by determined phenomena. On the other hand, if we view society as our creation, then we will be able to control and create the future instead of predicting it.[18]

Human Solidarity and Noöspheric Centration

As we probe into space, we discover that, of all the planets of the solar system, our Earth is the only one that carries complex living organisms on its

[18]Eugen Loebl, *Humanomics* (New York: Random House, 1976), pp. 43-44.

surface. Some of them cover the soil with moss and grass; some beautify the plains and the hills with shrubs and trees; some break the silence of the air with the songs of birds and the buzzing of insects; some introduce into the landscape the movements of beasts crawling, jumping, running, and flying.

Some fifty centuries ago there appeared a distinctly new type of living organism: it emerged from the animal herd and quickly took over. Curious, active, and full of initiative, it scratched the surface of the planet with a stick and later tore it open with a plow, to make it produce more abundant and better food; it pierced the earth's innards with mine shafts and long metal tubes to extract metals and bring up fuels. Unrestricted in a choice of habitat, the animal could live in the cold of the polar regions and in the heat of the tropics in the valleys and on the peaks. It traveled on the waters and plunged deep below their surfaces; it soared into the air and darted through it at high speed; it eventually broke loose from the hold of gravitation and make a bold leap into empty space to examine and possibly exploit other astral bodies that float at great distances from the place of abode.

This new form of life is *Homo sapiens*, the time-binder, accumulating experience and skill as numbers are multiplied from generation to generation, gradually mastering the lower forms that appeared before them, using for their own purposes the blind forces of energy that have developed in the course of chemical evolution from the simple atomic structure of hydrogen to the complex instability of uranium, improving the nourishing qualities of plants, vegetables, and fruits, domesticating animals, and changing their living habits to suit *Homo sapiens* own needs and fancies.

Conscious of activities and conscious of consciousness, they asked themselves, some 2,500 years ago, what made them different from the rest of existents that surround them. Some members of the kind who had the leisure to ponder over the workings of their newly discovered consciousness were able to formulate an answer that has satisfied curiosity for many centuries. They invented a mental construct they called "nature," and they offered it as the adequate picture of what makes a distinct lump of matter or an individual form of life different from everything else that exists. Thus they created a hierarchy of existents, layering them into three superposed kingdoms, the mineral, vegetal, and animal, above which man himself stood as the observer and master.

They saw that "human nature" present in each and every member of their species, and for generations they derived from this notion a satisfactory account of whatever individuals and groups planned and achieved.

The time has come to invent a new mental construct that includes that basic "human nature" but transforms it upwards to a higher level of complexity in the light of what the new sciences of man have learned in the last hundred years. Instead of describing *Homo sapiens* as simply an emergent from the animal herd, which can be dominated by time-binding capacities, we view them now as a complex dynamic unit, as a growing cluster of activities that occupies a unique place in the overall process of cosmic evolution. Individuals are different in age, experience and knowledge; they form groups that are also different depending on where they live and at what stage of development their tribe or nation happens to be. Their numbers stretch along the path of history as a continuous stream of increasing consciousness, power, and capacity to change the face of the earth. From small groups scattered over the surface of the planet in rare contacts with one another, they have gathered into a huge family of nations that are just beginning to realize their interdependence and to learn the political art of coexisting in a minimum of harmonious cooperation.

Teilhard de Chardin calls *noösphere* this new layer of living forms that envelops the planet and gives it a character that makes it different from all other members of the solar system. The third planet from the sun has become humanized, and it has begun to probe into the vastness of the space that surrounds it. It has become self-reflexive, shooting out of itself and keeping within the proper range hundreds of satellites with electronic sensors that observe what is going on at its surface in the natural interplay of atmospheric elements or in the technological inventions of nations bent on threatening one another with weapons of war.

Individuals are active cells of that huge organism, and their institutions—political, economic, technological, or educational—are its organs. Lines of transportation have provided the *noösphere* with a circulatory system; communication networks act as its nervous system, flashing information from one point to the other.

Humans are everywhere: all parts of the planet have been discovered and visited; most regions are inhabited permanently. Mount Everest was conquered; the Nautilus navigated under the ice of the North Pole; Antarctica is peopled all year round by scientists from various nations. The depths of the ocean are surveyed; the crew of Apollo 11 landed on the moon and left on it human-designed instruments that measure its seismicity; electronic probes have recorded the physical and chemical features of Mars and Venus.

This *noösphere* is a new phenomenon, humanly created. It is not the assumed workings of a Nature whose laws are predetermined and translatable into mathematical equations. It could be seen as the process of evolution becoming conscious of itself, emerging into a new order of existence, endowed with a brain, and enjoying the freedom to choose its own future.

The *noösphere* is the planet possessing human qualities, for good or for ill; it has reached a new stage of maturity long prepared by centuries of prehuman and protohuman life. It is the Earth come of age as a conscious entity and able either to commit suicide or guide its own future into experiences that surpass our brightest dreams. It is the embodiment of what

Whitehead saw years ago when he compared our universe to an organism, self-reflexive and self-renewing.

What has been said so far corresponds to what we call in general semantics the "verbal" level, or the discursive aspect of our semantic transactions to this latest phase of the ongoing evolution.

What of the nonverbal level, of the affective and value-laden aspect of our responses to what is happening around us and within us? What experience of ours, if any, corresponds to that seemingly valid theory? Is there within us a need, a drive, a felt tendency to bind ourselves together with other members of the human family in an awareness of a common fate, in a conscious realization that we share with them this speck of dust on which we travel through space-time during a relatively short flash of consciousness between the miracle of birth and the mystery of death? Do we observe and do we feel, in that *noösphere* of which we speak, a centering tendency somewhat similar to the drive for holistic complexity that we see in the atom, the molecule, the cell, and in all organisms? Is the attraction of human to human, or its polar alternative, the rivalry between human and human, a dominant feature of human experience?

It seems that it is. If we look at history as the drama of people attempting in various ways to bind together the whole of humankind into a single unit by conquest, religious conversion, economic penetration, or technological development, we see every such attempt is a manifestation of some deep urge that breaks out here and there at some points of the space-time plenum, is never fully satisfied and reappears again and again under some form or other. What do people want that they are ready to bring about by any means, fair or foul? What possesses them and works them into a frenzy that cannot be stopped, like that of the beast in rut obeying unwittingly the vital drive of its species to continue in existence?

The *noösphere*-binding urge reveals itself as the most powerful and ruthless form of energy that *Homo sapiens* displays. Under its impulse, people tear apart the atom itself and make it a thundering tool with which to subjugate the human race into a unity of politics and purposes. It makes people ready to take the ultimate gamble of being one in common mode of life or of not being at all. There was a time, not long ago, when we claimed that we were making the world safe for democracy, or for our own kind of noöspheric oneness. Others wanted to unify the world in the practice of Marxism-Leninism. All great religions claimed, each one in turn, to be world religions; all philosophical systems have so far striven to account for a common human destiny. What all these undertakings have in common is that they are determined to make the world one, happen what may.

At the same time as politicians, religious leaders, and military men attempt to make the human race one by propaganda or sheer force, some moralists and philosophers proclaim a oneness of a different kind, which they see as the obvious characteristic of humankind in evolution. "No man is an Island," writes John Donne; "To be is to be related," says the philosopher-mathematician Cassius Jackson Keyser. Confucius formulates the Golden Rule centuries ago, and Jesus repeats the commandment: "Love They neighbor like Thyself!" More recently Hermann Keyserling sees what he calls the "emotional" order, meaning the affective component of our behavior, as the most adequate replica of the order of the universe; Sylvan Tomkins speaks of the "logic of feeling" as a truer picture of the universe than the logic of strict intellection.

> Love has always been carefully eliminated from realist and positivist concepts of the world; but sooner or later we shall have to acknowledge that it is the fundamental impulse of life, or, if you prefer, the one natural medium in which the rising course of evolution can proceed.[19]

When the world was seen as made of distinct natures distributed in a hierarchical order and interacting with one another according to definite laws, its overall oneness, though taken for granted, was not studied as a special phenomenon deserving explicit attention. Then came Jan Smuts, in the twenties, who spoke of holism as "the concrete character which distinguishes all natural objects in the world of experience."[20]

At the level of the *noösphere,* that concrete character of holistic centration becomes the awareness of our solidarity as a species sharing a common experience on a small planet and a feeling of togetherness to be fostered and transformed into actual love given and received.

Whatever happens to the world of humans, in events that are divisive like wars and rivalries or conjunctive like joint international enterprises or love-ins, we had better see them as the cyclical pulsations of the evolutionary urge working its way in laborious self-renewals and creating step by step its own transformation into a transcending unity.

People of today stand at the growing tip of this vectorial process. Their main concern is to acquire the knowledges and the skills necessary to become experts in the art of living, working, and growing together in a felt relation of loving unity.

Perceiving-creating My World

From these broad and clearly visible aspects of our role in making the world in which we live, we may now advance toward the consideration of phenomena closer to our everyday life and look at them from a viewpoint quite different from that of generally accepted common sense. This brings us

[19]Teilhard de Chardin, *The Future of Man* (Harper & Row, 1964), p. 54.
[20]Jan Christian Smuts, *Holism and Evolution* (Viking, 1961), p. 122.

to one of the most baffling problems of epistemology, one that philosophers have been wrestling with from time immemorial. Until the present conceptual revolution and without the freedom to speculate that is normal at what I shall later describe in Chapter 10 as *stage four* of the epistemological profile, it had remained a haunting paradox.

The problem can be presented in a number of ways. There is the age-long conundrum that goes like this: if lightning strikes a tall tree and sends it crashing to the ground on a mountain where there is nobody within hearing distance, is a noise produced or not? Or, in Dr. Harry Weinberg's slightly different version:

> Suppose you and I are in a room. We see before us a desk which appears to have color, texture, shape. I leave the room. Question: Is the desk still there? The empiricist says yes, the skeptic no.[21]

Finally, we could word the problem in more abstruse language—as I saw it recently in a psychological journal, where a well-known psychologist complained that nobody has yet answered the important question "What makes the 'thingness' of a thing?" The man was asking this in all seriousness, apparently unaware that the question, as worded, is unanswerable. Evidently, there are still people who believe that if you can string words together in grammatical order and put a question mark at the end, you have asked a question to which an answer is possible and should be found. If we accept this view, what prevents us from asking "How much is much?," "How far is far?," "How many miles from near to far?" Or, as in the Middle Ages, "How many angels can stand together on the point of a needle?"

No, this is not a matter of juggling words, nor a contest of cleverness at manipulating abstract ideas without any connection with worthwhile issues. The underlying question is serious and the problem is fundamental, and we cannot evade it in a book on the art of awareness. If we cannot take a good honest look at our original contact with the outside world, we are not ready to come out of the delusive obviousness of common sense.

One way of dealing with the apparent difficulty is to come back to the central notion of abstraction and orders of abstraction. From what is going on, I pick and choose, consciously or unconsciously, certain elements that are within the range of my senses, unaided or aided by instruments. This is my first-order experience; this is here where I collect the raw data of my experience. For instance, the green patch of color that I see against the background of lighter shade on the wall in front of my desk is the raw visual impression on my retina. My brain will quickly analyze the impression in terms of its relative shades, of its shape as learned from other senses, of its perspective, its texture. It will cut it out of the surrounding colors as a dis-

[21] Harry Weinberg, *Levels of Knowing and Existence* (New York: Harper & Row, 1957), p. 59.

tinct object, in this case a sofa bed. If the room were in darkness, I could not
start the series of activities with this green patch on my retina, and my brain
could not abstract the sofa bed from the whirling dance of electrons that
surround me. It would have disappeared in the colorless world of atoms and
radiation that we now accept as the background texture of the universe.

What we make of that background texture is a creation of ours, made
possible under certain circumstances. It is a joint product of what is going on
and of what we are and do. This product is kept in existence by the simultaneous action of two forms of energy. One is the energy of the cosmos of
which we are a part, and the other is the specific energy of the part that we
are, both interacting, and by this interacting initiating new levels of existence. This new level of existence, created by me and bound to disappear
when I fade out of the picture, is my world, my personal contribution to the
enrichment of the cosmos, a world that is and will forever remain a unique,
irreplaceable, and nonrepeatable feature of the total space-time cosmos. I
create my world as I perceive it. My world is me-in-action from the moment
I was conceived to the moment my last living cell will stop functioning. It has
the same dimensions as I have; it lasts the same number of years as I do; it
covers the space that I have covered; it is populated by the people that I
have known; it is located in history where I happen to be located; it is part of
the cultural phenomenon to which I belong. It invades other personal worlds
to the extent that I generate enough human energy to irradiate to them, into
them, and through them.

This world of mine is distinct from the world that *you* create and of
which *you* are the center. Our worlds may overlap to some extent, as they do
now as I write and you read, but they never coincide exactly in their space-
time totality, and seldom do they fuse into a common experience. When
fusion occurs, however, it is an unutterable experience, clearly beyond
words, at a level of existence that words cannot reach. There is the total
surrender and the ecstasy of reciprocated love, and less spectacular degrees
of unity in living are experienced when a common insight makes two or more
persons share in a discovery and enjoyment of a notion that reaches deep
into their world of values.

It is at the level of values that our individual worlds have a greater
chance of fusing. We are observer-participants in the world, and it is as
participants, rather than as observers, that we share a common experience.
This participation can be seen as just below the verbal level as the flesh is
just below the skin, feeding it, supporting it, and protected by it. Within the
flesh are buried the vital phenomena of metabolic exchanges, renewal, and
growth. Below the verbal level are buried the metabolic exchanges of values
that are internalized and expressed in behavior. Buried also are the felt at-
tractions and repulsions, the yieldings and resistings, the commitments and

detachments, all the moving, interacting, and growing elements of life-in-depth.

When we start speaking about these, we quickly realize that our vocabulary is inadequate, metaphoric for the most part, and laden with connotations that distract our capacity to observe with a fresh vision. And yet, if we look well, this is where we can detect the connective colloidal tissue that binds our human world together. In science, common acceptance of a theory is what makes it "objective" for a time, until it is replaced by a more acceptable one. In human affairs, it is the sharing of values and the common adherence to their requirements that make understanding and cooperation possible. Yielding to love instead of holding on to the rules of discursive logic is what makes *vie-a-deux* (life-of-two-for-two) possible, enjoyable, and fruitful. A common dedication to a core of values is what holds "movements," institutions, and organizations together during periods of intensive and difficult growth. Later, the values may harden into sets of rules and procedures, the interpretation of which gradually assumes a "logical" character. When this goes too far, we speak of the "letter of the law" versus the "spirit of the law."

Now that we speak of matter-energy, or of energy assuming a tangible form and being called "matter" when it reaches the level of compactness necessary for our sensorium to become aware of it, could we not speak of the energetic-feeling-purposive-evaluating element of human functioning as the microscopic and submicroscopic levels of what we are? Our knowledge of these levels and our consequent techniques would then give us a mastery of human affairs somewhat comparable to our growing mastery of the physical world through our knowledge of its atomic substructure.

The verbal level—in the spoken word, the written word, the taped word, the works of art, and the monuments—would correspond to matter as opposed to energy, to apparent stability as opposed to everchanging motility, to "reality" that is sensed as opposed to "process" that is postulated. The atomic value of a person, of a book, of an organization would be measured in terms of its "radioactivity," not of its bulk in weight, not of its surface finish in shine or color.

Summary

We began this chapter by discussing the evolution of human extensions in the form of technology, methods of thinking-feeling acting, and theories and doctrines. The world of extensions has become the humanized world in which we live and guide ourselves in a limitless "unknown."

The evolution of this superorganic universe takes place by what Korzybski called time-binding. This refers to the frequency with which humans use their capacity to invent and innovate by combining the elements of different periods of time to create a life-space that did not exist before.

Teilhard de Chardin called this an activity of the *noösphere*, which he saw as the humanizing of planet Earth. The *noösphere* is evolution become aware of itself. When we, as individuals, tune ourselves to this phenomenon, we become aware of our solidarity as a species; we become participants in a common experience. Participation of this order can change the very quality of an individual's experience. This is multiordinality in action where the higher orders pattern the lower.

I wanted you to know that we make the world in which we live to a greater extent than previously realized. Now we can see how determinism, laws of nature, predictability, as high order abstractions of the past, would not allow us to think in terms of creating and inventing our environment. With the present conceptual revolution, it has not only become "thinkable," but an imperative value to be implemented in every area of our lives. As a start, I wish to introduce "Semantic Stages of Development" as a way of considering how we may enter into this new creative process.

multidimensionality and complexification

Bees build their honeycomb in six-sided cells that are marvels of engineering. They do not have to learn how to do it; the plan according to which they work is programmed in their organism, and they follow it faithfully, without changing it or improving it.

Beavers are born builders. The dams they throw across streams are of solid construction, and their huts are also masterpieces of convenience and usefulness (for beavers, of course).

Birds build their nests in similar fashion. Naturalists tell us that there is a limited range of variation and initiative in their work. Swallows have adapted their mud nests to the eaves of buildings, which did not exist in their natural habitat before people came upon the scene.

In these and similar cases, the plans are given by Mother Nature; the process is instinctive. Unconscious drives trigger series of ordered activities that establish working relations between the needs of the animal and the conditions of the environment.[22]

The Structured Unconscious

Humans, as semantic transactors—as thinking, feeling, self-moving, and electrochemical processes—have a *first* nature that determines some of their

[22]The theory of instinctive behavior is limited to whatever information is possessed by the author at the present time. This world is in a state of rapid change, and no theory propounded can assume a permanent stability.

behavior, just as it does for the bee, the beaver, or the birds. But, humans also acquire a *second* nature, which we may call the *structured unconscious* and which determines—prior to intelligent and volitional control—the manner in which they transact with people, things, situations, language, and symbols. They assimilate, in their unconscious, patterns of activity that are not inherited through the chromosomes they received from their parents. These patterns are cultural patterns that vary from one culture to another. They differentiate a Chinese from a Westerner, a German from a Frenchman, even an Englishman from an American—although in the last case the languages are practically identical. Cultural differences are found in vocabularies, in social mannerisms, and in the way people eat, cook, furnish their houses, play games, dance, greet one another—do whatever is done, as we say, "spontaneously" or "naturally."

This cultural second nature reaches an even finer degree of differentiation: the cultural unconscious becomes a distinctive *personal* unconscious, a dynamic pattern of attitudes, habits, internalized values, and modes of thinking by which each person relates to the world of things and people, observes and judges that world, and expresses himself to himself and to his surroundings.

Because *unconscious* is usually taken as a psychological term, we may fall back into the old rut of the distinction between mental and physical and may overlook the fact that this acquired second nature goes deep into our muscular tissues and our glandular and nervous systems.

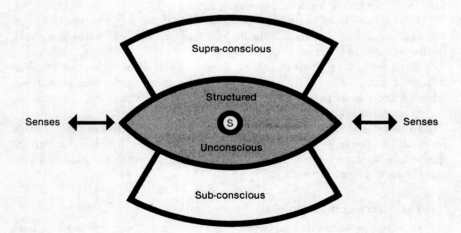

Figure 9.1. The structured unconscious. Sensations, dreams from the subconscious, and intuitions from the supraconscious have to go through it to reach the inner Self (S).

A well-known psychiatrist put it as follows.

Though obvious, it is also perhaps well to emphasize that fact that distinctions between organic and psychogenic are sometimes far from absolute. Organic changes in the organism must occur not only in the psychopath, the schizophrenic, and the hysterical patient, but in all people in response to every item of experience. He who learns French, gets married, dissects a cadaver, is frightened by a dog, or looks for a new word in the dictionary can scarcely be conceived of as emerging with the synaptic patterns of his nervous system entirely unchanged. It would not be profitable to confine our concept of what is organic to the cellular level with so much already known which indicates that molecular and submolecular changes (colloidal, electrochemical, etc.) are regularly resulting from our acts of learning or, if one prefers, from all our conditioning. He who ever saw a miser, an honest man, a bigot, a golf enthusiast, or a person who genuinely loves another will not have to be told that such changes can be enduring.[23]

The consequence is that an adult who wants to practice the art of awareness quickly discovers that the organism within which she finds herself has many built-in features, some that are useful and some that are obsolete for our day and age. It is like an old house whose plumbing and wiring require close inspection, and perhaps complete renovation. Kahlil Gibran uses a stronger simile: "It is not a garment I cast off this day, but a skin that I tear with my own hands." Indeed, the built-in features of our personal unconscious have become parts of ourselves, like the skin that stands between our flesh and the outside.

There are many strands to that unconscious, woven through the very fibers of our semantic organism. At the thinking level, we call them hidden assumptions, ideas, theories, and methods of thinking that we take for granted. They form the warp and woof of our logical consistency.

One who has explored this "hidden dimension" is anthropologist Edward T. Hall:

We have been taught to think linearly rather than comprehensively, and we do this not through conscious design or because we are not intelligent or capable, but because of the way in which deep cultural undercurrents structure life in subtle but highly consistent ways that are not consciously formulated. Like the invisible jet streams in the skies that determine the course of a storm, these hidden currents shape our lives; yet their influence is only beginning to be identified.[24]

Hall then goes on to state some of the difficulties involved in these new probes past conscious, explicit, manifest culture into what we are calling

[23]Hervey Cleckley, *The Mask of Sanity* (St. Louis: Mosby, 1950), p. 442.
[24]Edward T. Hall, *Beyond Culture* (New York: Anchor Press/Doubleday, 1976), p. 9.

here the structured unconscious, or what we will refer to later as the semantic or epistemic dimension:

> Recognition of the cultural unconscious is a relatively recent development in Western thought, so recent in fact that understanding out-of-awareness cultural processes is rare. Some of my most learned and erudite colleagues reject the notion that there is even anything to discuss in man's unconsciously structured temporal and spatial system. Talking about unconscious culture in concrete terms is a little bit like talking about writing systems for language prior to the development of writing. The reader should ponder a moment on what it would be like to live ten thousand years ago or more, trying to grapple with the analysis of language. Of course there would be those who verbalized freely, yet were completely unaware of the fact that there was a system that regulated their speech.[25]

We will see in later chapters that the words we use and the manner in which we link them together in grammatical sequence determine some of our behavior. We remember how the scientists of the late eighteenth century were delayed in their advance toward the discovery of thermodynamics by the unconscious assumption that heat was a chemical element because its name was a substantive. But there is another language that we take as a revelation of what is "really" going on in the "objective" world, the language of arithmetic as we learned it in grade school.

I am not speaking here of superstitions about numbers; most of us are free from these primitive reactions (except, perhaps, the owners of the many modern buildings and hotels that pretend to have no thirteenth floor). Nor am I speaking of advanced mathematics, where the methods are not confined to the manipulation of "quantities" (that natural numbers stand for) but extend to things that do not even resemble numbers, such as relations or even propositions. I limit myself to what is called "linear" and "additive" thinking, to the apparently sound commonsense view that one and one is always two, two and one is always three, two and two is always four, and so on. In other words, the additive thinker believes that "one more" means exactly "one more" and nothing else.

It does not! One more may mean a spectacular increase in structural complexity, a new order of existence that the step-by-step additive mode of thinking fails to reveal. One more, in such a case, is not an additive "more." Years ago I suggested that it be called a *structural* more.[26]

The Structural More

When we think with natural numbers, we can add and subtract; this is a fundamental operation of arithmetic, and it is wonderful as long as we re-

[25]Hall, *Beyond Culture*, pp. 143-144.
[26]J. Samuel Bois, "Introducing the Structural More," in *Explorations in Awareness* (New York: Harper & Row, 1957), Chap. 25, pp. 160-65.

main in the world of arithmetic. The trouble begins when we unwittingly use additive thinking in human affairs where it does not apply. For instance, it is true that two plus one makes three, but it is not equally true that two persons who are joined by a third person while they are in an intimate rapport consider that third person as a mere addition to the pair. Their "twoness" is disturbed (or perhaps relieved) by the "threeness" that replaces it. Here two plus one is not a case of addition, it is a case of total change, of transformation. And the important characteristic of the process is precisely that transformation.

This transformation is an empirical fact that *more* in "three is one *more* than two" fails to reveal. The word involves a comparison between two groups of units that are of the same kind, one being smaller than the other in size but not different in structure, as in "Five dollars is *more* than four dollars" or "There is room for one *more*." More does not adequately express what happens after the size of the smaller group has reached the critical point beyond which it becomes a group that suddenly acquires a structure and a whole set of properties that were nonexistent before the increase. As a consequence, it belongs to the category of terms of which Korzybski said:

> With our present low development and the lack of structural researches, we still keep an additive Aristotelian language, which is, perhaps, able to deal with additive, simple, immediate and comparatively unimportant issues, but is entirely unfit structurally to deal with principles which underlie the most fundamental problems of life.[27]

His suggestion was that we must create new terms.

> If facts cannot be covered by given linguistic forms and methods, new forms, new structures, new methods are invented and created to cover the structure of facts in nature.[28]

To convey the idea that the smaller group has been absorbed and transformed into a larger one, I suggest that we give *more* a new meaning when circumstances require. Apart from the generally accepted *additive more*, let us have a *structural more*. This would imply two things: (1) In the case of the two persons whose rapport had been interrupted by the addition of a third person, the second group, that of three persons, contains—additively—one unit more than the original pair; (2) the three units, including the two original units, are now in a web of relationships that did not exist when the pair was alone; the new group is not only larger, it is structured according to a different and more complex pattern.

The structural "less" corresponds to the structural "more," depending on whether we go up from the simple to the complex, or down from the

[27]Korzybski, *Science and Sanity* (Lakeville, Conn.: International Non-Aristotelian Library, 1933, 1941, 1948, 1958), p. 265.
[28]Korzybski, *Science and Sanity*, p. 172.

complex to the simple—from the parts to the whole or from the whole to its parts. Analysis is a search for the simple, for the elements that are devoid of the structure that made them a complex whole; synthesis is an attempt to put them together again in a structure that transfers them to a different order of existence.

Many analogies derived from the physical sciences show how the structural *more* corresponds to transformations that take place in the world of material things. Sand, water, and cement, when mixed together in the proper proportions and allowed to set, become a solid block of concrete, with properties that none of the three components, taken singly, could ever have. Gunpowder, made of charcoal, sulfur, and saltpeter, has a power of explosion when ignited that none of the elements could develop by itself.

In chemical compounds, the structural "more" is more evident still. Water is entirely different from the two gases that it contains. Sulfuric acid has properties that none of its constituents, sulfur, hydrogen, and oxygen, possesses. In the case of chemical elements, the structural proportion of the elements is a characteristic of the whole; it does not allow the addition of a single element outside the proportion expressed by the formula.

In biology, the transformation is even more evident. A seed put in the soil becomes the seat of an abstracting process: it chooses from the chemical elements that surround it, measures what quantity of each it requires at what time, and absorbs and combines them with the oxygen of the air and the photons of the sun to form a complex product—the plant or the tree—that will become something different from the seed itself.

The Structural More and Our Genetic Self

Additive thinking, where *more* and *plus* have a linear meaning, and where they fail to suggest a transformation of the constitutive elements of the emergent whole, pervades most of our built-in unconscious; it often exerts a harmful influence on our semantic transactions.

In the standard definition: "man, a rational animal," it suggests a linking of two heterogeneous entities, an addition of two elements: a body and a mind, a physical organism and a soul, an animal that is less self-sufficient than many but one that has an enlarged cerebral cortex that makes him superior to his fellow animals. If we think additively, as we do more often than we realize, we may conceive of our difference from animals as a plus or minus affair; we may use comparatives, and say—for instance—that orangutans are stronger, dogs have a wider range of hearing. Continuing our comparison from the human side, we may say that we are more intelligent and more resourceful than any of these animals.

All these expressions are inadequate, even misleading. The differences between humans and animals are not differences in degree, as the additive *more* implies, they are differences in *kind*. Human vision is not to be compared to the falcon's, but it is part of a seeing capacity that can use the Palomar telescope, the radio telescope, and the electron microscope. The human capacity for speed is not different in degree from the cheetah's, but it is part of an endowment that overcame gravitation when astronauts went into orbit. Human strength is not a matter of muscles, as is the orangutan's; it is the resultant power of our skills, theories, and knowledge of energies when we release the power of nuclear forces. We amplify our hearing to the point of listening to conversations across the oceans or to signals from the deep reaches of space.

If we introduce the structural more in our thinking, this new and more adequate picture of our species becomes easy. We do not result from the juxtaposition of animal characteristics and reasoning powers or from the superposition of an elaborate cortex on top of an animal brain. We have no purely "animal" and no purely "spiritual" characteristics. We have characteristics that are unique to us. They are *human* characteristics. All our reactions, even those that resemble animal reactions, such as hunger, sex, homeostatis, are shot through and through with meaning; they are related to what we think of ourselves, of our place in the world, of our function as individuals, as a marriage partner, a professional, an employee or an employer, a young woman or man or an old woman or man. Our transactions are *semantic* transactions. A man may go on a hunger strike; a woman may deprive herself to keep the youthful figure that is shown on TV commercials. They may both suffer from sexual frigidity for reasons other than the physiological condition of their gonads. As is the case in chemical compounds, it is the structure of the whole that determines what elements will be accepted into the structure and in what quantity. The whole, in the case of humans, is not simply the psychophysical activities that we have in common with all other members of the human family; it is the individual as a highly differentiated semantic transactor with a unique past, environment, anticipated future, and with unique thoughts, feelings, values, and bodily habits.

The Structural More and Human Activities

Our formulation of the structural more applies to a variety of situations in which an increase or a decrease of a certain element beyond or below a critical point changes the whole picture. I am thinking now of the breakeven point in cost accounting, where a small difference, above or below, means prosperity or bankruptcy. I am thinking also of the "straw that breaks the camel's back," when a trivial incident brings about an unexpected emotional explosion. I am also thinking of something that may appear quite different at first sight: the disproportionate influence that an uncooperative individual may have in a working group.

Let us amplify a bit on this last example. A group of four men, Fred,

Tom, Dick, and Harry, are jointly responsible for the survival and development of a small company. Let us assume that one of them, Harry, is habitually noncooperative, or systematically negative in his approach to common problems, or so mentally deficient that he cannot follow the rest of them. Arithmetically speaking, he is one of four, or 25 percent of the group, but he can interfere with more than 60 percent of the group activities. In fact, each of them has a direct influence on over 60 percent of their joint activities. This is another case where plain additive thinking fails to cover the empirical facts of the situation.

Figure it out for yourself. Count the number of possible interactions among the four of them, taking them two or three at a time. If two at a time, we have six possibilities: Fred with Tom, Fred with Dick, Fred with Harry, Tom with Dick, Tom with Harry, and Dick with Harry. If three at a time, we have four alternatives: Fred, Tom, Dick; Fred, Tom, Harry; Fred, Dick, Harry; and Tom, Dick, Harry. Now count how many times Harry appears in these ten possible groupings: six times out of ten. Harry can interfere with 60 percent of the work although he is only one of four partners. In fact, his nuisance value is higher than that because I did not include a third alternative: that of the whole group in a joint session. Does this not also show the terrific power the right of veto gives one nation in the Security Council? Does it not also show the historical importance of the few votes that made Senator John Kenedy the president of the country?

When one applies for a job, experience is counted in years. Ten years of experience is taken as five times two years—or surely as much more than two years. This assumes that one year of experience is a unit that is comparable for one individual and the next and that each consecutive year has added one more degree of efficiency. What of the person whose fifteen years mean simply a routine repetition of her first year, without change and without personal growth? This is a case where fifteen times one is not fifteen but only one. It makes me think of one of my philosophy professors: by looking at our lecture notes we could tell the students of the following year what he would talk about on a certain day, what examples he would give, and what jokes he was going to tell. Each year was an exact replica of his first year of teaching.

Years ago I agreed to give a seminar on executive methods to a group of young executives. In discussing the arrangements I had stated that I wanted no more than fifteen participants, and I explained why. On the first morning of the seminar I found fifty-four students in the lecture room. I protested, but in vain. The reasoning of the man responsible for the arrangements was simple: if I could talk to fifteen persons, I could as well talk to fifty-four, and the company would get more than three times as much for its money. The actual difference was that it got less, because with such a large group the necessary participation was not possible.

Another fallacy is "the more books you read the more you know" or "the more words you can read in a minute the more material you can handle." There is a catch in this, and no comprehension test will convince me that it applies to all kinds of reading material. If one reads to add items of the same kind as those he has already filed away in his memory, well and good; but the information that one fails to assimilate may make the difference between routine reading and creative reading. The comprehension test is itself a counting of individual items, not an evaluation of the structure of the total message. Professor Whitehead, the mathematician and philosopher, once said to his friend, Lucien Price:

> I read very, very slowly. Sometimes I see myself referred to as a "well-read" man. As a matter of fact, I have not read a great quantity of books; but I think about what I read, and it sticks.[29]

Arithmetic is a language, a very sharp and precise language; it is useful for purposes that are in line with it but misleading for purposes that are foreign to it. Additive thinking is unable to deal with most human problems, but it is embedded so deeply in our cultural unconscious that we are seldom aware of the manner in which it shades our thinking. To know its limitations is not enough, however; we have to devise new means of dealing with the complexity of human situations. The formulation of the structural more is a tentative step in what I consider the proper direction. Much structural research is needed if we are to invent language forms less inadequate to the empirical facts they are intended to cover.

Semantic Jumps

For the structural more—or the structural less—there is a corresponding change in our semantic transaction pattern. This change, even if very slight, involves a modification of our outlook on life. In some cases it may be spectacular; it may mean a genuine revolution in our inner world of ideas and values. I suggest that we call it a *semantic jump*.

It reminds me of the rapid flight of a squirrel I disturbed in a pine forest. It ran like lightning to a tall ponderosa, climbed it in a flash, and jumped from its highest branches to the next tree and then to the next, when it stopped and looked at me from a world I could not reach. Or it may be like the experience of the astronaut who suddenly finds himself weightless after the blast that tore him out of the web of gravitational forces. It may feel like entering a new world, where relations among things and people have assumed new dimensions and new proportions.

If we look deeply into our experiences, we can find many such changes, although it may take some time to become aware of some of them. Indeed,

[29]Lucien Price, *Dialogues of Alfred North Whitehead* (Boston: Little, Brown, 1954), p. 170.

we may have failed to profit from them as much as we could have because we did not know enough about them and about their significance. They may have been brought about by any change in any of the seven aspects of our semantic transactions (Fig. 3.1).

Let us begin our examination by looking at the electrochemical aspect that takes place at the level of our organs, glands, and nervous system. Some changes came about spontaneously and naturally, as when our sex glands became active at puberty and suddenly revealed to us a world where sex and love gave a peculiar glow to everything. Some change agents were human discoveries, as when opium, hashish, or a bout of drunkenness sweeps away the clouds of anxiety that darken our inner world. Some change agents are studied in laboratories and are sharpened as scientific instruments for producing specific results: tranquilizers, energizers, LSD, peyote extracts, and such. In these biochemical experiences there are definite changes in the outlook on the world held by the subject, most of which are permanent and irreversible. One does not regress physiologically from puberty back to infancy, and the nervous system of a person who has taken LSD or submitted to electroshock treatment cannot be the same as it was before.

Now, the environmental aspect. We all know that a change of scene often brings about a change in outlook. We may not all be equally sensitive to small changes of furniture arrangement, or to decorating or landscaping, or to the arrival of different people in our immediate neighborhood, but most of us will remember changes of environment that have made a great difference in our life. For example, people compare California to the Middle West or to the East, where they lived before, but their home of earlier years does not mean the same as it did before they knew what it is like to have a home in the Western part of the country. Or, if we take environment to mean a semantic milieu, we may have a case like that of a young woman, born in a German-Swiss protestant family, sent to a Spanish Catholic boarding school, and later on marrying an American, nonchurchgoing husband. This change in the evaluation of the environment is, again, what I call a semantic jump.

When our deep feelings are involved, the face of our world undergoes a significant transformation. Whoever recalls what it means to be really in love, what it means to have a life's companion wrenched away by the hand of death, whoever has dedicated herself to a cause or witnessed the defeat of a cause she held dear, all know that their world before the event was not the same world after, and the world after could not bring back the world of before. Their world either expanded or shrank, moved its focus from one center to another, or disappeared entirely to be replaced with one they had not anticipated. The change in outlook and personal reactions that takes place is also what I call a semantic jump. It may be forward or backward, toward more freedom or into a dark pit of misery.

At the thinking level we have such things as brainwashing and religious conversion. Accepting a new theory may mean a new reorientation for a whole life; and the psychotherapeutic process could be described as a chain reaction of successive insights that are so many jumps out of the darkness of confusion into the light of awareness and self-understanding.

The acquisition of a new skill, or any change in our self-moving activities—whether it be relaxation, the practice of sensory awareness, or the sudden realization of how it feels to sketch, to paint, or to create in an art form—is likely to bring about semantic reactions that may surprise us by their deep-reaching significance.

Our past may have kept an iron grip on our feelings and on our thoughts. A sudden insight, achieved by psychoanalysis or otherwise, may release that grip and give us a freedom of action that we never dreamed possible before.

Finally, the prospect of a bright future is a stimulant that rejuvenates—as the anticipation of a defeat saps our energies, dulls our mind, and spreads gloom all through the world in which we live.

There is much talk about security nowadays. For many persons security means living in a world that stays put, a world in which we can organize our life on a routine basis—with just enough distraction to relieve boredom. We expect a static core of existence as we expect people to have a static core of personality, which we can define and with which we can establish relations that are predictable in all details. If people don't stay put in the pattern of behavior that we have assumed is in keeping with their nature, we blame them for being inconsistent, changeable, purposeless, or crafty.

All this goes back to the old Aristotelian view of the world that fits nicely with the language we speak. Things are what they were, what they are, and what they will be. Whatever happens is thought to happen as a movement in space or in time. It does not happen through them, and does not transform their intimate structure as it happens, but pushes them unchanged along the road of history from year to year. From this simple view of things and persons moving along, the practice of semantic jumping makes us pass to a learned awareness that the world and ourselves are swirls of restless processes. Our bodies live because they are complexes of actions, circulation, chemical exchanges, respiration, and electric charges in constant variation. If we stopped breathing, we would die. This moving flux of changing processes is the dynamic warp and woof of our existence. As Alan Watts puts it: "The only way to make sense out of change is to plunge into it, move with it, and join the dance."[30]

This "dance of life," as Havelock Ellis called it, has styles and fashions that vary from one generation to the next, from one part of the world to

---

[30]Alan Watts, *The Wisdom of Insecurity* (New York: Pantheon, 1951), p. 43.

another, from one theoretical set of postulates to a different set. The art of semantic jumping consists of skills: (1) the skill of keeping in step with the evolving style of the dance of our own culture, (2) the skill of adopting, when needed, the basic patterns of the most exotic dance styles of other cultures and blending them with our own; and (3) the skill of participating in the creation of the new styles that the evolution of humankind requires, for instance passing from nationalism to internationalism, from traditional religion to genuine ecumenism, from competing philosophies to congruence in the enterprise of making the most of the best that humans have invented so far. We can substitute *thinking* for *dance* in these statements and the theme will remain the same, transposed, as it were, into the key of accepted Western intellectuality.

This brings me back to the structural more that we discussed in the previous pages. What I meant to convey, when I chose the words *structure* and *more* was not only a change that is obtained by a mysterious legerdemain from one fixed pattern to a more complex pattern that would also be fixed. It *was* that, but something else as well, and this something else is that particular operation that I am now attempting to describe as semantic jumping. It is by practicing it that one eventually gets the feel of what I mean.

For instance, you are reading a page on which each statement makes sense by itself, or at least you feel it does. Sometimes you may find that a whole page is full of such statements, but they sound commonplace and trivial. They file past, in front of your eyes, as so many obvious truths with which you are already familiar. They fail to click together, to form an original pattern that would glow and give you an insight. You begin to wonder why the author, whom you happen to respect, is making such a fuss about it all. If you don't watch yourself, you may pass judgment that she or he was in a weak moment when writing that passage, and you dismiss the whole message as too simple, too banal to deserve your sophisticated attention.

If the writer has otherwise stimulated your thinking, this is precisely the place where you might try semantic jumping and might integrate, in a structure of higher dimensionality, the elements that you see scattered in front of you. Or, to change the analogy (and at this stage of mental operations we do not have to follow the strict rules of consistent analogies), you may read in depth, doing your best to internalize the underlying structure of the whole message. This is the time to use your constructive imagination, to rocket yourself out of the gravitation of common sense with its earth-hugging weight.

These jumps vary according to the semantic barrier over which they take us. Some of these barriers are within our own culture, separating areas that for many years we arbitrarily classified as closed to outside interference; for instance, science and religion, pure science and applied science, psychology and physiology, mental and physical, business and pleasure, freedom and authority—in fact, all the dualisms that divide our mental world in "prospectors' lots" that are jealously guarded by the holders of properly registered titles.

There are higher barriers between cultures themselves, as between Eastern and Western philosophies, or between the communist and the capitalist economic and political theories. These require long practice in semantic jumping, up to a higher level of abstraction, where the Iron or the Bamboo curtains fade into relative insignificance, like farm fences viewed from the windows of a high-flying plane.

Finally, there are historical jumps, transitions from one method of soaring into speculation to a more powerful one that raises the ultimate ceiling of our ascension to the stratosphere of scientific generalizations. We first use these heights for the limited purpose of advancing the physical sciences, without imperiling—as we think—the fate of human beings. Now the time has come to bring the human sciences to these heights of adventurous speculation, way above the most exalted peaks of accumulated common sense. There the artist, the mathematician, and the nondoctrinal philosopher may meet in orbit, well above the highs and the lows of terrestrial weather, but with the hope of eventually influencing that weather and taming its hurricanes.

In the world of thinking, humans have achieved jumps even more spectacular than those of the astronauts and cosmonauts. When these jumps occurred, they were turning points in the history of our progress. From the days, not so far distant, when Bishop Berkeley ridiculed Newton in the name of common sense, we have freed ourselves from the laws of logical gravitation that shackled us to what we could sense or imagined as sensed. Berkeley expressed his down-to-earth view of the world as follows:

> Now, as our sense is strained and puzzled with the perception of objects extremely minute, even so the imagination, which faculty derives from sense, is very much strained and puzzled to frame clear ideas of the least particles of time, or of the least increments generated therein. . . .The further the mind analyseth and pursueth these fugitive ideas the more it is lost and bewildered; the objects, at first fleeting and minute, soon vanish out of sight. . . .They are neither finite quantities, nor quantities infinitely small, nor yet nothing. May we not call them ghosts of departed quantities. . . ?[31]

So said the good bishop of Cloyne as he upbraided Newton for proposing his *method of fluxions,* which was to become *calculus,* one of the most powerful thinking tools ever invented by Western culture. Berkeley could not accept what he derisively called "ghosts of departed quantities." As a

[31]Bishop Berkeley, "The Analyst," in *The World of Mathematics,* ed. James R. Newman (New York: Simon & Schuster, 1956), pp. 289, 292.

commonsense philosopher, he had not acquired the freedom to soar beyond what he could see, hear, or feel, or imagine as seen, heard, or felt.

Let us contrast Berkeley's views with those of a mental cosmonaut of our generation, Sir Arthur Eddington, the British astronomer.

> We have pictured the atom as consisting of a heavy nucleus with a number of nimble electrons circulating around it like planets around the sun. . . . You must not take this picture too literally. The orbits can scarcely refer to a motion in space . . . and the electron cannot be localized in the way implied in the picture. . . . The physicist draws an elaborate plan of the atom and then proceeds critically to erase each detail in turn. What is left is the atom of modern physics. . . . There is not enough to form a picture, but something is left for the mathematician to work on.[32]

What a difference—what a jump—between the statements of Berkeley and those of Eddington. Ten generations ago Berkeley protested against "straining and puzzling" our imagination beyond what we can picture easily. Today we accept as normal the prescriptions of Eddington and his fellow scientists when they say (in effect): "Take away the mental picture; come out of your sensory imagination into the outer space of pure abstraction. This is where we, mathematicians, work in the freedom of a non-Aristotelian logic that is not bound any longer by the gravitation of common sense."

Too few of us have been sufficiently identified with the scientific development of the West to get the feel of what this intellectual jump means. I have to use similes to convey that feeling, and unless you take time to meditate upon them, you may think that I am just indulging in a literary exercise, which I am not. I see the bishop's outlook on the world as that of a country squire surveying his estate as he rides on horseback; I see Eddington's outlook as that of an astronaut orbiting silently around the planet—or as commuting freely from the earth to any point in the universe where he happens to have to work that day. To quote Eddington again:

> We must seek a knowledge which is neither of actors and actions. . . . The knowledge which we require is knowledge of a structure of pattern contained in the action. I think that the artist may partly understand what I mean.[33]

No Aristotelian system that rationalizes a subject-predicate language and therefore conceives of the world as made of actors engaged in actions can meet these requirements of up-to-date thinking. Our Western culture has gradually—and painfully—disengaged itself from the shackles of Aristotelianism by a series of historical semantic jumps. These will be studied in the following pages.

[32]Arthur Eddington, *The World of Mathematics*, pp. 1560, 1561.
[33]Arthur Eddington, *The World of Mathematics*, p. 1559.

semantic stages of development

Humans, as functioning elements of the cosmos, were not at the beginning what they grew to become in the course of history. The different methods used to create answers that humans gave in the quest for knowing how to deal with the world and with themselves may be summarized in stages of cultural development. The semantic jumps of a culture are seen as recapitulated in each individual until he or she can reach the full maturity available in the cultural environment.

stages of cultural development: an epistemological profile

Professor Gaston Bachelard (1884-1962) for many years taught the history and the philosophy of science at the Sorbonne. He was the first continental scientist-philosopher to comment outspokenly and favorably on Korzybski's work, and he became an honorary trustee of the Institute of General Semantics. He was a prolific writer whose books ranged from treatises on physical chemistry to poetry and essays on art. One of his books is *La Philosophie du Non*, which describes a philosophy that says *no* to its own formulations because it remains an open-ended system, constantly denying the finality of its own conclusions. It is not only non-Aristotelian, as is the Korzybskian system, but it is a bold attempt to make the negative feature of all progressive theories the characteristic of a new type of philosophy.

According to Korzybski's theory of time-binding, human beings become structurally more than their ancestors as they add to their brainpower from generation to generation. In the course of history Western men and women have taken semantic jumps that have altered their outlook on the world and their capacity to deal with it. As semantic transactors, they became different from their predecessors after each of these jumps, which are tantamount to cultural variations, to transformations of what is commonly called our *second* nature.

Bachelard saw these semantic jumps recapitulated in the life of each individual growing from infancy through childhood and adolescence, eventually reaching—in some cases—the full degree of maturity available in our cultural environment. If we fail to reach this stage, we will live technologically in the twentieth century while remaining psychologically in the Middle Ages, or further back. Or we may grow to the sophistication of our time in some areas of our life and react as a primitive in some other areas. One of the purposes of Bachelard's scheme of thinking, called the *epistemological profile* (which we are now going to display), is precisely to evaluate these differences among the various aspects of our mental life. Korzybski claimed that these differences are due not to the relatively greater amount of information about ourselves and our surroundings that we modern humans possess but to the invention of new linguistic structures and new methods of thinking.

> History shows that the discovery of isolated, though interesting, facts has had less influence on the progress of science than the discovery of new *system-functions* which produce *new linguistic structures and new methods*. In our own lifetime, some of the most revolutionary of these advances in structural adjustment and method have been accomplished. . . . There seems no escape from admitting that no modern man can be really intelligent in 1933 if he knows nothing about these structural scientific revolutions. It is true that, because these advances are so recent, they are still represented in very technical terms; their system-functions have not been formulated, and so the deeper structural, epistemological and semantic simple aspects have not been worked out. These aspects are of enormous human importance. But they must be represented without such an abundance of dry technicalities, which are only a means, and not an end, in search for structure.[1]

General Semantics and Bachelard's epistemological profile is an answer to Korzybski's wish for a simple representation, devoid of dry technicalities, of Western culture's advances in thinking methods—from the crude animism of the primitive to the cosmic consciousness of the creative scientist of today.

We count five stages in the development of Western culture. The first four will be described in their order of appearance; the fifth will be the object of a separate section in Part IX.

Four Stages

1. THE SENSING STAGE

At stage one, individuals took their sensations and feelings as an accurate revelation of what the world was like. Their semantic transactions were *evaluative* transactions, and they did not question their objective value. *The world was what they felt it was*, threatening or inviting, beautiful or ugly, depressing or exhilarating, yielding to human whims or resisting human efforts. Things and events were personified, and ruled by arbitrary gods and spirits whose designs humans had to discover by divination—and whose easily provoked anger they had to assuage by offerings and sacrifices.

[1]Korzybski, Science and Sanity, p. 148.

In our twentieth century, people who still react at this sensing stage may not indulge in the religious rites and the magic practices of aborigines, but they have retained superstitious practices. They go to fortune-tellers; they wear good luck charms; they read the astrological column in the daily newspaper; they build buildings that have no thirteenth floor. Our commonsense language contains vestiges of primitive beliefs that personify natural phenomena. We say "There is a storm coming over the mountain," or "I cannot get rid of that stubborn cold," or "How could this happen to me?"

The term *sensing*, as used here, is not limited to sensory experiences. It also covers feelings that are unquestioned and uncontrolled, feelings to which we expect people to yield, feelings that are their own self-justification, and that we do not even dream of changing because we are convinced that they have been provoked by other people—or by circumstances—over which we have no control. If I feel hurt by what you say or do, it is evident that *it is you who hurt me!* You do it, probably, because you want to or because you feel I am not worth paying attention to. What shall I do? Propitiate you as primitive early humans propitiated their gods, or destroy you as they destroyed their enemies?

Here is a less tragic description of stage one that a participant in a seminar I was conducting gave me years ago.

A little toddler who is within hailing distance of his second year has a vocabulary of about ten words—mostly nouns—and he uses them in a way that greatly amuses his parents. He attaches the word "me" to anything he desires—"me cookie," "me milk," "me up," "me down." His whole conception of reality up to this present moment consists in himself and what he wants. His life oscillates between these two poles. This is cute in a toddler, and of course quite natural, but it is neither cute nor natural in an adult. Yet there are many adults whose whole lives consist in nothing beyond establishing contact between themselves and certain things they want—"me pleasure," "me liquor," "me money," "me sex," "me power." These are the people who bedevil their home, their employees, their friends, and anybody who is unfortunate enough to set himself in opposition to their desires.

The basis of moral and intellectual growth is the capacity to criticize oneself. But there are millions of people whose thoughts run along only one line: themselves and the things they want. How to get these things becomes the end of their existence, the only project in which they have interest. They are little "me cookie" people who have never grown up.

Now for a final example, which will also introduce stage two. Years ago we spent a summer on the shores of Lake of Two Mountains, my family and I. Our daughter Johanna was eight and her brother Leonard was twelve. One sunny morning they woke up early, and their first thought was for a swim. Johanna, the quicker of the two, ran to the end of the landing pier, and stopped. From his cot, her brother called: "How is the water?" She dipped her toe into the lake, withdrew it quickly, and brought her shoulders together in a shiver. "It is cold!" she yelled.

When she shouted, "It is cold!" she was reacting at the sensing stage: *what she felt was for her the objective measure of the temperature of the water.* She *felt* the water was cold, therefore the water *was* cold.

"Check with the thermometer hanging on the post," I called from the porch: "see how many degrees it reads." "Seventy-two degrees," she answered; "it is not so cold after all; come on, Len!" Soon they were both swimming and splashing without any thought of the cold.

I had invited her to jump to stage two. The message that my words implied was somewhat like this: "Be objective and logical. The thermometer is there to tell you the 'real' temperature of the water. Correct your first impression. Since it is seventy-two degrees, it cannot be cold. The water was at that temperature yesterday afternoon, and you enjoyed it."

2. THE CLASSIFYING STAGE

Of course, they had no thermometers in the days of the Greek philosophers who introduced the classifying stage. The difference between stage one and stage two is not a matter of instruments, it is a matter of what we call "objectivity." It was a great advance when our forefathers took the jump from stage one to stage two. They made the great discovery that the world of nature does not change with the moods of the gods or with human reactions. The world of nature has a stability of its own. A thing is identical with itself. It is human privilege and duty to use human powers of observation and to find the "real" nature of things. There are *substances,* and there are *qualities.* Substances are the "real" stuff the universe is made of. Qualities—or actions—may vary without changing the *essential nature* of persons and things.

A man's nature is that of an animal endowed with reason. Two people possess opposite qualities, and yet both are human because they have the same nature. One may be tall, the other short; one may be free, the other may be a slave. They may perform different actions while their essential nature remains the same: one is sitting, the other is running; one is awake, the other is sleeping.

There is no doubt that this conscious and logical classification was extremely useful; it was the beginning of science and philosophy. As time went on, substances were classified with finer discrimination; qualities were measured more accurately and compared on statistical tables. Today we say that Johnny has an intelligence quotient (a quality) of 120, a mechanical aptitude (another quality) at the 75th percentile of the boys in his grade, a *high* degree of aggressiveness, of extraversion. Our language has a structure consistent with that stage: it has nouns or substantives that refer to persons and things; it has adjectives that refer to qualities of nouns and adverbs that refer to qualities of actions expressed by verbs.

This structure of our subject-predicate language reveals the structure of our commonsense thinking. Every sentence in this book has this structure, and whoever wants to practice thinking within the confines of strict verbal logic is locked within the house that Aristotle built when he accepted Greek language forms as the adequate expressions of man's "natural" thinking capacities.

It does not take much observation to see that commonsense theories belong to this stage of cultural development. For people functioning at stage one, things are what they feel they are; for people functioning at stage two, things are what our language *says* they are. The difference is not as great as it might appear because our choice of words is often determined by habits, feelings, prejudices, and conditionings that we seldom reexamine. Stage-two people are under the impression that the collective brain of their culture mirrors the world: for each word in the dictionary there is a corresponding fact, a thing, a person, an action, or a quality that is somewhere, somehow, in the objective world. If their thinking goes from one thought to another according to the rules of logic, they are sure that it goes from one fact to another in the real world. Within their brain there is a miniature of the world.

Whenever we take as ultimate truth a "clear," "positive," or "fixed" notion, we think at stage two. Whenever we think in terms of opposites, of black and white, of for or against, of either all good or all bad, of freedom versus slavery, of 100 percent this or that, we are at the classifying stage. What we call clear thinking is oversimplified thinking. When we count, we are even more impressed by our conclusions: if the Russians orbited a satellite five times the weight of our last one, we conclude that they are superior in many other respects.

Since the human mind is seen as a storeroom of facts about the world, stage-two individuals have a great respect for persons who know many things, persons with a powerful memory, persons who can answer quiz-show questions, persons who have read many books, persons who can read two thousand words a minute. They believe in speed, in making many decisions within a short time. Whether these decisions solve problems or only create new ones is another question. They are conformists who sincerely believe they have ideas of their own, and they are ready to defend their opinions.

They quibble on the meanings of words because words, for them, are actual pictures of things and events, and they want to use the "right" term that gives the "exact" picture of what is being talked about. They look for what they call the "real" meaning of words; they expect sharp, clear-cut definitions; when they ask a question they demand a definite yes-or-no answer.

They believe that any question that can be worded grammatically—and therefore logically—should have an answer. Because they can ask "What is

the cause of my illness . . . my success . . . my failure?" they are convinced that
one cause accounts for their illness, success, or failure. If they fail to find that
cause, they must be lacking in intelligence, knowledge, or wisdom. This
search for simple causality lies behind many *why* questions—and behind the
many wild theories that are given and accepted as answers.

Kurt Lewin called this stage-two mode of thinking Aristotelian, and he
contrasted it with stage three, which he called the Galilean mode. He
claimed that much "scientific" psychology was still marooned at stage two.

> Present-day child psychology and affect psychology also exemplify clearly the
> Aristotelian habit of considering the abstractly defined classes as the essential
> nature of the particular object and hence as an explanation of behavior. What-
> ever is common to children of a given age is set up as the fundamental character
> of that age. The fact that three-year-old children are quite often negative is
> considered evidence that negativism is inherent in the nature of three-year-
> olds. . . . The classificatory character of its concepts and the emphasis on fre-
> quency are indicated methodologically by the commanding significance of
> statistics in contemporary psychology. The statistical procedure, at least in its
> commonest application in psychology, is the most striking expression of this
> Aristotelian mode of thinking.[2]

Classifying is a necessity in thinking and communicating, and there is no
suggestion here that we should avoid it; the suggestion is that we should use
it with full awareness of its limitations, remembering at all times that what
we say of a thing, a person, or a situation does not reveal its "real nature." It
is simply a way of talking about it.

3. THE RELATING STAGE

When certain segments of Western people took the semantic jump from
stage two to stage three, they did not give up their quest for objectivity; in
fact, they redoubled the intensity of their drive for a more adequate knowledge of the universe as they believed it existed independently of human
knowledge. From the dichotomous language of subject and predicate, of
substances and qualities, of agents and actions, they passed to the language
of mathematical formulas. The object of their science was no longer *what
things are*, it became *what things do*—or better, *how they do it*.

It meant a strong reaction against whatever smacked of metaphysics,
against mere intellectual understanding that does not lead to practical ac-
complishment. It meant systematic observation and rigorous experimentation, both guided by the laws of induction. It meant theories that could lead
to further discoveries. The human mind-in-action became attuned to a universe seen as a huge machine and developed methods to force nature to
reveal its secrets.

[2]Kurt Lewin, *A Dynamic Theory of Personality* (New York: McGraw-Hill, 1935),
pp. 15, 16.

It was the age of a science that questioned the authority of the Scriptures and of the philosophers of the past. It was the age of humans gradually assuming control over the forces of nature that they were discovering as they were perfecting their methods and their instruments.

It was the age when they were inventing an array of instruments to multiply their powers of perception: telescopes, microscopes, stethoscopes, X rays, oscilloscopes, Geiger counters, radar, radio, television, transistors, electron microscopes, Tiros and Earth satellites. They also constructed machines to multiply their powers of action: engines, explosives, railroads, automobiles, ocean liners, airplanes, assembly lines, spaceship boosters, lasers, cyclotrons, atomic reactors, A-bombs and H-bombs, earth-moving equipment, automation. In the biological field, new breeds of plants, such as frost-resisting wheat or hybrid corn, were invented; new breeds of animals were established; and old breeds were stimulated to levels of production that unhumanized nature could not reach. Medicine increased the average span of active life; transfusion of blood became a routine procedure; serums and vaccines curbed epidemics and antibiotics controlled infections; surgery performed quasi-miracles; allied research worked on organ transplantation and plastic substitutes for vital organs. For the common person, science and technology are practically the same: progress introduces more progress, increasing mastery over nature, improving predictability in weather forecasting, and controlling economic cycles.

The world is seen as a complex of interrelated parts, as a huge machine whose workings we keep discovering one after the other, and we learn to control them more and more efficiently. We long ago gave up the naïve belief that there is a single cause for any single phenomenon; we know that whatever happens is due to the convergence of many antecedents. We are devising better and better means of taking such a dynamic complexity into account: we build computers that can predict what will come out of the interaction of several space-time factors. The general public is so impressed by these accomplishments that these machines are called *electronic brains.* They may even listen to the claims of those who speak of *human cybernetics,* repeating early *Homo sapiens'* idolatrous gesture of making a god of what is planned with their brain and fashioned with their hands.

For many persons this is humankind's top achievement, and Science (with a capital *S*) becomes the supreme value, just as Religion was in the Middle Ages. To oppose Science is to be heretic in today's world.

It is evident that stage-three thinking is a distinct advance beyond stage two. Wendell Johnson, when he compared the static world of stage two to the dynamic world of stage three, put it this way.

The fundamental scientific assumption is that reality has a process character; if you reject that, you remove practically all the purpose and point in everything the scientist does. In a perfectly static world the only requirement for adjustment would be a good memory, and everyone would have that, if one might speak of memory as existing in a world in which tomorrow and yesterday would be identical. What most fundamentally characterizes the scientific, or well-adjusted, or highly sane person is not chiefly the particular habits or attitudes that he holds, but rather the deftness with which he modifies them in response to changing circumstances. He is set to change, in contrast to the more rigid, dogmatic, self-defensive individual who is set to "sit tight."[3]

4. THE POSTULATING STAGE OR CREATIVE PROCESS

Just as the individual who functions at stage three is ready to change his behavior when the scientist shows him new aspects of the real world, the scientist who functions at stage four is ready to change his own methods of thinking as he keeps experiencing himself in transaction with the world. In fact, he has no set beliefs but only a human-made structure of postulates that he accepts as a workable system of assumptions for guiding him in the conduct of his life as an individual and as a member of any group, large or small, to which he is conscious of belonging.

If we compare stage two to stage three, we see that the first was just a rough sketch, an oversimplification of the order of nature, a reduction—to a static picture—of the dynamic processes of the world. Stage three, in its turn, is now revealed to be an oversimplification of a human being's relation to the world and to herself. The concept of a "reality out there," of which a human is a detached observer, and which she explores and controls with an ever-increasing wisdom, must yield to much more abstract conceptions. The "laws" of nature that we mathematically formulate deal not with nature itself but with our knowledge of nature, with our relating ourselves with nature. "There is no quantum world," Niels Bohr is reported to have said; "there is only an abstract quantum description. It is wrong to think that the task of physics is to find out how nature *is*. Physics concerns itself with what we can *say* about nature."[4]

As a consequence, language—or any system of symbolization that we use—becomes central again, as it was in the days when Aristotle created his language-derived logic and metaphysics, but this time with the important difference that we are now aware of the situation thus created. We now know that "we are suspended in language," as Bohr would say. We know that the structure of our human world is the structure of the postulates our language presents to us; we know that it could be any alternate structure that another language presents to members of a different culture; and, finally, we know that it could be any alternate structure that we might create as we transform the world with our technological inventions.

[3]Wendell Johnson, *People in Quandaries* (New York: Harper & Row, 1946), p. 45.
[4]Reprinted from "The Philosophy of Niels Bohr," by Aage Petersen, with permission, from the September 1963 issue of the *Bulletin of Atomic Scientists*. Copyright 1963 by the Educational Foundation for Nuclear Science, Inc.

Yes, our verbalizing creates difficulties that a change in verbalizing could remove. In stage four, we are flexible in that regard; we do not have to stick to one kind of verbalizing as if it were the only accurate picture of the situation. We should not change the wording as a mere trick for fooling ourselves or the other person; we should change it and accept the new terms as a possibly valid alternative to an objective description. This is what physicists do when they view the atomic nucleus through the shell model, the liquid-drop model, or the visual model. Each model serves a purpose, and shifting from one model to another makes it possible to solve problems that the original model could not encompass.

Stage four is the stage where we learn to be independent of mental categories, "accurate" words, and exclusive theories. It is a preparation and often results in creative acts. The great discovery that ushered in stage four is the awareness of our self-reflexiveness, or the way we experience our experiencing, being self-reflexively aware of what goes on in our semantic transactions. It could be described as the awareness of our awareness itself.

We have at last understood that our mental constructs, linguistic or mathematical, are not images of an "objective" world, they are mirrors of ourselves looking at the world. Objectivity, as we took it to be, has now disappeared. Rational absolutes are crumbling. We are actually in the throes of a rebirth to a new form of human life the like of which history has never seen. Reason and rationality have reached their limits, and we are aware of this; proud dogmatism has to make room for humble uncertainty; predictability becomes possibility with an unmeasurable margin of unknowns.

At the present time it is among natural scientists (turned philosophers and epistemologists) that this discovery is most often discussed and commented upon. Here is how one of them, Werner Heisenberg, describes what led to this discovery.

> Profound changes in the foundations of atomic physics occurred in our century which lead away from the reality concept of classical atomism. It has turned out that the hoped-for objective reality of the elementary particles represents too rough a simplification of the true state of affairs and must yield to much more abstract conceptions. When we wish to picture to ourselves the nature of the existence of the elementary particles, we may no longer ignore the physical processes by which we obtain information about them. When we are observing objects of our daily experience, the physical processes transmitting the observation of course play only a secondary role. However, for the smallest building blocks of matter every process of observation causes a major disturbance; it turns out that we can no longer talk of the behavior of the particle apart from the process of observation. In consequence, we are finally led to believe that the laws of nature which we formulate mathematically deal no longer with the particles themselves but with our knowledge of the elementary particles. . . . Natural science always presupposes man, and we must become aware of the fact that, as

Bohr has expressed it, we are not only spectators but also participants on the stage of life.[5]

This does away with self-evident truths, with axioms as we learned them in Euclidian geometry, with shared perceptions that are supposed infallibly to bring about agreement. Whether we know it or not, our most obvious observations and our most solid and lasting knowledge have grown from a set of postulates.[6]

The highest achievement of our rational mind, when it reaches the postulating stage four of today's science, is to acknowledge its own limitations. No formulation that we can devise is 100 percent valid; no truth as we conceive it is *the* truth. As a consequence, we are ready to accept that, when dealing with a single phenomenon or a simple situation, we may use two descriptions and explanations that appear utterly different if not contradictory. For instance physicists may speak of light as the result of waves of energy or of showers of particles; philosophers may account for human behavior in terms of strict determinism or of its opposite, freedom of choice. Their relation of mutual exclusion is brought to a higher order of abstraction and this is called complementarity.

This does not mean that our mind is blank, or that we are uncommitted and without a philosophy of life. We make choices, we adhere to certain values, and we observe certain rules and regulations in our thinking, but, at the same time, we are aware that our choices may change as our experience of life accumulates, that our value system may expand to include what we formerly rejected, and that our methods of thinking may reach new orders of dimensionality. We are ready to use definite mental models to form within ourselves a mental picture of the world; we manipulate these models according to the rules of the system to which they belong; and we interpret them and draw conclusions that we translate into policies, plans, and actions. But we are not, for all this, deceived into believing that what we see could not be seen differently, what we understand could not be explained otherwise, and what we consider the proper thing to do could not be done in a different manner.

This freedom of interpretation and choice in the transverse direction of our march forward goes with the freedom of jumping ahead of the well-organized body of pioneers who keep advancing at the slow tempo of in-

[5]Reprinted from "The Representation of Nature in Contemporary Physics," by Werner Heisenberg. Reprinted by permission of *Daedalus*, Journal of the American Academy of Arts and Sciences, Boston, Mass., Summer 1958, *Symbolism in Religion and Literature*.

[6]Many passages in this book demand, on the part of the reader, more than cursory reading. This is doubly true of the statements concerning self-reflexiveness. Here we reach the vital nexus of what makes general semantics and epistemics totally different from the sciences mentioned above in stage three. I suggest several periods of meditation spaced over several days.

stitutionalized culture. We make use of available knowledge, but we are free to go beyond it (at our personal risk) to search deeper, to seek higher viewpoints, and to act as scouts who suggest to the main group of explorers where there might be a possible breakthrough. We become suspicious of the value of rigorous thinking along well-established channels.

> The creative order is not an elaboration of the established, but a movement beyond it, or at least a reorganization of it and often of elements not included in it. The first need is therefore to transcend the old order. Before any new order can be defined, the absolute power of the established, the hold upon us of what we know and are, must be broken.[7]

What such an orientation could achieve at all levels of human relations, from the life of the married couple to the forum of the United Nations, we can only surmise. Our philosophy of life, limited by the still-undeveloped human sciences, has not yet begun to renovate itself as our outlook on the physical world has been doing for the last two generations. One of the purposes of general semantics is to help people function more often and more easily at stage four. It takes time, but it proves to be an exhilarating experience.

The important thing to know and take into account is that refined rationality and elaborate induction are *not* the sources of creativity; but this does not mean that creativity is born of ignorance—quite the opposite. A great deal of preparation is necessary to equip oneself for an excursion into the not-yet-surveyed regions of a particular field of knowledge. This requires work—good, honest, pedestrian work. "Genius is a long patience," said Pasteur; and, to paraphrase Edison, "It takes more perspiration than inspiration."

We have to observe, explore, experiment, and learn if we are to make the fine differentiations that escape the casual observer. Then, and then only, are we ready to take the risk of entering the world of the unknown and to make sense of our experience in that world. It is like going into Antarctica, or climbing Mt. Everest, or piloting the X-15. We have to profit from the experience of those who preceded us and make use of the information they have gathered, yet be ready to take chances beyond what they ventured.

Because we take it for granted that the object of our observations, thoughts, constructs, is "out there" for us to see and theorize about; we miss the fact that the original singling out of the object is an act of our own choice and creation. The choice may not be entirely personal and conscious, it may be determined (in part) by the culture in which we were reared, by the purposes we have set ourselves, or by the circumstances in which we happen to be; but it is our choice in the sense that we could, if we wanted, abstain

---

[7]Brewster Ghiselin, *The Creative Process* (New York: Mentor Books, [New American Library], 1955), p. 14.

from it or make a different choice. For instance, if I say "I accept such-and-such a theory because it sounds sensible to me," I am actually choosing a particular theory because it fits with the "growing tip" of my experience. It is the "natural" expansion of what I am at the moment, as the flower in spring is the natural development of the bud on the branch of the tree, as the fruit is the natural expansion of the flower that disappears in producing it.

At stage four, the growing realization of choice makes the creative process central to everyday human functioning. Innovating becomes integral to the life cycle of cultures and individuals. This means that out of the experience and knowledge of an individual, his or her acquired semantic state at a date, emerges a new untested idea, a postulate that seems plausible. This is a creative act using the "material" of the individual's total life experience. The process of shaping the postulate is called abduction.

Next comes deduction that infers a pattern of planning consistent with these postulates in order to test them. This leads to experimenting by carrying out the previously arranged plans. Here, "experience" and "experiment" become synonomous. At a certain point in the experiment or experience, through a process of induction, we interpret what we have observed; we check our results.

Finally, we evaluate what we have been through, including the interpreted results, and see how our original set of postulates held up. They are either confirmed for the time being, or they may be corrected in order to plan a new cycle of experiments. Or, the postulates may prove to be inadequate for the purposes involved; in such a case, a new process of abduction is called for—a new creative act.

The experience of going through this cycle brings about a differently structured semantic state. The total life experience of the individual is renewed; this renewal is a structural more that increases the complexity of the person's wisdom. I put it this way in another of my books:

> As this renewed and enriched wisdom rises to a higher level of organized complexity, the creative loop (postulating-planning-experimenting-interpreting) bends in the time dimension and becomes the spiral of human cultural advance, or personal and cultural evolution.[8]

We will now examine in a bit more detail the creative process from which our postulates emerge.

Precreative Excitement and Confusion

Creative science involves the whole person, and so does creative learning; both experiences run along parallel lines. To make advances that de-

[8]J. Samuel Bois, *Epistemics: The Science-Art of Innovating* (San Francisco: International Society for General Semantics, 1972), p. 5.

serve to be recognized as creative, a scientist has to free himself or herself from the hold of the theories that are generally accepted in the cultural environment. To make personal advances in knowledge that deserve to be called creative learning, an individual has to be free from the hold of theories that have been uncritically accepted, from the hold of assumptions that often disguise themselves as common sense. Too often, we do the reverse: when we read or hear a theory that is new to us, we quickly pooh-pooh it if it appears to challenge some of our commonsense notions.

In the creating process there is a stage of confusion, of groping, of trial and error that is not always described when scientists and inventors report on their insights and discoveries. We are apt to think that they have passed suddenly from the pitch-dark of not-knowing to the bright midday sun of clear understanding. We still believe in magic, in miracles. This is not the way things really happen.

> Creation begins typically with a vague, even confused excitement, some sort of yearning, hunch, or other preverbal intimation of approaching or potential resolution. . . .Production by a process of purely conscious calculation seems never to occur.[9]

There is a corresponding stage in the process of learning. It is a stage during which we cannot clearly describe what it is that has stirred up our interest and created in us a state of excitement, expectation, and confusion. When I read *Science and Sanity* for the first time there was very little of it that I could accept consciously; in fact, the few statements that stood out in my conscious memory were those that flatly contradicted some ideas of mine that seemed basic and uncontrovertible (the principle of nonidentity was one). Yet I was stirred to the very depths of my sense of truth and values. The quotation from Ghiselin's *The Creative Process* perfectly describes the condition in which I found myself if we replace "creation" by "new understanding," and "production" by "learning." It would then read as follows: "New understanding begins typically with a vague, even confused excitement, some sort of yearning, hunch, or other pre-verbal intimation of approaching or potential resolution. . . .Learning by a process of purely conscious calculation seems never to occur."

Because we ignore this unavoidable phase of confusion that marks the first stage of real learning, we mismanage our learning experiences and we mismanage those of others. We expect learning to be a conscious process, a collection of new, well-differentiated items that we can show to inquirers who ask to see them—or that we can store up in compartments of our memory, from which we can pull them out at will.

We may have heard a lecture or read an essay that has stirred us deeply. If we are asked—or ask ourselves—immediately afterwards "What are the

[9]Ghiselin, *The Creative Process*, p. 14.

main points of what was said?", we feel embarrassed when we cannot give a clear-cut answer. We blame ourselves for having let ourselves be carried away by enthusiasm, feeling, idealism, or what-have-you, which is considered very bad form in our logic-worshiping culture, and we crush without compunction that delicate and precious link in the chain of learning reactions that was just beginning to form a living sequence. Because we do not accept the state of "imaginative muddled suspense" (as Whitehead calls it) that precedes successful creation and creative learning, we fail to reach the final stage of transformation and confirmation in new knowledge and belief.

I have seen the same disregard of this unrecognized phase of creative learning snuff out a whole program of executive development. The vice-president of a large corporation had been sent to a workshop I was conducting on Executive Methods (which is nothing but up-to-date epistemology applied to administrative work) for the purpose of evaluating whether the top staff of the company should go through that program of training. He was a well-informed person, very bright, and capable of feeling the impact of such a workshop, but, when the session was over, he was in that period of vague and confused excitement, of preverbal readjustment of his ideas and values, so that he could not yet translate his experience into clear-cut formulations.

His superior, the president of the corporation, who had great respect for his vice-president's intelligence and judgment in matters of this kind, but who had never suspected that creative learning involves a stage of mental confusion that is often allied to an unexplainable emotional condition, asked the vice-president for a quick and short report on "what this course could do for the company, what problems it could help solve, and how."

This time the vice-president, who was known to respond with clear-cut answers when asked such questions in matters of his competence, felt that he could not come out with a "one-two-three" type of report. He had been so stirred by the experience of the workshop that he was still in that initial stage of confusion and suspense (which he had not anticipated, and which, to a better-informed observer, would have been indicative of an impending revolution of his inner world of knowledge and values).

His answer to his chief was: "It was a very stirring experience, but I cannot at this moment tell you exactly how it could be applied to any specific problem of ours." "Well," said the president, "if a man of your knowledge and experience cannot see its practical application to any of our problems, I don't see how others, less well-prepared than you are, could profit from it. Let us forget about it."

Had the president known that creative learning is not simply adding to what we already know, that it is not the extension of the well-established but an expansion beyond it, that it involves initial disturbance and hesitation, he would have recognized that his vice-president's reaction was a strong indication that—for a man of his caliber to report such an unusual disturbance—he might have hit upon something of unexpected but real value. The president had never learned that there is a wide difference between rote learning and creative learning.

The same fallacy of expecting clear-cut, measurable results from a creative learning experience lies behind the tests of comprehension that are inserted in a course of rapid reading as a check of the progress achieved. If we comprehend and remember a high percentage of what we have just read, it is a sure sign that our reading was not of the order of creative learning. It was additive learning, it was inserting new facts in a classification system already established, it was filling in compartments already made in our memory warehouse. It was not creative learning, not a revamping of our classification system, not a reorganization of our store of knowledge, not a reshuffling of what we know and what we are.

There are many praiseworthy attempts to foster creative thinking in business and in the professions, and I am all for them. I find something good in all these efforts, from the occasionally childish game of brainstorming to the more sophisticated practices of group dynamics, role-playing, socio-drama, and the like. Some of them are very impressive, and they sometimes achieve results that are really spectacular. It is the function of epistemological research to determine the operative process in the various practices that accounts for the results. Once this process has come to light, we could make training in creativity part of our normal curriculum at the college level, or its equivalent in adult education and business training.

Semantic Psychoanalysis

It is relatively easy to accept the fact that the same word may trigger different semantic reactions in different persons. The dictionary meaning of a word is only an approximation of what the word has been taken to mean up to the time the dictionary was published. Being an "average," it does not apply exactly to every use of the word—no more than, say, the average height of a ten-year-old boy applies to every boy of that age in the neighborhood. Every word that we use has a meaning-to-me value at the time and under the circumstances that we use it. We saw this illustrated in Figure 4.1, p. 41. This value may vary from one situation to another, but the variations usually remain within a recognizable pattern. If I can make that pattern visible, it will give me a picture of what the word means to me. By comparing my pattern of meaning with yours, we may come closer to an understanding, perhaps to agreement. Or we shall be able to determine more accurately how and why we disagree.

To bring out this pattern of the meaning relation between a word and its user is the purpose of what Gaston Bachelard called *semantic psy-*

choanalysis. It has nothing in common with psychoanalysis as it is known in psychiatry—classical Freudian, neo-Freudian, Jungian, Adlerian, or whatever—and it does not deal with the subconscious, with complexes, fixations, repressions, and such things. It deals primarily with *thinking*, not with *feeling* activities, but it does not exclude feeling activities (which, as we have seen, are an undetachable aspect of our total semantic transaction). A second difference is due to the fact that it does not deal with neurosis and such conditions, but with our "normal" behavior. It endeavors to bring out the relative degree of wisdom of our habitual thought process.

We could compare semantic psychoanalysis to spectral analysis, a well-known procedure in the physical sciences where it has achieved spectacular success. It started some three hundred years ago when Issac Newton performed an experiment, which he reported in his *Opticks*. He saw what he called "a colored image of the sun" like a rainbow on the wall opposite the closed window through which a narrow beam of light was allowed to enter. Newton's original experiment was the beginning of a development that has reached a high degree of refinement and usefulness today.

Our study of the semantic spectrum is three hundred years behind our discovery of the spectrum of light—and some may now maintain that the former is a false start. It may be, but I am ready to give it up only if something more promising presents itself. I have used it in clinical work, in business, and in philosophical investigations, and others have also used it, and I know of no adverse reports.

Although our techniques of semantic analysis are still primitive, we are beginning to discover the main areas of the semantic spectrum. Bachelard suggests five areas, which we call the sensing, the classifying, the relating, the postulating, and the participating stages of human development. We are far from the measurement of anything that might correspond to the Angstrom units of the color spectrum, but, crude as it is, the procedure is already a significant advance. It shows that, despite their appearance of homogeneity, our most common mental constructs are made of elements that do not always form a balanced whole.

When we say that we are biased, would it not be interesting to be able to measure in what direction and to what extent? When we say that we see through rose-color glasses, would it not be good to evaluate the tint of these glasses in terms of psychological wavelengths? When we put together, in one semantic transaction, the blind impulsiveness of the primitive, the dogmatism of the medieval thinker, the critical attitude of the experimenter, and the indeterminacy described by Heisenberg, how can we determine which of these four elements dominates this assemblage? Perhaps we may find why some twentieth-century humans may suddenly indulge the barbarous pleasure of snuffing out an enemy's life with a nuclear bomb, whereas their primitive ancestors used a rock in the stone age. Until we have learned to differentiate these very dissimilar ranges, we shall find it difficult to manage ourselves and almost impossible to manage world events, which may mean the end of humankind as a whole.

The idea is to examine the thinking aspects of some of our basic semantic reactions—Bachelard calls them our "concepts"—and see how they are distributed on the semantic spectrum or epistemological profile: from the infrared of sensing to the ultraviolet of participating.

Bachelard did not speak much of a semantic spectrum, nor did he insist on the analogy of spectral analysis. He reported his finding of his semantic analysis of two terms familiar to him in his profession, matter and energy. On histograms where the highest bar represents the most frequent level of semantic transaction, he revealed that stage three was dominant for him on both concepts. This meant that his personal development was mostly at stage three, although he could report of experiences at stages four and five. This relative frequency of experiences at different stages corresponds to what we call here stages of development. They remind us of what Korzybski calls semantic states. And we could describe them as types of responses that have hardened into habits not easy to change.

Some Examples of Semantic Analysis

Let us begin with a simple example from life. Suppose you say "My boy is a problem to me." Let us analyze your semantic response to *problem*.

If the term, or the situation, makes you anxious, puzzled, or uneasy, and that seems to be as far as you can go with it, you are marooned at stage one. You have not started to think; you have let your uncritical, unconditioned reaction to the word *problem*—and to the situation thus labeled—dominate your organism. Value terms such as "It is awful," "It is terrible," "Oh, my God!" may well come out as verbal responses. You may shiver, sweat, cry, become fidgety and distracted. You may reach for a tranquilizer, or for a drink if you have a propensity for that type of relief.

At stage two, however, you begin to think. You make an attempt to classify the problem and the boy. You look for *the* cause of the trouble. You ask yourself *why*, expecting to find behind that *why* the *what*-to-do. You look for *the* solution, a clearcut, radical solution. You may ask yourself such questions as: "Is he lazy?" "Is he going with bad companions?" "Did he resent what the teacher told him yesterday?" "Is he neurotic?" Or, if your mind is already made up about the boy, you may interpret what happened as a proof of what you already think of him.

At stage three, you begin to realize that things are not so simple; many factors might be involved in the situation. You may ask yourself: "What is going on at home, at school, or elsewhere that may have some connection with the present situation?" "What is he heading for in his own expectations?" "What went on last week, last month, or in recent years?" You do not see this human problem as similar to an arithmetic problem in which the data are definite and there is only one correct answer. You think in terms of relations, of a balance among various determinants, and you choose to act upon whichever one is within your reach and likely to influence the situation for the better.

At stage four, you become aware that you are part of the problem-in-process. You are the only factor over which you have immediate control. To solve the problem becomes, for you: "How shall I manage myself as I transact in this situation, doing my very best and hoping for the best?" You are ready to look at the situation as the boy sees it, knowing full well that there are many possible versions to the story.

The original and staple meaning of *problem* disappears at stage four. Instead of being "the problem of the boy," which you could observe and solve in an "objective" manner, the situation has become a complex, interrelated cluster of events, things, and persons of which, you discover, you are one. This is where relativity comes into play: every situation forms a gestalt, a configuration, that is different for each participant and that involves a different participation from each. At stage four, Whitehead's statement becomes a necessity.

> The old foundations of scientific thought are becoming unintelligible. Time, space, matter...structure, pattern, function, etc., all require reinterpretation....If science is not to degenerate into a medley of *ad hoc* hypotheses, it must become philosophical and must enter a thorough criticism of its own foundations.[10]

If science must undertake a thorough criticism of its own foundations, what shall we say of plain common sense? What shall we say of our everyday language, and of its subject-predicate structure that dates back centuries before even classical science was born? The function of semantic psychoanalysis is precisely this: by revising our thinking models, it brings our semantic transactions in tune with the world that our technology has created.

Let us take another example and analyze a word that is often used in public discussions: *leader* or *leadership*.

At stage one we have the charismatic leader, who is appointed by "the gods" or anointed in some religious ceremony to become the head of a state, a church, or a group. This type of leadership is still accepted as valid in many institutions, although the degree of acceptance will vary, of course. The queen of England is formally anointed in the coronation service; she is the head of the nation "by the grace of God," but she does not rule. The Pope,

---

[10]Alfred North Whitehead, *Science and the Modern World* (New York: Cambridge University Press, 1933), p. 21.

another charismatic leader, has effective quasi-legal powers over his subjects. Modern dictators have also assumed this type of leadership; Lenin, for example, is glorified as such a leader in a burial monument that reminds us of the Egyptian pharaohs.

The stage-two leader is different; he or she represents the "objective"—and later the "scientific"—view of the characteristics of a born leader. Studies of whether he or she is intellectually bright or dull, a glib talker or a silent schemer, tall or short, healthy or sickly, emotionally balanced or slightly neurotic, are legion. They were continued during World War II for the purpose of selecting the most promising candidates for positions of responsibility, but many of these studies contradicted one another. We can recognize this thinking and purpose in such questions as "What makes an *ideal* student...an *ideal* teacher...an *ideal* marriage...an *ideal* parent?" These questions lead to a sharper definition of the ideas we form of a leader, a teacher, an ideal anything. They show our symbol-manipulating inventiveness and are no more real than the "snark" that Lewis Carroll created by combining the words *snake* and *shark*. They have no necessary connection with the actual performance of a leader, for example.

At stage three, the leader emerges from interactions between people and circumstances. We pass from leadership as a quality bestowed by the grace of God (stage one) or as a quality inborn in the individual (stage two) to leadership as a function, as a dynamic set of relations that operate at a certain moment in a certain situation. A corporation's organization chart may show that heads of divisions are formally appointed with well-defined authority and responsibility (stage one); they may have been selected and appointed because it was felt that their general ability, their work experience, and their "personality" fitted them for these positions of leadership (stage two); but the person who has the most telling influence on a particular decision may be far down the line or at a great distance to the right or to the left of the department concerned. The decisive influence may even lie outside the company; it may be a chance occurrence of minor events, none of which is intentionally set going by a leader or schemer. This brings us to stage four, where the notion of leadership evaporates in the thin air of probabilities.

I remember that once, when I was trying to introduce a new procedure in the Canadian army (where I was in charge of Research and Information), my long-prepared and tested scheme never reached the desk of the minister of national defense. His awareness of the problem and his decision in the matter were brought about by an article he happened to read in the *Readers' Digest* on a trip from Montreal to Ottawa.

Here we see that the rather primitive notions of leader and leadership do not apply, and we can better describe what happened by using another term. The term that is popular today is *decision-making*, the pinpointed meeting of energy vectors at the proper time and the proper place that sparks the decision event.

This makes us realize that the personality or the action of the leader is not necessarily part of the decision-making process. The leader concept may apply to stages one, two, and three in face-to-face situations, and, even then, the decision that we credit to a particular leader may well be only a critical point in the multidimensional network of vectors that unfolds itself under our eyes. In other words, the "time had come" for that procedure to be introduced in the Canadian army. Many chains of events—all unknown to me—were leading to it, but the chain that brought about the decision was not the one on which I had worked. If it had been, I might have been given more credit for the result than I actually deserved.

Let us apply this scheme of analysis to *communication,* as a word and as a process. We shall see, then, how this analytic technique spreads, deepens, heightens, and expands—in several directions—the standard definition in the dictionary: "Communication is the imparting of thoughts, opinions, or information by means of speech, writing, or signs."

At stage one, communication has not reached the level of explicit exchange of thoughts or information. It resembles the spinal reflex: the brain is short-circuited and the discriminating power of the cortex is not called into action. This type of communication may be described as either ritualistic or explosive, but in both cases it is meaningless in the sense that what is really meant or intended has no logical relation to what is being said or expressed.

Here is an example of the ritualistic type. You say "Good morning! How are you?" and I answer, "Fine, thank you!" Did you actually mean to inquire about my health, and do I feel that I should inform you about it? Of course not; what is meant is something like mutual recognition. You said "I am paying attention to you and I expect you to do the same." My answer was "Very well, I understand and I agree." When a salesgirl calls an old lady, "honey," the "sweetness" of the message is bland. When we write "Dear Sir" at the beginning of a letter and "Sincerely yours" at the end, we do not commit ourselves to any kind of affection or subservience, and our recipient knows it.

Strictly speaking, this type of communication is false to facts, but only sticklers for accuracy show concern for the falsehood. Yet, there may be cases where the ritualistic formula reacts upon its user and dampens spontaneity. You cannot say "Mr. President," "Your Majesty," or "Your Holiness" to the bearers of these titles without feeling a psychological distance between you and them. The parliamentary practice of calling an opponent "The honorable member from so-and-so" helps maintain decorum in verbal fights.

I also consider as a stage-one communication the polite chit-chat of casual social encounters in which one is expected to be pleasant, to avoid embarrassing silent spells, and to make conversation but to say nothing of significance. Some call it an art; to me it looks more like verbal doodling to avoid boredom or embarrassment.

Stage-one communication may be explosive as well. It is then an outburst of feelings in statements that are peppered with value terms, uttered rapidly in a high-pitch voice. It happens when we give the other fellow a piece of our mind, or bawl him out, or tell him off. No doubt this relieves the sender of the pressure of his feelings, but whether it delivers a message that the recipient accepts or profits by is another matter. If we cannot make ourselves understood in a foreign country, we repeat our English-worded message in a louder voice or we articulate it with determined emphasis. In a discussion, we can hardly wait for "our turn" to burst into speech; we interrupt the other person and trip him up with rhetorical questions. If a lecturer invites comments from the audience, we jump up and ask a question that is nothing but a thinly veiled revelation of a personal problem or an attempt to show off. These and similar instances of so-called communication are nothing but the uncontrolled semantic reactions of an individual who is concerned with herself, her feelings, and her set of personal values, and who wants the rest of the world to satisfy her need for approval, recognition, or domination.

At stage two, the message itself becomes the focus of attention. We want it to do justice to what we mean, to give the recipient a clear-cut picture of what we have in mind. We look for the right and the telling word; we take lessons in public speaking or in the dramatic arts to learn how to modulate our voice, how to pause at the psychological moment, how to gesticulate effectively, how to arouse the emotions of our listeners. In a written message we observe the rules of Rudolph Flesch or of the *Elements of Style;* and we make sure that the layout of our typewritten page brings out the salient points of our argument. We watch over the display of our printed announcements or our advertising copy. We use flip charts and the flannel board, and we draw diagrams. In a dialogue, both discussants may use such a procedure as role reversal to make sure that their statements interlock without a gap—like the pieces of a neatly cut jigsaw puzzle. The idea is that the more sharply defined the pieces and the better structured the message, the better the communication. That there is value in such practices, nobody can deny, but to take them as the crowning refinement of the art of communication is to reduce a living experience to the mechanical matching of cut-and-dried statements.

At stage three, one realizes that it is not sufficient to make his message a clear-cut picture of what he wants to transmit, it must also fit the requirements of the recipient; it must be in accord with his interests, his purposes, his attitudes, his knowledge, and his mental capacity. We then see communication as a process of relations, where the role of the receiver is no less important than that of the sender. We secure as much information as we can about the prospect we are going to meet. Once with him, we make him talk, make him say yes to noncommittal questions and thus induce in him a receptive mood. In a group, we invite suggestions from the audience, we write their statements on the board, we warm up our listeners with quick-fire questions that require simple answers, we set up role-playing skits, we break the large audience into "buzz groups" where individual members will have a better chance to participate and become involved, and we have them answer questionnaires, fill in forms, and write their impressions on slips of paper. The main purpose is not to commit ourself to take so many discordant views into account; it is to involve the listeners, to stir them up, to make them think, to bring them out of a state of passivity.

Stage-three communication also covers the case of the salesgirl who offers us a piece of sausage in the supermarket "just to have a taste of it," of the salesman who brings an "improved" vacuum cleaner to our house and invites us to vacuum our rugs with it, of the auto salesman who hands us a car key and suggests that we take a test drive, of the skillful lawyer whose relentless questioning extracts from a reluctant witness the evidence he is looking for. This communication is tailor-made to an individual, a group, or an audience whose interests have been evaluated by the best available means and whose participation in the interchange is taken as of prime importance.

Stage two paid attention to the "sending end" of the communication; stage three concentrates on the "receiving end." Stage three involves training in the art of listening. It also involves the art of reading—not necessarily at a high speed but at a pace in which the difficulty of the subject matter and the capacities and circumstances of the reader are set in harmonious balance. It brings to bear on the communication process the resources of many sciences and technologies.

Stages two and three are in keeping with the dictionary definition of communication, and they remain within the Aristotelian system. They also agree with the mechanical mode of thinking including certain types of feedback that is still prevalent in our most highly rated logical activities. There is a sender, a message, and a receiver. The message is like a package of information, thoughts, and opinions that is neatly wrapped and then passed on from sender to receiver. It is a matter of doing something to somebody by the use of words, signs, and symbols. These are psychological tools that one learns to manipulate with skill. Communication is what one does with words and what they do to us.

At stage four, communication assumes an entirely different form. Instead of being similar to an exchange of goods between two independent dealers, it becomes a vital transaction in which both participants feel involved to the very depths of their innermost selves.

To enter into communication is to enter a dynamic process that engulfs both the sender and the receiver, and from which they may emerge in a condition that neither can foresee nor control. It is the encounter of two semantic transactors who hold their thoughts, values, attitudes, and purposes, their past experiences, their present feelings, and their anticipations of the future in sensitive contact. The success of the entire undertaking will depend not so much upon their readiness to reach a detached objective understanding as upon their willingness to accept whatever change this joint experience might bring about in their respective outlooks on life and their ensuing behavior.

The communicator, aware that her "map" does not represent all the "territory," gives opinions that are open-ended; the communicatee listens with all the welcoming attention that she can muster, realizing that to evaluate what she is told she has to internalize it to some extent. Both see themselves as learners in the sense that they are ready to accept the lesson of this unrehearsed experience—the probability being, of course, that the better-informed, better-prepared, and more experienced of the two will derive more personal enrichment from the encounter.

In many instances the communication process is an intimate intercourse, as when we deal with values and feelings that lay bare the most sensitive parts of our unprotected self. The more intimate the contact, the more likely, if it is not properly handled, that it will cause bruises that may make more precarious subsequent relationships. It may also, when managed with skill and mutual respect, create a stronger bond of reciprocal appreciation and trust. Stage-four communication transcends the techniques of pure logic—Aristotelian and two-valued, or modern and multivalued. It is a phenomenon of psycho-logics, where feelings, values, and purposes have to blend in agape—mutual trust.

In the stage-four type of communication between a speaker and an audience, the speaker will of course observe the rules of stages two and three, doing his best to present a clear message in terms that the audience will understand and accept. The main concern, however, will go beyond the technical aspects of performance, it will focus on his own overall attitude and behavior. The important thing is for the speaker to relive the experience he had when what is now being expounded became a discovery, insight, and fresh learning experience for the speaker as an individual.

The members of the audience join in the speaker's experience of discovery; the occasion is an experiment in listening. For the time being, they let their minds harbor ideas that may appear strange or even threatening; they keep their perturbances subdued when their most cherished values are challenged; they forgo, for a while, as much as they can, their need for semantic security. They are not simply permissive, for permissiveness, like tolerance, implies an attitude of superiority over the other person, who is allowed to rave and ramble. They are ready to question their own views and to give credit to the speaker for superior information and wisdom on the topic he is discussing. It is only after the entire experiment is completed that they resume their semantic autonomy—either confirmed in their previous stand or enriched by the insights they have obtained while listening.

Our mental constructs are not limited to a particular stage; most of the time they are a mixture of thinking models that belong to distant epochs in the history of Western culture. If we represent in a bar diagram the relative amounts of various types of thinking that enter into a particular concept, we would have Bachelard's epistemological profile, a picture of the spreads and peaks of our semantic transactions. This picture is not static, it varies from moment to moment. For example, I may be violently shaken at the first news of a personal disaster, and for a short moment my thinking may be dominated by a stage-one type of reaction, but I may regain my balance very quickly, particularly if I have trained myself in the practice of higher stages.

This training requires a conscious and constant effort at the beginning. It is a gradual ascent from the unconditional reactions of animals to the fully conditional behavior of humans who are intelligent and free. As we make that ascent, we have to pass through a period in which primitive doctrines and languages must be revised. Mathematics and physics have made great strides in recent years because they have abandoned the thinking methods of earlier stages; they have done away with the old elementalism and the two-valued semantics of stage two. In Chapter 19, we will discuss creative communication as an advanced practice. It is suggested as a preparation for stage five, the participating stage of development.

CHAPTER 11

a reformulation

A Reformulation of Objectivity

There are many prescriptions of common sense that very few people object to, particularly when they are supported by what is generally taken as science. Two of them are: (1) take facts into account, and (2) be realistic. Both have an assumption that is firmly rooted in our culture, and this assumption has two elements: (1) There is an objective reality "out there," around us or within us, and (2) It is desirable to conform our thoughts and behavior to that objective reality. If we ask ourselves what prevents us from seeing and accepting them as they are, the commonsense assumption, confirmed by the psychology that floats freely in our cultural atmosphere, is that we have needs and desires—possibly hidden from us—that make us react in an unrealistic manner.

There is some truth in this assumption, of course; it is in keeping with sound psychological thinking. Let us consult the *Comprehensive Dictionary of Psychological and Psychoanalytical Terms* by English and English (published in Longmans in 1958) for two definitions related to this subject.

Realism. An attitude of being sensitive to, and guided by, *things as they are,* rather than as *one wishes them to be.*

Irreality-reality dimension. A dimension along which behaviors can be ordered according to the degree to which they are *regulated by needs and desires,* on the one hand, and by *the objective situation* on the other.[11]

[11]English and English, *Comprehensive Dictionary of Psychological and Psychoanalytical Terms* (Longmans, 1958). Reprinted by permission of David McKay Co., Inc. (italics added).

On one side we have "things as they are," or "the objective situation"; on the other side we have "as one wishes they were," or "behaviors regulated by needs and desires." It is either realism or delusion, objectivity or wishful thinking.

Our previous study of the epistemological profile has warned us of the dangers of stage-two "either-or" thinking. We have become suspicious of explanations by unicausality, and we are looking for more than one explanation—in fact, for a limitless number of postulated explanations. We therefore ask ourselves: What else, apart from our needs and desires, could possibly account for our lack of "realism," for our reacting to things *as they are not?*

One answer is: Our *structured unconscious* has something to do with this. By structured unconscious I mean the complex network of methods of thinking-feeling-acting, the theories and doctrines that we have internalized more or less consciously all through life. Many of these are embedded in the language that we use in thinking, listening, and speaking. This structured unconscious is different from the subconscious of psychoanalysis; it is the sound and sane nonconscious of common sense. It stands as a filter between our inner self and our perceptions, our subconscious, and our supraconscious (Figure 11.1). We do not react to things as they are, we react to whatever our structured unconscious makes of our perceptions, of our subconscious drives and affects, of our supraconscious illuminations and insights.

Here is an example of how it transforms our perceptions and rules over our physiological reactions. Read—preferably aloud, and slowly—the following paragraphs.

> I am particularly fond of lemon juice. I enjoy sucking the juice of a really ripe lemon. It has such a clean, sharp taste. Last week, we went to the supermarket, my wife and I. As I walked past the fruit counter, I saw a pile of big, fresh, ripe, juicy lemons that appealed to me. I bought a dozen of them and put them in the shopping cart.
>
> When we came home, it was hot, and I yearned for the tart taste of lemon juice. We unpacked the groceries in the kitchen. I picked one of my lemons, held it in a plate, took the bread knife, and cut the lemon in two. I could see the juice oozing in clear yellow drops. I took one half, brought it to my mouth, and sucked the cool fresh juice with delight.

Now you may continue reading in silence. As you do, observe carefully what is happening to your salivary glands. If your mouth has a tendency to water, are you reacting to things as they are? Are you tasting lemon juice?

This, evidently, is not wishful thinking. To call his reaction a delusion is a bit too strong, suggestive of abnormal psychology, of neurosis or psychosis; but this reaction is a normal phenomenon. One way to account for it is to say that the words "lemon" and "juice" transacted with a structured unconscious that permeates your whole organism, and this transaction, like all semantic transactions, has its electrochemical aspect. If I had described the experience in a language that you do not understand, the response would not have taken place. It therefore seems legitimate to conclude that language had something to do with it.

The Structure of the World

One of Korzybski's favorite statements was "The only contents of knowledge is structure." He once gave me an objective lesson about it, and I think it is relevant to what we are now studying.

Driving back from New York to Montreal, I had stopped for a couple hours in Lime Rock, Connecticut, where he was living. When I came into his study, he was busy with a kaleidoscope. After the usual salutations, he put the instrument in my hands and told me: "Look!"

I had looked through kaleidoscopes so many times in my life that I was not ready to play with this one very long. I put my eye to it, aimed at the light of the window, and gave it a few turns. "It is just a kaleidoscope like any other," I said to myself; "it gives an eight-sided pattern to whatever happens to be in the end piece. What's this idea in putting me through this child's game?"

I put the instrument back on his desk and made an attempt to have him talk of something else, but he was not in a mood to talk about anything else; he was in a mood to put me through an experiment. He took the tube, removed the end piece, and reached for another one in a box that contained half a dozen more. After he had fitted the end piece, he handed the instrument back to me. "Look!" he said again.

I looked, turning the tube two or three times with my fingers. Same pattern, of course. What was the old man's purpose, I wondered. Was he getting senile? Or was it just plain cussedness, of which I suspected he had quite a bit. I put the kaleidoscope back on the desk. He grabbed it, put on another end piece, and handed it back to me with the same injunction: "Look! Look!"

I was getting annoyed; but, annoyed or not, I had to go through the performance a third time—and as many times as there were end pieces in the box. Then he showed me his collection of end pieces: one contained bits of macaroni; one was half full of tiny nuts and bolts; one had, of course, the usual assortment of colored glass, and so on. "Well, what do you say now?" he asked, as he lit another cigarette.

I did not say anything. I felt I had better stay at the silent level than burst into speech and give him a piece of my mind for those wasted twenty minutes.

He waited with a quizzical smile for what appeared to me a very long time—and a further waste of the precious minutes I had set aside to talk with him about serious matters. Then he took the kaleidoscope in his hands with deliberation, put the eyepiece near my face, and pointed his finger to the far end. Sententiously he grumbled: "Chaos *there*, structure *here!*"

I still did not understand, and I was too upset to try to appreciate the lesson, but on my way through the Adirondacks that night, it dawned on me. *The structure we see of the outside world is made by the instrument through which we look at the world!* This instrument is our structured unconscious.

Many people are convinced that, as science proceeds, we are learning to perceive better, and we are coming nearer and nearer the point where we shall be able to describe reality in very exact terms. They miss the fact that describing something is to distort it, shrink it, and betray it to some extent. All our contacts with the world around us are acts of abstraction, and a description is an abstraction from first-order experience.

Wittgenstein put it this way: "What can be shown cannot be said." Korzybski said it a bit differently: "Whatever you say it is, it is not." These two statements are diametrically opposed to the medieval definition of objective knowledge, the "equivalence of the mental image and of the thing it pictures." Korzybski developed his entire system from three premises that contradict the medieval view:

1. The map is not the territory;
2. The map does not represent all the territory;
3. The map is not a map of the territory but a map of the mapper himself in interaction with the territory.

The opposition of the two viewpoints is much more radical than appears at first sight; it took me many years to see how different they are, and I am at a loss to convey my experience with words. One way of becoming aware of it is to put side by side two meanings of a simple verb that forms the basic link in most of our propositional statements, the verb "to be." The stated "to be" and the existential "to be" are not of the same order; the first refers to what we say of a thing, the second belongs to the silent level. The first refers to a man-made situation, the second does not.

The central notion is that we have no way of determining whether the world is structured according to the pattern we ascribe to it. And, even if we could do this, our mental picture would not *be* the structure of the world; the two would always be of a different order of existence. In many cases our descriptions—or mental models—satisfy us fairly well as rough approximations, and we feel proud of ourselves when they do. A successful experiment does not prove that our hypothesis is right, it simply demonstrates that we have not yet brought its weak points to light. It says that what we construct in our mind has some resemblance with what the real world is like, but the trouble is that we never know how closely our thinking and the event fit in a particular case. There is always a margin of difference that we cannot even measure.

On one side is the "objective" situation; on the other side is the mental image we form of it. Which of the two guides our behavior, the situation itself or our mental image of it? The answer is clear: Our behavior is determined by what we believe the situation is, by the mental image we have of it. We act according to what we know, and we never know everything that could be known about any event in which we are involved. The part that we don't know may be the significant part, and, if we could become aware of it and accept it, it might change our semantic response completely.

If this is so, what is the difference between a normal human being who believes that the world is what he says it is and a mental patient who follows his delusions and hallucinations? The difference is not a difference in kind, it is merely a difference in degree. Neither mental image is 100 percent accurate. The percentage of the normal person is only higher than that of the mental patient.

As far as we know, the "is" of existence covers a limitless ocean of possibilities; the "is" of what we know and control is like a small volcanic island that has emerged from the boundless sea. "We are immersed in a world full of energy manifestations, out of which we abstract only a very small proportion."[12]

The Limits of Observation

If we draw a spectral band of the full range of known energy manifestations, we have at one end the very short high-frequency cosmic rays and at the other end the long low-frequency radio waves. In the center of this band is a small region of light and color that we can perceive with our eyes, the "peephole" through which we can observe what is going on around us. Compared to the full range of energy manifestations of which we know something, this peephole is very small indeed. What lies to the right and to the left of it was unknown to our great-great-great-grandparents; it was the world of the mysterious, which they interpreted with magic, mythology, or astrology. Today we have instruments with which to peer into the world of subtle energies that lies on both sides of our unaided vision. We have even harnessed some of these powerful energies and made them serve us: in X-ray machines, radar equipment, and other inventions.

Within the narrow range of visible light itself; it was only twelve generations ago that Newton started the analysis of white into its component colors. Until then, very few people suspected that the beautiful colors of the rainbow were sunlight spread out in the sky by its refraction in raindrops. From Newton's discovery a new science was born, spectroscopy, with which we can make a chemical analysis of distant stars and galaxies.

[12]Korzybski, *Science and Sanity*, p. 238.

Many other devices have sharpened our vision and made it penetrate into realms that formerly were closed to it. There are microscopes, electron microscopes, telescopes (with or without photographic plates), infrared photography, oscilloscopes, and so forth. We abstract from the world of cosmic energies more phenomena than our ancestors could; we know much more of what is going on in the physical world around us and within our bodies. The more we know, the better we realize that much more is left for us to discover (Figure 11.1).

Figure 11.1. The energy spectrum.

Looking at the physical world is a form of inspection in order to understand and manage the forces of nature. For ages, we have been engaged in another form of inspection, which is called introspection, or looking into ourselves. We introspect with the unaided eye of common sense. We observe our thoughts, our feelings, our emotions, our desires, our purposes, our frustrations, and our anxieties. We try to differentiate them, to understand them, and to manage them.

How broad is the band of human energies that we can observe with the unaided eye of common sense? How clearly can we differentiate within that narrow band? Not much, I think. In the psychological realm, we are just beginning to widen the range of our observations and to probe deeper within the limited band of introspection.

To visualize what I mean, let us imagine a spectral band similar to the one on which we spread the range of physical energy manifestations. The range of human energies goes all the way from the subconscious on the left, through the conscious in the center, and to the supraconscious on the right. Our commonsense introspection is limited to the middle range, that of the conscious (Figure 11.2). Within this conscious range, humans have tried for generations to probe in depth, to fathom the secrets of their own souls, to differentiate the currents and the whirlpools of activities that surge within people. To use the analogy of the spectroscope, humans meant to let the light of self-knowledge go through the prism of self-analysis and spread itself into a spectrum that they could differentiate and measure, from the ultraviolet of creative thinking to the infrared of feeling and emotion.

The prism for self-analysis is our language and the logic we derive from it. As Werner Heisenberg put it in speaking of the physical world: "We have to remember that what we observe is not nature itself, but nature exposed to our methods of questioning." We must remember that what we see in ourselves—reason, memory, feelings, drives, and needs—is not human nature in the raw but human nature seen through the lens of commonsense language, the structured unconscious. There are probably a great many manifestations of human energy that cannot be detected through this lens, just as the cosmic rays and the radio waves are invisible within the narrow band of sunlight covered by the spectroscope.

Within the conscious range, a flock of psychologists, linguists, cultural anthropologists, and sociologists are working hard to increase our awareness. I would compare them to the physical scientists who use the spectroscope and the microscope to penetrate the secrets of the molecule and the cell.

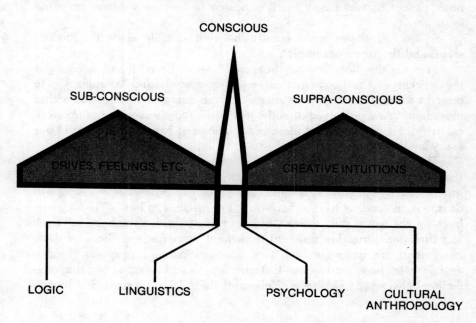

Figure 11.2. The semantic spectrum.

One of their early discoveries was that our language is a very imperfect instrument through which we look inside ourselves and report what we see. If we have no name for a phenomenon that occurs within us, we are apt to ignore it, or we describe it to ourselves so imperfectly that we miss its particular significance. If you go (and I strongly recommend that you do) to William James's classical *Principles of Psychology*, and read his chapter "The Stream of Thought," you will see how keenly aware he was of this difficulty.

> Suppose we try to recall a forgotten name. The state of our consciousness is peculiar. There is a gap therein, but no mere gap. It is a gap that is intensely active. . . . If wrong names are proposed to us, this singularly definite gap acts immediately so as to negate them . . . and the gap of one does not feel like the gap of another. . . . When I vainly try to recall the name of Spalding, my consciousness is far removed from what it is when I vainly try to recall the name of Bowles.[13]

Here is something within the range of the conscious, something that we can notice if we pay attention to it. Call it a gap, a movement of the mind in search of a memory that we feel is there; call it an attempt to recall, or what you will. None of these terms exactly describes what I am referring to; each is a figure of speech. Which term will eventually be accepted as the name of this particular phenomenon, I don't know. In the meantime, such an occurrence cannot be taken very much into account because we have no name for it.

So much for the conscious band. What of the outside bands, the subconscious and the supraconscious?

Freud is the pioneer who discovered/invented ways for us to consider the workings of subconscious drives, repressions, and complexes. He brought within the range of awareness human energies that operate within us without being perceived directly, just as the radio waves do in the physical world. His findings, and those of his followers, have become part of our everyday thinking.

There is a milling crowd of such elements of our semantic transactions that keep stirring within us anonymously. There are transactions that go unrecorded by our conscious mind. Some look to me like simple changes in direction, like indicators of a sharp turn. For instance, if I say, "He is clever, but . . .," the word "but" shows that I am going to back up or bend my track in a direction altogether different from what was expected. Some of these movements are not expressed; they are anticipations, purposes, hidden agendas, strivings, motivations that give a push and a pull to our thinking-feeling behavior. As George A. Kelly puts it: "A large proportion of human

---

[13]William James, *Principles of Psychology*, I (New York: Rinehart, Holt & Winston, 1950), p. 251.

behavior follows nameless channels which have no language symbols, nor any kinds of signposts whatsoever."[14]

These nameless channels operate as powerful controls upon our semantic transactions. They are outside the field of logic, because logic has to use symbols and words, and these phenomena have no names nor symbols by which they can be designated in a syllogism or an equation. Within this band of potential awareness are also the many ideas, principles, attitudes, and cultural determinants that we take for granted, that we do not question, that we accept as "essential" components of our human nature. It is the area of "of course" statements, of what we take as axioms of common sense, of basic principles that brook no contradiction.

Our structured unconscious is like a screen spread over the range of our awareness. We observe our transactional responses through that screen; we abstract only the bits and parcels of experience that are visible through it; we lump together disparate phenomena that our symbols fail to differentiate; we take as separate elements whatever our language dissects; and we order these elements and relate them to one another according to the structure of our syntax.

What appealed to me in general semantics is that it is an attempt *not* to take our language for granted, *not* to yield to the belief that there is a point-to-point correspondence between what we say we are and what we are in reality. By "what we say" I do not mean only what we say to others but also what we say to ourselves—what we think. It is not a question of sincerity or insincerity, it is a question of having no adequate symbols, and no adequate structure of symbols, to picture what is going on within ourselves. Some of us draw a picture in black and white; some take color pictures. Some register sharp details; some simply sketch a rough outline. None of us has yet mastered the skill of revealing, to himself or to others, the dynamic complexity and the throbbing tension of a single semantic transaction.

The third part of the psychological spectrum, the supraconscious, is veiled in an even greater secrecy. Many people believe in the supremacy of reason and logic and simply refuse to accept the existence of a supraconscious. For them, it is the realm of imagination, of sentimentality, of mysticism—if not a misty smog produced in the mental sky by the morbid exhalations of a repressed libido. For them, you are either sane, unsane, or insane. There is no room in their philosophy for the supersanity of creative scientists, artists, and genuine mystics.

I do not share these views, although I realize that we know very little about the supraconscious. What we know is not yet sifted from the dross of

[14]George A. Kelly, *The Psychology of Personal Constructs, I* (New York: Norton, 1955), p. 130.

allegories, figures of speech, or sententious statements that sound like co-
nundrums. Most of the time, those who strive to behave "scientifically" do
not welcome metaphors and generalities.

Science (with a capital S) has become the metaphysics of a great many
among us, and, when Science is made commensurate with strict logical rationality, we limit ourselves to a narrow range in the spectrum of self-knowledge. We interpret the standard definition, "Man is a rational animal," as a
complete description of what we are. "Rational" easily becomes the equivalent of "reasoning," and logical reasoning becomes the measure of what we
are ready to accept as human in the full sense of the word.

In the ages of faith there was a way out of this human-made prison. Most
people accepted rationality as the upper limit of human nature, but they also
accepted a whole realm of suprarational phenomena—an order of existence
beyond the reach of unaided human nature. This was the world of the supernatural. If "supernatural" means an unlimited world of untapped possibilities, I am ready to accept it. That this world has dimensions well beyond what we can imagine at the present stage of our development, I admit
as well. The thinking tools we know are probably inadequate for surveying
the world of the conscious, let alone the world of the supraconscious. We
have to create new tools as we proceed.

This is what chemists and physicists had to do as they penetrated deeper
and deeper into the atomic world. When they saw atoms as round balls with
hooks on them, they were using models that were too simple. These models
were borrowed from the world of the gross objects of common experience;
they did not belong to the world of the atom.

Later, chemists and physicists compared the atom of hydrogen to a simple planetary system. More complex atoms were compared to more complex
systems of a similar type. These analogies helped give results that the analogy of balls with hooks could not give.

Scientists eventually discovered that the planetary system model had
limits, and they invented other models, of a more abstract nature—some
expressible only in mathematical formulas. In the process, the term "atom"
became a misnomer. By etymology it means "unsplittable," and this was the
reason for its choice at the beginning; it was intended to be a descriptive
name for the ultimate particle of matter that would resist fractionation. We
now know, from experience, that atoms can be split, with a great release of
energy. But nobody seems to care about the contradiction that the unsplittable of the Ancients has become the fissionable of the Moderns. We accept
that what commonsense says it is, it is not.

When shall we question the "objective validity" of what we say of mind,
soul, personality, and such? The physical scientists would not have split the
atom if they had believed that it is what the word implied.

Science as a Human Enterprise

The story of Pygmalion falling in love with the ivory statue he had carved is a classical picture of man's idolatrous worship of his own creations. We forget that our institutions, our religions, and our sciences are human-made, and we eventually endow them with qualities and powers that are superhuman. We no longer claim that they have a supernatural origin and were revealed to us by some divinely appointed messenger, but we keep behaving toward them as if they were God-given and endorsed by God.

Of the idols that are so worshiped today, probably none holds such an exalted position as Science. I do not object to having a high regard for it provided we do not detach it entirely from its makers, human beings.

We are convinced that all problems can be eventually solved if we have the necessary personnel, equipment, and money. But this is an oversimplification and a generalization, although it is true that break-throughs have sometimes been achieved by concentrating the work of many experts in a chosen area (the production of the atom bomb is an example that nobody can deny). But it remains that there is something unpredictable in the advances of science. When the scientists go into the laboratory, they are very much like the fisherman who goes fishing. They may come out with a tremendous catch, or they may come out empty-handed. Science as it is lived by those who are in it bears little resemblance to science as seen by outsiders. When one of the most highly respected physicists of our generation, Professor Erwin Schrödinger, calls science a fashion of the time, we are so startled that we wonder if he is being facetious. But his statement, in a talk he gave to the Physics and Mathematics Section of the Prussian Academy of Sciences (February, 1932), is explicit: "Science is dependent on the fashion-able frame of mind of the epoch of which it forms a part."[15]

Of course, there are sciences and "sciences." In general, we acknowl-edge that the human sciences—the humanistic, behavioral, or social sciences—are greatly influenced by the culture in which they grow. But another class of sciences, the exact sciences—of which physics is the out-standing member—is considered free from subjectivity. It is claimed that the findings of the exact sciences are the same all over the world; they are not influenced by the political creed or the religion of the experimenter.

Why Experiments Are Made

The exact sciences are the sciences that Schrödinger—a physicist in the same class as Einstein, Bohr, de Broglie, and Dirac—said are a fashion of the time. He admits that experiments in the exact sciences have a high degree of

[15]Erwin Schrödinger, *Science, Theory and Man* (New York: Dover, 1957), p. 104.

objectivity (or "intersubjective testability")—which means that a physical experiment or observation will be the same for all observers if the conditions and the technical methods are the same—but *how many* of these experiments are carried out, and how many are *not* carried out that could or should be? A subjective choice is made right here. Science, in its totality, does not claim to give us the rounded picture of all reality, it gives us *a* picture of *some* reality, pictures of the segments of reality scientists have decided to study.

A thousand and one reasons, many of which are not scientific at all, cause scientists to perform certain experiments and not to perform others. Some experiments are not practicable until the appropriate techniques are available. What can today be done in Antarctica was not feasible in the days of Scott and Shackleton, and we could not send a man to the moon until we had (first of all) a booster that was powerful enough. There are also cases where the available finances determine what one can do; even if one of its citizens were the most creative genius of our times, a small and poor country could not build a cyclotron.

Many experiments have "suggested themselves" to scientists but have not been deemed interesting enough or sufficiently related directly to their actual undertaking. In some cases, a scientist may have felt that he knew what the results would be and that it would be a waste of time and money to check and verify.

Other experiments have been performed successfully, but were so in advance of the thinking of their time that they were not considered significant. Schrödinger cites the case of Grimaldi, whose experiments in the seventeenth century on the diffraction of light could be interpreted as the first demonstration of the indeterminacy principle, formulated by Heisenberg in 1927. At the time, however, nobody attached any importance to Grimaldi's experiments.

If a theory is diametrically opposed to what is generally accepted in the world of professional scientists, it has a very bad reception. In fact, it may be so disturbing to the official scientific community that some of its most respected representatives may forget their dignity and behave like the religious zealots of the ages of faith. An outstanding example of this type of aberration is the case of a book, *Worlds in Collision,* by Dr. Immanuel Velikovsky (published by Doubleday in 1950).[16]

Finally, we must remember that any advance depends on the data already available, and data, in turn, are the results of the work of previous generations. We therefore go back to the original decision of primitive people to begin a search for the understanding of nature's secrets.

---

[16]For the story of this incident, you may consult "The Sociology of Science" in the monthly periodical *Current* (February, 1964), or the sources mentioned in *Current: Harper's* (August, 1963) and the *American Behavioral Scientist* (September, 1963).

What was the purpose of primitive people when they made their first attempts at understanding nature? It was simple and practical: they wanted to survive; that is, to preserve what was already good in their way of life and to discover what could be better. Science is both conservative and creative. It has to be consistent with the common sense of the day, and it has to improve our condition. In other words, science does not exist for its own sake; it is a human enterprise with a practical purpose.

What of *pure* science? Is it not a disinterested search for the truth? Is it not born of pure curiosity, irrespective of the practical consequences? Yes, it is; but this search for truth is directed and sustained by the values that are important for the individual scientist. It is an attempt to translate into concrete terms what he or she considers to be of greatest importance. The choice of a field of research and the evaluation of findings are very much a matter of values.

Professor Schrödinger illustrates this in the following manner. Suppose you have just given a lecture on some research that you have completed and a colleague asks why you are making such a fuss about this particular topic.

> Then you will try to show all the connections your theme has with the others. You will try to defend your own interest in the matter. I mean that you will try to defend the reason why you are interested. Then you will probably notice that your feelings are much more ardently aroused than they were in the lecture itself. And you will become aware of the fact that only now, in your discussion with your colleague, have you reached those aspects of the subject that are, so to speak, nearest to your heart.[17]

"The aspects of the subject nearest to your heart"—didn't we discuss this earlier when we spoke of the cortex that intellectualizes and of the thalamic region that integrates all our behavior? Doesn't this remind us of the emotional order, which Hermann Keyserling takes as the basic pattern of our relations with ourselves and with the cosmos? And so we have gone full circle and are back where we started, with people alive and struggling in a world where they want security and mastery. Science is not an end in itself, it is simply another means of achieving our purpose.

The Acceptability of Scientific Theories

What makes a semantic transaction in a scientific theory or otherwise acceptable to other semantic transactors? At a symposium held in Boston and cosponsored by the National Science Foundation and the American Academy of Arts and Sciences, Dr. Phillip Frank, lecturer in physics and in the philosophy of science at Harvard, flatly contradicted the generally held view that science is a discipline that stands on its own.

---

[17]Schrödinger, *Science, Theory and Man*, p. 95.

Among scientists it is taken for granted that a theory "should be" accepted if and only if it is "true"; to be true means in this context to be in agreement with the observable facts that can be logically derived from the theory. Every influence of moral, religious, or political considerations upon the acceptance of a theory is regarded as "illegitimate" by the so-called "community of scientists". . . .This view tells the truth, but not the whole truth.[18]

Frank then explains why science cannot be evaluated in isolation.

If we consider human behavior in general, we look at physical science as part of a much more general endeavor that embraces also psychology and sociology.[19]

Humans, even as scientists, cannot divorce themselves from their semantic world taken in its entirety, and they cannot ignore the fact that their fellow humans are also semantic transactors.

Dr. Frank mentions many historical facts in support of his statements. He discusses at length the problem the scientists of the seventeenth century had in accepting Copernicus' theory of the sun as the center of our planetary system. Francis Bacon, the most conspicuous adversary of Aristotelianism in those days, refused to accept it—and even fought against it. Later on, Galileo—the most frequently cited advocate of progress in science of his generation—failed to accept Johann Kepler's theory that planets move along an elliptical orbit and not along the circumference of a circle. So it goes: unanimity in science is often long in coming.

Newton's physics supported belief in a God who was an extremely able engineer and who created the world as a machine. Darwin's theory of evolution was attacked on religious and moral grounds. The emergence of life from nonliving matter is rejected by people who feel it would weaken belief in the existence of a soul. The quantum theory is interpreted by some as a refutation of mechanical determinism in the workings of the universe and as an argument in favor of free will.

This brings us back to Schrödinger's statement that science is a fashion of the time. In other words, it is one of the outward expressions of the prevalent culture.

Our civilization forms an organic whole. Those fortunate individuals who can devote their life to the profession of scientific research are not merely botanists, physicists, or chemists, as the case may be. They are men and they are children of their age. . . .In short, we are all members of our cultural environment.[20]

The consequence is that, in all our activities, a general world outlook is dominant, or tends to dominate. A civilization is not at peace with itself until

[18]Philip Frank, "The Variety of Reasons for the Acceptance of Scientific Theories," *Scientific Monthly* (September 1954), p. 139.

[19]Frank, "The Variety of Reasons for the Acceptance of Scientific Theories," p. 140.

[20]Schrödinger, *Science, Theory and Man*, p. 99.

its various institutions align themselves according to a common world outlook. This world outlook, in turn, may be brought about by technological developments as well as by ideological movements. If the two fail to advance at a comparable speed, there is tension and misery. For instance, the Industrial Revolution was mainly a technological development, and it took many generations for employers to attune their sociological attitudes to what was going on. I remember the days when labor unions and collective bargaining were opposed by well-meaning people, and in the meantime, our civilization witnessed useless fights between segments of our population.

We are now in the midst of another technological revolution, the revolution in communications. It has shrunk the planet to the dimensions of a federation of small independent states without a central government, and this technological revolution necessitates a radical change in the methods of thinking that were in fashion generations ago. Western humanity is not the prototype of humanity at its best; our particular brand of democracy is not the highest form of political wisdom for all people in all places; our logic is not the only reasonable brand of logic. Finally, and this is most important, our science is not the highest human achievement. We must not worship science—it is a servant that may easily take the whole household.

The worthiest objective for us is to be human; and the great human enterprise is just that. All the knowledge that we may acquire, all the techniques that we may invent, all the skills that we may master are subservient to this main enterprise. Science is a powerful means for achieving our ends, but it is only a means.

Korzybski also saw science as a technique at the service of human interests.

> The greatest men of science have always had wide human aims and interests. From the non-elementalistic point of view, they probably became productive because of this broad human urge.[21]

"This broad human urge" calls for a broad formulation in our days, when the great religions of the world face one another and are forced to admit that none of them is *the* world religion. Whether we call this formulation a common outlook, a common metaphysics, or a common religion, the term is not important after all.

Some have suggested the term "New Humanism" to distinguish it from the old humanism rooted in the now obsolete scientific attitude of pre-Einsteinian years. A French writer, who succeeded in bringing together a brilliant group of scientists, artists, and writers, and who made them willing collaborators in his ultramodern magazine *Planète* (now published in

---

[21]Korzybski, *Science and Sanity*, p. 728.

French, Italian, Spanish, German, and Dutch), compares the old humanism to the new:

> At the level of the old humanism, all we have in this world in mutation are some useless good intentions, and all we can do with our intelligence is to see in despair the absurdity of everything and the threatening signs of a dark future.

In contrast to this pessimistic view, he proclaims a new faith, consistent with, and nourished by, an evolutionary view of the entire cosmos.

> What is beginning to infiltrate up-to-date consciousness is that we are here solely to facilitate the passage of something that will come after us. We are not here to enjoy what we are and what we have achieved. *We are here to be and to help the development of being.* And everything that detaches us *from having* and brings us *to being*, to being more as individuals and being more as humankind, must be taken as an advance toward the humanism of the third millennium. . . . In a certain sense, the notion of evolution gives a broad and messianic meaning to the idea of Man the Maker of the World, and I think that we shall mobilize more effectively the men of tomorrow by reminding them that we are here to push—as far as we can—our knowledge, our powers of action, our understanding, and our contacts with outside universes so that there may take place the changes that will give birth to a new form of humanity.[22]

The Self-questioning and Self-correcting Character of Science

There is a characteristic of the scientific enterprise that is becoming more and more evident and influential as people are growing to cultural adulthood. Science is the one human invention that possesses a built-in capacity for self-correction through self-questioning and maintaining a constant self-renewal of honesty in purpose. In the long run, this capacity takes over and it satisfies our sense of fairness and justice.

Generations ago, it took a long time for the wrongs done to pioneering scientists by their fellow intellectuals to be acknowledged and corrected. Galileo was made mute for the rest of his life, and Giordano Bruno was not even allowed to live and wait for recognition. Things are different today: libel, vilification, and character assassination are still possible, as in the case of Immanuel Velikovsky who we mentioned earlier; but new discoveries come fast, and people are not scared any more by theories that appear far-fetched. Velikovsky was, for many long years, *persona non grata* on college and university campuses. Lately, he is receiving widespread recognition as his views on the Sun, Venus, comets and meteorites, Jupiter, Mars, the Moon, the Earth, and Ancient History are confirmed. He is invited to speak at such places as Yale, Harvard, Columbia, and Dartmouth. In February 1972, the Canadian Broadcasting Corporation had a full hour program on his

---

[22]Louis Pauwels, "What We Are and What We Believe In," *Planète*, No. 21, translated by J. S. Bois (italics added).

life and work. To quote Velikovsky when he was publicly acknowledged at Harvard: "I did not come for revenge or triumph, I come to find the young, the spirited, the men who have a fascination for scientific discovery." Both he and his audience were exemplifying science as a self-correcting and self-renewing enterprise.[23]

Summary

In this chapter we have explored structural complexification in human life and proposed an epistemological profile as a way of evaluating that complexification, from the level of the human race to the level of the human individual. We also proposed stage four, the postulating stage of creative processing, as the level of functioning most appropriate to our present stage of development. This is the main thrust of this text and introduces the seed notion of Epistemics as the art-science of innovating. Later, we will describe stage five, participating, for which a stage-four orientation is suggested as a necessary preparation.

Consistent use of the epistemological profile by an individual can produce, over a period of time, an awareness not possible by any other means that I have encountered.

One of the things that I have tried to emphasize here is that each time a scientist, or any creative individual, creates a postulate, she or he invents a nonmaterial structure, a program of action that will determine the conditions of future experiments. This is the tuning of one's whole self to the ongoings of the cosmic process as revealed by the work of one's predecessors.

We can humanize all of our institutions, including science, by giving up practices held in high honor for centuries: instead of philosophy of "the world out there" standing in the objective light of dispassionate observation and whose structure is discovered by the strict logic of induction and deduction, it will be what Lancelot Law Whyte called an *organic* philosophy; a description of human beings as the makers of their world within the limits of their capabilities and for the purpose of satisfying their need to participate.

I now want to go more deeply into the notion of structure. With the use of a mental model that I have borrowed from Kenneth Boulding, we will see that structure connotes something more than static or mechanical. A deeper understanding of structure can help to bring us into new awareness in regard to the systems at work in human affairs.

[23]See the special issue of *Pensee*, a periodical published by the Student Academic Freedom Forum, P.O. Box 414, Portland, Oregon, Vol. 2, No. 2, May 1972, entirely devoted to the topic: Immanuel Velikovsky—How Much of Yesterday's Heresy is Today's Science?

structuring fields of activity

To know something is to see it as belonging to a structure, to a system, to an organized whole in which it has a definite place and function. The world may be seen as a hierarchy of wholes, of energetic structuring fields of activity, superimposed upon one another in an increasing order of complexity. Thus, structure is multiordinal in that it means something entirely different within different levels of existence. This is important in our use of mental models, analogies, and in our use of language structures.

CHAPTER 12

mental models and their use

Thinking Models as Standardized Analogies

The word *structure* occurs again and again in Korzybski's *Science and Sanity*, and it seems almost to dominate his thinking. Of the ten parts of the book, seven have *structure* or *structural* in their titles. Part VII (whose title has apparently nothing to do with the notion of structure, but deals with non-Aristotelian training) contains a detailed description and a long explanation of a diagram that has become something of a trademark for the whole system. This diagram, the *Structural Differential*, is intended to convey the author's central message of *consciousness of abstracting*, and its name clearly shows Korzybski's concern for two key ideas: (1) *differences*, which make each person, thing, or situation unique in space and in time, and (2) *structure*, which accounts for the inner arrangement of parts, or elements, of each unique person, thing, or situation abstracted as a distinct whole from the cosmic spacetime flow—from what we called *WIGO* in an earlier chapter (p. 78).

In varied forms of expression, Korzybski repeatedly stated his belief that "in structure we find the mystery of rationality, adjustment, etc., and we find that *the whole content of knowledge is exclusively structural.*"[1] Nor is he alone in feeling this way: fitting thought elements into the proper structure has become one of the main concerns of the epistemology of our generation.

[1]Korzybski, *Science and Sanity* (Lakeville, Conn.: International Non-Aristotelian Library, 1933, 1941, 1948, 1958), p. 61 (italics added).

Many new words, or old words used in a new way, replace such simple terms as "idea," "thought," "concept," or "reasoning." We now hear of *Gestalt*, *configuration, conceptual organization, constructs, patterns, schemas, conceptual coordinates, closed and open systems, maps, structures, multidimensional manifolds*, and *models*. Reasoning is no longer seen as a chain of propositions that are linked to one another by the laws of syllogism, as the old terms "therefore" and "non sequitur" imply. Thinking and reasoning is an activity that involves movements in many directions, like building a house, adjusting a complicated piece of machinery, or piloting a plane with an eye on a panel of dials and lights.

Through some sort of telepathy, scientists who have no personal contact with one another work in a similar fashion to overthrow the old order of things. They are revising their methods of thinking, each in their own field. Whether they know of Korzybski does not matter so much; if they are progressive, they have to rediscover what he discovered years ago, and they have to push forward in the direction he indicated.

Two such scientists, who would deny any affiliation with the general semantics movement, are Montreal psychologists, well known as experimenters and writers in their field: Drs. Hebb and Bindra. In 1952 they contribued an article to the *American Psychologist*, the professional journal of the American Psychological Association, that dealt with the problem of communication by means of the spoken and written word; and one of their statements sounds as if it had been written by a general semanticist.

> The fundamental difficulty of verbal communication remains: to get an overview of a *complicated structure* that must be apprehended bit by bit.[2]

Words come out of a speaker's mouth one at a time and enter the listener's ear in the same serial order, but they are really labels that express elements of a structure in the speaker's mind, and they are intended to create a similar structure in the listener's. This they often fail to achieve.

> The task that a speaker sets his listener is to achieve a two- or three-dimensional structure from a series in one dimension. It is the task of making a house *at once* out of a series of nails, boards, scantlings, and bricks delivered one at a time in a rapid series. Conversely, at the speaker's end, it is the task of taking the house to pieces just as rapidly, and shipping the parts in the right order to allow the receiver to put it together right.[3]

This reminds us of those American millionaires who dismantled European monuments stone by stone and rebuilt them on their estates in this country. A speaker takes apart the structure of his own mental construct and

---

[2]D. O. Hebb and D. Bindra, "Scientific Writing and the General Problem of Communication," *American Psychologist*, October 1952, p. 571 (italics added).

[3]Hebb and Bindra, "Scientific Writing and the General Problem of Communication," p. 571.

ships the parts one by one on the air waves. The listener, who has not seen the whole construct before it was dismantled, has to rebuild it by figuring out how the parts interlock with one another.

Analogies

It is now recognized that formal logic is something artificial, something for show, like the marching past of military parades; it is not used on the fighting lines of political debates, labor negotiations, addresses to the jury, or family arguments. In actual life, we do not use formal syllogisms, we think with analogies.

> The idea of some philosophers that logic has anything to do with the mental processes of the great majority of men is totally wrong. . . .The rules of logic are abstractions which in practical life are rarely used—so rarely, indeed, that flagrant logical errors pass by easily and are often not detected even by specialized minds trained in abstract thinking. Every political speech is full of such instances. Men do not think in logical terms; men think predominantly in the elastic terms of analogy.[4]

This apparently radical quotation is nothing but an echo of the exclamation of one of the rigorous followers of the inductive method, Johann Kepler, who said:

> I cherish more than anything else the Analogies, my most trustworthy masters. They know all the secrets of Nature, and they ought to be the least neglected in Geometry.[5]

According to Dr. Hebb, the well-known research psychologist, the use of analogies is not restricted to popular and practical thinking. He repeats Kepler's views and relates them to today's conditions.

> The worker in the laboratory does not merely report and expound by the aid of analogy; that is how he thinks, also. The atom was once a hard little round particle, or later one with hooks on it. Recently it was a solar system. The classical dispute of physics about the nature of light was really asking, Is light like a shower of pebbles, or like ripples in a bathtub? The ultimate answer, Both, was one that was hard to accept. Why? Because it fitted into no preexisting conceptions; waves are waves, and pebbles are pebbles—there is nothing in common experience that has the properties of both.[6]

This shows that, although analogies are useful, they can also be a source of difficulties. They give our thinking processes a pattern from which it is not easy to break free. We must therefore use them with discretion—and "hang

---

[4]Rudolph Jordan, *The New Perspective* (Chicago: University of Chicago Press, 1951), p. 267.

[5]Quoted in George Pólya, *Mathematics and Plausible Reasoning* (Princeton, N.J.: Princeton University Press, 1954), p. 12.

[6]D. O. Hebb, *The Organization of Behavior* (New York: Wiley, 1949), p. 119.

loose." When the mental pattern of an analogy has little in common with the empirical pattern of the phenomenon we are studying, it is dangerous to be too rigorously consistent; for this may take us farther and farther away from reality. The skill to choose adequate analogies is important for sound thinking.

As an example of suggestive analogy, George Pólya asks us to consider the hand of a human, the paw of a cat, the foreleg of a horse, the fin of a whale, and the wing of a bat. These limbs are differently used, of course, but they are composed of similar parts similarly related to one another. "Two systems are analogous," he concludes, "if they agree in clearly definable relations of their respective parts."[7]

In recent years, a new discipline called synectics has been developed that makes use of metaphorical analogies in creative activities, mainly in business and industry. They are now extending their work in the field of education. To quote one of their publications:

> Over twenty-five years ago, Synectics research was directed toward the possibility of increasing the innovative and learning output of individuals and groups. This research resulted in the Synectics Technique for the conscious use of metaphor in problem-solving situations.[8]

To abstract a set of "clearly definable relations of parts" is what we meant by relational abstracting (p. 102). When we compare two or more such abstracted structures and find that they have common characteristics, we reach a higher order of abstraction, that of *mental models,* or standardized analogies. These become tools for further thinking, and the better the tools the better the thinking. A skillful thinker is like any other skilled artisan: he has the most modern set of tools available, he knows which tool is best suited to what he has to do, and he uses every tool with professional dexterity.

Empirical Systems and Mental Models

How many such tools, or general patterns of structural thinking, are now available to us? An economist-philosopher of our generation, Kenneth Boulding, suggested a list of eight.[9] In each case he points to an empirical system, after which a mental model is designed.

In the following pages we deal with only seven empirical systems and corresponding mental models. Boulding was speaking of levels of organization, and he described human society as level eight, that of a most complex

---

[7]Pólya, *Mathematics and Plausible Reasoning*, p. 13.

[8]William J. J. Gordon, Introduction to Synectics (Cambridge: Porpoise Books, 1972), p. 1.

[9]Kenneth Boulding, *The Image* (Ann Arbor, Mich.: University of Michigan Press, 1956), Chaps. 2, 3, and 4, pp. 19-63. The whole book is most interesting and challenging. The author suggests the name *eiconics* as the name of "an abstract discipline consistent with a great many metaphysical or epistemological viewpoints."

structure made of human beings as elements. We stop at the human individual as the most advanced system-model that has come into existence in the
process of evolution.

SYSTEM-MODEL NO. 1: STATIC

The first empirical system is of the *framework* type, like a house, a table,
a chair, a monument, a machine standing idle. It could be the whole word
seen as made of permanent, or relatively permanent, things—mountains,
lakes, roads, towns, forests, continents; or as a living organism that is mentally dissected into anatomical parts: the roots, trunk, branches, and leaves
of a tree, or the limbs and the organs of the human body.

From this framework system we form a static mental model. This involves a simple enumeration of the constituent parts of a whole with descriptions of their size—which is larger, which is smaller—and of their relative
positions in space—which is above, which is below, which is to the right,
which to the left. There may be a statement of their function, but not of their
functioning.

The plans of a house are of this type; they tell where the kitchen, the
living room, the bathroom, and the bedrooms will be in relation to one
another. For a static structure such as a house, the static mental model is
quite sufficient; a three-dimensional mockup would be a bit better, of
course, but it would still be of the same static type.

We often reduce to such a static model structures that are too complex
and too fluid to be adequately represented in this form—and if we think
about them with such a mental tool, our thinking is necessarily inadequate.
The standard organization chart is such a static model: it shows what we
could call the anatomy of a company—where the president stands with respect to the other officials (at the top, of course), how many divisions there
are (each one headed by a vice-president), who reports to whom, who is
responsible for what.

This type of thinking model belongs to stage two of Bachelard's scheme
of human development; it is merely classification, both horizontal and vertical. It has the rigidity and the "either-orness" of what is unfortunately taken
as clear and straight thinking. We may stay marooned at this level when we
look at such diagrams as the Structural Differential (p. 93) or the semantic
transaction diagram (p. 29), which are intended to convey a much richer
message.

This type of thinking model also deals with the world of nouns that we
became acquainted with at home and in the elementary grades, the world of
substances that stand by themselves and that we tend to see in isolation. This
type of structure does not really exist in a world of processes. The boundaries
that we assign to "objects" are determined by our sensory equipment or by
the categorizing that is determined by our language.

We dissect nature along lines laid down by our native language. The categories and types that we isolate from the world of phenomena we do not find there because they stare every observer in the face; on the contrary, the world is presented in a kaleidoscopic flux of impressions which has to be organized by our minds—and this means largely by the linguistic systems in our minds. We cut nature up, organize it into concepts, and ascribe significance as we do largely because we are parties to an agreement to organize it in this way—an agreement that holds throughout our speech community and is codified in the patterns of our language.[10]

The only binding energy that holds together the parts of a framework empirical system is gravitation, or inertia. The parts stay in their respective positions simply because they are all stuck to the earth by the law of attraction. They are passive; their characteristics are determined by the conditions of their environment.

Whenever our thinking is classificatory and hierarchical, we are unwittingly using a static mental model. The stratification of socioeconomic classes in upper, middle, and lower; of management in top management and middle management; of formal education in graduate, undergraduate, high school, grade school, kindergarten; and the distinction between superior and inferior; between master and slave; between high-grade and low-grade; between first class and second class; between lofty theories and earthy objectives; between high ideals and down-to-earth practices; these and similar stratifications and distinctions belong to an up-and-down view of the world that dates back to the time when the earth was thought of as a flat plain, with heaven above and hell below. All have a tendency to make our thinking static and stratified.

SYSTEM-MODEL NO. 2: MECHANICAL

The empirical system from which we derive the second mental model is the *clockwork*, a machine made of parts that are interdependent in activity and kept going by energy supplied from an outside source. *Mechanical structure* is the corresponding mental model.

This is the level of the predetermined dynamic structure repeating its movements because of some simple law of connectedness among its parts. The great clock, of course, is the solar system itself, endlessly repeating its complex motions in the majestic wheel of the firmament. This is the world of mechanics. It is governed in the small by Newton's Mozartian equations; it is governed in the large by Einstein's atonal system. This is the universe of eighteenth-century deists—wound up by the great Clockmaker in the beginning and unwinding ever since.[11]

---

[10]Benjamin Lee Whorf, *Language, Thought, and Reality*, ed. J. B. Carroll (Cambridge, Mass.: M. I. T. Press, 1956), p. 213.
[11]Kenneth Boulding, *The Image*, p. 20.

With this mental model we pass from elementalistic thinking, from analysis of parts, to consideration of the whole as a working unit. It is the clock working as a whole that keeps time—no individual axle, cogwheel, spring, or pendulum does it by itself. Every part is necessary, of course, and every part has its individual function, but no part can be dissociated from the group of coworking elements; the value of each part is determined by its contribution to the working of the whole.

Mechanistic thinking of this type is prevalent in our industrial culture. Our analogies are derived from whatever we are familiar with, and, because we live in a world of machines, we get many of our analogies from machines. This type of thinking is a first step towards a further understanding of how we function. It is better than static analogies but still very short of adequate in human affairs. No single organ of our body, no single component of our personality can account for the total value of our behavior. In a team, each member has a contribution to make that may be necessary to achieve what the group has been assembled for, but no member can claim full credit for the achievements of the group. If we push this type of thinking far enough, we become keenly aware of our interdependence with the people who are, as we are, parts of a common organization. When we spread our outlook over the planet—the sputniks and the Explorers force us to do so—we see that no nation is self-contained any longer. If a nation fails to work in proper timing with the rest of the huge political and economic machine that is humankind today, the whole system may come to a standstill or damage itself badly in a third world war.

In a business company, a type-two mental model would not limit itself to the enumeration of functions; it would describe the relations between them in terms of relative autonomy and role responsibility; and it would draw flowcharts to show the movement of goods and the accompanying circulation of paperwork—as well as the mutual control they exercise. A more truly holistic model will take shape in our minds if we visualize, apart from the formal rigid organization, the informal organization, the spontaneous clustering of people around personal centers of leadership, influence, prestige, or competence that appear, disappear, weaken, or wax stronger, depending on circumstances that they themselves may have helped arise or that they resist stubbornly.

This clockwork model is a model of action and reaction, of cause and effect, of movement in space and time. It applies to humans as well as to machines whenever human "faculties" are taken to operate according to the laws of Newtonian physics. We see the world as a stage where actors either join in a common game or push one another in a contest. This type of thinking lends itself to an evaluation of opposing forces, to strategy and tactics, and to a balance of power.

Machines are inactive until they are set going by the proper form of energy; indeed, the world of machines is a static world waiting to be stirred into action, gathering and maintaining momentum as long as energy is poured into it and slowing down when energy is withdrawn. In our terrestrial world, where gravitation works relentlessly, inertia eventually brings every machine to a stop; perpetual motion is an impossibility. Our thinking about machines is still in conformity with Aristotelian physics: nothing moves unless it is set moving by the action of a mover.

Our language is replete with mechanical analogies that we often take as adequate descriptions of human behavior. We speak of stimulus and response as if our organism was habitually at rest like a motor that needs a starter to get going. We *formerly* described *a human being* as a semantic *reactor* as if the initiative for our behavior always came from an outside source of energy. We set up an organization as we put together the pieces of a mechanical contraption, and we pour our energy into it to *make it work*. We speak of decision-*making*, a process by which we *weigh* the pros and cons; we *keep in balance* the many factors that *are at work* in a situation; and we *plan a course of action* in a sequence of steps *to be taken in the proper order*.

Establishing an assembly line, organizing a crew of men that will fight a fire, and keeping a restaurant functioning smoothly at lunchtime are operations that make use of dynamic thinking. This means thinking in four dimensions, adding timing to the spatial relations of parts or units. Quite often, this fourth dimension, timing, is the key to success. In industrial operations, it has become a major concern, and it is the reason why time studies, flowcharts, and a variety of other techniques are applied in a methods department.

This type of space-time thinking has achieved what much of the general public admires when they think of science. A large airport is a good example of clockwork thinking in operation: there has to be room for all the big jets that wait for their loads along passageways that stretch out from the main building, landing strips that are clear of obstacles, service trucks, garages, refueling facilities. In the air, there are lanes and corridors that are invisible to the common observer but definite for the pilots and for the men in the control tower. This moving complex receives travelers from all corners of the world as it sends other travelers in all directions at the rate of hundreds per hour.

In human affairs, we have the thinking of a surgeon in the operating room, of a moderator in a group discussion, of a politician in a campaign, and of a public servant in decisions of international and historical importance. This is multidimensional thinking of a multitude of space and time factors that are weighed and combined into one operating mental unit as trigger-sensitive as the booster of a satellite. Our generation has achieved unprecedented technologies by building a powerful adjunct to the human brain, the electronic computer.

SYSTEM-MODEL NO. 3: SELF-REGULATING

The empirical system in this case is a machine with a feedback control, and the corresponding mental model is called a *self-regulating structure*.

There is nothing absolutely new in this type of mechanical system—mechanical governors have been in use for many years—but our attention has recently been drawn to the regulating feature by the increased use of servomechanisms and by the appearance of the science of cybernetics. The world is no longer seen as being made exclusively of actors and "acted upon" and of causes and effects, which, in their turn become causes of other effects *ad infinitum*. Causes may produce effects that react upon their own causes, that increase their activity in the case of positive feedback, or keep it within a specified range in the case of negative feedback.

We now speak of steady states, of homeostatis; of which is the tendency for an operating system to keep itself within a range of optimum activity, below which it will not stay for long and above which it will not allow itself to go. A simple example is that of our furnaces and refrigerators with their thermostats, which maintain a level of temperature within a preset range. A more complex mechanism is installed in a guided missile, which can enable it to pursue even a shifting target. Such a machine has what we could anthropomorphically describe as a purpose, an objective, and a degree of self-control. It does what it is designed to do, judges whether its performance is in keeping with its assigned purposes, and corrects deflections from its proper course.

Feedback thinking is closer to living systems, and it becomes extremely rich in possibilities when we apply it to human situations. At the physiological level, animals and humans are clear examples of feedback systems. If we run, our heart beats faster to accelerate the circulation; if we are hot, we perspire to cool off; when we are satiated, we feel no more appetite; when we are tired, we want to lie down and rest. Whatever happens to our body, it reacts to keep itself in functioning condition.

At the psychological level, culture is a kind of steady state that is not easily disturbed; in fact, all habits of sensing, feeling, thinking, and moving can be seen as steady states that provide for automatic corrections of whatever interferes with them. People can accept only so much change at a time. If we try to feed them too substantial a diet of rich ideas, they will stop assimilating them. They will easily digest what they are used to, but they may not even taste a different but healthier fare. In some cases, the feedback system itself is preset against the long-range welfare of the individual, but it nevertheless keeps working—and we have alcoholism, drug addiction, compulsory eating, and such. If feedback is taken into account, we can understand why some people do not want to think. They want to be entertained. They have developed an addiction to stories of sex and violence, to plain gossip, or to shallow vituperation against a common enemy.

As an organization grows older its feedback mechanisms grow more powerful, and it acquires a momentum that keeps it on a steady course. We can see this phenomenon in churches, in business firms, in educational institutions, in political parties, in professional associations, even in schools of thought.

When we use this model to evaluate the behavior of individuals or organizations, we understand many phenomena for which the previous models could not account. We see human beings, singly or in groups, as self-preserving and self-regulating systems that offer an inertial resistance to outside interference. This applies to teaching, preaching, persuading, and the like.

In the light of this knowledge, self-control ceases to be the result of strenuous efforts to keep our instincts and our emotions in check by sheer will power; it becomes, instead, a matter of intelligent skill in manipulating the feedback loops within our organism. It could be positive or negative feedback. Positive feedback works like the amplifier in a radio or television set; it increases the awareness value of reactions so faint that we may not even suspect we have them. It is sensitivity training in action; it is a simple, and too often a neglected, way of increasing the strength of constructive attitudes. If we love somebody, we should tell the person; it will make our love stronger and better. If we are depressed and we talk about it—to ourself or to others—we will make it worse for ourself. The difficult thing is to keep the negative feedback functioning and to stop talking about it. People quite often think they can talk themselves *out* of something, but it is still talking, and talking—either pro or con—induces a positive feedback and amplifies the trouble.

Physical Models in General

All three of the preceding thinking models can be classed as systems. In the framework model, we enumerate and classify the parts of a system. In the clockwork model, we see the parts interacting upon one another in a sequence of reactions that may reach to the very limits of our historical and geographical world. In the feedback model, we see systems as self-regulatory. Our own inner world may be seen as a feedback system: it maintains itself in a steady state of self-consistency, and this may interfere with its adaptation to changing conditions and to its own development.

Thinking is an aspect of our semantic transactions. It mirrors the pattern of the organismic processes that involve our feelings, our habits, our physiological condition, our evaluative relations with our environment, our past experience, and our expectations. By a singular phenomenon of circularity, *it determines the shape of these transactive patterns as it mirrors them*. Depending on how we formulate them, our semantic transactions are made static or dynamic, or they are narrowed or broadened, shackled or set free. Our thinking projects as it reflects; it plays the part of a living template that gives a shape to our behavior. To understand this is to find a new meaning in the classical saying "As a man thinketh in his heart, so is he." If we train ourselves to think differently, we change our view of the world; we give a new direction to our activities; we actually transform the world in which we live.

This reveals the importance of the mental models we habitually use. The richer they are, the richer our life will become. Model-making and model-handling has become one of the most powerful tools of today's technology.

In the old days, when an inventor wanted to build a machine—as when the Wright brothers built their biplane—the procedure was first to "guess" a design that might work, then build it, then test it, then make changes and test it again. The process of designing, building, testing, and rebuilding went on until a satisfactory product was obtained—or until the inventor's funds ran out.

Today, the first design is translated into a mathematical model, which is a set of equations that represents the required performance of the future machine. Instead of building an actual machine and testing it, the designer tries many possible alternatives in the variables of these equations and uses a computer to figure out the answers. As many mental models as necessary are built, tried, and modified instead of going through the labor and the cost of building a machine that might cost millions. I read somewhere that with only a slide rule an engineer could "construct" and "test" a model of an electric motor in two days of work with no expense of material.

Operations research is concerned with mathematical models as well; it deals with human activities inasmuch as they are determined by technical and situational factors. We know how valuable these techniques were in the last war, and we have seen them spread all over the business world in recent years.

The purpose of the thinking models we are now describing is different; they are far from having reached the sharp formulations of mathematics. They are intended to deal directly with semantic activities. They are an attempt to put order and system in what we do when we plan an interview, prepare a speech, handle a professional problem, manage a delicate situation, or attempt to stimulate our ability to think creatively.

The static model is simple and consistent with our language structure. The mechanical model goes beyond the subject-predicate structure of our language; it corrects elementalistic thinking. The third model takes some time to get used to because it introduces the rather new notion of circular causality. All three models are within the range of mechanical thinking.

If we limit ourselves to them, we are dealing with ourselves as if we were mere robots or guided missiles. One of the most valuable results of the present classification of empirical systems and mental models is probably that it prevents us from accepting as adequate a level of thinking that is below the empirical world we are dealing with. The world of humans lies beyond the world of mechanical models, cybernetics, operations research, or computers; it requires the use of mental models of the biological type, which we will now describe.

Thinking with Biological Models

The closer the mental model is to the empirical system of which it is the analog, the more realistic is the thinking. A model that is much more simple than the phenomenon it is intended to illustrate shrinks our thinking to the model's dimensions and causes us to miss the complexity of the phenomenon.

A Zen master is quoted as having said: "Can thought review thought? No; thought cannot review thought." He then attempts to prove his point by an analogy. "As the blade of a sword cannot cut itself, as the fingertip cannot touch itself, so a thought cannot see itself."[12]

I would say it differently. The Zen master takes a mechanical object, the sword, as the mental model of the mind, a living object, and he ascribes to the mind the limitations of the sword. Of course, a sword cannot cut itself; but are the mind's capacities or limits the same as the sword's? What are we describing here: the mind, which is of a higher order of existence, or the sword, which is of a lower? What is the measure of what? If one takes the sword as the measure of the mind, he reveals nothing of the mind that makes it different from the sword—and he imposes upon the mind the limitations of the sword. A static model, the sword, is a misleading analogy in dealing with a living process. (The analogy of the fingertip is a bit better; the fingertip cannot touch itself but it can turn back on the inside of the hand and feel it.)

If we content ourselves with the mental models that we have described so far, we are imposing upon life processes the limitations of mechanical thinking. All human enterprises are expressions of living activities. When we attempt to manage them as we would manage machines, we take life out of them. Humans become robots; natural flowers are replaced by plastic structures. We look for stability, but we create fixity; we plan progress, but we suppress growth.

To overcome these crippling limitations of physical mental models, let us see what mental models of the biological type have to offer. Kenneth Boulding proposes four of them.

[12]Alan Watts, *The Way of Zen* (New York: Pantheon, 1957), p. 53.

SYSTEM-MODEL NO. 4: SELF-REPRODUCING

The basic unit of all living organisms is the *cell*. The mental model that corresponds to it could be described as a *self-maintaining and self-reproducing structure*.

The cell has the characteristics of all previous systems plus something different and distinctive; it is made of many parts that interact among themselves, as we saw in clockwork models. It is a feedback system as well, reacting to whatever imperils its existence. This feedback system is not limited to an objective set by human beings, however; it has within itself a program of self-maintenance. In fact, it is this activity of survival that constitutes the very texture of its existence. The cell can never be at rest, like an idle machine. For the cell, to exist means to keep functioning, to ingest an input, to transform it into its own substance, to eliminate the waste matter, and to prepare for reproduction. In the three systems that we studied earlier—the framework, the clockwork, and the feedback—the parts had an existence of their own. They could exist independently of the system into which they had entered. Each beam, each board, each nail that is part of a building, each piece of metal that makes a machine, existed independently before it was brought into the structure of the building or the machine. It could again exist by itself if the structure were dismantled.

Not so for the parts of the cell; their existence depends on the existence of the cell itself. They are not independent bits that were put together to from the cell, and they cannot be kept in storage once the cell has disintegrated. They are functions that were made material, as it were; for the cell and its parts to stop functioning is to cease to be.

When we build in our mind a mental model that is an analog to this cell system, our cognition becomes permeated with change as its very texture. We do not operate as mechanical systems that move within the arches of time, we internalize time as an integral dimension of our own being. We become time-bound and time-binding, emerging anew from our former self at every beat of our heart.

In the measure that we are aware of this, in the same measure are we able to differentiate between live and dead issues. Married life, for instance, could be of the framework type: a static cultural organization that endures for years without noticeable changes. It could be of the clockwork type as well: a preordained interactive play of common interests and purposes. It could be of the feedback type: keeping within the bounds of civility the expressions of feelings that might endanger the partnership. But in all these cases, marriage is not a living process. It does not renew itself as it goes along. It is not an actual experience; it is a memory that is kept going like a machine that needs rewinding or refueling every so often. A clear distinction between the mechanical and the biological type of thinking makes one aware of these differences and enables a conscious adjustment to circumstances.

Cells are open systems, feeding on the resources of their environment but selective as to what elements they abstract from this environment. They bring to a higher level of potentiality the energy they absorb. They have a definite *within*, an autonomous functioning inside the membrane that separates them from, and at the same time relates them to, the milieu in which they exist.

Finally, they reproduce themselves once they have reached the proper degree of maturation. If their reproduction is kept under the hierarchical control of the organism to which they belong, we have normal cells for growth and repair; if they start reproducing themselves wildly, they become cancer cells that may eventually destroy the organism.

I do not know why or how Communists chose the word cell for their organizational units, but I am impressed by the aptness of the word. It suggests life, growth, and multiplication. For them, it may mean the development of a sound organism; for many of us, it is viewed as the beginning of a cancerous growth that threatens our body politic. To continue the analogy, we know that there are various procedures, some more drastic than others, to destroy cancer cells, but prevention is better than cure. If our science of the human organism had reached the point where we knew how to keep it functioning perfectly—or almost so—we might not have to deal with malignancies. The application of all this to any organism or organization is obvious.

SYSTEM-MODEL NO. 5: SELF-EXPANDING

Here the *plant* is the empirical system, and the mental model is a *self-expanding structure*.

This system-model is exemplified, on a large scale, by a pepper tree that I planted five years ago. The tree has characteristics that make it different from the systems I have described so far. Unlike my study, and unlike the furniture and the machines it contains, the pepper tree is made of parts that have kept changing from the time I planted it. They are not the same as they were years ago: the trunk is bigger, the branches are more numerous, the bark has changed from smooth to scaly. It is—and it is not—the tree that I planted. It has become, by its own activity, something that cannot be represented by a purely mechanical mental model. If we use a microscope to study its ultimate structure, we discover that its basic unit is the cell, which we took as the empirical pattern of our first mental model of the biological type.

This system-model includes all the previous ones and combines them into a complex whole. As a physical system, the tree has a definite shape, and, if I take a picture of it, the picture can easily be identified as that of a pepper tree. It functions with the rhythm of the seasons; and it has feedback properties as well: it repairs damages done to its bark and limbs, and it keeps within its trunk and branches the humidity necessary to survive and to grow in this dry climate. The tree, like every cell of its structure, is an open system; it maintains itself by feeding on its environment, and it gives back to its environment the results of its life processes.

Finally, the distinctive characteristic that makes the tree different from the cell system is that all its parts, although they came from a unique mother cell, have kept on differentiating themselves from the very beginning. The cells of its leaves are different from the cells of its roots; the cells of its seeds are different from the cells of its bark; the cells of its flowers are different from the cells of its wood. Its phenotype is different from its genotype. It is an organization that is not put together by humans, it is an organization that has grown according to a pattern buried in the chromosomes of its mother cell. This pattern evolved as the tree grew; and the tree stayed within the general pattern of the species while becoming individual and unique.

Here we have not only activity as we had in the clockwork model, self-control as we had in the feedback model, and self-maintenance and survival as we had in the cell model, we also have growth and patterned development as essential features of the system. We have time as an integral dimension; we have balance and symmetry that are free from rigidity and stylization. We have an organization of cells, each of which has become specialized; each receives something from the others and gives something to the others, all working for the maintenance and the growth of the organism as a whole. We observe changes that are not proportional. A seed does not grow evenly in all directions, like an inflated toy balloon; it grows roots that dig down into the soil, a stem that breaks through to the air above, and branches, leaves, flowers, and fruits that follow their own form of development within the general pattern of the species to which the tree belongs.

How much more meaningful as a telling analogy is this system compared to the dumb interrelatedness of parts in a human-made machine, even a feedback machine! Here we have a wealth of dimensions far beyond the usual categories of space and time. We have movements along vectors that defy reduction to plane or solid geometry and any form of visual representation. No wonder that growth, as a distinct phenomenon, has been so little studied up to now: it involves a self-propelling complexity that our physical thinking models cannot represent.

Life involves a resourcefulness that no human-made machine and no human-contrived organization can provide. A robust tree makes the most of its environment; its roots reach for bits of soil through the cracks of a rock, or lift and break walls that press them down; its branches spread their leaves to absorb as much sunlight as possible. Life is a resourceful and cooperative process that is endowed with an innate rhythm. By drawing our analogies from its workings in grass, weeds, bushes, and trees, we can enrich our mental resources and reach a fuller understanding of our own behavior.

Learning, for instance, could be seen as a growth process. If we admit that every human is as different from his fellows as every plant species is different from another, we easily accept the fact that no two persons learn the "same" subject in the same manner. In the spring, almond trees shoot out flowers before they grow leaves, while their neighbors, the pecan trees, produce leaves first and flowers afterwards. The leaves of some amaryllis turn from intense green to pale yellow, and dry up and die before the main stem grows and opens its long bud to form the deep chalice of its elegant pink flower. Similarly, of those who study general semantics, or any subject, in the same class and under the same teacher, some will exhibit various orders of assimilation of the topic; for example, one may take as fundamental what another judges to be secondary. Many students produce more "flowers" than "fruit"; and the proportion of seeds that will reproduce their kind is infinitely small.

Some plants propagate themselves as weeds and demand little or no cultivation, as do many popular ideas and fashions. Other plants require expert care and cultivation because they are delicate and valuable; they are like the arts and the theories that are a challenge to the climate of our culture. The cultural climate is more amenable to human control than the geographical climate; moreover, we can develop cultural species, such as hybrid corn and frost-resistant wheat that thrive in whatever conditions the environment offers. As a consequence, problems of education, propaganda, and cultural change become matters of semantic ecological planning.

The same mental model could be used to study the growth of an individual's philosophy and style of living. Cultural heredity could be compared to organic heredity, the difference being that the cultural progenitors, parents, teachers, leaders, heroes, great individuals, "stars," transmit to the young ones what we could call a pattern of semantic genes, of accepted "truths" and values that play the part of the genotype from which they will develop as phenotypes. For example, deep below the phenotypic individual characteristics is a distinct genotypic pattern that makes a Mormon different from a member of any other well-defined cultural group. The same is true of any other cultural heredity. As a consequence, problems of close personal association, including marriage of course become matters of symbiosis like grafting branches to trees of a similar family, and not simply matters of "give and take," bargaining, or mutual concessions.

SYSTEM-MODEL NO. 6: SELF-MOVING

The empirical system is the *animal* form of life, and the mental model that corresponds to it is a *self-moving structure*.

In the course of evolution, life forms reached a point when they could detach themselves from their moorings, move about to discover the world on their own, and modify outside conditions to suit their purposes. Animals are not rooted to a spot like plants and trees; they move about to find and create more suitable environmental conditions by which to live, grow, and multiply.

They receive information from a distance by means of their sensory organs. They show consciousness of self: they flee danger, they stalk their prey, they recognize who is kind to them and who does not want them around. They are capable of expressing moods and needs. They can be conditioned like Pavlov's dogs and trained like circus performers; they can learn by insight like Sultan, the great ape of which Köhler wrote. They have a limited anticipation of the future, like the mountain lion who jumps where the fleeing deer is likely to be and not where it is now. They react to the clapping of an appreciative audience; they play for their own enjoyment; they practice courtship and they make love. Plants and trees ensure their individual survival and that of their species, but animals go one step beyond this: they enjoy living for its own sake.

This empirical system is so close to the human form of life that we are easily led to derive from it a mental model of ourselves that we imagine is adequate. As Korzybski would repeat again and again, "We copy animals in our nervous system." We even limit our ambitions to a lower ceiling, to that of the plants, when we speak of survival as a human objective. We often fail to accept as desirable some of the characteristics that distinguish animal behavior from that of lower forms of life. Mothers try to keep their grown children psychologically tied to their apron strings, while the mother bird pushes her little ones out of the nest in due time. Fathers keep interfering with the day-to-day planning of their child's life, while animals let their progeny shift for themselves as early as their senses and their limbs can manage it.

If we use the self-moving mental structure as the analogy through which we observe and interpret the behavior of individuals and organizations, we accept more easily certain phenomena that a lower type of mental model cannot account for. A company may, as the common saying goes, "have roots in a community," as the cotton mills did years ago in New England; but if conditions elsewhere are more likely to ensure their survival and growth, as the mills found was true in the South, their manufacturing plants are bound to move someday, somehow, when circumstances are judged to be opportune.

A school of thought, a cultural movement, a religious organization, and other semantic biota can be seen as families of self-moving members, none of which has to remain close to the place of origin, geographically or psychologically. They do not simply "branch out," like the limbs of a tree, they go on their own, sooner or later blending themselves with different environments and undergoing variations that modify the outward features of the phenotype, or even bring about radical mutations of the common genotype.

When we think in terms of system-model No. 6, we find this most normal. Tradition that prevents emigration from the original flock reduces a biological system to a lower form of life. It is bound to fail in the long run.

A world of considerations invites our survey when we meditate on the vistas spread before our gaze by the acceptance of the self-moving biological structure as a mental model. To the characteristics of earlier standard analogies, it adds the capacity to seek and to choose the location that makes possible the preservation of the self and the self-image. Behavior is determined by a value system that is culturally inherited, almost as animals' instincts are transmitted from one generation to the next by the genes of the mother cell. Adaptability to the environment is limited by the range of cultural inheritance; modification of behavior is restricted by the guidance of tradition; and resourcefulness remains at the service of conservatism. There is a flexibility as to means, with inflexibility as to ends. Anticipations are patterned on the summation, by statistical means or otherwise, of past experiences. Tradition assumes great importance.

SYSTEM-MODEL NO. 7: SELF-REFLEXIVE

We have now reached the human level, that of the *self-reflexive* living structure.

Human life is the most complex process that we know. We are conscious of our functioning within a hierarchy of multiordinal units, all special to our species: family, community, nation, cultural group, and humankind as a whole.

We are conscious of time as an integral dimension of the experiences of each of these units: time-bound and time-binding. We abstract relations among items of experience (objects), and establish relations among them that are other than those offered by unaided nature (plastic compounds, transuranian elements, transformation of waterfalls into electric power, organization of economic and political units, etc.). We express these relations, whether discovered or invented, in symbols, and this web becomes the texture of the world in which we live.

We are autonomous to a high degree, and conscious of our autonomy. We are capable of changing our environment, including other forms of life and energy, to suit our purposes, our ambitions, or our passing fancies. We are capable of self-observation, self-criticism, and self-management. We may be conditioned, but we are capable of overcoming conditionings that were self-imposed or induced from outside.

We have gradually eliminated from the planet, our place of abode, practically all threats to our existence from lower forms of energy, physical or biological, and we are left with one overawing danger to our survival and happiness. This danger lies within ourselves and within those of our kind. It comes from the fact that some human organizational units are bent on making their human-made self-image victorious over all other self-images, at whatever cost to themselves and to the rest of humankind.

It is the purpose of general semantics and epistemics to play a part in the laborious creation of a human mental model that will facilitate the impending metamorphosis that most advanced thinkers are hoping for. From the rather pessimistic *Man, The Unknown* by Alexis Carrel,[13] we pass to books more symptomatic of optimism about ourselves, such as *Human Potentialities* by Gardner Murphy,[14] *The Next Development in Man* by Lancelot Law Whyte,[15] *The Phenomenon of Man* by Teilhard de Chardin,[16] that formulate, each in its own manner, the same purpose that Alfred Korzybski held—the development of a new kind of human being.

What are the advantages of such a graded enumeration of seven empirical systems and their mental correlates? Boulding answers:

> One advantage of exhibiting a hierarchy of systems is that it gives us some idea of the present gaps in both theoretical and empirical knowledge. Adequate models extend up to about the fourth level [the cell level] not much beyond. Empirical knowledge is deficient at practically all levels. . . .One of the most valuable uses of such a scheme is to prevent us from accepting as final a level of theoretical analysis which is below the level of the empirical world we are investigating. . . .
>
> The level of the "clockwork" is the level of "classical" natural science, especially physics and astronomy, and is probably the most completely developed in the present-stage of knowledge, especially if we extend the concept to include the field theory and stochastic models of modern physics.
>
> Beyond the second level adequate theoretical models get scarcer. The last few years have seen great developments at the third and fourth levels. The theory of control mechanisms ("thermostats") has established itself as the new discipline of cybernetics, and the theory of self-maintaining systems or "open systems" likewise has made rapid strides. We could hardly maintain, however, that much more than a beginning had been made in these fields.
>
> Beyond the fourth level it may be doubted whether we have as yet even the rudiments of theoretical systems. The intricate machinery of growth by which the genetic complex organizes the matter around it is almost a complete mystery. Up to now, whatever the future may hold, only God can make a tree.[17]

If the mental models in use stop at level four, how far are we from thinking about ourselves in a manner consistent with our empirical level seven? The gap is frightening, now that the whole planet may soon become a mere plaything for our unpredictable species, the unknown, whose reactions

---

[13]Alexis Carrel, *Man, The Unknown* (New York: Harper & Row, 1935).

[14]Gardner Murphy, *Human Potentialities* (New York: Basic Books, 1958).

[15]Lancelot Law Whyte, *The Next Development in Man* (London: Cresset, 1941).

[16]Teilhard de Chardin, *The Phenomenon of Man*, (London: Collins, 1959).

[17]Kenneth Boulding, "General System Theory—The Skeleton of Science," *Management Science* (April 1956): 205-7, *passim*.

we cannot anticipate because we have as yet no adequate mental model to guide us. We have just begun to observe ourselves through model three, that of the electronic brain, and we are so proud of our achievements along those lines that we are almost ready to take that machine as the ideal of what we should be.

When we play at being scientific in our human self-study, we ignore the realm of values because our most advanced physical model of ourselves, the electronic computer, is not responsive to values as such. And we try to deal with system seven by using models at level two.

We are just beginning to put some order in our thinking by means of this hierarchy of mental models. When we join the mental model we use to the empirical system, with which we have to deal, paradoxes disappear. The "physical" models are so dominant in our culture that we have used it more often than is appropriate in this textbook itself. The time has come to be aware of their danger and to profit from every opportunity to translate "physical" analogies into biological ones. For instance, if I am tempted to say that the notions in this book are useful *tools*, I remind myself that it would be more profitable to bring it to higher levels. This training is not a matter of "tooling our brain," it is a matter of growing to a degree of maturity sufficient to bear fruit. We cannot produce oranges with tools; we cannot solve a level-five problem with a level-two procedure. If we want oranges, we have to wait for the tree to produce them. The fruits we expect take time and proper cultivation to grow and ripen.

Starting with the plant all biological units require (1) time to function and grow properly, (2) proper soil and climate, (3) proper feeding and care, and (4) occasional pruning. This simple enumeration is more suggestive than a long list of do's and don't's.

Postscript to the Use of Mental Models

In light of the experimental science known as virology, the categories of "inanimate" and "animate" have been experimentally invalidated. Thus, in using the distinctions of "physical" and "biological" to describe the two general types of mental models, we must be careful *not* to make the following dichotomous assumptions: (1) that the physical models (static, mechanical, feedback) refer to "dead" inanimate objects and (2) that what we call biological (cell, plant, animal, human) are "alive" and animate. This is not so surprising if we remember that in the abstracting process *any* verbal category is at least two steps removed, or a higher order abstraction, from what is going on (WIGO).

The sharp dichotomy between "inanimate" and "animate" was a product of stage-two thinking that took what we see as what *is*. With the naked eye we do not see the "movement" of a rock or a piece of metal; therefore we assume that they are "dead" and "inanimate." Buckminster Fuller, in his volume *Synergetics*, has this to say on this matter:

> Atoms and crystal complexes of atoms were held to be obviously inanimate; the protoplasmic cells of biological phenomena were held to be obviously animate. It was deemed to be common sense that warm-blooded, moist, and soft-skinned humans were clearly not to be confused with hard, cold granite or steel objects. A clear-cut threshold between animate and inanimate was therefore assumed to exist as a fundamental dichotomy of all physical phenomena. . . .Virologists have found that no physical threshold does in fact exist between animate and inanimate. The possibility of its existence vanished because the supposedly unique physical qualities of both animate and inanimate have persisted right across yesterday's supposed threshold in both directions to permeate one another's—previously perceived to be exclusive—domains. Subsequently, what was animate has become foggier and foggier, and what is inanimate clearer and clearer. [18]

The implications of this are far-reaching, especially in relation to the semantic responses that we have developed around the word "life." But for our present purposes in learning to function at stage four of the epistemological profile, it is important to eliminate any absolute distinctions as positive conclusions. As shown in the use of animate and inanimate, acceptance of these as final can prevent us from further differentiation of integral organic operations, not only with those "inanimate objects" of our environment, but also with the processes of our own organisms. Mental models and analogies that are patterned after such verbal artifices can severely limit our participation in the worlds in which we live.

[18]R. Buckminster Fuller, *Synergetics* (New York: Macmillan Publishing Co., Inc., 1975), pp. xxix-xxx.

CHAPTER 13

languages as shapers of ideas

I look at a textbook for the study of Spanish, and it is like most language textbooks: each chapter or lesson consists of a few rules, a vocabulary, and some exercises. The vocabulary presents, in two parallel columns, the English term on one side and the equivalent Spanish term on the other side. In one column is "the family" and on the same line in the other column is *la familia*, on one side "the husband" and on the other side *el esposo*, "the wife" and *la esposa*, "the mother" and *la madre*, and so on.

Back of this parallel presentation of English words and their equivalents in the language we want to learn is a hidden assumption, a seemingly obvious truth that we are taking for granted. The assumption is that the two languages are nothing but equivalent and alternative methods of naming the same objects, of expressing the same thoughts. The objects are there, in the outside world; the ideas are there, in people's minds; all one has to do is to learn what to call objects or ideas in the new language: "brother" or *hermano*, "I have a bad headache" or *me duele mucho la cabeza*.

If, later in our studies, we hit upon a few experiences that cannot be translated in such a direct, equivalent manner, it does not change our basic assumption. We know that these exceptions—like all exceptions—"confirm the rule"; and the rule is that the two languages are simply two different ways of naming the same object, expressing the same idea, describing the same event. The objects, the events, and the ideas do not change; only the words that we use to refer to them change in spelling and in sound. The mother of a family is the mother, whether we call her "mother," *madre*, or *mère*.

If we want to express an idea, the words may not fit so snugly in exactly the same slots; we may have to say, for instance, *ud tiene razón* to mean "you are right," but the objective meaning is so obviously the same that our former assumption is not disturbed. It still seems evident that two different languages are two different ways of reporting the same human experience. In our current *episteme* (see Chapter 2, page 15), when this experience is "pure thought," free from emotional bias, we take it that we have strict logic, rock-bottom human common sense, and we deem it independent of whatever language we may use.

All this sounds quite reasonable, but it is not the way up-to-date science sees it; in fact, it is just the opposite of what is accepted today. Listen to Clyde Kluckhohn, the late Harvard anthropologist:

> Every language is a special way of looking at the world and interpreting experience. . . . One sees and hears what the grammatical system of one's language has made one sensitive to, has trained one to look for in experience. This bias is the more insidious because everyone is so unconscious of his native language as a system. To one brought up to speak a certain language, it is part of the very nature of things.[19]

Another scientist, Benjamin Whorf, the linguist, says:

> Each language is not merely a reproducing instrument for voicing ideas, but rather is itself a shaper of ideas.[20]

There is no such thing as *pure* logic taken as a set of rules for pure thinking. There is no logic that is independent of a symbol system. What is logical in one system may or may not be logical in another.

> We cut up nature, organize it into concepts, and ascribe significance as we do largely because we are parties to an agreement to organize it in this way . . . this agreement is, of course, an implicit and unstated one, but *its terms are absolutely obligatory;* we cannot talk at all except by subscribing to the organization and classification of data which the agreement decrees.[21]

We cannot talk and we cannot think *discursively* without making our thinking agree with the structure of our language.

The languages that most of us are familiar with—English, French, Spanish, German—have so much in common that the differences stressed by linguists and cultural anthropologists are not striking. Whorf called these languages Standard Average European, or SAE languages. To become aware of the control that language has on our thinking, we have to compare SAE to

---

[19]Clyde Kluckhohn, *Mirror for Man* (New York: McGraw-Hill, 1949), p. 159.
[20]Whorf, *Language, Thought, and Reality*, p. 212.
[21]Whorf, *Language, Thought, and Reality*, p. 213.

languages belonging to entirely different families, such as the Indo-Chinese, the Japanese, the American Indian, the Semitic, and such. Once this is done, it becomes evident that different languages have different logics and different maxims of common sense.

We seldom question the common sense of our own language; it seems that whatever lies within the range of common sense needs no further proof, no further check, no further explanation. This common sense is woven in the very texture of our every day speech. For instance, everybody knows that the past is gone, the present is here, and the future has not happened yet. This undeniable fact is the basis of the tenses of our verbs: the past, the present, and the future. They are part of the conceptual framework within which we study history, manage the present, and plan for the future.

What is evident for us is not at all evident to people who belong to a different culture: they can get along very well, planning their lives and communicating among themselves, without using our conceptual framework of past, present, and future. I take the word of the anthropologists, for this; they have found, for instance, that the Hopi language has no tenses like ours. In that language, writes Laura Thompson,

> ...the duties of our three-tense system and its tripartite objectified "time" are distributed among various verb categories, all different from our tenses; and there is no more basis for objectified "time" in Hopi verbs than in other Hopi patterns; although this does not in the least hinder the verb forms from being...adjusted to the pertinent realities of actual situations. [22]

If one says that the case of the Hopi language can be ignored on the grounds that it is part of "primitive" culture, anthropologists will give us examples from highly "sophisticated" cultures that illustrate the same point; namely, that our conceptual structure of the world is an arbitrary construction, an invention of our prescientific ancestors. Our dealings with the world and with our fellow humans have to follow patterns that were established centuries ago.

> You cannot say in Chinese, "Answer me yes or no," for there are no words for yes or no. Chinese gives priority to "how" and non-exclusive categories; European languages to "what" and exclusive categories. [23]

In other words, assumptions about the nature of reality and patterns of thinking are embedded in every language, and they do not necessarily correspond to equivalent assumptions and patterns of thinking embedded in other languages. These patterns of thinking vary from culture to culture. The Hopi get along very well without saying "I was," "I am," or "I shall be." The Chinese can wiggle out of a yes-or-no alternative without losing face. To many people in our culture, both sound illogical, nonsensical; to them, it is

[22]Laura Thompson, *Culture in Crisis* (New York: Harper & Row, 1950), p. 162.
[23]Kluckhohn, *Mirror for Man*, p. 160.

plain common sense, and they might justly wonder why we should quibble about it. For them, as for us, "it is as natural that experience should be organized and interpreted in these language-defined classes as it is that seasons change."[24]

Please take some time to ponder this last quotation. It is natural that seasons follow one another in a certain order: spring, summer, autumn, winter. Spring is between winter and summer; it comes again and again, always holding the same place in the yearly parade. We take it where it is, when it is; we did not choose its place.

Time as a succession of past, present, and future seems just as natural as the seasons in their yearly sequence. We see the present between the past and the future as we see spring between winter and summer. But the present is there only because somebody created it as a pattern of thinking about a process-happening that had no definite place, borders, or size. Somebody put it there long, long ago. Once the thinking pattern was invented and put into circulation, nobody thought of inventing a different one to modify our reaction to that process-happening. Time (past, present, and future) became the good and only pattern. It reigned unchallenged in that segment of human experience until a long-haired scientist recently questioned the wisdom of our primitive ancestors and linked time with space. But in the commonsense transactions of daily life, time is still "past," "present," and "future," as the grammar dictates. It follows a sequence, just as the seasons do.

When a science writer, Melville Thistle, appears to ignore the "natural" sequence, as in one of his serious-humorous talks entitled *We Can Change the Past,* it sounds more paradoxical than common sense would allow. It is like putting summer before spring on next year's calendar. We can imagine it, if we want; we can joke about the incongruous thoughts it triggers; but "Don't fool yourself," says commonsense "you cannot change the natural order of things, therefore you cannot change the past."

This "natural" order of things, invented and established by the unwitting creators of our culture, corresponds to what we have elsewhere called the system-function, the overarching vault that encloses all our doctrines, theories, and statements.[25] Our reasoning self denies the existence of whatever fails to fit within this system, which is the solid structure of absolutes that limits our world as it holds it together.

How did you and I happen to accept this system-function? How old were we when we did? On what evidence did we decide to accept it? You

---

[24]Kluckhohn, *Mirror for Man,* p. 159.
[25]J. Samuel Bois, *Explorations in Awareness* (New York: Harper & Row, 1957), "Statements, Theories, and Doctrines," Chap. 5, pp. 28-34; and "An Important Distinction," Chap. 8, pp. 51-58.

cannot answer these questions, and neither can I. We did not accept it, we were born and reared with it. It emerged with us as we emerged into conscious life. We took it for granted, as we took our hands and feet for granted, in an implicit act of faith that this is the way things are since this is the way everybody sees them and speaks about them all around us. Some of these things were there as results of nature's activities, and we had to accept them as our ancestors had. Some were there because our forebears had put them there, but we did not know the difference. We took for granted the world as presented to us, growing with us, and limited by the articulated wisdom of the language our parents spoke. It is through the screen of that language that "logical" evidence has been filtered ever since.

At the origin of our conscious life there is an act of faith, an unwitting acceptance—without antecedent evidence—of the interpretation of the cosmos made by some primitive ancestors who happened to react in a certain way to the world around them. This blind act of faith is at the bottom of the most supercilious logic. As Dr. Vannevar Bush put it in his report as president of the Carnegie Institution of Washington in 1955: "Our reasoning appears sound to us only because we believe it is and because we have freed it from inconsistencies in its main structure; for it is built on premises which we accept without proof or the possibility of proof." We believe that the way we have grown to react is the only way, the genuine "human" way. Our formal logic improves that way of reacting, makes it more efficient; it does not change its foundations. Something is set in advance in the mechanism of our thoughts and feelings: they will operate within certain limits.

The pervasive influence of the interpretation of the cosmos implied in our SAE languages is something like gravitation in the physical world: it is everywhere, acts everywhere, and, as a consequence, is not easily detectable. It took centuries for scientists to discover gravitation. First, they had to note phenomena that escaped the attention of the common person, and from these observations they devised a theory. Then they tested their theory by experiment. Today, they have reached the stage where we can rocket ourselves out of the earth's gravitational field and experience weightlessness.

The pulling force of the logic in which we were born and reared was not any easier to discover. Anthropologists and linguists took note of phenomena that escape the attention of the common person. For instance, Benjamin Whorf observed that our behavior is in part determined by the manner in which we describe the circumstances in which it occurs. From this and similar observations a theory was devised:

> No individual is free to describe nature with absolute impartiality but is constrained to certain modes of interpretation even while he thinks himself most free. The person most nearly free in such respects would be a linguist familiar with very many widely different linguistic systems. As yet no linguist is in any such position. We are thus introduced to a new principle of relativity, which

holds that all observers are not led by the same physical evidence to the same picture of the universe, unless their linguistic backgrounds are similar, or can in some way be calibrated. [26]

I know of one case where a scientist rocketed himself out of our cultural logic and reported on his experience, as the astronauts and cosmonauts report their experience of weightlessness in space. The scientist was Dr. Clyde Kluckhohn, the anthropologist, who studied the Navaho Indians. In spite of his careful observation and his open-mindedness, he could not make sense of their value system and their legal norms, but after he began to think as a Navaho and not as an American, their system of values and their rules for settling disputes became logical and obvious. After these Navaho concepts had been brought into the open, they formed a consistent philosophy. Without that philosophy, the facts that he saw could not be understood as the Navahos understood them; with that philosophy, the Navaho way of understanding them was the only one that made sense.

Another example is that of Carlos Castenada, who, in four well-written volumes, provides us with an illustration of the many difficulties that a member of one culture encounters when attempting to assimilate a system of a completely different structure. Castenada, who started out as an anthropologist on a research mission, became an apprentice to a Yaqui Indian shaman named don Juan Matus, who referred to himself as a sorcerer. Their relationship took place over a period of more than fifteen years.

In the introduction to *Journey to Ixtlan*, Castenada said:

> ...don Juan concentrated the best of his efforts into leading me to a genuine conviction that what I held in mind as the world at hand was merely a description of the world; a description that had been pounded into me from the moment I was born.
>
> He pointed out that everyone who comes into contact with a child is a teacher who incessantly describes the world to him, until the moment when the child is capable of perceiving the world as it is described....From that moment on, however, the child is a *member*. He knows the description of the world; and his *membership* becomes full-fledged, I suppose, when he is capable of making all the perceptual interpretations which, by conforming to that description, validate it....
>
> Fortunately, in the case of my apprenticeship, don Juan was not concerned at all with whether or not I could take his proposition seriously, and he proceeded to elucidate his points, in spite of my opposition, my disbelief, and my inability to understand what he was saying....My difficulty in grasping his concepts and methods stemmed from the fact that the units of his description were alien and incompatible with those of my own. [27]

When an astronaut returns to earth, we are ready to accept his version of

---

[26]Whorf, *Language, Thought, and Reality*, p. 214.
[27]Carlos Castenada, *Journey to Ixtlan* (New York: Simon and Schuster, 1972), pp. 8-9.

how he felt when he was freed from the influence of gravitation. Similarly, we have to accept the anthropologist's report when he tells us how it feels to live in a world of thought where our logic exerts no influence. He is one who knows that we can remain human without clinging to our particular brand of logic; and from this we can conclude that our value system and our norms for settling disputes are not the only possible ones in a world in which human-kind can continue to exist.

It is not easy for us to get the feel of cultural logics very different from our own. All we can do, at the moment, is accept the fact that they exist and peer into some of the regions that are within our understanding.

Looking at our own language "from the outside" makes us realize that it is not consistent as we are wont to believe. For instance, we divide most of our words into two classes, nouns and verbs, as if nature were clearly divided into two classes: (1) a class of things that are rather permanent and (2) a class of actions that are transitory. "House" is a thing; it stands there perma-nently. "To enter" the house is an action, the movement from outside to inside; it is transitory. The trouble is that we also use nouns to describe transitory events, to which we thus give a sort of permanency that they do not possess. We speak of "waves," "sparks," "flames," "storm," "noise," "emotion," and we use verbs to describe lasting and stable events such as "to keep," "to continue," "to persist," "to dwell." We even use nouns to refer to something that does not exist until an action takes place to bring it into existence. For instance, nobody "has" fists, and "to have" fists you have to close your hands. Instead of saying "I have fists," it would be more logical to say "I fist my hands."

The Hopi have a way of using numbers that I believe is more logical than ours. They use cardinal numbers, 1, 2, 3...only for things that form an objective group. Thus they say "two horses," "three men," "four trees," and so on, because there can be such actual groups of these. But when it comes to things that cannot form an objective group, they use ordinal numbers, *first, second, third,* . . . .Thus, they will not say "ten days" because ten days cannot be collected as an objective group. "They stayed ten days" becomes "They stayed until the eleventh day," or "They left after the tenth day."

Back of our own picture of the world is the Aristotelian concept of matter and form, which makes it difficult for us to accept the ultra-modern view that matter and energy are one and the same. In Hopi, this difficulty does not exist because the warp and woof of their cosmos is not matter but something that is much more fluid and process-like. To express it, Whorf uses the gerund of a verb that is now obsolete in English, the verb "to event," and he speaks of "eventing." This is much closer to the physicist's concept of energy and action—without reference to a substratum of that energy or an "actor" who does the action. I want to convey something of the kind when I speak of the world of general semantics as a world of *happenings-meanings.*

If we look into other cultures, we will find still other methods of mental functioning, which are different from ours and different from the Hopi. Here is a passage from a personal communication that I received a few years ago from a general semanticist who teaches languages in Japan.

> In the East, the world within which man lives and moves and has his being is apparently perceived as a great indeterminate esthetic continuum of space, intersected and cut up by "objects" or "things" of *beauty*, large and small, of definite shapes, sizes, colors, hues and textures, which form varying and ever-changing patterns of space between them, clearly seen as entities of *beauty* (for which there are words in the vocabulary). The whole is set in a background of space which is a thing of beauty in its own right. In terms of Western logic, "the beauty of empty space" is for practical purposes a non-sense expression; it is a basic principle of Eastern esthetics—which is the same as saying that it is a basic principle of Eastern life.[28]

Are non-Aristotelian logics more inclusive than the SAE logic that gives shape to the "thought-world" in which we live, move, and have our being? Dr. Lanier is inclined to think so.

> Just as the Aristotelian logic is a special case of the all-inclusive non-Aristotelian logics (as the Euclidian geometry is of the non-Euclidian geometries, and the Newtonian physics is of the non-Newtonian physics), so the particular structure of the world which characterizes the Western languages and culture is but one special case of the more inclusive worlds of the non-Aristotelian languages and cultures of the East.
>
> The West is stymied by the symmetrical patterns of its own Aristotelian logic, by the values in which it cannot see, cannot understand, cannot enter into the structures of the East, because it cannot pierce the walls of its own culture. Conversely, however, the Language-Logic and the Thinking-Feeling structures of the East, and the cosmological world to which they are geared, offer no essential barrier to an understanding of those whose neuro-linguistic system comprehends within its delicate complexities the Western—and perhaps—other structures and points of view.[29]

This brings vividly to mind a remark that another general semanticist, my friend the late Charles Tarver, made to me one day as we were contrasting our views on a topic that I don't happen to remember just now. "Charlie," I said, "I see you locked behind the bars of the Aristotelian mental prison." "I do see bars between us," he rejoined, "but I wonder who is in and who is out."

Who is in and who is out? Who is locked within a restraining system that he accepts as the system of the whole world, and who is free to move from his system to any other? Dr. Lanier's opinion cannot be dismissed lightly: we know that the Japanese copied our technology with great ease not long ago and are not behind us any more; and what of the Chinese?

[28]E. A. Lanier, a private communication to the author (December 2, 1955).

[29]Lanier, private communication to author (December 2, 1955).

Most of us know no more about the linguistic forces that bear upon us than the savage knew of the forces of gravitation. We imagine that thinking and talking are free activities, of which we can be masters as long as we keep our emotions in leash. Nothing is farther from the truth. Thinking is still a mystery, as the movements of the planets and the comets were mysteries in the Middle Ages; we are just beginning to survey the tremendous energies that are at work in our "inner space." The study of the cultural determinants of logic is one of the avenues that is open to us. In a world of a plurality of cultures, we have to accept a plurality of logics.

Summary

In this chapter on structure, I described mental models using Kenneth Boulding's levels of organization. This presents "structure" in terms of fields of activity in ever-increasing levels of complexity. This construct makes it possible to detect the baleful implications of the static and mechanical thinking models that we use most of the time in human affairs, and alternatively to begin to profit from the biological models that introduce the notions of growth, development, and maturation in our thinking about ourselves and about the institutions we live with and create.

I also discussed how various languages are different in structure, not just in vocabulary, some languages more than others; and that there is no one-to-one logical correspondence between such language systems.

Self-reflexiveness in the use of analogy and language keeps us out of the "gravitational pull" of assumed "objective realities" independent of human participation that are buried in our language structure. With analogy, we forget that they are analogies. We take them for an accurate description of what is going on. Without awareness of our self-reflexiveness, we unconsciously expect what is going on to fit our units of discourse. This can lead to great difficulty in human affairs, and to some rude awakenings when we expect the expected.

At stage four, we realize that we are the model makers; that when we invent a human model, we are that which is modeling itself. We are structurally more than any model that we can make of ourselves or of our experience. This and other postulates of the current conceptual revolution call for a new kind of participation with oneself and with others. This involves an intimacy and thorough familiarity with those aspects of our functioning that are other than discursive, such as the self-moving, feeling, and electrochemical aspects of our semantic transactions. This will be the subject of the next chapter.

PART VII

"silent" determinants of behavior

The activities covered by the ellipses X, A, and B in the semantic transactor diagram (p. 29) (drives, needs, habits, motives and feelings) are like the regions of which we have no clear geography. To deal with them we often have to depend on the unsystematic observations of previous generations and on unduly moralistic directives.

The propulsive force that keeps the universe in existence manifests itself at the human level as love—the natural medium in which the rising course of psycho-social evolution can proceed.

CHAPTER 14

nonintellectual aspects of semantic transactions

Of the various aspects of our semantic transactions, thinking is the one to which we have given most of our attention so far. We studied the process of abstracting, developed our awareness of orders of abstraction and of circularity, learned to analyze our mental constructs by means of the epistemological profile, listed mental models in increasing orders of complexity, have given consideration to the human time-binding capacity—from the primitive who invented symbols by a kind of elemental intuition to the scientist of today who chooses postulates from a much richer intuition sanctioned by conscious design.

The fact is that the many human sciences that are supplying us with information about ourselves are just beginning to study the self-managing aspects of our feeling, self-moving, or electrochemical activities. In these areas our vocabulary is not yet with the technical sharpness of scientific constructs; we are still using commonsense expressions in most cases. When new terms are chosen or invented by a school of psychoanalysis or psychology, it takes some time for them to be accepted, if they are at all, by the general public. For instance, what percentage of people with better-than-average knowledge have a clear idea of what is meant by Lewin's *life-space*, by Murray's *succorance*, by Maslow's *self-actualization*, by Selye's *adaptation syndrome*, by Alexander's *primary control?* How often do we use these terms, or similar ones, in ordinary conversation or in thinking about ourselves? How often do we, rather, use plain, commonsense, indeterminate terms to refer to such phenomena or their assumed equivalents?

For most of us, the areas covered by ellipses *A, B,* and *X,* in the seman-tic transaction diagram (Figure 3.1) are like regions for which we have no clear geographical map; we have to depend on the often fanciful reports of nonsystematic observers. It is said of Hottentots that they had no number classification beyond one, two, and three; whatever was more than three was "a lot," or "infinity"—without any possible differentiation between four, a dozen, or many more. We are still at a comparable stage when it comes to differentiating our feelings and our body sensations. We quickly stop short once we have said that we love, hate, or trust someone. The various forms of love are lumped together, like all the "more-than-three" were by the Hot-tentots. Love is easily taken to imply an erotic element when the two "lov-ers" are of different sexes, and it may well be that this lack of distinction reacts upon the "lovers" themselves, creating problems that are purely symbol-derived. In French, the commonsense vocabulary is even poorer; it does not even include the obvious distinction between "to love" and "to like."

Does this mean that no work is being done in these areas? Quite the contrary. Research reports, experimentation schemes, and theories of all sorts are abundant in professional periodicals. Self-help books appear many times a year that promise happiness, health, power, creativity, to everyone who accepts their psychological, mystical, religious, or *new* "scientific" recipes.

A choice has to be made among these offerings, and it is not easy. Even after we have discarded the schemes that are blatantly advertised, in which we suspect that the purpose is not so much to help the reader or the sub-scriber but rather to exploit his misery and his credulity, we are left with an abundance of theories and methods that overlap or clash, or that require the help of an expert for their application. In the pages that follow we shall describe theories and methods that our experience has shown to be of some use.

Primary Control and Relaxation

We are now dealing with what we called, in our semantic transaction dia-gram (Figure 3.1), our *self-moving activities* (ellipse *A*). They include the autonomic functioning of our organs, our voluntary movements, our sensory experiences, and our muscular skills. We have a recording in our writing. We may meet a friend on the street, and a noticeable change in the way she walks, holds her head, shakes hands with us will reveal that something im-portant has happened in her life. Our moving activities reflect and, by circu-larity, influence our semantic transactions

Persons who are trained in observing human behavior, who have learned to detect the slight differences in muscle tone that escape the common observer, are able to see conditions of which the subject herself may be unaware.

Is it possible for the unskilled person to develop an awareness of his *A* activities from the inside, as it were, so that he may learn to manage these self-moving activities much as he learns to manage his thinking and his feeling? Do moving activities, voluntary and involuntary, fall within the range of awareness, as the subtle changes in the face of a sitter fall within the range of observation of a painter?

I think so. The art of awareness includes the awareness of our physical self, of the quality of our sensations, of the balance of our posture, of our muscular tension or relaxation, of the way we move, walk, and gesticulate. A certain degree of this general awareness is desirable for anyone who wants to save his energy and be fully productive.

We may quote here a statement of John Dewey:

> It is not such a simple matter to have a clear-cut sensation. The latter is a sign of training, skill, habit.[1]

Was this statement of the great educator-philosopher influenced by his personal experience in the training he received from F. M. Alexander, the Australian discoverer of primary control, who was practicing his art in London at a time when Dewey, George Bernard Shaw, Sir Stafford Cripps, and other outstanding people were consulting him? It may well be, for the same book has ten pages of comments on Alexander's method.

Alexander's technique of primary control appealed to such persons as those we have cited because it was based on sound scientific observation, which was later confirmed by independent experiments in laboratories. In a 1924 treatise entitled *Körperstellung* ("Body-Structure"), Professor Rudolph Magnus of Utrecht, Holland, announced that he had discovered what he called "central control" in animals of all kinds. This control exists in a complex of muscles in the region where the head joins the neck. From this point the entire system of animals is controlled, as can be seen in slow-motion pictures of falling cats always reaching the ground on their four feet.

Dewey quickly saw how the discoveries of Alexander, confirmed by the experiments of Magnus in Europe and later by Coghill in this country, threw a new light on Pavlov's conditional reflex theory. Alexander's work demonstrated that certain basic and central organic habits and attitudes condition *every* act we perform, *every* use we make of ourselves. Hence a conditioned reflex is not an arbitrarily established connection, such as that between the sound of a bell and the eating reactions of a dog; it goes back to central conditions in the organism itself.

Here is the point where General Semantics and the Alexander

[1]John Dewey, *Human Nature and Conduct* (New York: Modern Library [Random House], 1930), p. 31.

technique meet: both agree that the organism works as a whole, and that we have to think about it in a nonelementalistic manner. Its activities are integrated in a central pattern that reveals the general orientation, the style of living of the individual. To develop awareness is to unearth this central integrating pattern that is buried in our cultural unconscious. Once it is brought to light, we can take control of it. At the thinking level this pattern is the system-function of our subject-predicate language; at the feeling level it is the set of values that we do not question; at the self-moving level it is the primary control that is lodged in the muscle system where the head joins the neck.

My personal experience with the Alexander technique is limited to five training sessions under Dr. Frank Pierce Jones, of Boston, which I took many years ago, and to prolonged private training by means of the exercises devised by Dr. Robin Skynner, of London, a medical practitioner who applies General Semantics to his work.

One of the interesting points made by Alexander, and emphasized by his American disciple, Frank Pierce Jones, is that our organism is misused because our culture has developed habits of posture that do violence to our bone, muscle, and organic structure. I see a parallel between this and the habits of strict logic that have taken over in the thinking areas. In the feeling areas, we either disregard the constructive function of sentiments and emotions, or we shamefully admit that we are neurotic when they get beyond control. The art of awareness is the art of living in full consciousness of these energetic drives and habits, seeing that they stay in tune and in harmony with one another.

According to Dr. Skynner, it may take up to eighteen months of practice for a person to train himself in primary control by means of the program he suggests. It may be so, but I can report from personal experience that noticeable results can be achieved earlier. These exercises have nothing in common with the usual setting-up exercises; they are not a strain on the system. George Bernard Shaw was eighty years of age when he first went to Alexander, when he could hardly take a step without agony because of angina. In less than three weeks he was able to walk a mile and to resume the daily swim that he had given up. He lived another fourteen active years, and died of a fall while pruning a tree.

There is no doubt that the help of an instructor makes a great difference in the training for any skill. The better the instructor, the better the training, of course; but even if the former acts merely as an observer and encourager, he or she—or a training pal—may be of value.

I have acted many times as an instructor in training people in organismic awareness by means of another technique: Dr. Edmund Jacobson's progressive relaxation. Dr. Jacobson, a physiologist at the University of Chicago, began to study the effects of muscular relaxation about fifty years ago and has published many reports of his experiments in scientific journals. In 1929 the first edition of his scientific treatise, *Progressive Relaxation*, was published by the University of Chicago Press. In 1934, he published a popular description of his experiments and techniques under the title *You Must Relax*, which has gone through several editions. A few years ago a foundation was established to promote the application of Jacobson's findings to business and industry. In 1964, he published a book intended principally for his confreres in the medical profession, *Anxiety and Tension Control*. In it he introduces "Self-Operation Control" or self-training in habits of efficiency by means of neuromuscular control.

Jacobson's main theme is the cultivation of the muscle sense, of the ability to differentiate—at the silent level—how our muscles feel when they are tense or relaxed, and he insists on a daily practice of from one to two hours over weeks and months. It may be that some persons have the persistence to keep at it that long, but I have never met a person who did it all by himself with the help of only the book. With an instructor, the practice time can be reduced to half an hour a day, and the initial phases of training—to the point of clearly differentiating between tenseness and relaxation—take no more than three or four sessions. From that moment on, trainees are on their own; all they need is encouragement to keep practicing until they have reached the degree of expertness that is indicated in each case. This proficiency, once obtained, requires further practice of course, as does expertness in any other skill. There is an anecdote about Paderewski in the days when he was acknowledged as the top pianist in the world. "If I fail to practice one day, I notice the difference. If I stop two days, my friends notice it, too. If I abstain for a whole week, everybody in the audience detects it!" The same is true of relaxation: this skill requires constant practice if one is to reach the virtuosity that certain situations demand.

There is no attempt to use suggestion or hypnosis in the Jacobson method; quite the contrary. It is a matter of conscious muscular training, like learning to swim, to dance, to typewrite, or to play a musical instrument. In my own practice, the results were uniformly good and had a marked influence on the clients' ability to face their problems with an easier mind. This ability, with the use of report language to describe situations instead of interpretive language to evaluate them, made it possible to face the most touchy issues without going into emotional panic. No patient who had been in the habit of taking sleeping pills felt the need to continue taking them after three or four exercises in supervised relaxation.

Dr. Jacobson has made the claim that, with enough practice in the relaxation of the muscles of the eye and the throat, one may eventually stop one's thinking at will. I agree, but I insist that it takes much practice. What is of particular interest to me in this, from the point of view of general semantics, is that this achievement becomes quite understandable once one agrees that thinking is not simply an affair of the mind, the spirit, or what have you. I cannot resist quoting a rather lengthy passage from Jacobson's popular book concerning this. It shows that earnest workers in the human sciences are not general semanticists in a formal way, but they are participants in the conceptual revolution of our time. Listen to this, and ask yourself what your thinking has in common with that of John Doe.

> All of his life, John Doe had been accustomed to distinguish between his mind and his body. When he worried, he believed that he did so with his mind, not with his body. No doubt, he assumed, worry occurred as an act of the brain. To this extent, worry, was something, he reflected, that went on in the body but it was in a particular part of the body, namely: the skull. What was true of worry, he believed, was likewise true of his memory and his attention, his fears and other emotions and especially his imagination. He yielded to the belief that mental activities occur in the mind and when muscles become tense, this is only a result or expression of what goes on in the mind. He maintained, therefore, that while relaxing might do him a lot of good, it could hardly be expected to take care of his mental ills. To this he added a further objection and difficulty. He found that when he was emotionally upset, he could not relax. From this he concluded that he lacked the willpower to relax. From this objection he passed on to another, namely: that he could not be expected to relax in the presence of so much distress unless something was first done to improve his mental state.

> John Doe came by his views honestly. He inherited them from his forefathers, including those of the nineteenth century. As he learned to observe accurately what took place at moments when he worried, imagined, recalled or engaged in some other particular mental activity, he became enlightened. . . .Experience taught him that the mind was not what he had believed it to be, following tradition. He acquired a new working conception and with the aid of a little explanation, he no longer assumed that whenever he worried it was an act of the brain alone. For one thing, he learned that as he relaxed, he ceased to worry! This surprised him![2]

Yes, as you relax, and the better you have trained yourself to relax, the less you worry. There is no magic or miracle in this: the organism reacts as a whole. If we are too upset to think logically, and if we have practiced the art of muscular relaxation, there is a fair chance that we may be able to relax in spite of the mental and emotional upset. For the time being, this is the most direct way of controlling our thoughts and our emotions. Learning muscular relaxation is like learning to swim. If we are an accomplished swimmer, the chances are that in an emergency we will be able to do almost automatically what a nonswimmer could not possibly do even if he tried hard.

One of the most interesting features of the Jacobson method is what he

[2]Edmund Jacobson, *You Must Relax* (New York: McGraw-Hill, 1934), p. 159.

calls *differential* relaxation, or relaxation while being otherwise active. We may identify relaxation with lying on a couch or lounging in an easy chair, but this is not necesarily so; and there are many things we can do without engaging all the muscles of our body. We can read, write, sew, engage in a conversation, or even in a debate, without having to tense up the large muscles of the limbs or the trunk. What often happens is that we let a generalized tension run over our whole organism when a limited effort is all that is needed. The consequence is that we spend more nervous energy and we perform less effectively. A good acrobat, or ballet dancer, or musician performs with ease because his or her whole system, instead of stiffening in a generalized tenseness, relaxes where it should and when it should. Similarly, most of our work calls for less expenditure of energy than we exert. Once we have learned, by experience and practice, the difference between a tense and a relaxed muscle, we can let part of our organism rest while some other part is active.

If while at our desk—writing, telephoning, conversing, or reading—we make sure that the unused muscles of our legs, thighs, and arms are in a state of relaxation, we will soon notice that we do not tire so easily, we remain more habitually calm, and our thinking is more alert. If we try to do all this before a basic training in the fundamentals of relaxation, of course, it won't work; we will have added one more preoccupation to what we are busy with. Remember the swimmer: he feels at home in the water because he has learned to manage his movements in the fluid element; a nonswimmer may become frantic and might drown. Relaxing is not a matter of good intentions and willpower; it is a matter of simple learning and constant practice.

On Motivation

What gives unity and consistency to our behavior is not so much the logical meaning of the theories we hold true as the value-meaning of what we hold dear. The cortex is at the service of the centrencephalon, and not vice versa. As a consequence, the *B* aspect of our semantic transactions—which covers not only affects and emotions but also attitudes, purposes, desires, ambitions, and values—has an importance of its own.

How do we analyze and measure feelings and purposes? The task is not easy; it requires finding a common dimension for those hard-to-define urges, drives, and affects that give movement, direction, warmth, and color to our life. In textbooks on psychology, this usually comes under such headings as "personality," "motivation," "personal development," "levels of aspiration," and so on.

There is a plethora of theories of personality that are current in psychological literature. Some of these theories stress hereditary factors, but not so much nowadays as was the fashion years ago; it has become less acceptable to blame our ancestry for what we are. "I was born that way" does not carry much weight today. Many theories take into account the early experiences of the individual, and they remind us that these experiences have created unconscious determinants that remain active all through life. This view is quite popular with general semanticists, who speak of a cultural unconscious, of methods of thinking-feeling-acting that we take as natural because they grew with us as our body did. They know that our methods are patterned after the syntax of our mother tongue and after the mechanical models that are prevalent in our culture.

In theories of personality, we read about such topics as personal development, emotional maturity, self-identification, individuation, self-actualization, self-concept, and other explanations where the self is at the center of things. The theories based on association and reward—of the early Pavlov type—that were once so prevalent have not disappeared entirely, but they have receded into the background. Today we emphasize purpose, drive, and direction of the organism-as-a-whole, influenced by and influencing its environment.

To decide which of the many theories to adopt is very much a matter of consistency with one's outlook on life. In general semantics, we are aware of multidimensionality and abstraction: a situation may be studied under one of its many dimensions by conscious choice. This does not mean that other dimensions are completely ignored; they are there, of course, and we know that they could be taken as alternative scales of measurement.

The personality dimension that I have found the easiest to detect and measure, at least qualitatively, is *motivation*—as described in Dr. Abraham Maslow's *Motivation and Personality*. [3] Motivation is what impels us to do certain things rather than others; to wish for certain things rather than others; to react to persons and situations in a manner peculiar to ourselves.

Maslow has devised a scale of five needs that he calls instinctoid. Whatever has been researched and published on the hierarchical order of these needs, it seems that one notion is emerging that is gradually being accepted: self-actualization, mentioned as the top and overarching instinctoid need. Self-actualization as primary motivation subsumes the lower needs of physiology or hunger, security, belonging, and recognition. Self-actualization covers a cluster of urges, drives, tendencies, and characteristics that are not easy to describe. It corresponds roughly to what other personality theorists call the "mature person"; and to the notions of emotional balance and self-acceptance it adds a notion of drive, of open-ended achievement.

The self-actualizing person is attracted by the new, the unfamiliar, the challenging, the mysterious, the difficult to understand, the not-yet-known.

---

[3]Abraham H. Maslow, *Motivation and Personality* (New York: Harper & Row, 1954). I recommend a careful reading of the whole book.

He accepts being thrown into situations that he cannot rehearse beforehand. If he is kept at a job that offers no more challenge, he may become disinterested and may quit for what may appear to be trivial reasons.

He has a high degree of self-acceptance and a low degree of self-defensiveness. He does not expect perfect performance from himself or from others; he accepts what happens; he does not fret and fume over losses; he does not make an issue of minor things.

But he is not a Milquetoast, either. At times, he may appear ruthless, fatalistic, and heartless. He will take a stand, against all opposition, if he feels that it is his duty to do so. He will do it in apparent disregard for the feelings of persons who view the situation differently. When he does so, he does not mean to fight and crush persons as individuals, he wrestles with situations he feels he has to correct and recreate.

He is from a culture and within a culture, but he has grown to be independent of the shibboleths of this culture. He lives in a wide frame of reference, has a code of ethics that may appear unconventional, is deeply religious without strong institutional affiliations. There is nothing solemn about him; he has a sense of humor that can be sharp without hostility. At times he may let himself become too involved with neurotics, bores, and unhappy people. He is open-minded but not easily led. He is willing to seek all the information he can get on a problem of great importance, but he realizes that, in the end, life is made of a series of gambles.

Our instinctoid needs may all contribute at the same time, in various degrees, to the motivation of a particular course of action. We could trace a profile of our needs as we can trace a profile of the intellectual skills that we use, from the sensing reactions of the primitive to the sophisticated wisdom of the relativistic scientist. By tracing such a profile of instinctoid needs, we learn to differentiate them. This give us a clue as to how to manage our energies both for immediate results and for long-range objectives.

Maslow relates to the basic values held dear and sees them eventually dominating our behavior, so it is important to take them into account. Our conscience is not simply a list of do's and don't's that mirrors the law or some code of conduct transmitted by tradition, it is also, and in great part, the urge to gratify certain instinctoid needs as they surge within ourselves under the impact of time and circumstances. The art of managing these needs is no less important than the art of sound thinking.

Viewed in the light of biological models, self-actualization becomes the easily assumed advanced stage of the growth process, common to human beings as well as to all living things. It is the tendency to achieve maturity, to insure the continuation of the species while giving the individual a feeling of achievement to the fullest of her potentialities. In the case of humans, full achievement is never reached as a closure; it invites new rebirths in a never ending evolution. The study of this area of human activity is the subject of epistemics as a science-art of innovating. George A. Kelly is working in a common area when he suggests to do away with the whole notion of motivation as usually discussed in psychology. He views it as the conative manifestation of the very broad cosmic urge with which we participate.[4] In such a case, various theories of motivation could be seen as alternate descriptions of how we obey that urge, depending on the culture we exemplify unwittingly or in an expanding awareness.

We have not yet reached, and it may possibly be a long time before we reach, the stage of knowledge in the study of feeling and purpose at which we can use refined scales of exact measurement. We are still at the qualitative stage, where our main task is to invent new classifications that are free from the implications of our commonsense language and to devise original patterns of thinking about the whole set of phenomena thus reclassified. This has to be done without ignoring the empirical and experimental findings of previous generations, but also with a definite attempt to order them differently.

Another approach to the study of *B* activities is that of Sylvan Tomkins.[5] There is much that is old and much that is new in the two volumes that emerged from Tomkin's more than twenty years of research. The work is laborious, as any report of a new orientation is bound to be and is hard to read, which may save it from a facile and spurious popularity; but they contain a great deal that may help general semanticists organize their thinking and direct their observations in matters of feeling, purposes, and values.

The behavior processes that activate our organism and direct its activities may be considered at three different levels. At the lowest level, that of the nonconscious, are biological mechanisms (of the feedback type) whose function is to keep our electrochemical and self-moving activities in harmonious balance. To this level belong the general adaptation syndrome of Selye[6]; blood-clotting when a vessel is cut, convergence of leucocytes to combat infection, muscular tension to achieve postural balance, elimination processes through fasting under supervision. Most of these adaptations operate below the habitual level of awareness. Their action is of the reflex type, automatic and undelayed.

Next comes the level of drives. Drives may be considered the conscious expressions of the physiological activities of an organism that manages to remain alive and functioning, both as an individual and as a member of its species. The most urgent drive is the drive for air; next comes thirst, or the drive for water, and sleep, or the drive for rest; next the drive for food and for the elimination of waste; then the drive for avoidance of pain; and finally the sex drive.

[4]George A. Kelly, *The Psychology of Personal Constructs* (New York: Norton, 1955).
[5]Sylvan Tomkins, *Affects, Imagery, Consciousness, I and II* (New York: Springer, 1962).
[6]Hans Selye, *The Stress of Life* (New York: McGraw-Hill, 1956).

Drives provide information about the condition of the organism and the motivation to do what it requires at the moment. "They know what they need to know, to do what they have to do."[7]

Drives are specific; they are felt where the consummatory response is likely to produce results. The drive for air is felt in the respiratory organs, for food in the mouth and stomach, for defecation in the lower intestines. When a drive is repressed for too long, however, it spreads its disturbance all over the organism. It then reaches the level of affects and of thinking activities.

In drives there is awareness, increased variability, and possible delay of consummatory responses, as well as activation of the learning system—reactions that can be modified by experience and conscious training. For instance, the drive for air may be delayed because of the conditions of the environment, such as being under water or in a poisonous atmosphere. Through training, a person can learn to delay his breathing for longer periods.

Affects are different from drives. They do not operate in or on an organ, but are responses of the whole organism. "The specificity of the drive system is such that it instructs and motivates concerning *where* and *when* to do *what* to *what*."[8] Affects, on the contrary, are general in structure, and may find their consummatory responses in a variety of outlets. Your distress and my distress may vary more than your hunger and mine.

> Since the affect system has a more complex structure than the drive system, we should expect to find a greater range of inherited variability within the affect system than within the drive system.[9]

Apart from inherited variability, affects are made different in their manifestations and in their expected satisfactions by the culture in which we are brought up. An American company had succeeded in making a low-price, perfectly clean and hygienic protein flour from whole fish. But, for many years, the company was not allowed to sell or export it—not even to countries where people are starving for lack of protein—because in our culture we simply don't eat fish that has not been eviscerated and cleaned.

Affects may amplify the energy of the motivational system. Hunger plus impatience is more uncomfortable than simple hunger.

> A knowledge of pain perception goes beyond the problem of pain itself: it helps us understand the enormous plasticity of the nervous system and how each of us responds to the world in a unique fashion.

> In higher species at least, there is much evidence that pain is not simply a function of the amount of bodily damage alone. Rather, the amount and quality of pain we feel are also determined by our previous experiences and how well we

[7]Tomkins, *Affects, Imagery, Consciousness*, I, p. 31.
[8]Tomkins, *Affects, Imagery, Consciousness*, I, p. 172.
[9]Tomkins, *Affects, Imagery, Consciousness*, I, p. 179.

remember them, by our ability to understand the cause of the pain and to grasp its consequences.[10]

Affects may also attenuate, mask. or interfere with drives. Disgust, distress, or apathy may interfere with hunger. Surprise, fear, distress, or apathy may interfere with the sex drive.

Learning has more to do with affects than with drives. The objects of affects become values that stand in a hierarchical order, depending on their importance in the training we received at home, at school, in the church, and in our general cultural environment. Values can be defined in terms of affects: "Whatever one is excited by, enjoys, fears, hates, is ashamed of, is contemptuous of, or distressed by, is an object of value, positive or negative."[11]

Affects influence thinking activities as much as they influence drives. They are influenced, in turn, by the words we use to describe them. By the use of properly chosen words we may amplify positive affects or attenuate negative affects.

Self-management depends very much on the skill one has acquired to choose *ex tempore* the words with which to describe, to oneself and to others, the affects that surge within. At times, a violent description of negative affects—hostility, hate, anger, and the like—may have a cathartic effect, as some psychological theorists still claim, but it reminds us of the drastic purges that were in fashion centuries ago and that were deservedly ridiculed by Molière at the time when the medicos of his days were prescribing them with pompous solemnity. Modern medicine has emerged from this stage of ignorant violence. It is about time that we learn to eliminate our negative affects without tearing apart our psychological innards. Instead of being afraid of a possible repression, as if it were something like ptomaine poisoning, we can keep our whole system functioning freely if we learn to delay our reactions in the proper manner. To delay them does not mean to ignore them or to curb them by sheer will power, it means to be aware of our spontaneous affects without interpreting them right away, without passing a quick and uncritical judgment on who or what caused them. They can then be managed, or even transformed, by a conscious choice of appropriate responses, verbal or nonverbal.

A neutral response that is plainly descriptive of what is happening may work "miracles" more easily than one might anticipate. For instance, instead of saying "I hate you for what you think of me!" try something like "I feel uneasy about what you just said." Instead of saying "It was stupid of me!" try "I wish I had done it differently." Instead of tearing your hair, pat it gently; instead of banging on the table or clenching your fist, just relax your shoul-

---

[10]Ronald Melzack, "The Perception of Pain," *Scientific American* 204 (February 1961): 41.
[11]Tomkins, *Affects, Imagery, Consciousness, I*, p. 329.

ders. You won't "blow a fuse," you won't break a blood vessel, and you won't be poisoned by swallowing your own bad feelings. Your affects will not sour within you; you will find, with amazement, that it really feels good.

Instead of enumerating affective components of behavior as simple units, such as love, hate, fear, jealousy, Tomkins presents them as continua along which a gradient of intensity may be visualized. For example, we have an affective continuum of interest-excitement, of interest growing into excitement, or of excitement dwindling to mere interest. He lists two positive affects: interest-excitement and enjoyment-joy; five negative affects: distress-anguish, fear-terror, shame-humiliation, contempt-disgust, and anger-rage; and one that he calls "interrupter"; surprise-startle.

With the exception of startle, affects act in a self-reflexive way and become specific activators of themselves. In terms of the first order experience represented by the circle below the parabola in the structural differential diagram (Figure 6.3, p. 93), we see that self-reflexiveness does operate and can be trained at this first level of abstraction.

> The experience of fear is frightening, the experience of distress is distressing, the experience of anger is angering, the experience of shame is shaming, the experience of disgust is disgusting, the experience of joy is joying, the experience of excitement is exciting. [12]

The reduction or interruption of a positive affect is punishing; the reduction or interruption of a negative affect is rewarding. The toxicity of negative affects, such as anger that makes us have our own way for the time being, may be compared to the toxicity of certain drugs that destroy some bacteria or relieve some intense pain but at the same time produce side effects that are damaging to the whole system in the long run. Such damaging affects, if left to run their course, may be more damaging than the situation that was the occasion of their appearance.

Our time-binding capacity, or the capacity that we have to keep the past and the anticipated future within the range of our conscious now, is not an unmixed blessing. It demands more skill than the instinctive running away from trouble or danger. It makes possible the continuous activation of unpleasant past experiences and anticipated fears, disgusts, or humiliations, whose very presence produces anxiety. To reduce it, it is useful to learn the skill of intentionally narrowing the span of awareness to a limited now by whatever nonverbal means are available, such as sensory awareness, muscular relaxation, living at the silent level. Trying to do it by directed thinking or feeling activities, such as "trying to forget it" or "telling oneself to be sensible about it" and other such commonsense suppressions, leaves the negative affect within the range of awareness and lets its self-reflexive activation continue by amplifying feedback. This reinforcing feedback of negative affects

[12]Tomkins, *Affects, Imagery, Consciousness, I*, p. 296.

was formerly called the "law of the reverse effort," meaning that the more one attempts to control them by mere willpower, the stronger they become, eventually turning into chronic moods or into semantic states.

There is another way in which negative affects can be reduced or transformed, and it was described years ago in Dr. Matthew Chappell's *In the Name of Common Sense* (Macmillan, 1949 [rev. ed.]), later published as a paperback (by Collier) under the title *Worry and Control*. I have often wondered why it is not more generally recommended in books on clinical psychology. I have used it more than once in particularly resistant cases, and it helped produce rewarding results.

The idea is to surround the centrencephalon (the thalamic region in Korzybskian terminology) by a cortex made active with memories, cold and unemotional at the start, that were once concomitant with the affects, now absent, that we want to bring back to life. If we keep at it for a sufficiently long time, *without any willful attempt by the subject to stir up emotions by autosuggestion or otherwise*, the former affects will grow—where they apparently had left some traces—and, in time, they will refresh the whole organism. An example will illustrate what I mean.

A self-declared homosexual came to our office in Montreal; he had been forced by his family to leave England and start a new life in Canada, if he could. He said that he had had one year or so of psychoanalysis and wanted some help. To my question whether he had ever had any interest, however slight and passing, in persons of the other sex, he answered with definite no's and never's. I kept telling him to look deep in the recesses of his memory, and one day he told me he recalled that, when he was seven or eight, his mother had spent a summer at the seashore, where she had a friend who was the mother of a girl of about his age.

He was quite sure, he said, that they had played together on the beach. "There was really nothing heterosexual about it, as far as I can remember," he said, "but since you insist so much on my relating any experience with persons of the other sex, this is one that technically belongs to that class." I asked him to write a description of whatever he remembered of that vacation, the cottage, the beach, the sea, the games they played, his mother, her friend, anything at all. He came back with only three lines, and I urged him to write more details. "Well," he said, "it may be mere invention on my part, but I shall do my best to follow your prescription."

After three or four weeks, he had more than two single-spaced typewritten pages. A bit later, he came to me in a state of mild excitement. "That season was not the only one I spent with Sissie at the seashore," he reported. "I had forgotten all about another summer I passed with her, and that time it was more than neutral games."

A few years later he died, still a bachelor, but he had neutralized his tendency to form homosexual liaisons with adolescents and had established satisfactory relations with more than one female friend.

The Central Assembly

This is not the place to enter into a detailed study of the few affective continua that Tomkins discussed in his two volumes: interet-excitement, enjoyment-joy, surprise-startle, distress-anguish, and fear-terror; such a study is beyond the scope of a general methodology. There is, however, an integrative approach to the whole semantic transaction system that fits with what we have already stated in earlier chapters on the role of the centrencephalon and on psycho-logics. Our semantic reactions are controlled in direction, intensity, duration, and stability by an idiosyncratic patterning that we may call the *central assembly*.

This central assembly is not strictly anatomical; it is not limited to a neural feedback firing in reverberatory circuits, cell assemblies, and phase sequences. It integrates, at a more comprehensive level of existence, the various aspects of our semantic transactions: thinking, feeling, self-moving, electrochemical, environmental, past, and anticipated future. Of all these aspects, logic—whether classical, symbolic, mathematical, or metaphorical—deals only with thinking. Psycho-logics add new dimensions to the thinking phenomenon, taking into account orders of abstraction, multiordinality, differentiation of mental models, the structural more, the semantic jump. It also postulates a translogical order in the whole complex system of semantic transactions.

The description of the role of the central assembly could be taken as an attempt to formulate the psycho-logical, or translogical, order. The central assembly could be seen as a dynamic self-reflexive system that integrates the various types of activity as a set of so many subsystems. Thus the central assembly reactivity pattern, or central assembly set, of the whole space-time individual integrates the dynamics of thinking, of feeling, of perceptive and muscular habits and skills, of electrochemical functioning, of transacting with the environment, and of binding together within the now memories of the past and anticipations of the future.

Each of these subsystems has its own pattern. None of these patterns can be assumed to correspond structurally to the syntactical order of our subject-predicate language, refined or not by the wisdom of common sense or by the techniques of logic.

CHAPTER 15

the human equivalent of the cosmic propulsive energy

Love, or Altruism as a Passion

One of the nonintellectual aspects of our semantic transactions on which the new human sciences have not yet cast much light, comes under the much-abused terms *love* and *loving*. For the general public these words cover a multitude of activities, from the lofty dissertations of Eric Fromm in *The Art of Loving* to the gross memories of Henry Miller in *Tropic of Cancer*, from the studies of good neighbors, saints, and mystics made by Pitirim Sorokin to the lurid tales of the whorish achievements of a Fanny Hill. On the opposite side we have the daily recounting of crimes of violence, the persecutions and destructions due to the human refusal to accept all humans as related, small wars and preparation for the "big war," covert hatreds within families, open feuds between generations. Love and loving, and their opposites, hatred and hating, refer to a phenomenon that spreads from the narrow circle of the individual to the billions of human beings all over the globe, a phenomenon that manifests itself at the heights of detachment and heroism and at the depths of the most sordid selfishness. Can we make sense of all this?

Taking a fresh view of humankind as a natural phenomenon that cannot be dissociated from the ongoing drama of cosmic evolution, a modern scientist-philosopher wrote that

Love has always been carefully eliminated from realist and positivist concepts of the world; but sooner or later we shall have to acknowledge that it is *the funda-*

mental impulse of life, or if you prefer, *the one natural medium in which the rising course of evolution can proceed.*[13]

That "fundamental impulse of life," why should it be kept out of our scientific picture of the world? How does it fit with what Korzybski had in mind when he spoke of "the *affective, personal raw material*, out of which our ordinary meanings are built"?[14] If love—or whatever we mean when we use this word—is the pulsating and propelling energy that keeps evolution emerging from lower to higher forms of life; and if the affective element in our own life is what gives substance, cohesion, and value to our ordinary meanings, what prevents us from acknowledging its supreme importance when we claim to develop a system to make awareness possible and practical? The time has come when we must face this central human phenomenon with a mind that refuses to be disturbed. Surgeons operate without a tremor in the brain and in the heart of living subjects; why can't we, with the same scientific calm, explore the most vital parts of our thinking-feeling self?

Some speak of love as a matter of interdependence that we have to accept as a fact of life. This is true, no doubt, but it sounds cold and dispassionate. I prefer Sir Charles Sherrington's expression, *altruism as a passion* (from *alter*, the "other"), which means concern for all other human beings simply because they are human. This concern must become more than a so-called attitude, or a readiness to act in a definite way, and something more than a mental recognition that we are interdependent; it must be a real *passion*, something like a personal need that feeds on itself, on its own gratification as a source of greater intensity.

It began, thinks Sherrington, when the lowest form of life, the solitary and independent cell, took the first jump to a richer level of existence, that of the multicellular organism. Each individual cell gave up something of its heretofore previous independence to become joint possessor of a higher form of autonomy from its environment and was enriched by the multiplication of energies as it became integrated in the organism in formation. From that eventful moment, which marked a definite quantum jump in the evolutionary process, "union differentiates" as Teilhard de Chardin put it. It brings individuation to a higher level: from being one among many individuals, similar in nature and function, to being one among many differentiated coparticipants in a nature of a higher order and in functions that are richer and more numerous. Union differentiates, and raises to a new level of existence, what was only a distinct unit within a class—isolated and indepen-

---

[13]Pierre Teilhard de Chardin, *The Future of Man* (New York: Harper & Row, 1964), p. 54 (italics added).

[14]Alfred Korzybski, *Science and Sanity* (Lakeville, Conn.: International Non-Aristotelian Library, 1933, 1941, 1948, 1958), p. 22.

dent, but restricted in function. Union differentiates and enriches what it joins together. It creates altruism as a new relationship on the cosmic scene.

> At first glance such altruism may strike the biologist as contrary to the broad trend and polity of life. That makes the more notable the fact that evolution nevertheless has brought it about. . . .Biology cries, "The individual for itself." What are the most successful individuals which Life has to show? The multicellular. And what has gone in their making? The multicellular organism is itself a variant from the perennial antagonism of cell and cell. Instead of that eternal antagonism it is making use of relatedness to bind cell to cell for cooperation. The multicellular organism stood for a change, insofar, from conflict between cell and cell to harmony between cell and cell. *Its coming was, we know now, pregnant with an immense advance for the whole future of life upon the globe. It was potential of the present success of living forms upon the planet.* [15]

But individuation and self-centeredness quickly reappeared. Multicellular organisms, made of the cooperative interaction of many individual cells, began fighting among themselves, each to ensure its survival and that of its own species. Nature became the scene of predatory living.

> Predatory living has prospered and prospered hugely. It has brought into existence countless millions of lives which otherwise would not have been and but for it would forthwith perish. It has produced beautiful types of form and motion. It attaches as corollary to "zest-to-live" a "lust-to-kill." It develops its own gift of killing to heights of skill and ingenuity which astonish. [16]

Nature became "red in tooth and claw." Life, as such, was no sacred thing. When *Homo sapiens* appeared, in their turn, they made room for themselves and their broods by the same methods of predatory living: fighting and killing other forms of life or subduing them through domestication.

For generations we have kept this successful pattern of behavior, not only in dealing with animals but also in dealing with competing groups belonging to our own species. The tribe became a superorganism that equipped itself with weapons to fight and destroy other tribes. Nations became larger and more complex organisms that survived and prospered by the conquest of other nations. Eventually, we reached the present era, during which two world wars shook the whole planet and made it clear that the whole race runs the risk of total annihilation if it relies on conflict as the arbiter of its destiny. And now, we must ask ourselves: "What is the next step in evolutionary advance that will replace conflict as a mode of survival?"

The answer that the human sciences propose is altruism and intelligent planning. Altruism must come first. It must permeate all the activities of the individual and all the workings of the organizations that are created; other-

---

[15]Charles Sherrington, *Man on His Nature* (New York: Mentor Books [New American Library], 1964), p. 270 (italics added).

[16]Sherrington, *Man on His Nature*, p. 270.

wise, the planning will keep some old patterns of conflict that will vitiate the whole undertaking. Hidden assumptions in the realm of values have to be dug out and brought into the open; they form the tangled web of the roots of commonsense ethics, and they are just as difficult to eradicate as the commonsense logic of obsolete epistemology.

Conflict has to be ferreted out of our daily life, in all its most subtle manifestations, and replaced by an altruism that has to be cultivated, fostered, and developed until it becomes the acquired dominant passion. Once this passion has become "natural" for a sufficiently large number of members of our species, the metamorphosis of humankind into a higher form of life will take place as a normal stage of the evolutionary process. We are now in the throes of this transformation.

That it should be accompanied by a wild release of unruly behavior need not surprise us: the world of values goes through a stage of turbulence that portends the new order. Instead of fighting the turbulence with methods that have become obsolete, it is up to us to understand what is going on and to hasten the coming of the new order. That it should be viewed with pessimism by old-style humanists, who in despair see only the absurdity of everything and the threatening signs of a dark future, need not disturb us either. The old humanism that limited itself to fighting organized religion is bypassed, and a new synthesis of whatever is worthwhile in human experience is in the making.

It is true that the human condition is in peril at the moment, but it is also true that, for the first time since they have been on this planet, human beings know that their fate is in their own hands, and they know that they can develop the skills necessary to cope with the situation.

> Everything leads us to think that we are in a phase of explosive metamorphosis, which is not only the result of human intelligence and purpose, but which is a phenomenon due to the whole ascending movement of life on the parcel of the cosmos we inhabit. It is a great and pathetic event that men of today are beginning to become aware of. This fact transcends them and concerns them at the same time. It involves them in a responsibility at the level of humanity as a whole and of the cosmos itself.
>
> But this explosive metamorphosis may also turn into a regressive explosion if we slow down and remain in the old humanism instead of founding a new humanism, preparatory to a superhuman condition. A superhumanism, we may say. At the level of the old humanism, we understand only through a fog of ineffective good intentions the ancient religious precepts, the meaning of which is perhaps clear for none but the superreason and the superintelligence to come. For instance, "Thou shalt not kill" may perhaps correspond to a superhuman vision of the harmonies of life, and we shall not understand that commandment until our reason has progressed. "Love one another" means nothing. It is nothing but a pious wish, unless we substitute for it the transforming powerful effort

suggested by the other precept: "Accept and understand one another; help one another to develop and progress."[17]

Sherrington expressed himself in a slightly different manner, but his message has much in common with that of the French writer.

> It is as though the door of Nature had been pushed ajar and man were peeping through, there to get a glimpse of his own story and some fresh understanding of himself. In several ways his fuller knowledge has spelled disillusion, disenchantment. In him, evolving mind has got so far as to become critical of its way of life. . . . He is distressed by cruelty inherent in the economy of his own life. He is disillusioned the more to find he is part in that same dispensation. The regime is, if he asks his "heart," one for which he cannot seek his heart's approval. . . . But ancient trends die hard. . . . He must try to shed from his genecomplex some subhuman ingrained elements. The contradiction is that he is slowly drawing from life the inference that altruism, charity, is a duty incumbent upon thinking life. That an aim of conscious conduct must be the unselfish life. . . . Of all his new-found values perhaps altruism will be the most hard to grow.[18]

Whether we see the task that confronts us as shedding from our genecomplex some "subhuman ingrained elements" or as founding a new humanism to replace the despair of existentialism and the ineffectiveness of the theories of the absurd, the new postulates call for a dual operation. Part of it consists in doing away with whatever traces of conflict and conflict-fostering tendencies we still countenance more or less consciously in our life; part of it demands that we give unalloyed love—the fundamental impulse of life—the freedom to transform each of us into a new type of human being.

Conflict and Conflict-fostering Practices

Back of self-centeredness is a hidden mechanism that accounts for most of our readiness to enter into conflict with whoever comes our way. This mechanism is the projection of our self-image into the view we have of humankind and the disparaging judgments that emerge from contrasting the two images. The old precept used to be "Do not judge and you shall not be judged," as if it were proper to prevent the other person from judging us and permissable to judge ourselves. I prefer the shorter, "Do not judge, *period!*"—neither the other person, nor ourselves, because in both cases we run the risk of being wrong most of the time. If we again refer to the Structural Differential, (Fig. 6.3, p. 93), we will realize that none of our interpretations can be commensurate with our first-order experiences, and still less with what is going on.

---

[17]Louis Pauwels, "Ce que nous sommes et ce que nous croyons," in *Planète*, 21 (Paris, 1965): 11 (translated by J. S. Bois).

[18]Sherrington, *Man on His Nature*, p. 266.

Conflicts arise between what we think we are and what we think the other person is, between what we think she said and what she thinks we said, what we think she meant and what she thinks we meant. But all these are projections that both of us thrust forward like the lances of medieval jousters in tournaments. Drop the lances. Approach each other in a friendly and trusting contact, viewing each encounter as a new experience, unpredictable in all its details, which we can make more pleasant and fruitful if we don't prejudge it. Once the experience is over, let it flow in its place in the stream of life, without holding to it; otherwise, we run the risk of creating an eddy that slows us down or keeps us turning in circles.

Even when we have to make a decision, we should not judge it as the best, or the only one, we can or should make. It is the one we happen to see as the most expedient under the circumstances. Let life flow around, above, and below it, carrying it away in its ever-changing course. Again, all we can do is "hang loose."

Such a general attitude will reduce the potential conflicts to a tolerable minimum. It means that we will never be an exploiter of another person's foibles, of his ignorance, his fears, his anxieties, prejudices, or mistakes.

We will not make a display of a difference in social status if we enjoy the higher one, except if it might give more security to whomever we are dealing with.

We will not make a display of our skills, as in a wrestling or boxing match, or in a competition where others may be emotionally involved.

We will not play the role of a logician who picks on words that are poorly chosen, asks for sharp definitions, notes trivial contradictions, and poses rhetorical questions to trap the unwary.

We will avoid words or phrases that imply a contest and/or a victory in communication, such as "winning an argument," "fighting for one's opinions," "standing pat against all opposition," "convincing or persuading" the other person, "refuting an objection," "proving our point." Instead of this, we may "answer a question," "express our own semantic transactions," "explain what we meant"—and remain calm even when we feel we are misunderstood in matters that do not involve imminent danger to others or to ourselves.

We will avoid challenging questions, such as "Why don't you do it this way?" "Can't you see what is wrong with that?" or "Why do you act the way you do?"

We will avoid using terms that are tantamount to imposing our own set of values upon the other person. For instance, "You should . . .," "You ought to . . .," "You must . . .," "If I were you, I would. . . ."

Finally, we will abstain from terms that brand the other person's behavior or utterances as worthy only of reproof or condemnation. We may state that we don't accept them as we see or understand them, but there ends our freedom of evaluation. This does not prevent the self-actualizing person from not letting anything or anyone budge her from a position she thinks she has to assume, but it leaves her free to take a new decision when an apparently slight change in the situation gives it a new structure.

Love as a Transforming Agent

The avoidance of conflicts is not enough; the correction of practices that invite conflicts is not enough either. There is need of what Sherrington calls a "soul-growth," which will bring about a higher self.

One thing seems certain: this growth phenomenon is outside the field of science as we know it today. It is not an achievement of our discursive powers, of the two-valued logic of Aristotelianism, or of the infinite-valued logic of general semantics. In fact, for one who would limit the Korzybskian system to consciousness of abstracting, the remarks that follow are irrelevant.

It is one of the discoveries of the contemporary human sciences that our concerns are not all cognitive in the generally accepted manner. Insofar as many genuine human experiences have aspects that are affective, science— at least at the present time—does not relate to them as such. Have we any reason to believe that it will always be so, and that science will forever be kept outside the world of affects? I don't think so. We are just beginning to realize that intellectuality is only one of the many human characteristics. To our power of creating classes and organizing our world in a logical order, we now add a capacity to sense and grasp a different kind of order, the order of pure relatedness, nearness, and compatibility. No experience reveals that order more vividly than the love experience.

We are dealing here with one of these new investigations, where we have to create our methods of work as we proceed from postulates to experience and from experience to postulates. As a bold pioneer in this type of search put it:

> New verities are felt before they can be expressed; and when they are expressed for the first time they are unavoidably wrapped in a defective garb. At their birth they appear like a faint gleam in the dark, and they attract us. But, at first, we do not know exactly in what direction and at what level the source of light can be found. And so, we grope for a long time, hurting ourselves against dark obstacles, enticed by misleading reflections, until we come into the light that guides us to their source.[19]

We are far from the quantitative procedures of actuarial science at the moment; we are not looking for large numbers of phenomena that we can group in well-defined classes. We are picking, within our personal world of

---

[19]Pierre Teilhard de Chardin, *La Vision du Passé* (Paris: Editions du Seuil, 1957), p. 17 (translated by J. S. Bois).

readings, observations, experiences, and speculations, whatever seems to us worthy of further experiencing and observing.

Count Hermann Keyserling spoke of an "emotional" order and an "emotional" reality.

> The particular quality of emotional reality depends entirely on its being personally experienced. The world of emotions is essentially that of personal experiences; indeed, it is the world of experience par excellence; for it is only when feelings decide that the term "inner experience" becomes endowed with the meaning everyone involuntarily attributes to it. From this follows what is of essential importance: *the realm of the Emotional Order is one throughout and in all respects with what we call the Soul*....And everyone understands "soul" to mean an entity not only different from, but higher than reason.[20]

"When feelings decide," it is "an action of the soul, an entity different from and higher than reason." How can we translate this in terms that we are familiar with, say, in the description of the epistemological profile? We could say, gropingly and hesitatingly as Teilhard suggests, that the experience of being in love starts with what we shall later describe as a unifying or stage-five-type experience, with a feeling of supreme integration, of unity in diversity, that is experienced as the deep "reality" of human adult life. The task is then to take that newly experienced form of superunity as the basic postulate of an awareness of transcendent oneness and of a blending of individual differences. One does not have to create unity, unity is there at the start; but one must foster the growth of our awareness of it—the "soul-growth" of Sherrington—by letting educated "feelings" decide again and again, over and beyond reason and logic.

This brings us to what seems to me the main difference between love and rationality. We do not love because it is reasonable to do so in a particular case; we love first, and reason then adapts itself to the new conditions created by the love experience that has been accepted and is now willed deliberately. Things that appeared impossible before become possible and easy; interests and concerns that were nonexistent before become central and binding, without any feeling of pressure exerted from outside. It becomes a world of complete altruism and trust.

This type of trust held fast when the discursive minds of individuals are at loggerheads, is the powerful bond that makes love victorious in spite of violent conflicts at the level of strict logic. And when this type of victory has once been experienced, its creative power takes over and makes coming misunderstandings as nothing but the harbingers of greater unity and joint insight.

Love, as we understand it here, has very little in common with the culturally accepted way of making oneself lovable by pleasant manners, in-

[20]Hermann Keyserling, *South American Meditations* (New York: Harper & Row), p. 254.

teresting conversation, sharing of hobbies and interests, and sex attraction. "What most people in our culture mean by being lovable is essentially a mixture between being popular and having sex appeal."[21]

In this, as in many other things, the new humanism transcends the standards of our culture without, however, neglecting whatever it contains of lasting value. Sex, as we shall see, has a part to play in love as a growth experience.

We may help ourselves if we consider love under three aspects. They do not exhaust the characteristics of that peculiar transcognitive experience, but they put some order in our thinking about it. Love may be seen as (1) appreciation, (2) tenderness, and (3) commitment.

Appreciation refers to beauty, proportion, radiance, attractiveness, genuineness, alertness, intelligence, grace, and taste. All this is relative, of course, and it is more a matter of mutual compatibility than of conformity to some "objective" standard. Personal appreciation does not mean a Miss America or a Mr. America contest.

Tenderness refers to the affective-unitive aspect of the mutual relationship. Sex belongs here, but it cannot be divorced from the amenities of words and behavior that make life pleasant, free from petty clashes and trivial arguments, humorous and cheerful, filled with comforting sympathy when pain or trouble occurs, and that doubles the value of joy and success by sharing them as personal experiences.

Finally, there is the aspect of commitment, of determined choice and consistent perseverance. It gives love a stability that does not depend exclusively on attractiveness or on compatibility, which may be felt at times and missed at times. Commitment means a solid determination to "make a go" of the vital undertaking, whatever may happen. Eric Fromm puts it this way:

> To love somebody is not just a strong feeling—it is a decision, it is a judgment, it is a promise. If love were only a feeling, there would be no basis for the promise to love each other forever. A feeling comes and it may go. How can I judge that it will stay forever, when my act does not involve judgment and decision?.[22]

These three aspects—appreciation, tenderness, and commitment—have to be kept alive on both sides, and this is what makes the life of a human couple not a *state*, as is commonly said, but a *joint enterprise* of growing together through expanding experiences of stronger trust and fuller understanding.

In the revolutionary period we are going through, marriage is one of our institutions that is particularly affected. From being a permanent state, bolstered by religion, law, and social mores, it has become a private enterprise, the success of which depends mostly, if not exclusively, on the skill of

[21]Eric Fromm, *The Art of Loving* (New York: Harper & Row, 1956), p. 2.
[22]Fromm, *The Art of Loving*, p. 56.

partners determined to make it a means of self-actualization in companionship. It becomes a test of self-management shared night and day, an achievement in the art of living with another self whose autonomy we can't ignore. It is at the same time a marvelous opportunity to experiment with love as the experienced impulse of life in evolution.

This is what some scientists see as the new function of the human couple in this period of intensified human development. The human couple can experiment with love-energy under all its aspects and in all its modalities and can report the results of their growth experience to the interested scholars.

In some of his most penetrating speculations, Teilhard de Chardin ventures into this domain, when he discusses the role of sexuality at this moment of history.

> If man and woman were principally for the child, then the role and the power of love should dwindle as human individuality develops and as, on the other hand, the density of the population on earth reaches its saturation point. But if man and woman are principally for each other, then we understand that the more they humanize themselves, the more they feel by that very fact the increasing need of getting close to each other. This second alternative is the fact that is verified by experience. . . . Evolution does not come to a close; but it continues further toward a more perfect concentration, linked with an ulterior differentiation that is achieved by union. . . . The complete human molecule is already something more complex and, therefore, more spiritualized than the individual taken alone. It is a duality that involves both a male and a female element. It is at this point that appears the full function of the cosmic role of sexuality. . . . Love is an adventure and a conquest. It manifests itself and develops, like the Universe itself, by means of a continuous discovery. To love really means, for two persons, to be carried passionately, one by the other, towards a higher possession of their individual self.[23]

In other words, the human couple may be seen as an experimental plot of land where love, or altruism as a passion that embraces all aspects of life, is cultivated with care until it reaches maturity and produces the fruits of knowledge we need for playing our role as participants in the emergence of a new and better humanity. From being the "fundamental impulse of cosmic life," love would become humanity's powerful agent for its self-transformation.

A New Human Being in the Making

There is an abundant literature on the ideal state, the dreamland where people live healthy, happy, and wise under a government that is perfect in

---

[23]Pierre Teilhard de Chardin, *L'Energie Humaine* (Paris: Editions du Seuil, 1962), pp. 91-96 *passim* (translated by J. S. Bois).

its laws and in their application. All writers of utopias, from Plato in *The Republic* to the psychologist B. F. Skinner in his *Walden II*, built this world of fantasy according to their individual preferences. All, however, made it clear that the world they describe is nowhere to be found; it was their way of criticizing the world in which they lived and of expounding their own theories.

It is not my intention to add one more version of the human dream for a perfect world. Nobody knows what the world is going to be in the next generation; we are on the road to a condition that we do not know in advance, and all we can do is increase our chances of making it a bit better than the one we now have. We are on the road to a land that we never saw; let us translate into practical rules of behavior the desire we all have for better things.

If we take the long view of our presence on this planet and the presence of other forms of life, we see a slow process of evolution. For millions of years this evolution was strictly biological; recently, for only a few thousand years, it has been cultural. The form of life to which we belong seems able to exert a distinct influence on its own evolution and that of other forms of life. In reviewing this general process, we see definite jumps or mutations when new specimens are produced, most of which are doomed to die in a short time; very few survive to "possess" the earth. The strata of the soil show us, in fossilized form, the sequence of biological mutations.

A chemical and physical sequence had unfolded itself prior to the appearance of plants and animals now preserved in geological strata. It continues today around us and within us, all powerful and unrestricted. We have to extend our awareness of this evolutionary process to a world view, from whatever we picture as the origin of existence to the constantly receding limits of a future in ceaseless becoming.

Nothing can stop the evolution of humankind; but now that we are aware of it, thanks to sciences that have developed in the last hundred years, we are able to play intelligently the part that we had played before by mere instinct. We now know that *Homo sapiens* is not simply another species in the animal kingdom. With the appearance of our species on the planet a new age began, the age of life specimens able to reflect upon themselves and upon the universe. Teilhard de Chardin calls it the psychozoic era. For Korzybski it was the beginning of time-binding, of the cultural evolution of which we are capable and for which we are responsible.

This brings us back to the very first topic we discussed: the conceptual revolution of our time. We occasionally spoke of a gap that has been widening for half a century between our technology and our management of human affairs. The physical sciences tell us more about where we are than do the psychological sciences. People who still believe that a human being is an animal endowed with reason are as much behind our time as people who claim that the earth is flat and the center of the universe. I agree with Benjamin Whorf's comparison of the man who does not know what science has discovered about the cosmos to the man who knows nothing of the influence his language exerts on his thinking and behaving.

> As this man is in conception of the physical universe, of whose scope and order he has not the faintest inkling, so all of us, from rude savage to learned scholar, are in conception of language. . . .Natural man, whether simpleton or scientist, knows no more of the linguistic forces that bear upon him than the savage knows of gravitational forces. He supposes that talking is an activity in which he is free and untrammeled. . . .He implies that thinking is an OBVIOUS, straightforward activity, the same for all rational beings, of which language is a straightforward expression.[24]

One of the consequences of this ignorance is that, when we get into trouble in family life, in business, in politics, or in international affairs, we look for explanations and remedies everywhere but in our processes of thinking, evaluating, and communicating. The main purpose of these chapters is to remind us that the latter is where we should look first. General semantics is a collection of methods, derived from the sciences of this generation, for the purpose of guiding us in the study and the management of these processes.

In the understanding of the physical universe, the second conceptual revolution brought about the discovery of gravitation. Prior to this, gravitation was everywhere, of course, but it so thoroughly penetrated the workings of nature that it was practically impossible to detect its existence as something different from a property of matter itself. Now that it has been overcome in space flight, its existence is a matter of common knowledge.

There is an activity in the psychological universe that is as pervasive as the assumption that the activity of gravitation is in the physical cosmos. It is the activity of abstracting. To become aware of it is not any easier than it was to "discover" and to invent ways to see that material bodies are not light or heavy by nature but are simply gravitating.

Abstracting, the orders of abstraction, and multiordinality account for a dimension of our thinking that few people take into account, the vertical dimension. This dimension makes it possible for us to differentiate between first-order experience and description, between report language and interpretative language, between neutral terms and value terms. These dimensions do away with the confusion that arises from the use of such terms as "fact," "situation," "problem," "thing," "event"—of any term that is so general as to be like the infinite in mathematics, equal in extent to one of its parts. They make it clear that there are no impersonal statements, that whoever claims to speak in the name of the Law, Science, or Religion, or of any of the accepted personifications of Wisdom, Truth, and Goodness, is actually

[24]Benjamin Whorf, *Language, Thought, and Reality* (New York: Wiley, 1956), p. 251.

voicing personal thoughts and preferences. Wendell Johnson called this ventriloquizing.

> Ventriloquizing is usually an unconscious process, but it may be done deliberately by men who know quite well what they are doing. In fact, since the time of Aristotle it has been taught in universities as part of rhetoric. . . . For example, an American political speaker presents . . . proof of his views by declaring them to be the views of Washington or Lincoln and the very essence of American policy. He speaks, thus, as with the voice of the Founding Fathers.[25]

Abstraction shows us there are no purely objective statements either. When we say "This is a beautiful place," we are projecting our own evaluations, investing the place with beauty that is of our own making. If another person, with a different background, different tastes, and different standards of beauty, says "This is an ugly place," a General Semanticist would not be disturbed in the least. He knows that the place does not exist independently of the way the human participants relate themselves to it. It is seen as a different experience for two different observers; it is not that the place is either beautiful or ugly.

Awareness of abstraction would reduce the number of "why?" questions and "because" answers. Or it would at least make us realize that when we are dealing with whys and becauses we are dealing with interpretations, projections, and opinions, and not with bare facts. Should we entirely exclude whys and becauses from our talking and writing? I don't think we should; it may be very interesting or important to know what other persons think about certain topics.

The use of *I* and *Me* is natural for persons who are aware of abstraction and projection. They know that what they say is much more informative if it is not put, implicitly or explicitly, in the mouth of an all-knowing "goddess of supreme wisdom," the idol that stands behind most absolute statements. Here are some samples of absolute statements, and a suggested translation that uses the first person singular.

Instead of saying "Everybody knows that. . . ." wouldn't it be more informative to say "Of the four persons with whom I discussed that in the past week, three had this opinion about it"? Instead of "Nobody would put up with that," wouldn't it be more informative to say "I know of nobody who I think would accept that"? If, instead of "The real trouble is . . .," we say "From what I know of the situation, I think that this-or-that might help remedy it," wouldn't our statement be more within the range of practical wisdom? There is no limit to the possibilities of such an exercise in translation.

The second point to remember is that the technology of mental work has gone through many changes, comparable to the changes that have taken

---

[25]Wendell Johnson, *People in Quandries* (New York: Harper & Row, 1946), p. 67.

place in research and industry. A well-equipped medical laboratory of fifty years ago would not answer the needs of an up-to-date hospital. The locomotives that pulled the first transcontinental trains across the Rockies are kept in museums and not on operating tracks. Model T, even model A, Fords are practically never seen on our highways. The pot-bellied stove and the ice refrigerator are relegated to technologically underdeveloped settlements. In the short span of human life, we remember when the radio was a startling novelty and television was mentioned only as a distant possibility. All these changes we now take for granted when it comes to the physical aspect of our lives, but it is time that we take stock of our mental equipment, throw out what is definitely obsolete, and learn to use the most advanced techniques that the human sciences can offer.

The first thing to do is to determine the age of the mental tools we are now using; are they of the period of the Roman chariot or the period of the jet plane? (Professor Gaston Bachelard has given us a five-point scale against which we can measure the relative modernity or obsoleteness of our mental equipment.) Some of our tools may date back to pre-Aristotelian days, when primitive people took their uncritical sensory reactions as the measure of things; and there must be some people who still function that way, at least in certain areas of their life. My reason for saying this is that I see and hear many commercials that would appeal only to people who are still functioning at the primitive level. These advertisements cost money, and I don't think the sponsors would continue them if they were not worth what they pay for them.

If our mental technology is of the classificatory type, it belongs, at best, to the Middle Ages, when the Western world remained almost frozen in a certain pattern for many generations. If that type of thinking were entirely discarded, the segregation issue would not even exist; debates would be cooperative searches for truth or practical wisdom, not contests to bring out a winner; capitalism and communism would not be discussed as two diametrically opposed economic religions; noncommitment would be accepted as a justifiable attitude in international politics. Our newspapers and magazines seem to show little difference between the prevalent thinking of our times and that of the days when people were either believers or heretics, saints or sinners, civilized or savage, free men or slaves. The either-or manner of thinking is so deeply embedded in our habits that we find it extremely difficult to recognize it in ourselves. From the days of grade school, when we had to labor through long lists of synonyms and antonyms, we have been told that there are two sides to any question, a right one and a wrong one. No wonder our thinking is still of the black-and-white, yes-or-no type.

In the seventeenth century a new mental technology was inaugurated. It was the revolution that brought about the classical scientific methods. If we use that technology, we know that there may be not only two but many sides to any question, and that the more of them we take into account the greater are our chances of viewing a question in its proper perspective. We do not oversimplify things; we try to build mental models that are as similar to the situation as possible, taking time and change into account, realizing that every decision is a gamble and every step we take is an experiment with life. But we are confident that the accumulated knowledge of many generations has given us a backlog of precedents on which we can depend, and most of the practical issues with which we are confronted are decided by those precedents.

Finally, we may transfer to human affairs some of the mental techniques developed in the physical sciences since the advent of relativity and the quantum theory. Here we are aware that the backlog of information accumulated in the human sciences since the beginning of this century is limited, in most cases, to our own Western world and does not apply to humankind as a whole. We know that different cultural postulates will create different kinds of individuals. We search not so much for a residue of common characteristics in all cultures but for a formulation of a higher order that will transcend them all, while giving each an opportunity for genuine development.

There is a good deal of groping at this level. There are group dynamics, psycho- and socio-drama, client-centered therapy, psychosynthesis, studies of psychological constructs and creativity. The trouble is that they are far from having the resources and the backing that is given to the physical sciences. Many of the advances made in these areas had to be made outside our well-established educational institutions because these advances occasionally question the value of certain practices that are standard in these institutions. We are at the growing edge of the technology of human self-management.

Apart from a general awareness of abstracting and a conscious rating of the stage at which we function mentally, it becomes important to know how these intellectual activities are integrated around a core of active motivation. Here the motivational construct of Maslow becomes useful, making it possible to differentiate the self-actualizing persons who enjoy giving of themselves from the needy ones who still derive their psychological sustenance from what the environment can give them in security, belongingness, and recognition.

This brings us to what we may call the fully functioning "human nature," and Gardner Murphy, in his *Human Potentialities*, calls it the third human nature. The first one is the general biochemical and nervous organization that made humans able to be conscious of their consciousness, to think, to learn, to develop an individuality, and to accumulate experience from one generation to the next. We may call it the biological human nature, the original time-binding form of life. Every member of the human race, from the aborigines of Australia to the scientists and writers who receive the Nobel Prize, has this nature in common.

The second human nature in Gardner Murphy's scheme is the human being molded by culture, by ways of living not transmitted by heredity in the genes but standardized and transmitted as the normal way of life. This second nature is passed on to the young and is accepted by them as an essential part of their human heritage. It takes a high degree of awareness to differentiate cultural inheritance from genic heredity.

The third human nature is now in the making. It emerges from the present conditions that bring cultures face to face, cultures that have lived in practical independence and ignorance of one another from time immemorial. The new human being who is now emerging wants to understand these cultural diversities and to live her or his sense of purpose in the sweep of the cosmos. This third human nature is in sharp contrast to the second nature from which it emerges. The second human nature, if left to itself, tends to get more and more rigid and standardized through the stabilization of habits, through the fixation of values, and through technology that gives us more and more power over the nonhuman energies within our influence. The third human nature does not belittle this power but it gives priority to the understanding of ourselves and to the managing of a specifically human form of cosmic energy. This new human being sees this energy as a characteristic of the whole planet on which we live and understands what Teilhard de Chardin meant when he wrote:

> To a Martian capable of analyzing sidereal radiations psychically no less than physically, the first characteristic of our planet would be, not the blue of the sea or the green of the forest, but the phosphorescence of thought.[26]

This phosphorescence would be the radiation emitted by the *noösphere,* the covering of the planet that has spread over all the continents since *Homo sapiens* appeared on the scene, that shows in spots on the oceans, and even in layers of space that are close to the earth. It would be the glow of the increasing amount of nerve cells that surround the planet like a net, and which, if taken as mere physical substances, must weigh millions of tons. The incessant activities of these trillions of flashing units create the world of human thought viewed as a planetary phenomenon, the complexity of which defies all imagination.

From the correspondence I exchanged years ago with a semanticist friend of mine, I take some passages that give us an idea of that complexity. The free dissertation of my friend also reveals a mathematical formulation of

---

[26]Pierre Teilhard de Chardin, *The Phenomenon of Man* (London: Collins, 1959), p. 183.

time-binding that is different from Korzybski's, but certainly original and thought-provoking.[27]

I had written to him: "If time-binding is accepted as a 'law of nature,' and if transaction, as I try to describe it, is also accepted as a 'law of nature,' we come to the idea that humankind is an expanding universe of a kind, and our responsibility to participate consciously in this expansion becomes imperative and clear." He answered:

> Your letter served to trigger some ideas which I have thought about for some years. It is a healthy activity for me and I appreciate your reminding me that it is necessary from time to time to, so to speak, squeeze some juice out of the "fruits of meditation." In any event, the following is an attempt to present some of my ideas concerning the matters about which you wrote me.
>
> As often happens, it seems necessary to begin by speaking about something else. To greatly oversimplify one viewpoint, it can be said that we begin life as an organism subject to "impressions" both from out and from within. This organism is able to record, in whatever manner, the passing traces of these "impressions" and is able to relate these experienced "impressions" or their recordings to one another, along with some degree of whatever pleasure or pain accompanied the original "impression."
>
> We assign symbols to the organismic reactions of these "impressions," and other symbols to the relations or linkages between them. By the use of these symbols we manage to communicate to some degree with each other. I am sure that no more need be said about this, as we are both familiar with this viewpoint.
>
> Now, let us divide what goes on in the organism into two categories: (1) the category of "direct organismic impression-experience," and (2) the category of "relating of these experiences." The first one, "direct experience," being nonverbal, and the second, "relating," have in some degree symbol content.
>
> From this splitting there is then generated a third category; viz.; the "direct organismic impression-experience of the relationships—or linkages—thus created." These relational experiences, of course, are subject to being related; these, in turn, can be related, etc. At any level we are able to use the symbols of communication available to us.
>
> It is easy to see that this can be considered a cyclical process and that consciousness of the differentiation between direct experiences and relational experiences and the symbolic expression of these is of supreme importance; but with this we need not concern ourselves for our present purpose.
>
> We seem to organize and departmentalize our relational experiences into segments or clusters where pertinence becomes the criterion of inclusion. In other words, where the content of a segment is determined by some relationship of a

[27]The writer of the essay quoted here was Charles Tarver, Jr., a businessman of Dallas, Texas, who attended two advanced seminars that I gave at the Institute. At the time of his untimely death he was a member of the Board of the International Society for General Semantics.

different (higher) level. Ordinarily there seems to be very little cross-relationship between many of these clusters of relations. We often call these unrelated segments or clusters unrelated fields of knowledge, as for instance, what one "knows" about accounting and what one "knows" about psychology.

In this context, there arises the question of expressing, in some type of symbolism or formula, the structure of these relationships in any segment, and the relations between the segments themselves. There is an expression in symbolism, which seems to state the situation and the process going on, in a rather adequate manner. This symbolic codification is the Graicunas expression for "Relationship in Organization" (*Manhood ofc4, pp. 275-77*):

$$R = N \left[2^{(N-1)} + N-1 \right],$$

where N represents the direct experience factors and R comes to be the measure for our relational knowledge in a segment or cluster where pertinence is the criterion.

In a wider sense, the particular R's become the N's for a superequation which can be said to represent the state of the individual's intelligence—or overall knowledge—at a stage. The value of the N's, and therefore of the R's, grows as we progress through life and reevaluate our present and past experience.

This brings us to the question of a group interaction. It seems reasonable, in the context of the above, to view what happens in a situation such as an advanced seminar as follows: Each member brings to the group a unique set of experiences related in a unique manner. Each has organized the clustered segments of his experience in a unique complex, which may be said to include and limit his knowledge at this stage. When information and opinions are exchanged, relationships disclosed, differences of meaning brought out, viewpoints and attitudes exchanged, we all create for one another new levels of relationships, which allow and drive us to reevaluate, and reorganize our complexes of relations into new and different systems. The old patterns are *not* destroyed, but the new ones are rather superimposed.

There is this supremely important factor also. We are influenced to cross-reference the old content with the new. A moment's examination of the formula will show, for example, what this can mean numerically as to the size or scope of our intelligence-knowledge. It is as if we were to some degree able to multiply our existence, at least as far as our direct relational knowledge is concerned. The growth of pertinence surprises us. We have each to some extent lived the other's intellectual life, and have enriched one another's "knowing" by some such degree as R grows when N grows in the formula.

In a cultural context, the complex of all the R's at a particular stage would seem to represent the degree of civilization existing at a time. This complex would seem to correspond to the value of Korzybski's system-function at any stage of civilization.

Some other implications of the above occur to me, and I am sure will come to you; the tremendous impact of a new idea upon the thinking of a culture; how one novel contribution brings literally a flood of related formulations.

This has been the barest sketch of some of the implications of this notion, and in fact it seems to me that the subject deserves some extended thought. In the context of Korzybski's time-binding it seems to me that, from the viewpoint expressed above, each generation to some degree contributes its own experiences and reevaluates past knowledge in some such manner as the Graicunas relationship with its attendant cross-references.

And my friend Charlie went on, making the formula more complex, to include such factors as "a person's obtuseness at a stage" and drawing inferences relevant to the mentality of Eastern mystics. Each time I met him, there was a distinct increase in my potential wisdom in the now. He made me think, made me reexamine and reevaluate my wisdom of yesterday. As he said, "We were, in some degree, able to multiply our existence."

For me, Charlie Tarver was a typical specimen of what I understand Gardner Murphy to mean when he speaks of the third human nature, and what I personally mean when I speak of a "new human being in the making." He was active and successful in his business life, altruistic in his dealings with those near him, and devoid of any pretension of reforming the world. He found time to keep himself abreast of developments in mathematics, the physical sciences, and the human sciences occasionally engaging in a thought experiment—as we have seen. This type of free-moving, yet circumspect, meditation has an important role to play in the life of any person who feels responsible for a share in improving the human condition.

> The outstanding individual will tend now to merge again into the continuity of the social background, but in a new manner. Personality will mature further, but one aspect of maturing will consist in an awareness of the social and hereditary continuity which expresses itself in the thoughts and ambitions of the individual. Thus the special individual who contributes to the development of the tradition will not appear as an arbitrary or autonomous subject bearing a separate burden and responsible for a separate achievement, but rather as one of the many formative organs of the social process. This will enable the individual to be more straightforward in asserting his vision, since he can recover something of the innocence of the ancients whose creative powers were not disturbed by undue awareness of themselves. The burden of European subjectivity can now be discarded, the formative personality being aware not only of himself, but of all the social tendencies which make him what he is. The subjective loneliness, and its companion the messianic temptation of genius, may thus lose their intensity.[28]

Individuals of this third human nature are still few and far between, but they exist all over the world. When they meet, they recognize one another despite differences of language and cultural habits.

They do not form cliques; they are not much concerned with formal organizations and propaganda by means of mass media. They look for personal contacts, for the crossfertilization of minds in an exchange of tentative formulations that are free from the formalities of strict logic.

[28]Lancelot Law White, *The Next Development in Man* (London: Cresset, 1944), p. 213.

I think they can be easily recognized by the three characteristics we have reviewed in this section: (1) They are aware of the vertical dimension of thinking, whether they describe it as orders of abstraction or otherwise. (2) They are at home at the fourth stage of human development, as described in Bachelard's profile; in other words, they can translate one set of postulates into another set, and they can remain undisturbed if no translation appears possible for the moment. (3) They have the self-detachment and the self-commitment of what Maslow calls the self-actualizing persons.

Summary

To summarize this chapter, we discussed the nonintellectual aspects of semantic transactions at the level of muscular and postural habits by inserting the differential relaxation of Edmund Jacobson and the primary control of Mathias Alexander. From Dr. Abraham Maslow, I borrowed his postulated scale of instinctoid needs, from basic physiological drives to self-actualization. For an overall incipient theory of affects and for another integrative approach (the central assembly) to the whole semantic transaction system, I turned to Sylvan Tomkins whose work unfortunately stopped short in the middle of my presentation. Finally, I swung open the door of the world of values by introducing the topic of love as a transforming agent and dealing with the avoidance of conflict fostering practices.

When I speak of nonintellectual aspects of human behavior, I do not mean to belittle the intellect and the part it plays in changing personal values, but to emphasize that the X, A, and B areas of the semantic transactor are 'silently,' but inherently, involved in all of our activities. Intellect is not just a logical affair.

In relating this to all that we have covered so far in this book, I am quite willing to accept an analogy proposed by Alfred North Whitehead. He suggests that we see the immense mass of living human existence as a huge developing organism. This organism would consist of each and every human being as a distinct cell. Today we know that the overall health of an organism is closely linked to the cleanliness and freedom from waste of each of its constituent cells. This involves all the known activities of the human transactor; electrochemical, meaning proper nutrition; self-moving, meaning proper exercise; and development of unusual skills, feeling activities that reflect the realm of values, where altruism as a passion or plain love for one another are gradually replacing conflict as a normal constituent of commonsense behavior; and the thinking activities where we work to create a genuine ecumenism in thoughts and philosophy of life.

And so, the apparently humble and limited action of the individual, who profits from the accumulated science and best-tested practices of our timebinding predecessors, contributes as much as he or she can be expected to do toward the healthy growth of the whole humankind.

Other practices such as acupuncture, acupressure, polarity therapy, and reflexology demonstrate the so far unheeded, dynamic interactions of various parts of the organism. The scientific basis of what is known in the East as *kundalini* is being explored; and the field of parapsychology is moving far beyond the pioneering work of Dr. J. B. Rhine, who originated the term *extrasensory perception* while working at Duke University in the 1930s.

All these findings do contribute to make us hope that the day is near when the plain individual will have more influence than she or he expected on the health and vigor of the human race. In fact, the individual eventually becomes aware of his or her personal responsibility for the overall peace, smooth functioning, and welfare of all participants in the psycho-social evolution. This in turn may be seen as the growing tip of cosmic evolution itself.

PART VIII

the practice
of awareness

The practice of awareness demands an orientation based on the awareness of a control unit that can structure the "messages" coming from the various aspects of our semantic transactions and can, in turn, guide our experience. To express it differently, it calls for the multiordinality of the self, involving self-reflexiveness, feedback, and self-participation.

Through advances in science and other fields, more and more indicators are coming within the range of cultivated sensitivity, and there are many more than we suspect that can be observed by the person who wants to know, manage, and participate in his or her own experience.

our many selves

A major practice proposed by General Semantics is to make an effort to free ourselves of the logic of Aristotle, of the Ideas of Plato, and of the many offshoots of Greek philosophy that have been cultivated all through the ages in our Western world; to live in a mental world that is as up to date as the latest advances of technology, a world of semantic Early Bird satellites and supersonic transport planes. General semanticists focus upon humans, whom the biologist Alexis Carrel still considered the "great unknown" not so long ago, the powerful searchlights of all the new human sciences can mobilize. With Teilhard de Chardin, they consider our humanness not as a "nature" among other "natures," but as a phenomenon unique in its class and worthy of being observed with an entirely fresh mind. With Gaylord G. Simpson and Julian Huxley, they place our species back where they found it, in the stream of evolution, where they see it as a key element at the present stage of cosmic history. Here is how *Homo sapiens'* role was described at the close of a scientists' symposium held at Princeton in 1955.

> As man has gone on with his own development, he has become more conscious both of the general process of organic transformation and of the important role he himself has come to play. Instead of bowing himself out of the picture, as he did when he followed the canons of seventeenth-century science, he now takes a central position in the stage, knowing that the performance itself, in the theater of consciousness at least, cannot go on without him. He begins as an actor, singling himself out from his animal colleagues, already something of a prima donna, but uncertain of what part he shall learn. In time he becomes a scene-

painter, modifying the natural background and finding himself modified by it, too; and he is driven to be a stagehand likewise, shifting the properties to make his entrances and his exits more manageable. It is only after much practice in all these roles, as actor, scene-painter, stagehand, costumer, that he discovers that his main function is to write the drama, using many of the old plots left by nature, but giving them a new turn of the imagination and working the events up to a climax that nature without his aid might not have blundered upon in another hundred million years.[1]

How long would it have taken for evolution, unaided, to endow us with the capacity to fly faster than sound, to dive under the polar cap, or to orbit the planet on which we live? It might never have happened had we not envisioned these achievements with our imagination, planned them with our thought, and made them materialize by means of the technology we have created. The more we know about our species and the better we recognize the importance of our role in changing the face of the earth, the better it will be.

But knowing is not enough. Socrates' prescription, "Know thyself," will be put in the museum of antiquities with the logic of Aristotle and the Ideas of Plato unless it is translated into rules of conduct. In this, as in any other field of endeavor, the time has come to pass from *knowing-what-it-is* to *knowing-what-to-do-with-it*, from science to technology, from theory to practice.

In the present case, practice does not mean "how to make friends and influence people"; it does not mean "leadership," "propaganda," the use of mass media, the display of force, or techniques of law enforcement. None of these reaches the core of a human being. We know now that humankind is made of radically autonomous units, each destructible of course but absolutely independent—as was demonstrated time and again in the concentration camps of recent wars and as is acknowledged by any therapist of experience.

No one, moreover, semantician or not, even if he holds a most exalted position in politics, finance, education, or religion, deals with "man" in general, with humankind as an integrated whole, or with "human nature" as a tangible unit that can be controlled, modified, or transformed. Each of us deals with individuals, singly, and finally with our own self as the *one* actor in the scenario of life of our age.

Each individual with whom we deal is the final and only arbiter of what he or she will think, wish, or do. And I am the final and only decider of what I shall think, wish, or do. Something can be done *to* me, of course, but nothing that is done to me is ever constructive unless I eventually accept it as my own.

[1]Lewis Mumford, "Prospect," in *Man's Role in Changing the Face of the Earth*, ed. William L. Thomas et al. (Chicago: University of Chicago Press, 1956), p. 1145.

And so, the technology that we have to develop is technology of self dealing with self, in the light of whatever the contemporary sciences have to offer.

Self-1, Self-2, Self-3 . . . Self-n

We hear a good deal about the self today. Psychologists speak and write about the self-concept, the self-image, self-actualization, self-acceptance, self-esteem, self-defensiveness. We seem to enjoy coming out of our skin and looking back at that "objective" somebody that looks very much like us, and whom we claim to observe in sort of a detached way. The self is like an actor on the stage, playing the main part in the drama of our life.

Who does the observing of that self who performs on the stage? Is it not my own self? Then which is my *real* self, the actor or the observer? If you look closely you may discover another personage who deserves to be called self: the director of the play, the one who decides what to do and how to do it. We may then discover yet another self, the one who is now talking about the actor, the observer, and the director. Since this self talks about the others, there is an implicit claim to be none of them. And what of the self that is actually talking and theorizing to us about those four initial selves? We could continue this without end, creating a new self every time we want to talk about the last one we have conceived in the series.

Self becomes a multiordinal term used on a scale of objective abstraction dealing with Self-1 as the actor, Self-2 as the observer; Self-3 as the director of the play; Self-4 as the theorizer who is now describing the situation in terms of multiordinality; and so on, the only end being the level at which we decide to stop our analysis, or Self-n.

Every one of these selves is as "real" as any other; every one of them is a first-order experience and, thus, a low order of abstraction, while being at the same time differentiable from every other one with respect to the order of abstraction that makes it the container or the contents. In fact, these selves are not separate "entities," as they say in philosophical parlance, they are orders of vertically differentiated activities that may be conceived as going on simultaneously, the higher ones managing the lower ones. When we speak of Self-1, Self-2, Self-3 . . . we are using a shorthand expression to mean "I-operating-at-level-one," "I-operating-at-level-two," and so on.

We may also condense two, or many, levels into one. For instance, we could combine Self-2 and Self-3, the observer and the director of the play described above, and create a more complex Self-2, an observer-director, producer, and scriptwriter, as was suggested in Lewis Mumford's statement. Self-2 would then be sort of a manager of Self-1, extemporizing constantly, as we have to do in life, passing from one unrehearsed situation to another. This brings us to a simplified diagram, Figure 1, that contains only three selves: *1, 2,* and *3.*

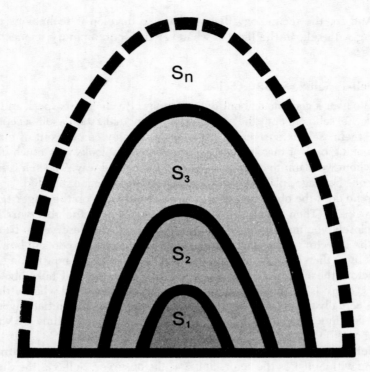

Figure 16.1. The selves in awareness. Self-1, Self-2, Self-3, . . .Self-n.

Self-1 may be seen as that pattern of spontaneous activities that does not change much after we have reached a certain age and react to people, things, and situations in a fairly predictable manner. It is sometimes called "personality." It is the "what-I-am," the assumed invariant that psychologists claim to measure with their tests. it is what we refer to when we evaluate Joe's I.Q., degrees of his personality traits, and for his mechanical, verbal, or mathematical intelligence. It covers set attitudes, well-established habits, manners, tastes, and preferences that makes one who knows Joe capable of guessing pretty accurately what Joe will think, say or do in most situations.

We may deal with Self-2 as the observer-director-producer-scriptwriter. This Self-2 is born of awareness and appears when the boundary between the organism and the environment "lights up," as it were. Self-2 acts like a scanning device that takes in what goes on in the organism and what goes on in the environment. It is ourself as the artist of life, finding and making the meanings that we grow by. Our life at this level consists in seizing what is relevant, interesting, and nourishing; in welcoming what is semantically significant; in rejecting what is threatening, unassimilable, or potentially

Figure 16.2. Self-2, or boundary between organism and environment becoming warm and bright in awareness.

poisonous. When we operate creatively, we are like sparks that brighten, warm, and bind together the organism-environment complex (Figure 16.2). When such an experience occurs, we may use various terms to describe it, depending on what aspect we want to emphasize. We may call it an insight, a discovery, a solution, a decision, an adjustment, an achievement, a relief from tension.

Self-2 has to be alert if we are to make the most of the transactions of which the organism and the environment are mere aspects to detect the blockages that stop or slow down the exchanges of energy. It has to reexamine the habits of thinking, feeling, and moving that have become obsolete. It has to look inside the organism to evaluate the short-comings of our thinking models, the poisonous character of negative feelings, the damaging muscular tensions that reveal stress, the bodily indices that warn of metabolic imbalance. It has to deal with situations as they develop and not as Self-1 wishes them to be, make the most of what is available, accept people as they are, and put up with conditions that cannot be changed without undue complications.

Self-2 is the becoming self in action. Self-1 is too often what we refer to when we say "I want to be myself!" Of course, it is reasonable to have a certain degree of confidence in Self-1, in the accumulated knowledge, experience, and wisdom that we have earned through years of labor, soul-searching and mistakes. But, unless our Self-2 keeps functioning, observing, and inventing ceaselessly, we quickly become has-beens in a world that keeps on burying the past and building the future. We had better differentiate our Self-2 from our Self-1. What Self-1 becomes depends very much on whether Self-2 makes sufficiently frequent appearances and does a constructive job. If Self-2 stays away, refuses to take into account what is going on, and fails to manage Self-1 in the proper manner, this person becomes an automaton with only the guidance and power of old habits of thinking, feeling, and behaving—all inadequate to the newness of actual life.

Next, we include in our model a Self-3, overarching Self-2 and Self-1. If we see Self-2 as an artist in action evoking creative behavior from Self-1, then Self-3 can be seen as a scientist-epistemologist that keeps Self-2 up to date in the methods and wisdom developed by the study of individuals and groups within cultures all over the world. Self-3 assimilates the basic theorems of the new epistemology and from them the practical directives that apply in each case are drawn. This means knowing about such constructs as abstraction and about the difference between description and interpretation; taking multiordinality and circularity into account; knowing of motivation and of the nonintellectual aspects of semantic transactions; noting the shortcomings of "physical" mental models; and using the epistemological profile as a guide at all times. Every new experience of Self-1 and Self-2 enlarges Self-3's knowledge by testing the plausibility of its methods. Maturity and wisdom derived from every piece of new information gathered out of reading, listening, meditating, and participating increases the value of Self-3 as a participating guide of Self-2.

Self-3 must also know of a possible situation when the directed activities of Self-2 may bring about a crisis in dealings with Self-1. This crisis could be compared to *withdrawal symptoms*.

It is well known that a person addicted to any kind of unhealthy behavior, be it drug taking, cigarette smoking, or compulsive eating, will go through a painful and occasionally tragic period of withdrawal when an attempt is made to break the bad habit. I saw recently in a magazine a picture of members of Synanon holding down on the floor a newcomer who was wriggling in pains in her desperate fight against her old drug-addicted self. Anyone who has stopped smoking cigarettes or who has taken coffee, sugar, or salt completely and suddenly out of the diet, knows from personal experience how the craving for the accustomed stimulants comes back with unexpected strength in the early stages of abstention and gnaws without mercy at their very vitals. Any psychological consultant knows very well how a neurotic will cling to a neurosis at the same time as begging for help.

All these cases could be interpreted as disturbances of an acquired semantic pattern that has become a habit with which they have learned to feel comfortable, even if it is detrimental to their health and development. Once that has been going on for a certain length of time—and in some cases it has lasted for years and years—any attempt to correct it and to restore the semantic system to a healthy state becomes a threat to the neurotic Self-1 and provokes all sorts of withdrawal symptoms. Some of these will appear at the thinking level, some at the feeling level, some at the level of dealing with the environment, and even at the physiological level. A person attempting self-reeducation, either alone or in a group training in general semantics or epistemics, may feel suddenly a surge of "good" reasons to give up the whole undertaking or "sound" reasons to question the wisdom of the whole system; feelings of distrust in the teacher may develop; the person may become easily irritated and even hostile in dealing with the human environment (family, friends, fellow workers, etc.); bodily symptoms like headaches, poor sleep, arthritis, bad digestion, heart troubles, and what not may occur. I even had one recently who reported he felt he was going to die and had a medical friend, with whom he was attending a professional meeting, quickly take his pulse and check on his heart condition.

All these are withdrawal symptoms, and Self-2 must not get panicky with their occurrence. Self-2 must deal with Self-1, who might be squirming in pain, like a drug addict as the Synanon members deal with newcomers who come to them to be delivered from the slavery of the needle. This means kindness, indeed, but unwavering firmness.

If we accept the views of Trigant Burrow, and of many other scholarly observers of our present human condition, that our whole cultural environment is permeated with semantic neurosis, we will not be surprised at the frequency of such withdrawal symptoms.

Self-Reflexiveness and Feedback

The above presentation of the three selves is only an elaboration of the theory of self-reflexiveness. This, in turn, refers to a mode of functioning that is so natural to people who speak a language that includes a middle voice that they are scarcely aware of its importance. The middle voice is described as follows in the *American College Dictionary*.

> [In some languages] it denotes a voice of verb inflection, in which the subject is represented as acting on or for itself, in contrast to the active voice in which the subject acts, and the passive, in which the subject is acted upon.

The mode of functioning implied in the middle voice is not easily accepted in English. We use it for gross physical operations, as in "I wash myself," but it does not cover the subtle psychological activities that involve many roles of the self as actor, observer, director, or commentator. In French, for instance, we can say, *je m' émeus*, from the infinitive *s' émouvoir*. Literally—and using what is considered by some a neologism—it could be translated "I emote myself," but this does not make much sense. When I use the passive voice to translate *je m' émeus*, I have to imply that someone or something is acting upon me, and I fail to give any inkling of the part I am playing in the process. Depending on the context, I may say "I am moved...touched...affected...upset" but I could not change the exclusively passive situation. In French, the middle voice means a complex process, which I might describe as follows:

1. An emotion surges within me, and at this stage I pass no judgment as to its origin.
2. I become aware of that emotion.
3. I acknowledge the experience as mine.
4. I let it, or help it, develop.

As a consequence, the final result is the joint product of two selves, the self that is stirred (Self-1) and the self that consents to be stirred and joins in the stirring (Self-2). I do not simply let the emotion take its course, I help it unfold itself to any "size" I judge proper.

In English, we can form a mental model of that self and of its activities by using the analogy of feedback systems. In recent years there has been a great deal of research in communications, automatic controls, and neurology, and because of this research the notion of feedback has become generally accepted. Feedback mechanisms are devices that watch and control performance. They answer the questions, "How am I doing?" "When shall I stop, start again, change course?" They set off actions and reactions.

In most feedback mechanisms there is a control unit that receives the messages from the operating system and sends out the orders that direct the ensuing performance. The pituitary gland in the body and the thermostat in a living room are examples of what I mean.

To make the art of awareness possible, we have to have a control unit, a second self superposed upon the original in a multiordinal manner, a center of cultivated sensitivity to the phenomena, clues, and indications that we have studied in this textbook. The function of this unit is not to ask "why" questions or to indulge in introspection. It does not ask itself "Why am I this way or that way?" "Why do I feel as I do?" "What is the matter with me?" "Am I a neurotic?" All it does is check on what the original self says or does, on how it says or does it, on relaxation and tenseness, and such things. This will provide it with many indicators that reveal how the semantic reactions of the original self are functioning and will give it a choice for appropriate correction when needed. We have already compared ourselves to a pilot with a control panel that shows how the plane is performing. From this continuous information, the pilot knows what to do to keep on the proper course and reach the objective.

As the human sciences keep progressing, more and more indicators of safe or dangerous semantic functioning can be observed by the layperson. They require no laboratory apparatus nor psychological testing devices. They are within the observable range of what we say, what we do, how we say it, and how we do it. They can be measured on a qualitative scale, from danger to safety, just as we can tell whether our gas tank is empty or full.

Danger and Safety Indicators

Indicators do not necessarily mean that one is in trouble when the danger indicators can be observed, but they mean that we are heading for trouble, whether we are otherwise conscious of it or not. These indicators are like the dashboard gauge that tells us our engine is overheating; it will warn us before our car stalls on the freeway and will give us a chance to attend to the trouble.

They are within the observable range of *what we say, what we do, how we say it,* and *how we do it.* They can be measured roughly on a qualitative scale from *danger signs* to *safety signs.* Here are a few of them. The danger indicators are in roman type; the corresponding safety indicators are in italics:[2]

1. We use absolute terms, generalities, abstractions of a high order, words that imply "allness,"

    or *we use descriptive terms and lower order abstractions, statements as to who, what, where, when, and how much.*

2. We use judgment terms, terms loaded with approval or disapproval,

    or *we use neutral terms, terms that are as free as possible from bias or slant.*

3. We use "either-or" arguments, pass from one alternative to its extreme opposite, describe things in terms of black and white without any gray shading in between,

    or *we speak in terms of more-or-less, give consideration to degrees and shades of meaning, avoid talking about opposites.*

4. We speak of the present situation as "just like" another one, of this person as "just like" So-and-so, of this problem as "just like" the one solved previously,

    or *we differentiate carefully between people, situations, and problems.*

5. We confuse facts that can be verified by anybody, and interpretations, opinions, and judgments that are exclusively our own,

[2]J. Samuel Bois, *Explorations in Awareness* (New York: Harper & Row, 1957), p. 186-188.

> or   *we distinguish between what is going on and what we feel or understand is going on.*

6. We ramble from one subject to another,

    or   *we keep to the subject under discussion.*

7. We quote authorities to uphold our viewpoint,
    or   *we try to evaluate the situation on its own merits.*

8. We quibble on the dictionary meaning of words,

    or   *we use words as mere tokens for what we wish to convey.*

9. We talk fast and/or loud,

    or   *we talk with deliberation.*

10. We interrupt, start talking before the other person is finished, we contradict with a quick "yes/but,"

    or   *we listen with genuine attention, wait for our turn to speak; even then we may allow some silence in order to absorb what was said.*

11. We keep muscles tense, move in jerks, fidget, twitch,

    or   *we relax, remain calm and quiet, and delay our reactions.*

12. We ask rhetorical and tricky questions,

    or   *we ask matter-of-fact questions that invite more information.*

13. We take ourselves very seriously,

    or   *we keep our sense of humor.*

Of course, these skills take practice, preferably one at a time. Start by working with one that is easy to recognize and control, and keep practicing until the new behavior functions almost by itself. It becomes more interesting and exciting as one becomes more sensitive to the fine points, and more expert in performance. Here are a few examples selected from the listed indicators.

Number 1: the percentage of absolute, sweeping, and general terms we are using, such as "Doctors are like this-or-that," meaning implicitly that we are speaking of *all* doctors. We should also check on words of a high order of abstraction, "freedom," "democracy," "religion," and know that we are heading for trouble if our talk includes 15 percent or more of these high-order terms. The correction is made by using descriptive terms and abstractions of a lower order. Expressed as a simple rule, our statements should deal with *who, what, where, when,* and *how much* or *how many.* For instance, "I know of one, two, or three doctors who charged more than Medicare allows for the same service."

Number 2: the frequent use of value terms, of adjectives and adverbs that describe much more how we feel than what is actually going on, such expressions as "you should," "you must," "you ought to," "the only thing to do is." These words show that we are attempting to impose upon the other person our own set of values, and this does not work as a rule. We should wait until we are asked to give advice, and, even then, make sure that the request is sincere. The corresponding safety indicator is self-evident: descriptive terms—terms that are as neutral and free from bias as we can think of. For instance, "in a similar situation I did this or that, and it worked."

Number 4: the tendency to identify; persons who boast of having experience are occasionally tempted to act this way; what they see now reminds them of something else, or looks like it, and they pronounce judgment without taking time to see the differences between the present situation and the one they identify it with. The safe way to handle this is to look, look, and look again for differences. We should not try to find similarities; they come to mind spontaneously, and what we add may simply confirm our prejudices. Instead, we should look for differences. They may be hard to detect, but they are significant.

Number 5: the confusion of first-order facts with second-order inferences. To observe this danger sign is not always easy because our choice of descriptive terms often involves covert interpretations. Our newspapers are full of such biased statements, presented as objective descriptions of facts. The remedy for this danger is to train ourselves—first in simple matters—to distinguish between what is going on and what we feel or understand is going on.

Number 10: the manner in which we carry on a conversation. Have you ever noticed how much overlapping there is among the statements that come from various members of a conversational group? When this occurs, there is no communication; all radio sets are broadcasting at the same time, but none of them is receiving.

As an antidote, I recommend the practice of the art of listening. Some go farther and suggest what they call role reversal. This consists of repeating in our own words what the other person has just said—and of making sure that our version is excepted before we begin to give our answer. I tried this a few times while moderating business meetings, but found it a clumsy technique; I usually took it for granted that I understood and left it up to the other person to object and correct me when he felt he was misinterpreted. But I found it useful to let a second or so elapse between the last words I heard and the first ones I spoke.

Number 12: "When did you stop beating your wife?" is more frequent than we realize. Although they may not be so obviously tricky as this one, they may involve an assumption that we want to force upon the other person. We can even make a collection of them, as a very instructive hobby, including "What would you do if you were in my place?" Of course, if another can put himself in our place, if he can see us as we see ourself, what can he do but accept our conclusion? If we translate this question into a declarative statement, we will see its real meaning: "Stop thinking the way you do and think the way I do: then, and only then, shall I agree with you because it will mean agreeing with myself."

Observing our behavior from Self-2 is useful not only in preventing trouble and waste of energy, it has proved to be a powerful means of discovering hidden assumptions and unearthing mechanisms that operate within ourselves in manners we seldom suspect.

When I held training conferences for executives, I would ask them (during the last period) to check one, or no more than two, indicators of safety and danger that they were going to observe in the following weeks. They did this entirely for themselves, without telling anybody of their choice. When I saw them individually a few weeks later, my first question was "Did you choose an indicator to observe?" If the answer was yes, I would ask which one, then asked him to tell me what he had observed as he had checked that item. Some of their observations were revelations for them and very interesting to me.

One, who had decided to check himself on his "yes, but" answers, said.

> The first thing that I found out is that I was using those words much more often than I suspected. In the majority of cases when subordinates came to me with a suggestion, that was my habitual reaction. It was an unplesant discovery to find out the way I was actually reacting.

I continued my inquiry. "What else did you find?" He answered with some embarrassment:

> I tried to cut out these "yes, but's" but I soon discovered that I was using paraphrases, tricky questions, or involved statements that meant really the same thing as my habitual "yes, but's." I was changing the wording, but my basic attitude was not budging easily. I had to work on that, too.

"Did you find anything else?" I asked.

> Yes, I observed that this yes-but practice is more general than I realized in this company. I yes-but my subordinates and my boss yes-buts me in his turn. The consequence is that nobody wants to stick out his neck and decisions are pushed upstairs. The boss has to decide so many details that he has no time to do his own job properly. And everything suffers from it.

These indicators are so closely related that if we pay attention to one we are actually working on the others. The organism works as a whole, and the careful observation of what appears to be a simple speech mannerism, as in the case just related, will soon bring us to a serious examination of our basic attitudes. This is where many people give up practicing general semantics. Those who thought it was just a matter of being more clever in the choice of words and of playing with a few devices, like the index, the quotes, or the like, leave it for some other passing fad. Those who are looking for an easy way to master the art of communication and to win arguments had better look elsewhere. The old saying, "There is no royal road to knowledge," remains true—even in our day when royalty is almost an anachronism. The translation could be: "There is no gadget yet invented to take the place of learning by persevering practice."

Between the organism and the environment, we may imagine a contact zone that envelops the whole organism (Figure 16.2). Within this space, patterns of interaction are already established, like programmings that are preset in a computer. When a stimulus from the environment comes to the organism, it is processed through these patterns. When the organism directs its energies to the environment, they have to go through the same patterns. As a consequence, we see as we have learned to see, we hear as we have learned to hear, we walk, we speak, we write in the manner we have acquired in earlier years and that has become a personal, unchanging characteristic of each of us. The sum total of this network of patterns is our "personality," our recognizable individual self, our structured unconscious (p. 142).

Some interaction patterns are inborn: if I run, I start breathing faster. Some are due to early conditioning: if I think of lemon juice, my mouth waters. Some are due to conscious training: when I see a red light, my foot presses on the brake. Some are buried way down in my body tissues, at the electrochemical level. Some are emotional habits, some are intellectual habits; they provide me with preestablished sets of ready reactions that have proved useful or gratifying over the years.

These interaction patterns would be all I need if the situations I have to face were simply repetitions of those I faced before. But they are not; occasionally I have to face unrehearsed situations. In fact, it is false to say that history repeats itself. It cannot. My life is an irreversible process, and every day I advance into the unknown, becoming slightly different from myself with each step I take. The art of awareness may be seen as the art of living.

Further Development of Self-1, Self-2, Self-3 . . . Self-n

To summarize what has been said so far on the self-reflexiveness of Self-1, Self-2, Self-3, we first postulated self-1 as the actor, or "personality" with its well-established ways of functioning, its habit patterns and acquired wants and needs. Self-2 was proposed as an observer-director of self-1. Self-2 is born of awareness and becomes an artist of living who participates by evaluating, managing, and guiding the semantic transactions of Self-1. But even more importantly by creating a vision that allows Self-2 to see in Self-1 potential talents, beauty, and resiliency, and to disengage that jewel from the slag of banality that surrounds it. A release of Viewpoints Institute dealt with this topic under the title, *On Obeying One's Vision.*

As an artist working on human material, I can work on my own self as well, bringing out the potential beauty that I see in my inner self, the available resiliency of my soul, the dynamic balance of my skills and values. To do so, I have to be capable of vision, and to disengage from the chaotic inconsistency of my behavior the hidden image of my latent excellence. I must obey that vision as it unfolds itself under my eyes. . . .

The act of creation is not the plodding achievement of a worker who follows slavishly a detailed plan prepared in accordance with preestablished rules; it is the unrehearsed activity of the artists who follows faithfully the expanding process of a form that grows under his eyes as he shapes it with his hands.[3]

Self-2 has to stay on the job to keep Self-1's attention in the ever-present, becoming activity of life.

Finally, we spoke of Self-3 as a scientist-epistemologist who provides Self-2 with up-to-date methods of thinking-feeling-acting that emerge from first-order experience, or from the lives of creative, time-binding individuals of all cultures. Self-3's participation helps to keep the other selves in an appropriate rhythm and flow with each other. All of these selves function as one and are not separate as our description might lead you to believe.

Now we come to a further development of this model. We can combine Self-2 and Self-3 as described, preceding into a single Self-2, now an artist-scientist-epistemologist; and we postulate a new Self-3.

To begin a description of this new Self-3, we need to remember that at the subatomic description of WIGO, or the ongoing cosmic process, postulated in high-energy physics, "objectivity" and "subjectivity" are obsolete categories. "Objects" and "things," causes and effects which seemed to logically link together our world "out there" end in the awareness of a participating observer. In the subatomic, or quantum world, commonsense appearances disappear out of the range of ordinary experience into a continuous creation where differences each uniquely seem to be describing this one common action. It is only within the Aristotelian system that we speak of this quantum world as a "level," "sub," "under," "behind," "beyond," or any other such description. The high order abstractions of stages two and three of the epistemological profile grew out of the assumptions of a time when we thought this world existed, had meaning and purpose, according to the way we abstracted with our "physical" senses; later, it was the way we abstracted with our language and mathematical symbol systems. This phase of human development could be described as objective identification. This means that I assume and presume that "things" "exist" objectively independent of me, or, conversely, that "things" "exist" only in my so-called mind. In either case, the assumption and primary value is that "things" "exist." One is a "physical" interpretation, the other "metaphysical."

[3]J. Samuel Bois, *On Obeying, One's Vision* (Los Angeles: Viewpoints Institute).

So, also, with our constructs of "self," and our habit of thinking in terms of visible, or considerable, objects. The self is either identified with "the body," or with the murmurings of "the mind."

With present-day science, we have come to the postulate that there can be no "metaphysics" on the grounds that there is no longer any basis for an objective physics. We cannot go "beyond" or "behind" or "back of" the "physical world" when we can accept that the physical world is a common-sense construct abstracted from the limited range of our senses, sensations, intuitions, and logical introspections. At stage four, the quantum world is a description or mental model of how individuals called physicists generalize their own semantic transactions. In their model there is no differentiation between "physical" and "metaphysical" or "body" and "mind" or "real" and "mystical." Theirs is a realm of unpicturable action—one ongoing process. We ourselves are integrated aspects of that action whether or not we ever come to accept this postulate or somehow have a first-order experience.

It is in this context that we describe a new Self-3 to begin to feel our way into bringing an awareness of ourselves as that living action into accepted experience. This is "self" without "objects," cause-effect relationships, and logical discourse as means of self-identification. This Self-3 cannot be pictured, but can become a first-order experience by learning what it is *not* as an initial step. Again, this is not something "mystical" or "meta" denoting something beyond or other than. I invite you to become familiar with this way of thinking-feeling by remembering that any "objects" or "images"— whether experienced as "physical" or "mental"—are our own abstractions and not what is going on. We must take the responsibility for our own abstractions. Objective identification of our first-order experiences can prevent us from fully participating in what is going on as a cosmic happening. Let us not make the obsolete interpretation that Self-3 as I describe here is something "spiritual," but can be an everyday experience of oneself as a whole, and not an object of thinking-feeling-acting activities. Rather, consider it as the action by which those activities can occur at all.

This Self-3 could be described as an emerging, creating self. Not creating in the sense of an artist or a scientist, but as a creative happening that "goes by itself." We might think of it as the "pure activity" or the felt presence of the overall growth movement of all selves in participation. If we could make a verb out of the word self, Self-3 could be called "selfing" as a cosmic event. In terms of the Structural Differential (p. 93), we could call it participating in the unity of what is going on (WIGO), represented by the parabola.

To get a feeling for this rather abstract description of Self-3, imagine what it would be like if the bud could feel itself blooming. It would not have to have a theory of motivation; the movement of blooming would be integral to the life of the bud and not have to be accounted for as a separate phenomenon. Or imagine a bird that could feel its song emerge from the depths of the group field of all birds. If you asked that bird why it sang, it would answer by singing. Or imagine if the earth could feel its own evolutionary activity in the appearing and disappearing of billions of life forms on its surface, beneath its surface, in its atmosphere, and in the activity of its human brain; or if cells could feel themselves differentiating and clustering to take on function in the form of a human nervous system; or, on a macroscopic level: if the solar system could be aware of the birth and death of itself in the form of stars. Each noun becomes inseparable from a verb; in fact, the noun becomes an inference from the activity identified. The bud becomes the budding, the bird becomes the singing, earth becomes the evolving, the cells become the combining, the solar system becomes living and dying in an ongoing process; the human self becomes the very act of creating itself.

The activity of Self-3 may be felt at the level of Self-1 as a surge of energy to accomplish a task, whether the task is immediate, or life-long; or, conversely, it might be felt as a deep depression or a feeling of "voidness" from the disappearance from one's life of what had previously seemed so important and around which we had structured the content of our living. In order to be an effective guide, Self-2 must be prepared to evaluate these kinds of happenings in light of Self-3 rather than limiting its awareness to the content of events in the realm of Self-1. Self-2 becomes aware of Self-3's activity by feeling the disturbance of established values, purposes, and seeing these disturbances as opportunities to invent new values, new purposes, and new methods to carry them out.

This whole participation of the three selves can be called a "journey." We could say that the direction of the journey is given in the "insistence" of Self-3's movement as a creative pressure that urges Self-1 and Self-2 to allow the renewal of what no longer serves a useful purpose in the evolution of the whole, whether that whole is seen as an individual, as a couple, as a group, as a culture, or as a species, and on, in a spiraling multiordinality.

We could see the three selves as different orders of unity. Each higher level of self presents new possibilities that were not apparent at the previous level. Thus, self-communication, or better said, self-participation, becomes vital to the evolution of the individual. Self-2 is key in being able to transform the "silence" of Self-3 into values and purposes that Self-1 manifests in space-time actions, or semantic transactions. The quality and method of self-communication depends on the stage of cultural development of Self-2. In semantic psychoanalysis (p. 171), we saw the word communication at each stage of the epistemological profile. At stage four, we saw the beginning of communication becoming participation. So we can now say that it is the inadequacy of means or even our possibilities of participating that impose a limit on the transactions within ourselves and with others.

This is presently accepted at the biological level. Francois Jacob, winner of the 1965 Nobel Prize in medicine, wrote, "For an organism to differentiate, for it to become more independent and to extend its exchanges with the outside world, there must be a development not only of the structures which link the organism to its environment, but also of the interactions which coordinate its constituents. At the macroscopic level, therefore, evolution depends on setting up new systems of communication, just as much within the organism as between organism and its surroundings."[4]

We could compare the three levels of existence of the self to levels of existence in biological life.

Self-1 would be analogous to the less complex forms of life who are totally dependent on external conditions, such as single-celled organisms. The life of these organisms are directly affected by the surrounding medium such as soil, air, or water. If conditions are favorable, life follows its course; if not, the organism dies or suspends all exchanges, activities, and all manifestations of life.

The "surrounding medium" of Self-1 could be seen as the psycho-social matrix, or the space-time *episteme*. The events within that medium such as where and when the individual is born, the social group within the larger culture in which he or she is identified, the genetic makeup of the parents, and so forth all influence and directly shape the "personality" of Self-1. They create a field of circumstances in which Self-1 acquires specific wants and needs beyond that of biogenetic requirements.

With the appearance of Self-2, Self-1 widens the possibilities for living with more autonomy in relation to space-time conditions. Self-2 could be compared to lower animals and plants where the internal medium is less dependent on external conditions. Environmental fluctuations still affect the life of the organism, that is, its vitality, but not suppressing it entirely. Generally, it is body temperature under the influence of the external temperature that regulates the movements.

The awareness of Self-2 at a certain stage of development can be seen as a membrane that protects a web of values, purposes, and felt significance. Relative to Self-1, the "inner world" of Self-2, while influenced to some extent by local happenings and events, remains untouched. Witness many people who survived the Nazi concentration camps. Psychiatrist Viktor Frankl was one of these and founded a new branch of psychiatry, known as existential psychology. In an article, he wrote, "Meaning sets the pace of being. Existence falters unless it is lived in terms of transcendence towards something beyond itself."[5]

---

[4]Francois Jacob, *The Logic of Life*, (New York: Vintage Books, 1976), p. 308.
[5]Frankl's article in *Phenomenology, Pure and Applied*, ed. Erwin Straus, Duquesne, 1964.

Translated in terms of the present model, Self-2 as a scientist-artist provides the "moment-to-moment significance" that makes all of Self-1's space-time activities *semantic transactions*.

The third level, or Self-3, could be compared to higher animals, composed of a large number of cells. In this case, only surface components are in direct contact with the surrounding medium. Dr. Jacob writes:

> Higher animals literally live within themselves...the most valuable components are buried deep in the body, because they are better protected from misadventures in the surrounding medium...all activities are entirely independent of external conditions. Whatever vicissitudes of their surroundings, organisms go on living in the same way, as if in a hothouse: it is the 'constant and free life, independent of variations of the cosmic medium.'[6]

Self-reflexiveness at the third level means being completely free from any space-time conditions and discursive values and purposes. This gives the "selfing" activity the freedom of living in an "atmosphere" that is out of the range of the gravitational field of subject-object and linguistic structures. Our Self-3 needs no "image" with which to identify itself. Thus practices at the "silent" level become necessary to one's evolution; in this way, Self-3 provides an opening into the "unknown"; by unknown I refer to what cannot be predicted nor understood within the established and familiar structures of Self-1 and Self-2. For the lower selves, Self-3 becomes the emerging unexpected. Finally, Self-3 provides an environment of constancy to protect the whole self from inopportune changes of daily living, sometimes called a sense of "center." In this case, center means the dissolving of "inside" and "outside" so that the self's "center" could be said to be everywhere at once.

One of my main purposes for postulating this new Self-3 involves how we participate within the environment. By "environment," I include the necessities of the shifting tides of human affairs, as well as the ecological processes. Of course this could be extended indefinitely to include the whole cosmic process as our "environment." If we limit our awareness to the events of Self-1 born of the affairs of the social environment, then we receive very limited information, and we can only respond and participate in a more or less determined way to what is going on. Self-2 as scientist-artist can increase our movement and openness by being sensitive and alert, not only to the semantic transactions of Self-1, but also to the quality of participation that can allow the evolutionary, creative impulse of Self-3 to play an active role in the life of the whole Self. This can be seen as self-reflexiveness in a unified state.

---

[6]Jacob, *The Logic of Life*, p. 188.

CHAPTER 17

practices in self-development and self-renewal

The Art of Listening

When we speak of communication, the first picture that comes to mind is that of the communicator, the sender of messages. The art of communicating is often understood to be, mainly if not exclusively, the art of making oneself listened to with attention and understood without confusion. Teachers, preachers, executives, and group leaders take courses in public speaking, even in dramatic arts, for the purpose of communicating more effectively.

All this is good, of course, provided the emphasis on the role of the sender does not make us disregard the role of the receiver. Communication is a two-way affair, and the receiver's function is no less important than that of the sender. In fact, we could say of listening what Emerson said of reading: "T'is the good reader that makes the good book."

Experiments have shown it is the good listener that makes the good speech. The same lecture presented to a group of students by an excellent speaker and to a similar group by a poor speaker (with motivation constant) produced almost the same understanding in both groups. To use an analogy from radio: a good receiving set, accurately tuned, is just as important as a good broadcasting station. The message, as a transmission of information, is the joint product of two sources of activity, one at each end of the transmission process.

Receiving messages also has particular importance because listening constitutes the major part of our communicating activities. A survey of a group of persons in various occupations revealed that, on the average, 45 percent of their communicating time was spent in listening, 39 percent in talking, 16 percent in reading, and 9 percent in writing. If this is true, and we have no evidence to the contrary, nearly half of the compensation an executive or a professional receives is payment for his performance in effective listening. If they are poor listeners, their knowledge and wisdom may be of little value because it may be applied where it is not needed.

We touched upon the topic of listening when we studied the functioning of the nervous system, and we learned that it takes time to internalize the messages we receive through the eye or the ear. We have also been reminded of the importance of effective listening as in the case of the executive who observed himself "yes-butting" his subordinates and being "yes-butted" by his superiors. In order to function efficiently at the Self-2 level, it is useful for us to think a bit more about the benefits of good listening and to describe in greater detail what an effective listener does.

The benefits of effective listening are many.

1. We get more from a conversation or a conference than the indifferent listener.
2. By avoiding snap objections that tangle the communication in knots, we save the time it would take to unravel these knots by laborious explanations.
3. We increase our chances of making more realistic decisions and giving more pertinent answers because we are better informed about facts, attitudes, and opinions.
4. By showing interest and asking nonthreatening questions, we may help the speaker fill in gaps in the presentation.
5. We discover what level of language the other person will best understand when our turn comes to speak.
6. We are better prepared to make our message fit with the knowledge, views, and feelings of those with whom we are communicating.
7. We learn to speak more effectively by observing how people convey, or fail to convey, their messages to us.

Now here is what an effective listener does.

1. The listener listens to understand what is meant, not to become ready to reply, contradict, or refute. *This is extremely important as a general attitude.*
2. The listener knows that what is meant involves more than the dictionary meaning of the words that are used. It involves, among other things, the tone of the voice, the facial expression, and the overall behavior of the speaker.
3. As the listener observes all this, he is careful not to interpret too

quickly. He looks for clues to what the other person is trying to say, putting himself (as best he can) in the speaker's shoes, looking at the world as the speaker sees it, accepting the speaker's feelings as facts that have to be taken into account—whether he, the listener, shares them or not.

4. The listener puts aside her own views and opinions for the time being. She realizes that she cannot listen to herself inwardly at the same time as she listens outwardly to the speaker. She is careful not to "jam" her receiving set.

5. The listener controls his impatience because he knows that listening is faster than talking. The average person speaks about 125 words a minute, but can listen to about 400 words a minute. The effective listener does not jump ahead of the speaker; he gives him time to tell his story. What the speaker will say next may not be what the listener expects him to say.

6. The listener does not prepare her answer while she listens. She wants to get the whole message before deciding what to say in her turn. The last sentence of the speaker may give a new slant to what she had said before.

7. The listener shows interest and alertness. This stimulates the speaker and improves performance.

8. The listener does not interrupt. When he asks questions it is to secure more information, not to trap the speaker or force him into a corner.

9. The listener expects the speaker's language to differ from the way she would say the "same thing" herself. She does not quibble about words but tries to get at what is meant.

10. The listener's purpose is the opposite of a debater's. He looks for areas of agreement, not for weak spots that he plans to attack and blast with the artillery of counterarguments.

11. In a conference, he listens to all participants, not only to those who are on his side.

12. In a particularly difficult discussion he may, before giving his answer, sum up his understanding of what was said. If his interpretation is not accepted, he clears up the contested points before attempting to proceed with his own views.

Like all skills, listening requires self-observation, time, patience, and practice. It is not enough merely to read the above and assent to it "intellectually." In fact, we may assume that, if we agree with what was said, we behave in the manner described; and this is one of the worst traps we can set for ourselves.

In a group that has the advantage of having an appointed moderator, the function of observing may be left to her or him at the beginning, and he or she should be free to interrupt whenever it is felt that a correction is appropriate. But, in the end, no participant can make real progress unless he checks on his own way of acting and keeps on checking until the skill of listening becomes a habit.

To check on one's performance while in action is very difficult for the beginner. It seems better to wait until a conversation or a conference is over, and then make a leisurely evaluation of oneself as a listener. But having a "listening partner" is even better, a friend who is also a participant and who is willing to give you an evaluation of how you participated in the exchange.

As I stated before, in this training, as in most cases, it is good to limit one's observation to a limited number of items, perhaps only two—or, better still, only one at a time. Aspects are so closely knitted together that improving one of them will mean improvement in all. But trying to observe ourself all across the line at the same time is more than we can do at the beginning; it may lead to discouragement, to giving up the whole undertaking and contenting ourself with "good," but ineffective, intentions.

Reading and Meditating

To his friend Lucien Price, who wondered how he had gathered so much information on so many subjects, Whitehead said: "I do not read many books, but I think about what I read, and it sticks." It is safe to assume that Whitehead was speaking of serious reading, but all reading need not be of this kind. It is good to enjoy humor, fiction, and mystery stories, but, even then, we may come across passages that invite us to stop, daydream, or think.

To read is to come into contact with someone. A writer often "talks" to us about something to which he has given a good deal of thought. We may stop him when we want, make him repeat a statement as many times as we wish, or keep him silent while we ponder what he has just said. The only thing that makes reading less satisfactory than a two-way conversation is that we cannot ask questions on points that are not clear; but, if we are patient, we may find the explanation we are looking for on the next page or in the next chapter.

Reading is not exclusively a matter of cortical activity. Of course, we have to think while we read, but fruitful reading is very much a matter of attitudes, feelings, motivation, and purposes. Our *B* activities exert a great influence on our *C* functions.

If we start reading with negative feelings, we may not get much out of it. Nor is it good to be critical too early; it is better to wait till the writer has completed the full structure of the message she attempts to convey and look for the meaning that lies behind the design of words, sentences, analogies, and metaphors. It may not be the way we would have drawn the picture, but it may imply more than appears at first sight. It may evoke thoughts that we have never clearly formulated before.

If a statement clashes or appears to clash with our cherished views, why take this as a threat to our mental security. Let us look at it with a steady mind and take time to examine it without being disturbed. We don't have to accept it in the end, but we may miss something valuable if we let our emotions becloud the scene.

Any statement that gives us a shock may be taken as an invitation to original thinking. Why not ask ourself: "What if this threw a new light on my hidden assumptions, on ideas that I am taking for granted, on areas of my inner world that I have not visited for years?" Even if we do not accept what is said or the way it is said, it may trigger a chain of feeling-thinking reactions and eventually burst into an insight that could not have come otherwise.

We should not let ourself be unduly impressed, for good or for ill, by the name, the reputation, or the political, scientific, or religious allegiance of a writer. If we do not like Jesuits, we may find certain pages of Teilhard de Chardin a hodgepodge of questionable science and obsolete theology; if we are in deadly fear of international communism, we may not appreciate Trotsky's literary style; if we expect a pearl of great price in every cryptic statement written by Korzybski, we may take as a revelation from on high what is just a passing thought of his.

So much for our *B* activities, our attitudes, feelings, and purposes; we can now pass to our *C* activities, to thinking proper. Should we maintain a passive role and simply file away what comes to us in linear sequence? Or shall we engage in active reactions to the thought structures that take shape before our eyes? Shall we act as spectators, or shall we get into the game? Of course, we shall get into the game. If we want our reading to be creative— and it should be—we have to become participants in a joint enterprise, ours and the author's.

For instance, we may stop at the end of what appears to be a key statement and translate it into different words. This is like turning a cut diamond under the light to examine its many facets. Here is an italicized statement in a previous book of mine, which I evidently meant to emphasize: *"Altruism is not a matter of choice; it belongs to the nature of man."*[7] Here are two possible translations. "To care for the welfare of others is just as necessary for man as to breathe, to eat, to sleep, or to perform any survival function." Or "As I did not choose to have eyes, ears, arms, and hands, I did not choose to depend on others or to have them depend on me; that's the way things are, though, and I cannot change them to suit my fancy."

We could develop the idea a bit further as we translate it. "There are things that I can choose, like living in the city or the country, smoking or not

[7]J. Samuel Bois, *Explorations in Awareness* (New York: Harper & Row, 1957), p. 195.

smoking, voting Republican or Democrat. And there are things about which I have no choice: my parents, being white or black, not growing older. If I pretend otherwise, I am just fooling myself and heading for a rude awakening. Similarly, I am fooling myself and heading for an unpleasant experience if I choose not to care about other people's welfare."

We may relate the statement to other statements that we are familiar with. In the present case, many thoughts come to mind. From Cain's question, "Am I my brother's keeper?" we may pass to Cassius Jackson Keyser's cryptic sentence, "To be is to be related," to the lines of John Donne, "No man is an island . . .," or to Hemingway's title, *For Whom the Bell Tolls*— which comes from Donne's essay.

We may look for analogies that illustrate the statement. The first that comes to my mind at the moment is a team of baseball players. Each one has to depend on the others and each has to support his teammates. The catcher may have a personal grudge against the first-baseman, but he can't let this interfere with the success of the whole team. If it loses, he loses.

We may analyze, on the epistemological profile, our transaction with one of the key terms in the statement. For instance, our notion of "human nature" may still linger at stage two, where it corresponds to the standard definition of a person as a *rational animal*, as an individual complete by himself. In that case, the statement about altruism will not be so easy to accept; we may think in terms of the survival of the fittest. a stage-three reaction is what the poet had in mind when he wrote "No man is an island . . ."; he was conscious of the fact that we are interdependent, that each of us is only a node of interrelatedness.

A stage-four reaction will go beyond the interdependence of individuals. It will take individuality and groupness as two complementary notions, apparently opposite to each other because each is inadequate for the complexity of the human process. When such a stage-four reaction dominates a profile, the statement becomes obvious.

Finally, we may have known the ineffable unifying experience, where our oneness with other humans is a sort of first-order contact, beyond sensation and theory. Here the statement sounds like a melodic tune that reduces to a simple design the overwhelming power of a full orchestration of trans-discursive feelings echoing in our souls. It is a reminder that evokes an experience beyond words.

We may let the statement, as it were, sink into the recesses of our innermost self. This may be facilitated by a repetition of the statement as it stands or by one of its translations. If this repetition is directed to ourself by using the first person as the subject of the sentence, its suggestive power will increase noticeably. For instance, "I am not fully human unless I willingly care for the other person." Use this personalized statement as a flashlight and direct it into the dark corners of your inner self. It may reveal remnants of old rancors that you have stored in a hidden crevice.

Anyone who is familiar with the practices of religious life, yoga, or mind-training will recognize that what I am proposing here has a great deal in common with these practices. I don't deny it and I don't apologize for it. Why should we ignore techniques that have proved effective? We can use them without necessarily embracing the whole philosophy of life of which they are a part. I don't have to believe in reincarnation to avail myself of some Buddhist practices; I don't have to become a Jesuit to profit by the powerful techniques of the Spiritual Exercises of Ignatius of Loyola; I do not have to adopt the code of a desert hermit to appreciate the values of inner quiet and meditation on fundamentals.

Meditation, under some form or other, can be seen everywhere in human history. Creative people withdrew from the commotion and noise of daily life to restore their personal balance with the cosmos and to set their sights above and beyond the movements of the crowd. Such great leaders as Buddha, Jesus, Mohammed, and Gandhi lived for hours and days in silence and meditation, accumulating reserves of semantic energies that they communicated to millions of minds and hearts for generations and generations. If we look at humankind as an organism born with the appearance of *Homo sapiens* and spread over the planet as part of the biosphere, we see the fruits of meditation and contemplation as hormones secreted at definite points of time and space by people who played an active part in the survival and growth of that organism. These hormones are transported here and there as packets of semantic energy that bring about advances in science, upheavals in politics, and the emergence of new ideologies.

We may see each individual as a miniature of humankind, of which each of us is a part. Each of us, too, is an organism developing in space and time. We have semantic centers that require occasional withdrawal from immediate preoccupations to function effectively. We all need periods of quiet, of time to clean up the psychological waste accumulated from unassimilated experiences and take an inventory of our stock of ideas, time to discard thinking and feeling methods that have become obsolete. It is good to nourish ourself with the wisdom that others have condensed in books and articles. This means reading and meditating, as described in the previous paragraphs.

It may be profitable to read the same book or article over and over again if it proved to be thought-provoking in our first contact with it. There are books and "books." Some are full of detailed information, which they keep available for us on our shelves or in the stacks of our libraries: reference books, such as the *Encyclopaedia Britannica*, a world atlas, the *Story of Civilization*. We read them when we need their information for a particular purpose.

There are books of a different kind, that are not catalogs of facts and data but the fruits of days, months, or perhaps years of meditation by an individual who has given special attention to a certain field of human endeavor and experience. They invite us to live that person's experience.

Some were published years ago, but are not completely outdated, such as James's *Principles of Psychology*, Montaigne's Essays, or Plato's Dialogues. Some are of present vintage and keep us conversant with the creative efforts of the thinkers of today, such as the reading references at the end of each part of this book. Some are not necessarily scientific or philosophical treatises: the poetry of Walt Whitman, the plays of Bernard Shaw, the fables of James Thurber. They start growth activities within our thinking-feeling self, and their stimulating power is not easily exhausted. Coming back to them, we often get a new experience from a page or a passage that we thought we had already squeezed dry.

Crisscross Reading

Another reading practice has also proved pleasant and helpful, which I call "crisscross reading." It has something in common with the *Syntopicon* of the Great Books, with the difference that it is a very personal and spontaneous form of cross-indexing. For example, I may be reading: "Science as it is thought of popularly is a stereotype that bears but little resemblance to science as it is known intimately by those who live it from day to day."[8] This makes me think of what I read in Schrödinger's *Science Theory and Man*, and I go back to his chapter entitled "Is Science a Fashion of the Times?" From there I may go to certain passages of Poincaré's *La Science et l'Hypothèse*, to L. A. Du Bridge's "Exploring the Unknown" in *Frontiers of Science* (Basic Books, 1958), to Korzybski's definition of science as the "generalized results of semantic reactions acceptable to the majority of informed and not heavily pathological individuals."[9] By doing this I bring together, in a common discussion, many people who have already told me their views on science. It gives me an opportunity to compare various viewpoints and to integrate them into a richer structure of my own.

This is what we do all the time more or less consciously. If we compare our memory to a filing cabinet, we can say that we have a certain number of folders in which we store whatever information and experience we gather on a few general subjects. There would be a folder on love, on justice, on sex, on freedom, on science, on mathematics. Some would be bulging with notes and clippings, some would be flat and seldom opened. The filing is done sporadically and unsystematically, and there is little or no cross-indexing—except what we might do by association.

[8] Harold K. Schilling, "A Human Enterprise," *Science* 127 (June 1958): 1324. Used by permission.

[9] Alfred Korzybski, *Science and Sanity* (Lakeville, Conn.: International Non-Aristotelian Library, 1933, 1941, 1948, 1958), p. 26.

What I suggest is occasionally taking stock of our memory files, putting them in better order, subdividing folders that are full of heterogeneous material, discarding information that is out of date, comparing notes, clippings, and experiences, cross-indexing when we discover relationships between topics that we had not noticed before. For instance, I recently cross-indexed the Hopi notions of "eventing" and "preparing" with the "intellectual passions" described by Michael Polanyi, the "centrencephalic system" of Penfield, the thalamo-cortical integration of Korzybski, and the *B* aspect of our semantic transactions. Obviously, this makes for a syntopicon that is extremely personal, that defies all the rules of classification by verbal lables, but each of us has a similar system whether aware of it or not. Why not take the fact into account and make the most of it?

Self-training in Silencing Oneself

Korzybski occasionally called his system an *empirical* science. Some have objected to this appellation and have made much ado about it. If we listened to them, however, we should start a stage-two discussion about what is science, what is an empirical science, what do general semanticists do that can be classed as genuine research—as is done in other sciences?

This apparent difficulty can be solved quite easily if we forget academic distinctions and take a fresh look at life as we live it. We can start with a postulate, already accepted by some workers in the human sciences, that "stems from an attempt to consolidate the viewpoints of the clinician, the historian, the scientists, and the philosopher"—according to Dr. George A. Kelly, one of its foremost proponents.

> Let us look at *man-the-scientist*. . . . When we speak of *man-the-scientist* we are speaking of all mankind and not merely a particular class of men who have publicly attained the stature of "scientists." We are speaking of all mankind in its scientist-like aspect, rather than all mankind in its biological aspects or mankind in its appetitive aspects. Moreover, we are speaking of aspects of mankind rather than collections of men. . . .

> Such an abstraction of the nature of man is not altogether new. The Reformation called attention to the priesthood of all men in contrast to the concretistic classification of certain men only as priests. The democratic political inventions of the eighteenth and nineteenth centuries hinged on the notion of the inherent rulership of all men in contrast to the older notion of a concrete class of rulers. In a similar fashion we may replace the concretistic notion of scientists being set apart from non-scientists and, like the reformers who insisted that every man is his own priest, propose that every man is, in his own particular way, a scientist.[10]

[10]George A. Kelley, *The Psychology of Personal Constructs* (New York: Norton, 1955), p. 4.

What do scientists do? They have hunches, translate these hunches into hypotheses, and carry out experiments to test these hypotheses. This is exactly what every one of us does all along. Every step we take on the road of life is an experiment; every decision we take when the road branches out in many directions is an experiment; every plan we make for the immediate or the distant future is an experiment. We start with a hunch that we rationalize in the light of what we already know; we figure out where it is likely to take us; and then we make an experiment with ourselves as the subject. This experiment is more often than not a bold jump into the unknown. Each of these jumps is an irreversible process; it restricts or expands the range of possibilities that we will find available for the next jump. So, in a sense, the life of the lay person is similar to the life of the professional scientist, but it is more serious: the lay person does not experiment with chemicals or with rats, but with himself, and the outcome may mean personal success or failure.

Each new life experiment is unique; no two of them are identical in their totality. You cannot repeat the experiments that I had to make in my life—I cannot repeat them myself. The best we can do is compare our *methods* of experimenting and profit from each other's experience. General Semantics and Epistemics incorporates the methods that the lay person, in the capacity as "man-the-scientist," has learned to depend on when we experiment with ourself, with those near us, and with our possessions; and this is the sense in which it may be called an empirical science.

Being a scientist could be compared to being a medical doctor. When we pass forty, we have to be our own doctor to some extent; we have to know what is good for us and what is not. Does this mean that we disregard medicine as a profession? Of course not; it simply means that we must acquire what the nonprofessional should know of medicine to take care of ourselves under ordinary circumstances. When we are faced with a health problem that goes beyond enlightened common sense, we go to a person who has made medicine their profession.

I am a nonprofessional scientist, I assume that you are too, and, outside our specialties, we both are nonprofessional scientists whether we are willing to admit it or not. We all have to experiment with our own life, and this calls for a special skill. Why not profit from the experience of those who have made it their profession to experiment, doing our best to transfer the special skills of a special branch of science into the general skill of experimenting with our own life? Why not study the philosophers of science, those practitioners who have made it their job to observe and rationalize what is common to all creative experimenting?

Of the basic skills that seem valuable in all experimental scientific work, there is one I would like to describe in this chapter. It is the skill of functioning at what Korzybski calls *the silent level* of perceiving, feeling, touching, and hearing without talking to ourselves while we are sensing. This is one avenue that leads into an experience that will be described later as a stage five experience. It is not easy, and it is not a psychological trick that works automatically; it is a skill that requires patient, consistent, and long practice.

The general purpose is to liberate ourselves from preconceived ideas, hidden assumptions, and rigid ways of thinking. It is intended to correct the bad effects of uncontrolled circularity. Remeber what we said of this before? "We see only what we are used to seeing; we hear only what we are used to hearing; we understand only what we are ready to understand." We live in a vicious circle, and the problem is to break out of the circle. Reaching for a silent-level experience is a way of breaking out of the circle. It involves two steps of increasing difficulty.

The first step is a simple exercise that I call *sensory deconcentration*. It is a way of loosening the concentration involved in whatever we do in earnest. Much of this concentration is a sheer waste of energy, just a bad habit, uncontrolled and ineffective.

As I am writing this, I may concentrate on what I have to say and pay little attention to what surrounds me. So far, there is nothing wrong in this; the trouble arises if I make a virtue of that concentration and think that the more I concentrate (and at the same time tense up unconsciously) the better. This is not true at all; instead I allow myself to "deconcentrate" instead, giving my system a release from tension without impairing my efficiency. I do this by looking cursively at a few objects in my study. On the end table in front of me I see a reproduction of Paul Klee's "Blue Head," with its two black eyes that stare at me. Then I look at the red flowers on the cushion at one end of the settee, at the attaché case at the other end, at the dater on my desk, at a pinhole in the shade of the lamp, at the green copy of a Clarkson letter showing under a scribbled sheet, and so on. I don't give much thought to any of these; I just glance at them and pass to something else, aware of what I am doing and registering my sensations as I go. This does not interfere with what I am doing; I am not "distracted" in the usual sense. I remain in control, both at the focus of my activity, which consists in writing, and at the periphery, which consists in looking around.

Once my day of work is over, when I come out of my studio, which is built on a slope in my orchard, to climb the stairs in the dark of the night, I may direct my flashlight to a distant tree, or to the roses that hang on the archway, or to the barrel cactus close to the barbecue. On entering the living room I may observe the design of the rug, or the way Baron, our boxer, stretches in front of the fireplace. None of this is important or is directly related to a particular purpose, or will hold my attention for more than a fleeting moment, but it prevents me from being too wrapped up in what I am busy with. Without such a technique, I may act like a sleepwalker who goes along unaware of what surrounds him, and not participating in the cosmic ongoing of which he, himself, is one aspect.

The second step, an exercise in sensory awareness, is different in the sense that, instead of stretching our perception to the periphery of our focus of attention, we make the exercise itself the center of our attention.

We can begin by listening to sounds that we seldom pay attention to; for instance, the chirping of birds that actually fills the air at times and that we take as a background noise of no significance. Or we can look at things in ways that are new and different from our stereotyped way of looking at them.

I remember an experience of this kind that I had two years ago when I dropped in at an art workshop at a youths' summer camp. The instructor told us to look closely and at length at anything within our reach, and I picked a leaf from a branch that was hanging by my head. I still remember that leaf: its finely veined structure, like a mosaic, where no two pieces had exactly the same shape or the same shade; its well-engineered ribs, the texture stretched between them and supplied with moisture through built-in channels; the shine of the upper surface and the pastel underneath, and the scalloped hem all around.

This type of experience is still a classifying experience (it involves some talking to oneself, I know), but its value is its newness; it shakes asunder our stereotypes: "a leaf is a leaf," or "green is green." It is a preparation for the more advanced stage of silent practice, where one feels, perceives, hears, tastes, and touches without—or practically without—any interfering word or mental category between oneself and what one is in contact with.

An outstanding surgeon told me how this practice made it possible for him, eventually, to master the technique of an extremely delicate operation that had proved too difficult for him up to that time. By observing himself carefully, he discovered that he had been talking to himself as he proceeded with his work. This talk, subtle and inaudible though it was, was like a screen that separated him from his work. He started practicing the silent level by training his ear to listen to sounds that he, like most of us, was burying in the background noise. He would practice when he was going to bed at night—and, in a big city, it is amazing how many different sounds fill the air, even at night. He told me that, eventually, he could differentiate twenty-eight sounds: some relatively loud, like the starting of an automobile engine in the street; some extremely faint, like the crumpling of the bedsheet as he breathed. He trained his other senses as well; and also practiced his operation technique on cadavers, feeling his way, as it were, instead of talking to himself to describe what he was finding. The results were beyond his expectations: he not only mastered the technique but he shortened the average time required for that operation from four hours to one hour and forty minutes.

Here is a clinical case from my own practice. A man thirty years of age, single, well-educated, had come to me in a state of acute depression, unable to do work of any kind, and was contemplating suicide. He had all sorts of problems, but one of these was homosexuality, not just a passing experience but a well-established liaison with a person of his own sex: a "falling in love," with all the vicissitudes of love-life and the heart-rending experience of separation when his lover had to leave town.

My method of working with cases of this degree of severity is based on a conviction that Korzybski expressed as follows.

> Personal difficulties always seem very personal, and no outsider can ever fully grasp the situation. One of the benefits of the present method of training in sanity consists in the fact that we do *not* dwell upon the personal affairs of the individual, but that we give, instead, a general structural semantic method, by the aid of which every one can solve his problems by himself.[11]

Therefore, once this client had told me (to his satisfaction and to mine) what he was concerned with and how the situation had developed, I asked him to dismiss his urgent problems as much as he could for a while and to listen to my explanation and description of how I had trained myself to think and react in ordinary circumstances. "By doing this" I told him, "we will be better able to work together on your problems." What I actually did was teach him the basic notions of general semantics. As I was doing this, I would carefully avoid any statement, example, or exercise that might appear to be related to his problems.

The practice of the silent level appealed to him. He would be looking, listening, observing, and "discovering" the physical world in which he lived. This helped him much more than reading books and magazines on psychology, as he had done formerly.

Later, he had the idea of practicing at the writing table in his room. He would take sheets of paper and color one sheet after the other with crayons, making spontaneous designs and mixtures of hues. He would look at these without verbalizing as to what they were, what they represented, or what they suggested.

In the course of our interviews I never discussed his "homosexual" problem, and, in a letter he wrote to me more than a year after we had stopped working together, he reminded me that I had mentioned it only once: let me quote from that letter, where he tells how he handled his homosexual ten-

[11]Korzybski, *Science and Sanity*, pp. 528-29.

dencies. He decided to test his manliness in a heterosexual encounter. After describing the scene, he wrote:

> I felt no revulsion, fear, etc., but for some reason—which I did not try to get at—I sensed there must have been some anxiety. I knew it was foolish to try and place it, or label it. I could not be aroused. So I resorted to my skill to react at the silent level. I ceased verbalizing to myself and let myself experience. Doctor, you were right; I am not a homosexual.

I followed his progress for a few years and found that the change was permanent.

So, these techniques work, and that is the beauty of it. I have used them with clients who were extremely worried, unable to think of anything else but their troubles, and I would give them a prescription that ran somewhat like this.

> As you come out of the building, notice as many things as you can that you would not notice otherwise: the width of the sidewalk, the finish of its surface, the material of the wall—brick, stone, or concrete—the number of persons who are waiting for the green light at the corner, the colors of the cars that are lined up along the curb, etc. Or register the sounds and noises that you seldom really hear because you take them for granted: the rumble of engines, the hubbub of a crowd, the whistle or drone of the plane overhead.

It is simply amazing how this simple prescription relieved their anxiety. One does not yield to a feeling of discouragement if the results to not become evident in the earlier stages. It takes time and persevering practice, but success is assured if one keeps at it.

The second step, in my experience, is a rather difficult achievement. It is an attempt to reach what Korzybski calls the silent level, the level of first-order experience without any naming at all, conscious or unconscious; and Wendell Johnson calls it nonverbal abstracting.

> Hold an object (ashtray, pencil, or anything else that may be handy) in both hands and look at it steadily, examining it. As soon as you begin to verbalize about it, put it down. Take it and try again. See how long you can stay "on the silent level" of abstracting. This should be practiced for a short time each day for at least a week or two, using different objects. You can also do it while watching a person, viewing a painting, listening to music, or watching a game of some sort. In such cases, of course you cannot hold in your hands what you are observing, and so you need to use a slightly different technique: before you begin to observe, cross your arms, and when you begin to verbalize uncross them. This is an unusually effective exercise for demonstrating the degree to which your observations are influenced by your verbalizations about whatever you are observing.[12]

It is not easy to attain the silent state or to maintain it for long; but the closer you come to it by practicing the simpler skills of "deconcentration"

---

[12]Wendell Johnson, *People in Quandaries* (New York: Harper & Row, 1946), p. 493.

and sensory awareness, the better you will be able to control your "worries," stop thinking in circles, uncover your hidden assumptions, and overcome such common bad habits.

To carry out a really fresh experiment we have to clear the environment of all the semantic impurities that we generally accept as the "normal" accompaniment of living. We have to prepare our environment—like the surgeon who makes the whole surgical environment as aseptic as possible before she operates on her patient. It requires no less care to venture into the vital parts of our inner self.

Now we come to a technique in "silent" training introduced to me by Verlin Heuton, a teacher of General Semantics and Epistemics at San Deguito High School in southern California. It is a simple procedure that is called "sitting." It is a practice that he does daily, as well as offer it to his students. The procedure is merely sitting in a sense of your own presence, as free as possible from any self-images with which you are usually identified. The only other directive is to watch your breath go out. You might ask, "What do you mean by that? How do you watch your breath?" Let your breathing come into your attention and get a sense of it going out; just be with it. Do not concern yourself with what happens on the in-breath; your breath will come in on its own; just be with it.

Sitting time can be anywhere from twenty minutes for beginners, and as much as two hours for those more experienced, and it should be done daily if possible.

After sitting, it is suggested that you write about what took place. You can use the semantic transactor diagram (Figure 3.1, p. 29) as a guide to writing about what you noticed. You may notice, especially at the beginning, that there is a lot of inner chatter or self-talk at the level of C activities. You might be thinking about what you had for breakfast that morning before school or wondering if you said the right thing to your employer yesterday; this is thinking in the past, or "pasting." Or you may be thinking of a date that you made for that evening, or thinking about how you can make some needed money to pay for an unexpected doctor bill; this is anticipating the future, or "futuring." But whether one is "pasting" or "futuring," you are involved with language structure, and thus speaking from the "past."

For instance, if you are "sitting" and noting your experience with self-talk, you will be creating content that conforms to the units of discourse. While you are doing that, whatever it was that you were paying attention to is already past. The content can be future or past in tense, or in the anticipation and recall of events, but at the verbal level, it is all past to some degree; thus, futuring can be seen as speculation based on past experience.

The compulsive use of language that indiscriminately "goes by itself," can keep us dangling like marionettes from the strings of our structured unconscious. I have found that when verbalizing and other discursive distinctions are not in process, my experience is all "presence." The minute I say to myself, "Look! I'm in my own 'presence,' " I am out of it, so to speak. Sitting can be another way of beginning to learn to differentiate without language, and the writing of observations afterward can help to make a new use of our ability to classify, relate, and postulate. Our discursive ability can be creatively used to clarify, heighten, and give an order to our 'silent' experience—but used very discriminately.

The reader might do well to review Chapter 13 on "Language as Shapers of Ideas" at this point.

After gaining some experience in sitting, you may begin to live moments where you can experience yourself functioning without the use of language. This can provide the opportunity to become intimate and familiar with yourself as a semantic transactor without the evaluative abstractions of the verbal level. This can be an education in which you are both teacher and learner, as well as the subject. The fruits of this education will become apparent in the writing after sitting, and eventually in your thinking-feeling-acting.

If one persists, sitting can be like a laser beam that cuts through our familiarly oriented, personal *episteme* to the supraconscious that I described in the diagram called "The structured unconscious" (Figure 9.1, p. 142); and also in the diagram called "The semantic spectrum" (Figure 11.2, p. 187).

In the first diagram, one sees the structured unconscious as the personalized dynamic pattern of attitudes, beliefs, habits, internalized values, and modes of thinking-feeling-acting through which all our experiences are processed.

As I have stated, the important factor in holding this dynamic pattern in a unit is our language structure and the values that emerge from living with it. This is represented in the second diagram as the slim range of commonsense introspection, or what is called the conscious range, in a limited sense of the word.

When second-order self-reflexiveness at the 'silent' level (i.e., when first-order experience is tuned to WIGO) becomes differentiated in our awareness, the "conscious," discursive range of the spectrum loses its exclusive semantic impact. When the verbalizing stops, and we can move out of the subject-object orientation into a felt oneness in WIGO, then we begin to move freely through the nameless frequencies of our semantic spectrum, the source of our creativity. To participate in our own "nameless frequencies" *as a way of life* is a life-long study and commitment. As an *experience*, this deeper awareness, or felt-participation is our introduction to the creative Self-3 that I postulated earlier on page 284. This can be described as the "supraconscious self" from which we receive creative intuitions that are necessary to self-renewal. Through its "laser power" we can transform the very structure of our *episteme. And when carefully integrated at a stage-four level of functioning,* a new self emerges. But if Self-2 functions at stages one, two, or three, experiences like that described above can confirm the individual personality, or Self-1, within his or her private world. The feeling of sureness or "revelation" can create the illusion of having found The Truth. All three selves as different aspects of a unity are integrally important to living on our planet.

Of the creating Self-3, Bhagwan Shree Rajneesh, one of India's most widely known spiritual teachers, has this to say:

> Out of this silence, every creativity comes. It is very pregnant. . . .So whenever I say "silence," I do not mean the silence of a cemetery, the silence of a house when no one is there. No! I mean the silence of a seed; the silence of a mother's womb; the silence of roots underground. There is much hidden potentiality that will be coming soon. Activity will be there, but now the actor is no more, the doer is no more.[13]

Finally, a word on "boredom" while you are sitting. You may find yourself looking at the clock and wondering if the sitting will ever end. You may fall asleep or invent some pain or discomfort to avoid the self-created pressure of "nothing's happening." We become very creative at the moment of "boredom." We develop content to our experience to keep the reticular activating system of the brain on the alert. There is nothing wrong with this unless it becomes a compulsive urge for novelty that runs your life.

But when we can become self-reflexive and see ourselves as the "container" of the "content," we can enlist "boredom" as a friend, for it signals the threshold of our habitual way of relating ourselves and provides an opportunity for self-renewal. When we go past those moments we find that "boredom" is a second-order experience; it is a remembered semantic state to which we give value in the present. On the 'silent' level, "boredom" becomes an unspeakable affect involving sensory/muscular activities without the discursively elaborated content. This can be a valuable lesson in any number of situations, especially involving pain of any kind.

The ability to function at the 'silent' level is vital to our next topic, that of abduction and creative innovation.

From Abstraction to Abduction and Creative Innovation

Until now when I described my own version of the process of abstracting, I have suggested that we see ourselves picking out of WIGO (What Is Going On) a certain number of point-events and gathering them in a set of perceived relations, which I called a first-order experience (Figure 6.3, p. 93).

This first-order experience I see as a felt relationship with a fraction of WIGO, this fraction being surrounded by an ETC. of limitless size.

[13]Bhagwan Shree Rajneesh, *Meditation: The Art of Ecstacy* (New York: Harper & Row, 1976), p. 21.

We say, repeating Korzybski's premise, "The map is not the territory," meaning that this first-order experience has not the same extension as WIGO and belongs to a different order of existence. We add the second Korzybskian premise, "The map does not represent all the territory," meaning that, even as a representation imprinted in our nervous system, this first-order experience does not cover all that is going on at that instant, but only a fraction of it.

This is good as far as it goes, as a first approximation of the happening that we are studying. But it may be advisable to stop at this point and reflect on the various assumptions that our procedure involves. They are at least three:

1. There is a WIGO there facing me;
2. I stand outside that WIGO as a detached observer;
3. The map, being self-reflexive, according to Korzybski's third premise, inserts itself into WIGO as perceived and makes it at least slightly different from what it was initially.

Instead of WIGO, Korzybski calls the phenomenon represented by the parabola the 'event' or the 'scientific object,' meaning a localized WIGO described in scientific language. His view is roughly equivalent to mine, the differences between us are that I take as 'background' the whole cosmic event at a moment, and I use commonsense language, which could vary in sophistication from individual to individual, as a workable description. Depending on the knowledge of the person I observe, his world is less or more complex, its size and its depth and the cluster of relationships that holds its elements together are determined by the mental span and grasping capacity of the individual. If he is a physicist, his world is likely to be the scientific world of physicists; if he is a Christian scientist, it is probably the world as described by Mrs. Eddy; if he is French or English, his world is one that can be described in either one of these languages and none else; if he is a child, his world is that of a child; if an oldster, the world of an oldster; and so on. In fact, the WIGO from which we abstract our first-order experience is our own unique world, structured according to our culture and personal experience. We live and operate within a space-time plenum out of which we cannot come entirely free.

Abstraction, by itself, does not take us out of the deduction-induction loop that closes upon itself within that cultural plenum. To come out of it, we have to undergo the emergence of a new self and of a new WIGO consistent with it. This demands an act that we label creating, or bringing into existence what was not before. I speak of it as *innovating*, and I call the process *abduction*. It means drawing out of the totality of my space-time self and establishing in the historical stream of happenings a new energetic existent, active, reactive, and bent on continuing itself as an expanding system.

This process of abduction may be triggered off by various forms of awakening to a new degree of awareness. We could see these awakenings as interruptions of our ongoing sequence of living (Self-1) where one's formerly held unconscious assumptions (i.e., what we took as spontaneous, "natural," and rock-bottom "reality") are shaken. The initial response to such disturbances can be anything from mild surprise to radical shock, depending on one's preparedness for the unexpected. It may be hearing or reading a statement that goes beyond or challenges what I am ready to say by myself; by meeting with conditions I am not prepared to face; by undergoing an experience that disturbs the smooth running of my habits of thinking-feeling; by any shock or sudden change in my functioning at any level. In such cases, it is not sufficient to abstract, "as is," the first-order experience to insert into my activities of the next instant; I have to assume the role of self-creator, or achiever of self-emergence.

If we take the structural more into account, we see that even a slight change means a self-restructuring, in fact a self-renewal. We have to postulate life as a never-ending succession of deaths and rebirths, of disintegrations and emergences.

We may study these structural transformations of the self by meditating on the chart *The Worlds in Which We Live* (Figure 8.1, p. 119). Each of its four concentric circles may be considered in turn.

1. *Senses.* A new sensation, particularly if it is intense and takes place when the system is in the mood of welcoming imprinting, will cause organismic changes that are extremely difficult to annul. Enslaving addictions can be created, as in the case of drugs, alcohol, cigarettes. This is also the case of habituation for certain foods—'the pies as my mother used to make them,'—the need for a background of music while working, the pleasure of skiing, surfing, swimming, the enjoyment of exercising, the thrill of caressing and being caressed, the tyranny of compulsive eating. It is easy to realize that a change in these and similar habits introduces a disturbance in the total semantic organism and calls for a careful restructuring of a 'self' patterned after a new design.

One of the strongest felt assumptions of our earthly existence is the daily experience of living in a relatively strong gravitational field. Our posture, the way we move about spatially, our sense of equilibrium, location, involves this "accepted-as-natural" experience. Whirling dervishes of the East interrupt this confirmed assumption in their spinning dances; this practice provides them an opening into another way of experiencing. As children, we twirled around to make ourselves dizzy. Imagine how the lives of the astronauts were affected in moving out of the earth's gravitational field and experiencing the relativity of the assumption that "bodies have weight."

2. *Instruments.* We abstract elements from the world of happenings as

they are presented to us by the instruments, tools, and appliances we are familiar with: the glasses we wear, the false teeth or the fillings in our mouth, the razor we use to shave, the typewriter we write with, the car we drive, the utensils we use to prepare our meals, and the practically endless variety of physical facilities our technology has put at our service: telephones, newspapers, radios, television sets; public conveyances such as buses, taxis, trains, airplanes, elevators; regulation of traffic by painted directions on the roadway, signposts and traffic lights, bridges, gates, revolving doors, and such. Pencils, pens, Xerox duplicators, tapes and recorders, washing machines and clothes dryers, automatic selling machines and coin-operated telephones, garage door opening devices, television control at a distance. Any change in these means of contact, control, and use of our surrounds, especially if it covers a complex of well-established activity patterns as when we move from a place of residence to another or from a work environment to a different one, does demand more semantic resiliency than we are likely to anticipate.

3. *Methods of thinking-feeling-behaving.* Here we are at the very center of our semantic makeup, of what Sylvan Tomkins had in mind when he discoursed about the "central assembly," and what I describe as the *episteme* that pervades all our activities, 'physical,' 'mental,' 'physiological,' 'affective,' and what not. Here, every operating factor in our organism—body and soul, to use the old terminology—is dynamically in active energetic relation with every other factor. Its workings are a vital contribution to the harmony or disharmony of the total orchestration of what we are and what we do. Here words and sequences of words affect actions and sequences of actions; underlying activities are not easy to detect, which we call unconscious thoughts, feeling, drives and needs, express themselves in speech, in bodily movements, tears, yells of pain or shouts of joy, brightening of the whole countenance in happiness or showing a mask of gloom in frustration or despair. The reciprocating action of these activities is one of the peculiar features of human functioning; expressing anxiety is anxiety amplifying, expressing distress is distressing, expressing fear is frightening, expressing anger is angering, expressing trust is inducing trusting behavior, speaking with calm and deliberation gives clarity and constructive consistency to communicating, listening without prejudgment facilitates exchanges of feelings in tense situations, muscular relaxation pacifies emotional disturbances. This is precisely the field in which we exercise ourselves when we study and practice the disciplines of general semantics and epistemics. This is the center where we train ourselves in the most comprehensive of the arts, the art of living as a self-actualizer dedicated to altruism as the ruling human passion. We all know from experience that it is a very demanding undertaking, but we also know that it becomes more and more rewarding as we progress in experience and skill.

4. *Theories and doctrines*. Formulations—theories and doctrines—are not to be taken as mere breezes that play lightly over the surface of happenings. They are integral parts of our world of striving, reacting, transacting, toiling, enjoying, and relating ourselves to one another. The old dictum, "Mens sana in corpore sano," "A healthy mind in a sound body," applies here to the full and with a much broader meaning: "Sound and Flexible Theories in shuttling interaction with Forward-moving Practices." This involves both new knowledge (circle 4) and new methods (circle 3). There is the growing fringe of each individual WIGO, and, we expand our view to the milling crowd of humans all over the planet, the growing edge of the general WIGO, which our commonsense language calls the WORLD or the UNIVERSE. We abstract from the WIGO what we have already achieved, and we cause to emerge by a process of abduction from our time-accumulated transactions, past and present, the 'new heavens and the new earth' that the apostle Peter was dreaming about in a moment of 'inspiration,' or a stage-five experience, which he had to express in the language of his day.

Thanks to our scientifically guided awareness, we now dissect this complex happening—without fractionating it in the least—in terms of abstraction, abduction, and creative innovation. In a recent book entitled *Epistemics*[14], I play freely with the notion of 'reality' proposing as reality—the highest abstractions of our time. I make of the trilogy abstraction-abduction-innovation the art supreme of the people of our generation. In this art they blend methods, theories, and values in a new consciousness of their cosmic role.

When I look at mathematics in the light of my experience with other arts, I am not awed any more by its techniques. Mathematizing becomes for me a human experience that has a great deal in common with other experiences that are not given equal credit for their share in human advancement.

This abstract art of mathematics has brought about in quick succession the atomic age and the space age. By what transfer of skill can we pass from the art of mathematizing to an equally effective art of living? We may do so by reversing the orders of reality with which we deal. In the world of prehistoric people, stones, plants, and animals were the realities that had to be taken into account to survive. These realities-1 were raised to the level of realities-2 when humans invented abstract classifications they thought revealed to them the 'real' nature of things. Later, they enriched the reality-2 of classifications by adding to it the reality of the 'laws of nature,' or reality-3. But, during all that time, poets, artists, mystics, and dreamers were fascinated by a reality-4, a realm of existence preternatural, beyond nature as known at that age. We are fashioning the key of the door that opens for us that world of wonders. We discover that from that world flows a form of human

[14]J. Samuel Bois, *Epistemics: The Science-Art of Innovating* (San Francisco: International Society for General Semantics, 1972), p. 88-89.

energy: the energy of values we hold supreme and the energy of scientific knowledge that gave us the control of the very heart of matter.

What if we took this reality-4 as a more immediate reality than the realities-1, -2, and -3 to which our predecessors were limited.

Summary

In this chapter, we have looked at the practice of awareness or self-participation. I presented a mental model that serves as a context for self-observation or self-management—or the guiding of oneself by a better informed and wiser self. This involves the recognition that we can function simultaneously at different levels of psycho-logical activity. The model is the Self-1, Self-2, Self-3 . . . Self-n multiordinal diagram, which includes the notions of feedback and self-renewal, taking cognizance of the indicators of safety and danger in what we say and do, and in the manner we say it and do it.

We said that Self-1 is the self that is guided; Self-2 is the self that guides; and Self-3 is the self that learns the theories and methods and masters the skills of self-management in guiding Self-2 in the art of awareness. Then I proposed a new Self-3, combining the previous Self-3 with Self-2. This new Self-3 can be seen as a self no longer shrouded in discourse. It could be taken as a continually creating self-presence without the sense of self as an independent unit; in fact, self at this level ceases to be a "knowing" or "known" self, but an activity that is at one with all processes, under the guidance of the binding force that holds the universe together.

To this we added the definite directives on how to listen, how to read, and how to meditate or live at the 'silent level.'

Finally, we spoke of the transformation of the self by means of creative innovation, which more or less summed up the pupose of the whole chapter.

The creative innovation of our self involves the interruption of habitual abstracting from a well-established personal *episteme*, or what don Juan referred to as the *tonal* in the book *Tales of Power* by Carlos Castenada, and what we also called The Worlds in Which We Live in the chapter on time-binding. This dis-integrative action can be seen as the beginning of a renewal that takes place through the integrative action of the creative process as described as stage four starting on page 164: postulating-planning-experimenting-interpreting. This is the evolutionary advance of the self, from the microcosm of the individual to the macrocosm of humankind.

In the postulating stage of human development, we know that individualism is only one way to speak of human units. Other ways were anticipated by the poet who wrote, "No man is an island," or others who spoke of the "family of man."

There is need to reconcile—by a sort of complementarity—the independent and the dependent aspects of individuality.

This brings us to the more advanced practices of epistemics that are concerned with what I call Participating, or stage five of the epistemological profile.

PART IX

introduction to participating

The experience of human participation in the ongoing cosmic process is an existential experience common to all generations, but it has been observed and described differently at different stages of human development.

Participating as I wish to bring it into awareness, has been going on all along. We are part and parcel of the ongoing world, whether we are conscious of it or not. Conscious participating has been the way of dissolving the self-made distance between ourselves and what is going on. Our ancestors did it by magic, by esoteric practices, and by religious rituals. We can do away with this human-made distance and learn the art of participating in consciously guided awareness.

participating: from experiences to a stage of development

Of the two activities of human life, observing and participating, the second is the one that stresses transaction. We can observe things and people that stand by themselves outside of us, and all that we have in common with them is coexistence. Participating involves a togetherness in functioning that gives our experience a quality perceived as at-one-ness, as the sharing of activities with an autonomous otherness that joins our world and enriches it with its living presence. We become aspects of a common process and we bring about the emergence of a new world that absorbs and transforms us both.

The science and art of participating demands first that each participant let go of all defensiveness. Not only the defensiveness that protects the self from threats, actual or possible, *but the defensiveness that strives to avoid the impairment of selfhood,* the feeling of self-destruction that we assume is involved in total surrender.

To rid oneself of defensiveness is only the preparatory condition for the next step in participation. This next and principle step is the actual gift of oneself to the other, a giving that is pure giving and not an anticipated exchange or "something for something."

When the other one gives in return, the receiver does not grab the gift as a treasure to possess, but receives it as a pure gift bestowed by the higher degree of life that manifests itself in the joint experience.

Then comes that act of mutual fusion into a transcending oneness; the symbiotic communion that creates the Super-Self, warm with renascent life energy, soft but strong, radiant and glorious.

Seen in this way, our experiences become more than just a matter of understanding, of having the same viewpoint as another, of joining together for practical purposes, or of trying to fill the "gaps" of knowledge left by unexplained phenomena with new rationales and theories. For me, it becomes a matter of developing the skilled sense of value through which we consciously live at-one within the energetic clusterings of the ongoing— whether of events, situations, individuals, or groups—and allowing ourselves to be affected to the very deepest core of values, purposes, and preferences.

It means to consciously participate with the mysterious binding force that holds all living processes in dynamic integrity. While we may not detect this binding force with our individual senses or with ordinary introspection and intuition, it can be a first-order experience of our total semantic self, which becomes our participating "organ of perception."

In this section we will explore some of the facets of what I call participating, first distinguishing it as an experience from the unifying or "peak" experiences of the first four stages of cultural development, and then as the fifth stage of the emerging *episteme*.

Distinction Between Stages of Experience and Stages of Development

In the first and second editions of this book, we had not yet reached the formulation of a distinction that we now consider very helpful in pursuing our overall objective. It is the distinction between stages of *experience* and stages of *development*, either personal or cultural. If we turn to the Structural Differential (Fig. 6.3, p. 93), we remember that we spoke of a first-order experience, the circle in the diagram, prior to whatever can be said about it in a description, interpretation, or conclusion we may derive from it. It is on that prior-to-be-spoken-about "raw" experience that we are now focusing our attention.

We could define stages of experience as transitory happenings-meanings, and stages of development as well-established ways of functioning. The intensity of any experience is not at all a measure of its value. This lack of distinction between experience and development has lead to a great deal of confusion. We may have a high grade of experience in a low stage of development, as for instance when Bachelard comments on Nietzsche's notion of energy and says that "On the basis of a false notion, it is possible to build a towering doctrine."[1]

---

[1]Gaston Bachelard, *La philosophie du non* (Paris: Presses Universitaries de France, 1940), p. 47.

The stages of personal and/or cultural development are seen as emerging from the relative frequency of the stages of such experiences, and we consider it vitally important to be aware of them. So far we have described that awareness in terms of stages one, two, three and four; or of identification with classifying, structuring, and self-reflexing our experience of that with which we are in contact.

In revising Bachelard's original scheme of thinking about the stages of human development, I labeled stage five the *unifying* stage because I wanted to emphasize the fact that creativity involves a certain degree of cosmic consciousness, of felt participation in the energy process that sustains the existence of the whole universe. I called it *unifying* to set it in sharp contrast to the divisive experience of strict objectivity, which we consider to be so desirable at the lay person's level, and to the scientific detachment that we take as the only proper attitude for the sophisticated research worker. I have now placed this view of the creative process at stage four.

We are now making a fresh start in attempting to be most conscious of a certain character of our experience that is most difficult to describe. It could be spoken of as a bold attempt to break out of experiencing according to a carefully formulated dynamic structure of words, diagrams, gestures, or any form of expression. We now limit the use of the term *unifying* to describe such an experience at stages one through four; this means that, while this type of experience synergetically reunites the individual with the cosmic ongoing, it is then valued and formulated according to a particular stage of development.

At stage one, a unifying experience is one of unquestioned sensations and unexamined feelings. At stage two, it becomes the experience of classifiers who may see it as a revelation of the "real nature" of things, people, and events, and who doctrinize it in words and symbols that are taken as the distilled "essence" of the experience. At stage three, a unifying experience is the experience of relators who see it as the "discovery" of the structure, function, and order of the world. This is the revelation of the "Laws of Nature" and is usually prepared through systematic observation and experiment. At stage four, a unifying experience can be described as a culminating experience of self-reflexiveness; the simple self-union of postulators who acknowledge that the world in which they live is structured by their semantic states-in-process. The experience is not construed as a revelation or a discovery of something "out there," but one that involves both subject and object in a transaction in which "truth" is no longer the equivalence of the subject's picture of what is going on. The subject recognizes the experience as one that unifies in himself or herself what had been culturally and discursively separated.

At stage five we no longer speak of "unifying" experiences; it is not necessary to unify what is already one. As a label for stage five as a stage of *development*, we suggest the term *participating*. Participating *experiences*, or stage-five *experiences*, can be seen as the fruit of guided awareness in being-at-one with WIGO (what is going on). One participates in the experience of participating itself. This differs from a unifying experience, as previously described, in that there is no need or urge to discursively process the experience in order to "know" it. It can be formulated as an event in space-time, but such a construct is, of course, only symbolic in value for purposes of communicating with those who have not recognized such experiences for themselves without attaching an abstracted meaning to them related to definite events or situations. In other words, a stage-five or participating *experience* is where the significance or 'silent' meaning is free from attachment to "objects," and can be assimilated directly without the instrumentality of discursive symbols and categories, whether classified, related, or postulated.

It is only when many such stage-five experiences are integrated into our awareness and become part of an overall functioning that we really speak of participating as a stage of development. At that point, it may be correctly said that participators no longer limit themselves to "experience" as a space-time conditioned duration with a beginning and an end.

We may now proceed to go into a bit more detail in regard to unifying experiences, participating experiences, and stage five, the participating stage of development.

It is not within the scope of this book to do an in-depth development of this subject; all I can offer here is an introduction. I see it as a vast and important undertaking to be creatively and boldly developed, as free as possible from the theories, doctrines, constructs, and methods of the past. In the section titled, "Practices in Participating," I offer some beginning suggestions that can be experimented with by any individuals, couples, or groups willing to undertake such a radical renewal of the self.

The Unifying Experience

From the primitiveness of prehistoric humanity to the most worthy specimens of humanness that we have had in recent centuries, Western culture has shown stages of development that we distribute along a scale. We called the first period the *sensing* stage of unquestioned feeling. The second period was the *classifying* stage of commonsense metaphysics. The third period was the *relating* stage of classical science. The fourth period is the *postulating* stage of relativity and the necessity of the creative process.

After we had described each stage, we discussed various types of mental models that can be used at stages two, three, and four. We divided these models into two main classes, the mechanical and the biological, and concluded that mental models of the biological type are better adapted to the study of human situations. We do not plan our life as we plan a house, and we cannot speed up our cultural development as we can speed up the construction of a highway. We do not put together an organization of people as we arrange machines for production. Human cooperation is much more a matter of symbiosis, of grafting together live elements that are capable of sharing common values.

Realistic thinking means that we choose a mental model that is as similar as possible to the object or the situation with which we are dealing. For a human-contrived system, a mechanical model may suffice; for a situation that involves factors that are beyond human control, models of greater flexibility are required. From the rigorous causality of stage two, we pass to the probabilistic models of stage four.

Is realistic thinking possible without mental models? Is there a way of knowing that transcends structural knowledge? Yes, there is; and this transcendent form of experiential knowledge is what we are attempting to describe as an important aspect of unifying experiences in a revision of Bachelard's epistemological profile.

If we look for a description of this type of knowledge in the writings of observers of human experience who lived centuries ago, we will see it often interpreted as something mysterious, magical, or mystical. It went beyond the powers of description and analysis developed in those days, but today we look at it with the unperturbed curiosity we have when we study any natural phenomenon, whether we can explain it or not. We don't believe in miracles any more, if by this we mean supernatural interventions that cannot be accounted for by present theories. We are both more humble and more daring; we freely admit the limitations of our theories, but we are ready to expand them until they cover what has previously been called miraculous and supernatural.

Here is how a contemporary epistemologist deals with what we call a unifying experience. He speaks of *contemplation* as an exercise that takes us beyond the world of definite mental models.

> The conceptual framework by which we observe and manipulate things being present as a screen between ourselves and these things, their sights and sounds, and the smell and touch of them transpire but tenuously through this screen, which keeps us aloof from them. Contemplation dissolves the screen, and pours us straight into experience; we cease to handle things and we become immersed in them. . . . As we lose ourselves in contemplation, we take on an impersonal life in the objects of our contemplation; while these objects themselves are suffused by a visionary gleam which lends them a new and vivid and yet dreamlike quality.[2]

[2]Michael Polanyi, *Personal Knowledge* (Chicago: University of Chicago Press, 1958), p. 197.

After comparing this experience with religious ecstasy as described in the writings of mystics of various faiths, Polanyi says that

> Music, poetry, painting: the arts—whether abstract or representative—are a dwelling in and a breaking out which lies somewhere between science and worship. Mathematics has been compared with poetry: "The true spirit of delight, the exaltation, the sense of being more than Man, which is the touchstone of the highest excellence," writes Bertrand Russell, "is to be found in mathematics as surely as in poetry." Yet, there is a great difference in the range of these delights. Owing to its sensuous content, a work of art can affect us far more comprehensively than a mathematical theorem. Moreover, artistic creation and enjoyment are contemplative experiences more akin than mathematics to religious communion. Art, like mysticism, breaks through the screen of objectivity and draws on our pre-conceptual capacities of contemplative vision. "Poetry," wrote Shelley, "purges from our inward sight the film of familiarity which obscures from us the wonders of our being;" it breaks into "a world to which the familiar world is chaos."[3]

You will have noticed that this long excerpt from Polanyi, a scientist-philospher, contained quotations from Russell, a mathematician, and from Shelley, a poet. These two men are highly regarded human beings, who possess a keen sensitivity to the finest differences in human experience. How much each of us has in common with individuals like these is a matter that deserves a searching study. It may reveal potentialities in the so-called average person that were neglected because they were unknown. The latent riches of humanness have not begun to be tapped.

Now let us listen to a neurologist, Ralph W. Gerard, doctor of medicine, philosophy, and science. In a conference held under the auspices of the New York Academy of Medicine and attended by forty-eight scientists engaged in human studies, he called holistic the stage of human experience that we call a unifying experience.

> The stage in which we try to identify the variables of interest . . .is like that of identifying the nouns of the language and the entities under consideration. The static stage is getting the simple static relations between them.[4]

Translated into the terms that we have used here, this contains stage two and a glimpse at stage three of Bachelard's epistemological profile, or Boulding's framework model. Dr. Gerard continues:

> The dynamic stage is the one where some of the verbs of existence come in. In it we enrich the language and we see how the variables interact in time and with changes. Finally, there is the holistic stage, the putting it all together with a certain amount of *Eingefühl*. In fact, I think at the very end we come back to the kind of amorphous feeling which is a deep understanding of the situation, which

[3]Polanyi, *Personal Knowledge*, p. 197.

[4]Ralph W. Gerard, *Integrating the Approaches to Mental Disease*, ed. H. D. Kruse (New York: Harper & Row, 1957), p. 281. With permission of publisher and author.

goes beyond the analytic, beyond the verbal, and beyond the definition. Then we really know it.[5]

This quotation from Dr. Gerard brings forth two characteristics of a unifying experience. (1) It is beyond the analytic, the verbal, the sharp definition. In other words, it cannot be glibly described; it is an experience too rich for a systematic logical presentation; and we may need to resort to poetry or some other form of art to transmit the message. (2) It gives the person who experiences it a strong feeling of assurance—as Dr. Gerard said, "Then we *really know it.*" As I said before, this feeling of assurance often becomes a trap for the person who goes through such an experience, and even more so for those who take literally what he may say about it, as if the formulation given is the ultimate revelation of "reality." When the knowing proper to a stage of development is taken as final and unchanging, such an experience thus becomes a confirmation of the finality of an earlier stage, instead of an opportunity to break through to a more advanced stage of development.

Dr. Abraham Maslow, well known for his *Motivation and Personality*,[6] has devoted a great deal of time to the study of the psychological aspects of the experience. He speaks of "peak" experiences, or moments of highest fulfillment. In these experiences, according to Maslow, our knowing assumes a peculiar form, a form that is different from the structural knowing of discursive stages two, three, and four. He calls it *B*-cognition, or being-cognition, to emphasize that it is not only an abstracting phenomenon of the ordinary kind but a contact of the whole person with whatever he is attentive to—fusion of the two in a kind of symbiosis.

In ordinary perception things are seen as parts of a world, already cut into pieces, and each one having a name attached to it. We see things through the pattern of the name they possess: a house, a tree, a person, a face. In *B*-cognition, the object is seen as unique, not as belonging to a class to which it conforms. The pepper tree that I see in front of my window is not *a* tree, it is this individual, unique tree; it is the irreplaceable part of the total cosmic process that it expresses in its own untranslatable way.

B-cognition is different from abstraction: it does not select certain aspects to the exclusion of others; it does not classify an object with others of the same kind. It is childlike in that the object is seen with freshness, as though for the first time. As the object takes its unique place in the unclassified flow of processes, the observer ceases to objectify his own self; he becomes aware that he is also part of the processlike cosmos that pulsates through him as it does through the tree. The peak experience in *B*-cognition thus becomes ego-transcending. It is unifying in sheer existence—not in purpose, motivation, or personal needs.

[5]Gerard, *Integrating the Approaches to Mental Diseases,* p. 281.
[6]New York: Harper & Row, 1954.

Do I advocate turning loose our wildest imaginations, or letting ourselves be run by free-roaming fantasies? Not at all. At an interdisciplinary symposium on Creativity held at Michigan State University in 1957, Maslow gave an answer that expresses what I have in mind.

> The great work needs not only the flash, the inspiration, the peak experience, it also needs hard work, long training, unrelenting criticism, perfectionist standards. In other words, succeeding upon total acceptance comes criticism; succeeding upon intuition comes rigorous thought; succeeding upon daring comes caution; succeeding upon fantasy and imagination comes reality testing.[7]

These experiences are not limited to poets, mystics, and creative scientists; they are the common heritage of all human beings. The problem is to know how to induce them, how to recognize them when they occur spontaneously, and how to derive all the benefits they offer.

The dominant characteristic of a unifying experience is that it is free from definite mental categories. Our mental categories are residues of transactions that took place in the past; they are dried up and stored in our memory. Instead of tasting the genuine flavor of a fresh fruit, we live on desiccated prunes and syrupy preserves. To see the world anew every morning, to discover the aspects of our life that we miss because we are in the habit of neglecting them, to stop for the pause that *really* refreshes is possible anywhere, anytime.

A unifying experience takes us out of any established order; it places us in the center of a world where the accustomed signposts of systematic rationality are missing. At the same time, it fills us with an assurance that this is the most genuine experience a human being can have; it is the fountainhead of the greatest achievements and discoveries in all fields of human endeavor: science, religion, philosophy, technology, ethics, law, the fine arts, economics, and politics.

There is an almost limitless variety of terms for describing that experience or accounting for its existence. Some speak of creative intuition, of genius, of inspiration, of the supraconscious, of the oversoul that takes control of the individual, of the state of *satori*, of divine madness, of enlightenment, of insight, of ecstasy, of transformation, intelligent agape, existential commitment, or some other term that is beyond sharp definition, depending on what aspect is emphasized and in what context—artistic, psychological, or religious—it is observed.

It is widely different from the sensing contact of stage one, which is uncritical and uncontrolled. It is accepted in full awareness of its dangers and is managed by all the resources of stages two, three, and four that are avail-

[7]A. Maslow, "Creativity in Self-actualizing People," *General Semantics Bulletin*, No. 24-25, p. 49.

able to the main participant. It is becoming alert to living as circumstances demand it.

In the self-reflexive creative process of stage four, we are aware that a unifying experience, or being at one with the cosmic process, does not unify what was by nature separated; it unifies what was by culture seen as separated. It is when we renew our fundamental oneness with everything that is, as we discover that we are both autonomous from and subject to an order that we recognize as most congenial to our innermost self. Our dichotomous culture, which stresses subject versus object, has thrown a veil of mystery over this vital oneness. In a unifying experience, the veil is rent asunder, and the wonderful unity in which we live is revealed through a felt participation in the energy process that sustains the existence of the whole universe. This experience has a "taste" of its own. It is a whole semantic response that gives a feeling of renewed youth, dispels fear and anxiety, and brings from our deeper self a desire to be loving and understanding.

Living to the full, whether in scientific research or in the practice of the most humble trade, is a matter of preference and choice in valuing, of commitment, of being in love with something, with somebody, with oneself, and with the whole universe in an entrancing embrace—outside of which there is nothing but emptiness and death.

It is from such an experience that scientists derive their new formulations, heroes receive their courage, artists secure their illumination, and saints take their victorious feeling of integration within the whole cosmic process.

> Creative scientists know very well, from observation of themselves, that all creative work starts as a "feeling," "inclination," "suspicion," "intuition," "hunch," or some other unspeakable affective state, which only at a later date, after a sort of nursing, takes the shape of a verbal expression, worked out later in a rationalized coherent, linguistic scheme called a theory. In mathematics we see some astonishing examples of intuitively proclaimed theorems, which, at a later date, have been proved to be true, although the original proof was false.[8]

This affective-intuitive element runs all through the chain of activities that makes life a consistent whole, and it can be detected throughout the traditions that animate the development of our culture.

Some Qualifications Regarding Unifying Experiences

For individuals living within the discursive stages of human development, which means the overwhelming majority of people, there is a danger in the use of terms to describe and classify or categorize the kinds of experiences discussed in the previous section. We choose a term as best we can,

[8]Alfred Korzybski, *Science and Sanity*, (Lakeville, Conn.: International Non-Aristotelian Library, 1933, 1941, 1948, 1958), p. 22.

not always being aware that our choice of terms in the old language is limited and biased. Unless we are aware of that, we are unaware that we are dealing with a new type of experience. I suggest that we be loath to attach a label unless we know in advance most of its connotations.

This kind of openness can make a unifying experience into a participating or stage-five experience from which the participants do not try to maintain or regain the sense of equilibrium of their at-home semantic state; in other words, they do not actively seek the comfort of the understanding characteristic of a former way of functioning.

I can call participating a *full* experience, meaning that at a certain moment I am not simply aware of the things that surround me sensorily, or of the theories, attitudes, and symbolic significances that are common in my culture. I have the full experience of being at one with the cosmos or all that exists. It is as if my "inward vision" had dissolved what had separated me from this plenum of energy of which I am an inherent aspect. I stop seeing "things" like galaxies stars, people; I do not see history as a series of events linked in chronological order, nor as battling governments that succeed one another. I live and "see" within the whole of the energetic ongoing as a full human experience, as full as I can live it at my stage of development.

Our ancestors, the cave people, had an experience. They could see the beast they were hunting, the fruit they were gathering; they could see ways to make tools out of rocks and sticks to achieve their purposes. Beyond that it was the mysterious, the mystical, the frightening unknown to which superstition was their way of relating.

The next group of our ancestors were not only able to picture to themselves the individual rocks, sticks, and whatnot, but the "nature" of those things as well, including the "nature" of the mysterious unknown. This "nature of things" was a construct of theirs, much as we have constructs of "energy" today. But since they did not see that "nature" as their own construct, they believed that they were seeing what was inherent in those things.

Some asked, "What is the locus of the nature or essence?" Plato said that it was in the Mind of the Supreme Being, and whatever we say and do is a materialization of that. Aristotle said that that was not quite so, that "nature" is really in the things themselves. Aristotle's was a tempered realism, not a pure idealism. Nor was his the gross realism of the appearance of things, but a metaphysical realism that could see into or beyond the physical appearance. Aristotle's method of "seeing" was deductive logic and classification.

Our ancestors of the next period had an even less concrete reality, more illusive and less easy to picture than the reality of those who preceded them. Instead of the "nature of things," whether it be somewhere in the Mind of God or in the mind of the individual corresponding to the "essence" in the thing itself, they invented the beginning of what the sciences today call *activity*. It was not the "pure" activity of today's subatomic sciences, that is, an activity without an actor; it was the activity of *something*. And that activity they saw as "laws" that held all things in relationship—the "Laws of Nature." This was a more abstract type of reality, and they accepted it and expressed it in such terms as interaction, acceleration, gravitation, attraction, repulsion, causality, energy. So much so that eventually they invented a picture of the cosmos as being held together by two forces: the force of motion, the origin or source of which was a mystery; and the force of attraction, which kept the planets at a definite distance from the sun.

The reality they presided over existed in the dynamic intervals of the phenomena observed, and, like their predecessors of the previous period, they considered their view an objective one; they saw themselves "discovering" the ultimate nature of reality.

Now we go one step further to an even more abstract world. The word abstract here does not mean a mere construct of the human mind, but the result of a more extensive and intensively deeper participation that takes us beyond the appearances of materiality revealed by our senses and manifest experiences. This abstract reality, which goes even beyond any symbol system or logic, can be described as a multidimensional, ever-active plenum of action. Some individuals of those earlier ages that I described were in contact with that action, but they spoke of it in terms that were available at their degree of epistemic development. That action had to logically fit into the familiar world in which they lived, even if that world was a very esoteric one. At times they spoke of it as their oneness with Nature, expressed by a totem pole, for instance. Later on, it was a term of possession, either by the devil or in a holy frenzy of the shaman, the priest, and the mystics of the Middle Ages; it became a visitation of God.

Now when we go back and study these conditions, we see that they were most probably relating in their own language the experiences that we are describing here as unifying experiences; the unifying experiences of discursively differentiated human beings. I do not question their experiences, but I do question the relating of the experiences.

At a much earlier time in my life I had experiences that baffled me. I did not know what to make of them. I knew that at certain moments of either deep recollection in meditation or complete absorption in contemplation, suddenly my "inside space" became an empty void. There was nothing to think about, nothing to contemplate. I was, as I could see it at the time, in a "space" that appeared to be made of light. It brought an unusual calm and warmth that penetrated me. I experienced an inner peace that was beyond anything I had experienced before. At the time, I was advised by those more experienced in such matters that I had experienced the stage of simple union, the first stage of what they called mystical experience. All of my studies in theological dogma and morals had not included studies of these experiences. I began to read the mystical literature of the West, and some of the formulations helped me to recognize and become systematically aware of what was going on in me.

From this stage of simple union—and you can see the description in William James' *The Varieties of Religious Experience*—one may enter into a phase where you have strong phenomena, of visions, of ecstacies, of insights, of enlightenment, which I see now as nothing but a projection from our felt experience in the screen of our structured unconscious, taking whatever is there and turning it into a dreamlike picture to make a vision out of it. This stage can be an extremely dangerous one, and later on in life I studied the detailed history of such experiences which, for some people, lasts a long time; sometimes ten to twenty years. Later, after studying general semantics, I still had opportunities to counsel people who were disturbed by experiences of that type and to guide them out of a very difficult period.

The third stage of the unifying experience (in the jargon of religious psychology) is called transformation. Suddenly the visions cease and the individual lives at peace with herself or himself and the rest of the world, and living what outwardly is a most ordinary life.

If I apply these stages of unifying experiences to present conditions, speaking not of individuals, but of that cultural entity made of people who earnestly are trying to understand themselves and the world in which they live, I would compare the second period, the period of visions and possible disturbances, the seeking for unusual experiences, to what is going on today. We go for "altered states of consciousness," various Eastern religious practices, unusual experiences in growth centers and assorted kinds of therapies and experiments; we seek the thrill of experiences way beyond what we thought we were able to have. Then we talk about them with terms that imply an exceptional experience. After these experiences, spontaneous or induced by special circumstances, we have a tendency to turn back and to try to revive them because they were the "peaks" we had reached.

My view is that there is no denying that simple union, of being in the "void"; there is no denying the second stage, being in the trances of an ongoing transformation that upsets the whole system. But integrating them in a super condition or structural more where one is no longer placing primary value in the everyday experiences of the social order, such as making money, eating, sleeping, working, developing prestige; we are in that, but at the same time we are habitually living in what I call participation, being able not to confuse one's self with the social, phenomenal, or living order of time-conditioned processes. When we are used to living that, it will not have the spectacularness of the first-time experience. We may confuse the new semantic state with the humdrum existence of everyday life—which it is not.

In a later work, Abraham Maslow made a differentiation between what he had labeled a "peak" experience and a "plateau" experience. He made a qualitative distinction between these two types of unifying experience; the latter being more voluntary than the other. The "plateau" experience is approaching in formulation to what I would call a stage-four type of unifying experience, which is emerging free from the discursive-affective stages of experience.

> I would now add to the peak-experience material a greater consideration, not only of nadir-experiences. . .but also of the "plateau-experience." This is serene and calm, rather than a poignantly emotional, climactic, autonomic response to the miraculous, the awesome, the sacralized, the Unitive, the B-values. So far as I can now tell, the high plateau-experience *always* has a noetic and cognitive element, which is not always true for peak-experiences, which can be purely and exclusively emotional. It is far more voluntary than peak-experiences are. One can learn to see in this Unitive way almost at will.[9]

In a great many cases, stage five as a stage of development was introduced by some kind of unifying experience, but the unifying experience is an experience only. I wish to repeat what I said earlier: a state or a stage of development is somewhat more permanent and is apt to be developed by our own initiative and skill. Related to this I again quote from Maslow.

> Very important. . .is the realization that plateau-experiencing can be achieved, learned, earned by long hard work. It can be meaningfully aspired to. But I don't know of any way of bypassing the necessary maturing, experiencing, living, learning. All of this takes time. A transient glimpse is certainly possible in the peak-experiences which may, after all, come sometimes to anyone. But, so to speak, to take up residence on the high plateau of Unitive consciousness— that is another matter altogether. . . .It should not be confused with the Thursday-evening turn-on that many youngsters think of as *the* path to transcendence. For that matter, it should not be confused with *any* single experience.

> All I wish to do here with this brief mention is to correct the tendency of some to identify experiences of transcendence as *only* dramatic, orgasmic, transient, "peaky", like a moment on the top of Mount Everest. There is also the high plateau, where one can *stay* "turned on."[10]

When Maslow writes that one can "*stay* 'turned on,' " he comes closer to what I mean here by a stage of development at stage five. I think that there are many of us who have had unifying experiences, but who have translated them in terms that deny their very possibility by speaking of them as unusual. Because of the circular reflexiveness of our language, using these terms to describe these experiences makes them difficult to maintain. When we insist on calling a unifying or "peak" experience unusual or exceptional,

[9]Abraham Maslow, *Religions, Values, and Peak Experiences* (New York: Viking, 1964, 1975), p. xiv.

[10]Maslow, *Religions, Values, and Peak Experiences*, pp. xv-xvi.

we keep it out of a program of living. As long as we keep it outside, it is outside, because we make the world in which we live. If, on the other hand, we are able to understand that this is an experiment in deeper living, and that we should do our best to keep it free from any mental categories or theories even while using them when the situation calls for it, a new kind of existence emerges that makes possible what previously could not even be imagined.

When for the first time physicists discovered that certain chemical elements emitted radiation, it was considered exceptional at first—the "peak" experience of chemistry. Those chemicals had no business radiating! That was left to the sun or to fire, but not to a dead, dull chemical element. But it did! Eventually, physical sciences came to the conclusion that what was exceptional and unusual was simply the revelation of a deeper reality. From this was born the science of nuclear physics, which revolutionized our technology and view of the cosmos. You cannot deal with that science using the rules of Galilean or Newtonian physics. Particle physics is not amenable to mechanical physics.

So it is with "peak" experiences that we have all undergone, which we sometimes undergo without recognizing them, due to the limited views we hold regarding ourselves as human beings. At times when we are able to perceive that inmost self, and it is not miraculous or "far out," we can begin to develop our skills in becoming habitually aware in that way. A new kind of human being emerges who no longer possesses the negative qualities attributed to us at earlier stages of development, such as our being inherently aggresive creatures of war and conflict.

I now wish to explore deeper into the participating experience as it emerges into a new mode of existence.

Duality and Oneness

The world in which I live appears to me as a phenomenal duality. At the center there is me, and all around there is the not-me's, persons and things that I observe, and to which I relate in my own unique way. Even when I look at myself, the objective me that I observe and deal with appears somewhat detached from a me that is more central, felt, but not seen. This feeling of immanent duality is the price I pay for what we call "objective" knowledge of what is going on about me, and within me. This is the condition I must accept to enjoy my awareness of being in the world and the flow of my own awareness. This knowledge is embedded in the language I have learned to speak. It is patterned after what my culture has taught me to see as the "real" structure of the world in which I live.

As a human being, I cannot be ingenuously at one with a Nature untouched by human hands. I find myself in contact with a human-shaped

Nature, as artificial as a totem pole compared to the tree out of which it was carved.

Other existants who have not yet reached a self-conscious level are at one in total immediacy with their own selves and with their environment. The flower is at one with its color; the water is at one with its wetness; the sun is at one with its radiation; the mountain is at one with its mass; the cloud is at one with its floating lightness; the rooster is at one with its crowing; the hen is at one with the eggs she is laying.

They are at one also with their space-time environment. The flower blooms or withers according to the time of the season; the rooster crows when the dawn begins to light in the horizon; the hen cackles when the eggs are laid; the river flows down as the slope directs it; the sun appears in the east, and disappears in the west; the mountain grows out of the plain.

For these to exist is to be at one with characteristics and activities from which they cannot dissociate themselves. It is also to be at one with the place they occupy at the moment they appear in the world of ongoings. They cannot come out of their unique being in the world. They are locked within the evolutionary process at a definite space-time location.

We are not locked up in this manner. As a reflexive existant, I live a life of abstraction, of detachment from the surround that I observe close to me or far from me; and I can abstract a self that I see as distinct from me, the observer, different from other existants that I know.

I am able to determine, to some extent, what my participating oneness with the world and with myself will be. I do so by relating myself to whatever is not-me, and even to me as an object according to my outlook on life, and according to a set of personal values. The relating that I thus establish between myself and what is going on becomes a human-made oneness out of which emerges the world in which I live. This oneness and the personal world that grows out of it is a mass of joinings that I weave as I choose, made tighter or looser as I wish.

Of all the existants that I know, I am the only one who has to develop the art of conscious relatedness to what is not-me and to create a new form of oneness that Nature, left to itself, has not provided for. It is a oneness that transcends the phenomenal duality of me and not-me.

I can practice the art of conscious at-oneness in a variety of activities. I can be at one with whatever I do. With this page that I am writing; with the painting that I spread on a canvas; with a sculpture that I mold with my hands and carve with my chisel; with the piece of furniture that I shape with my tools; with the house that I design as an architect; with a client that I lead out of a neurosis into the peace of self-understanding.

Arts are human inventions that have reached, beyond their initial worth, the beauties and the enjoyments that Nature unaided offers to the organisms that are capable of reacting to them. They transform and bring to a higher level of existance the potentiality inserted in our biological makeup. They bring about mutations of a new kind, exclusive to the domain of cultural evolution where humans participate in the act of creation, making of their own nature, blended with their environment, something that never existed before.

We have amplified the sounds of birds to the size and complexity of symphonic orchestras. We have turned the uneducated yells of joy and the sobbing of sorrow into the passionate arias of the overwhelming choruses of operatic composition. We brought out of the seven colors of the rainbow the thousand shades of synthetic pigments. We have made of primitive shelters the architectural marvels of residences, office buildings, temples, and stately edifices that we now take for granted. We made of simple tribal customs the elaborate system of our laws and our political institutions.

Can we make of the art of at-oneness a distinct and human creation, a definite enrichment of what Nature offers to us, as a challenging possibility? Can we establish a so far unknown form of oneness with the universe and with our fellow humans that will outrival the highest achievements of our other arts? Can we devise and practice a oneness with the whole cosmic process and with its human constituents that will transform our world of strife and violence into one of harmony, that we are not afraid to lose because its existence is of our own making? Can we free ourselves of the gravitational pull of separate individualism and attain the weightlessness of free-ranging trust and mutual exchange of unrestricted kindness?

I think we can, and I feel we must now that the whole planet has shrunk to the size of a small village, where distrust among villagers is still institutionalized as mutual deterents. The time is come when we have to learn the secrets and to practice the skills of the yet unknow art of being fully at one with our physical and biological environment by respecting its ecological requirements, and, above all, to be at one with all of the members of the family of humankind, above and beyond differences of race, culture, religion, and form of government.

Where do we start? The highest form of duality consciously building itself into a planned oneness is a human couple. By practicing the art of transforming this duality into a super unity, we may acquire a finer perception of the subtle strands that link into oneness lower forms of duality. We may thus learn how to create a human-designed, symbiotic oneness that will transcend the simple kinds of inborn unity.

From the workings of Nature that we saw groping through its holistic advances, from the particles to the atoms, from the atoms to the molecules, from the molecules to the cell, from the cell to the organism, from the asexual organism to the male-female transmitters of a more varied life, from the plant to the animals, from the animals to the conscious complexity of *Homo sapiens*, we venture a mutation of our species, of the world, and of the human world to the level of existence that no science fiction has yet anticipated.

It is for the human couple to pass from a sense of duality to a oneness consciously designed and achieved. This demands a constant exercise in the skills of human communion. From this exercise grows an art that becomes more and more demanding as it becomes more and more enjoyable. The two parties vie with each other in finding/creating forms of expression of at-oneness that reach to deeper and deeper levels of a fully participated life-in-common. Individuation gradually disappears, and out of it emerges a new form of symbiotic existence. From a consciously planned transaction of persevering unity, practiced a bit awkwardly in the beginning, they gradually pass to a stage of oneness that wraps them within a soft cocoon of warm tenderness, in which they lose their former separateness and are reborn in a joint life away from outside disturbances, interference, and anxieties that would threaten the unity. Once their inner selves are thus transformed into a oneness of free-ranging peace, they emit a radiant stability of feelings; they spread around themselves an atmosphere of warmth, ease, and trust. They have reached a stage of oneness supreme. They have conquered by their conscious efforts the basic oneness that holds together all the elements of the cosmos in process. They have experienced love as the medium in which the rising course of cosmic evolution proceeds.

Participating: As Experience and as Stage Five

When a woman and a man consciously express their oneness, through sexual intercourse, for instance, they can be seen as participating for the participation itself—the act is not in the center of their attention. The felt oneness in which they are joined, the renewal and celebration of their mutual commitment, and the deepening of trust are also secondary in the sense that they are aspects, or unifying actions, within the oneness itself. These actions are not "caused" to happen by the couple, nor are they something that they "have" or "possess." We could see them as *phases* of participation. In fact, any creative act can be seen as a unifying action phase that is integral within the value environment of participating within WIGO, or the ongoing cosmic process.

Susanne Langer, in speaking of human feeling (in the sense of anything felt) as a phase of a process or a large complex of processes within the organism, provides an illustration in the form of a physical analogy.

A phase is a mode of appearance and not an added factor. Ordinarily we know things in different phases as "the same"—ice, water and steam, for instance—but sometimes a very distinctive phase seems like a product. When iron is heated to a critical degree it becomes red; yet its redness is not a new entity which must have gone somewhere else when it is no longer in the iron. It was a phase of the iron itself, at high temperature. Heat is not a thing, but an agitation, measurable in degrees, not amounts, and when the iron is no longer hot there will be comparable degrees of heat, or of some equivalent process or sum total of processes, outside the iron. But the redness simply disappears; it was a phase of the heated iron.[11]

Another example would be the "objects" we see; by object I refer to anything that can be considered as an object of our attention. Any object can be seen as a phase of our own semantic process. Abstracted at stages one, two, or three of the epistemological profile, the basic sense of value is that of subject separate from object, either categorically or relatedly. At stage four, we may still experience "objects," but with the knowledge that they are derivitives of a discursive oriented mode of transacting; they can be seen as phases of our own abstracting process infused with values, purposes, and expectations.

From the individual to our species, we can be regarded as a phase of an ongoing evolutionary process, and not as a product of it. This view no longer contains the separation of Humans and "Nature." The evolutionary process is rising into a phase where individuals will more frequently emerge who can participate and combine their uniquenesses in a world where "objects," including one's own self, are not experienced as "things." They will directly feel the urge and oneness with the surging energy of being alive in a living world; of identifying with an activity that animates every process in existence.

This clustering action of unique individuals in conscious contact with their oneness we call participating. It eventuates in an obsolescence of isolated individuality and at the same time, a fusion into a new order of existence. The structural more, or stage five that emerges from these acts of participation can be seen as a phase of this very occurance as an established way of functioning. We can compare this to the resonance of a positron and an electron in subatomic physics. When they are brought into phase, the result is a fusion of "entities." What emerges is a flash of radiation that spreads indefinitely throughout all space. If our attention is limited to the field of the electron and the positron, we might conclude that the happening has the meaning of absolute annihilation. If we become more inclusive, we could experience the destruction of matter in one configuration—positrons and electrons—continuing in an entirely different state or activity.

The individuals, couples, and eventually groups who accept to actively participate in depth can be seen as miniature laboratories where new values are invented and given to what it means to be human. Through the centuries, various individuals have accepted this role in human evolution. We

---

[11]Susanne K. Langer, *Mind: An Essay on Human Feeling*, vol. 2, (Baltimore, Md.: Johns Hopkins Press, 1970), p. 21.

can illustrate this process in a biological analogy in which the viability of an evolutionary innovation is tested out in germ cells.

> The germ cell functions as a sort of test tube. The mutation can be tested here without endangering either the organism or its offspring. The "test" lies in finding out whether the mutation will prove compatible with the complex metabolic processes of the germ cell. Most mutations would contribute nothing useful to the organism; many are actually harmful. The germ cell screens and eliminates all these unsuccessful mutations in the most efficient way imaginable; if the results are "negative," the cell itself simply dies! Thus the mutation contained in the dead cell has been quietly discarded. Only the single germ cell suffers any ill effects; the organism itself remains unaware of the whole process.[12]

Oneness as participation is a "fact" that we accept; unity is a condition that we create and recreate whenever circumstances provide the opportunity. Each act of unity becomes a stage-five experience that leaves in the overall system, that comprises the organism and its space-time environment, a reverberatory trace that compounds and increases the oneness. To practice participating as unity is to make oneness more tolerable, fruitful, joyous, and increasingly compelling. Oneness is structurally more than union; participating is structurally more than unifying.

In human affairs oneness is a matter of commitment. Once established, it transcends the fluctuations of mood and the contingency of circumstances. To love in oneness means to establish a union that changes the semantic state of both parties and brings them to a higher level of shared existence. To practice participating means to train oneself in the attitudes and habits that are consistent with the rhythms of oneness thus established; to make semantic jumps required by the structural more introduced willingly into one's life.

The art of conscious participation can be practiced as an education in a new orientation. Undifferentiated oneness is not enough to "externalize" a new stage of development. The individual must learn to be free of the methods, trainings, and disciplines of the past that stop providing the proper support necessary to deal with the task of the "future." The epistemological experience of moving into the foundations of one's deepest beliefs takes the skill of an artist-scientist. To learn to differentiate within oneness is not the same as the classifications, relationships, and postulates of the previous stages. Yes, we can make use of those methods as we need them, but one's whole self as a method is of another order. To illustrate what I mean here, I wish to quote at length from Franklin Merrill-Wolff, a one-time mathematician and philosopher of academic standing, who left to go on his own journey, so to speak, back in the 1930s. He wrote at length of his "transformation of consciousness" in two books.

---

[12]Hoimar von Ditfurth, *Children of the Universe* (New York: Atheneum, 1974), p. 223.

At the time of the culminating Recognition I found myself spreading everywhere and identical with a kind of "Space" that embraced not merely the visible forms and worlds, but all modes and qualities of consciousness as well. However, all these are not There as disparate and objective existences; they are blended, as it were, in a sort of primordial and culminating totality. It seemed that the various aspects and modes that are revealed to the analysis of relative consciousness could have been projected into differentiated manifestation, if I chose so to will it, but all such projection would have left unaffected the perfect balance of the totality. . . .

There finally arrived a stage wherein both that which I have called the Self and that which had the value of Divinity were dissolved in a Somewhat, still more transcendent. There now remained nought but pure Being that could be called neither the Self nor God. No longer was "I" spreading everywhere through the whole of an illimitable and conscious Space, nor was there a Divine Presence all about me, but everywhere only Consciousness with no subjective nor objective element.[13]

Merrill-Wolff then goes on to describe how he experienced differentiation within the "recognition," as he called it. This kind of differentiating is not covered by the formulation of abstracting.

Throughout the whole period of this supreme state of consciousness I was self-consciously awake in the physical body and quite aware of my environment. The thought-activity was not depressed, but on the contrary, alert, and acute. I was continuously conscious of my self-identity, in two distinct senses. In one sense, I was, and am, the primordial Self and co-terminous with an unlimited and abstract Space, while at the same time the subject-object and self-analyzing consciousness was a sort of point-presence within that space. An illustration is afforded by thinking of the former as being of the nature of an original Light, in itself substantial, spreading throughout, but not derived from any center, while the latter is a point-centered and reflected light, such as that of a searchlight. The searchlight of the self-analyzing consciousness can be directed anywhere within the primordial Light, and thus serves to render chosen zones self-conscious. Through the latter process I was enabled to capture values within the framework of the relative consciousness and am thus enabled to remember not merely a dimly sensed fact of an inchoate transcendence but, as well, all that I am now writing and a vastly more significant conscious integration that defeats all efforts at formulation.[14]

I see Merrill-Wolff as one example of an individual as the "imagination" of evolution. I see in him, among others, the evolutionary process trying out a new kind of human functioning. I suggest that, while individual experiments will continue, with increasing frequency this quality of experience will be developed more easily, and will multiply as a value within the structural more of the unified couple; and eventually within ever larger groups.

[13]Franklin Merrill-Wolff, *The Philosophy of Consciousness Without an Object* (New York: Julian Press, 1973), pp. 66, 73.

[14]Merrill-Wolff, *The Philosophy of Consciousness Without an Object,* pp. 67-68.

In *Breeds of Men*, I put it this way:

Finally there is the full reciprocity of participation in the total union of two persons who have become accomplished performers in the art of being at one with each other at all levels of functioning. Such an experience gives birth to a form of psychic energy that belongs to an order of existence different from whatever an individual can sense by himself. It is achieved when two persons have abandoned for good their individual defenses in complete trust of each other; have accepted unreservedly what they are without measuring their respective qualities, shortcomings, or weaknesses; and have entered willingly the unrestricted fusion of their activities of thinking, purposing, remembering, and holding on to each other. This is oneness supreme, participation total and transforming. It makes of plain human beings the new sort of existents that Julian Huxley and Pierre Teilhard saw emerging at the present time from the common crowd of self-seeking members of the human species, as *Homo sapiens* emerged centuries ago from the herd of hominids bent on foraging for mere biological survival.

The experience of being at one in a felt symbiosis with things, people, and situations may be viewed as the initial phase of a new art, the art of participating with expanding awareness in the creative thrust of cosmic energy.[15]

To summarize my views of stage five, I would say that union or oneness is a *sine qua non* prerequisite for the "practice" of participation. This kind of practice does not proceed from a discursive *episteme*, nor from what is commonly thought of as "feeling" activities. In one sense, participating, as well as oneness, is something that we do not create. It could be described as a deep recognition and acceptance that participating has always been the case, and we now unabashedly accept it as our way of life.

As a stage of human evolution, we cannot limit participating to a stage of *development*, but, better said, a stage of *renewal*, unprecedented by the previous discursive stages. As a stage of renewal, stage five is the innovating of radiating centers of values in the form of people who, in themselves, become the necessary "methods" to bring about the conditions for oneness to be the world in which we live.

We now pass to the beginning practices of participating in everyday experiences. They were originally published in a pamphlet titled, "Communication as a Creative Experience," published and issued by Viewpoints Institute in Los Angeles. I see these practices as a stage-four preparation for stage-five experiences, and they have proven helpful in guiding people into a new feeling and valuing orientation that no longer accepts exchange of messages and conflict as a basis for communication.

---

[15]J. Samuel Bois, *Breeds of Men: Toward the Adulthood of Humanity* , (New York: Harper & Row, 1970), p. 125.

CHAPTER 19

practices in participating: communication as a creative experience

Communication and Empathy

When something goes wrong in human affairs, we often give as an explanation: 'The trouble was poor communication.' And communication, viewed as an exchange of thoughts, opinions, and information, becomes the focal point of interest of people who want to improve matters. Research is done, theories are proposed, experiments are conducted, new procedures are invented to help people express themselves clearly and listen with an open mind. We are now seeing encounter groups, sensitivity training, marathon sessions, awareness techniques, and even language as a psychedelic experience.

All this is good, and nobody should underestimate the work that is being done to improve the skills of would-be communicators and the environmental conditions that facilitate better communication.

It remains that successful communication is still, in too many cases for us to feel complacent about it, a matter of sheer luck. Its most advanced techniques work quite effectively in promoting deodorants, cosmetics, drugs, beer, cigarettes, and politicians, but often fail when vital questions are raised and personal values are at stake. Its failure becomes tragic when on the limited theater of home family life is torn apart, or when on the world theater of the United Nations diplomats declaim in empty palaver and keep

This section reprinted from J. Samuel Bois, *Communication as a Creative Experience* (Los Angeles: Viewpoints Institute, 1968), p. 13-32.

336

each other's attention away from the real issues of material destruction and human suffering.

What is wrong with communication as we practice it? What has to be done about it? Is it the communication process itself that is wanting? Or is there, back of this exchange of human thoughts and opinions, some broader and deeper disturbance, which, because it is unknown or ignored, makes possible and probable repeated failures in communication? An untoward happening may appear accidental to the casual observer, but a scientifically trained analyst of human affairs would rather see it as a symptom of a much wider and deeper set of unfavorable conditions.

In the present case, we may have to spread our attention to the overall conceptual revolution that is shaking our whole word of thinking and feeling and that makes the practice of the skills of effective communication extremely difficult. It is like the condition of the astronaut whose capsule starts tumbling wildly under the influence of cosmic forces cannot be controlled. It makes it impossible to manage movements with a precision that demands steadiness.

The world of humans is now going through a tremendous upheaval that renders altogether inadequate the methods of thinking and behaving that were satisfactory in the relatively stable conditions of the past. In that past, enlightened as we thought by the well-established theories of our most respected philosophers and by the experimental findings of our rigorously trained scientists, we believed that there is such a thing as 'human nature' common to all of us, a 'sound logic' that applies to the thinking of all members of the human species, and an 'objective truth' that can be discovered and is bound to be eventually recognized by all better educated and well-meaning individuals. In this solidly structured world of knowledge and understanding, communication in the most delicate matters was simply a question of refined skills and personal artistry.

It is now well established that these beliefs in 'human nature,' 'sound logic,' and 'objective truth' were mere assumptions shared by a limited group of people that we took as a representative sample of the whole human race. This group was our own, the Judeo-Christian, Greco-Roman portion of humankind that has practically mastered the world with its technology. Other groups developed independently from our own, and they also saw themselves as the representative sample of the whole human race. What these groups and ours had in common was that they accepted as characteristics of all humans what were in fact spontaneous inventions of some primitive ancestors and were later raised to the level of uncontrovertible truths.

As we began to learn about these cultural differences, we sharpened our vision and we eventually noticed that similar deep-reaching differences do exist among individuals who belong to a common culture, and that some of those personal differences are likewise irreducible. Individuals are just as different on the inside—in their thinking, values, and purposes—as they are different on the outside—in their height, muscular build, and general appearance. What is natural for one, in terms of both his first and second natures, is not equally natural for the other.

As a consequence, we see that peaceful coexistence is not a matter of finding a common denominator of human nature and logic; it is a matter of creating a supersystem of thought and values that will transcend, in this our age of planetary community, the isolated 'second natures' that we have developed each cultural group for itself, and took for the basic human nature common to all members of the *Homo sapiens* species.

The first requirement of the new world into which we emerge, by the very force of events that are now beyond the control of any group or of any individual, is to accept the existence of differences among cultures and among individuals. These differences show their contrasting character more clearly at the intellectual-verbal level: we speak languages that have no point-to-point correspondence, we have different views of the world, different theories to account for what happens, different methods of reacting to ourselves and to the world in which we live. It becomes extremely difficult to communicate at this intellectual-verbal level.

In fact, we know now that a perfect logical fit in mental processes is no more possible than an exact measurement can exist in physical matters. Observation and measurement are conditioned by the theory and the instrumentation that is used. Similarly, the 'second human nature' that each cultural group uses as its means of observation and evaluation conditions the relation that we establish between ourselves and whatever surrounds us in space-time. As a consequence, perfect objective viewing and understanding of oneself and of any other person can never be reached, and perfect agreement as to what is so or not-so is an impossibility. Everywhere and every time there is operating a mysterious element of indeterminacy that seems to belong to the very nature of things as grasped by human powers of knowing.

The failure of perfect agreement at the thinking level does not prevent mutual acceptance at a higher and more inclusive level of educated feeling. At this level of feeling, we are aware of the fact that we have to live together in interdependence on a small planet—or in a small family group, enterprise, nation—whose smooth functioning makes our own individual life tolerable and potentially enjoyable. It comes to a question of deciding what is the locus and the size of the group in which we want to participate. In the case of the whole human race living on a planet of which no part is now completely isolated from the rest, we have to accept to belong to it, or else. . . .Nobody can stop the world for you or me to get off.

If we make the necessary distinction between agreement with the other person's ideas and the acceptance of the other person's existence, we may solve many problems of communication. When both sides become aware of the importance of this distinction, the chances of succeeding will multiply, as if they were raised to a higher power.

Communication then becomes a by-product of our commitment to a mutually accepted common life, based on the awareness that we are joined in a common fate.

It is empathy in its pure state, not simply *a condition* of good communication, but *the source and origin* of all that is lasting and valuable in all communicative encounters.

Three Levels of Communication

To study communication, it may be helpful to see it as a phenomenon that belongs to what we may call the *behavioral* world.

What do we mean by the term 'behavioral world'?

We mean the complex whole of individuals-active-in-their total-space-time-environment. If we take all people into account, we have a complex whole that corresponds roughly to Teilhard's *noösphere*.

This behavioral world has many dimensions, including of course the space and time dimensions of our commonsense world, plus a limitless number of other dimensions that defy any form of graphic or imaginative representation. We may suggest some of the following: a 'psychological' distance dimension, of nearness or remoteness that is rather felt than measured; a vectorial dimension of 'directionality' in terms of objectives to be reached, of a thrust of energy towards ends and purposes, of levels of aspiration; a striving dimension of intensity of interest, emotional involvement, dedication, fanticism, commitment, and potential resolve; a dimension of inward movement revealed by turbulence, harmonious rhythm, or neutral quietness, of deep-surging tides of unconscious drives and tendencies, of preconscious affects and acquired needs or consciously accepted choices and decisions.

It is an ever-active plenum that is cumulatively time-bound and creatively time-binding, a space-time ongoing process that is conscious of itself, self-reflexive, responsible within a range of limited autonomy, ceaselessly expanding and advancing at its own speed and rhythm. It is the world of happenings-meanings, of semantic transactions coalescing into semantic states that are eventually expressed in institutions, works of art, organizations, cultural and religious movements, and political constitutions.

Within this behavioral world, communication as a semantic transaction is not limited to its verbal aspect. As a holistic human experience it may be considered: (1) as a preserver of preestablished distance, (2) as an occasion for mutual push-and-pull exchange of energy, and (3) as a symbiotic compounding of thoughts and values towards a common enrichment of participating personalities.

Communication-1

It involves the recognition of a presence-at-a-distance and a purposeful continuation of such a distance. You do so when you do not want to engage in a discussion, when you accept to 'make' conversation to entertain some one, when you keep within the established conventions of politeness and formality, when you keep on saying pleasant things that are noncommittal, when you do not want to alter the situation in which you find yourself.

You hear that type of communication from a politician—or diplomat—who has to answer a question in an equivocal manner, in a communiqué that limits itself to safe generalities, in the 'yes-dear' of the spouse who has accepted to live in a neutral harmony with his mate, in the empty compliment or the meaningless 'thank you' given to acknowledge a perfunctory performance. You see it in the correct but cold attitude of the saleswoman who suspects that you are just shopping and not planning to buy, in the calculated silence of the guest who does not make any remark to an unalert waiter but will cut down the expected tip, in the performer who damns his competitor with faint praise. You may stay at that noncommitted stage when you are introduced to a stranger to whom you don't know how to react, and whose reaction to you may turn out to be significant for your prestige, welfare, or happiness. It is communication that expresses the lofty detachment of a celebrity who shows polite cordiality but cannot be a pal to every one of his admirers. It is communication without engagement.

Communication-2

Here, the communicators engage in an exchange of semantic energies; it may even become a verbal wrestling match where the rules of the competition are those of clever logic, and where a draw will be accepted only if a culturally accepted practice demands it.

You hear the reverberations of such a communication in a debate, where each contestant does their best to prove a point, to convince the other person, to make him change his mind. You have it in an attenuated form in the various encounters called 'dialogues' by people and organizations who are sincerely convinced that the repeated friction of sharp statements against the flint of hard convictions will produce the spark of truth. You have it in most cases of teaching, preaching, demonstrating, explaining, in committee hearings, whenever questions are asked to probe, to trip the other person into a position out of which she won't be able to free herself, whenever feedback is invited to bring about further involvement. It becomes the skill of selling, the art of correcting employees and subordinates without hurting their feel-·ings too much or arousing their defensiveness. It becomes the boring practice of a person who keeps talking about what he did or what he said while his listeners try to run away from the noise he makes. It is the 'I-it' relationship of expert and subject, with which he or she keeps playing to their heart's content in the presence of some captive audience.

It is communication patterned after a mechanical model of action and reaction. The best it can do is to make things run smoothly thanks to an accurate adjustment of working parts and a generous oiling of good manners.

Communications-3

This one is a vital transaction, a blending of semantic transactions, a sharing of feelings, values, and purpose fully expressed and fully acknowledged in their undisguised condition. It is an 'I-Thou' relationship, a being together achieved bilaterally in spite of weak or strong differences of views and convictions, because these are taken as tentative and modifiable on both sides. This is better described as communion than communication, since the symbiotic experience is taken as the focal activity and the exchange of thoughts is seen as a mere byproduct of the feeling contact that is held fast and gently in site of temptations to break it loose.

It reminds one of the Rogerian permissiveness and concern, the holding of hands and the relaxed stroking of nonverbal group exercises. In more intimate occasions it involves the hugging and kissing of friends and lovers. In large groups of actual strangers it may involve the 'loving-in' practices that are becoming acceptable and planned to counteract the isolation from which we all suffer to some extent in our congested world. It may involve just being together, either doing simple things or silent in a felt common presence, with an occasional casual remark that appears now and then like a basting thread that holds the two together in a loose assemblage until a more elaborate binding of thoughts and feelings will, when the occasion presents itself, tighten them firmly in a solid continuous oneness.

It is communication patterned after biological models of vital exchanges such as grafting, transfusion, mouth-to-mouth respiration, transplanting of organs or losing oneself in the ecstatic experience of a fully shared orgasm.

The Gradients of Communication

These three types of communication may be pictured as three layers of a stratified block (Figure 9.1). The lower layer, represented in the accompanying diagram by the lowest rectangular section of the total rectangle, would be communications-1, or communication-at-a-distance. The middle one is communication-2, or communication-as-an-exchange-of-semantic-energy. The top one would be communication-3, or communication-as-a-vital-compounding-of-thoughts-and-feelings.

We may draw a diagonal to the total rectangle to show the gradient of communicating relationship. An arrow that goes up indicates growing inti-

Figure 19.1. The communication gradients.

macy, from communication-at-a-distance to communication-as-a-vital-experience. The arrow that comes down indicates the reverse process, from felt oneness, through argument, down to indifference. The middle layer is where most communication takes place in our culture. The movement along the gradient shows the improvement or worsening of the relationship.

From Communication-2 to Communication-3

Communication-2—and the whole cluster of words to which it belongs such as interaction, causality, smooth running, space and time, determinism, self-improvement—is readily accepted as common sense. Such commonsense terms go with reactions that are taken as 'normal,' or 'natural.' They involve assumptions and implications that we take for granted; they are habitual ways of thinking and behaving that everybody deems appropriate.

There lies a danger, and Korzybski wants us to become aware of it. He writes: "We do not realize what tremendous power the structure of an habitual language has. It is not an exaggeration to say that it enslaves us through the mechanism of semantic reactions. These structural assumptions and implications are inside our skins. . . . If unravelled, they become conscious; if not, they remain unconscious."[16]

What is the commonsense meaning of the word communication? We have the answer in the *American College Dictionary:* "Communication is the imparting or interchange of thoughts, opinions, or information by means of speech, writing, or signs."

This definition involves:

1. a sender;   2. a message;   3. a receiver.

The sender and the receiver may exchange places in turn, and there

[16]Korzybski, *Science and Sanity*, p. 90.

may be messages shuttling back and forth, but each unit of the exchange process involves the three elements in the following order: sender—message—receiver.

The *sender* is expected to:

1. make the message true to facts, accurate, objective;
2. make the message clear and logical;
3. deliver the message at the proper time, in the proper manner, under the proper conditions;
4. convince and persuade the receiver by fitting the message to the receiver's needs, purposes, attitudes, prejudices;
5. take the feedback (questions, objections, etc.) into account so as to improve the clarity and the power of the message.

The *message* is expected to be:

1. not too long, but rather short and to the point;
2. clear and logical;
3. built in such a way that the receiver will be led to accept the conclusion that is offered.

The *receiver* is expected to:

1. listen with critical attention;
2. compare the opinion of the sender with his own;
3. express dissents as clearly and logically as possible.
4. become a sender in turn and perform as the sender (above) is expected to do.

The game continues until one of the two gives in—for whatever reason—at least outwardly. The word *compromise* has a bad meaning in our culture; the chances are that both players will do their utmost to avoid such an ending. Each does their best to win the argument.

The game lends itself to the display of verbal fencing skills, such as pushing the antagonist into a corner, tripping him with rhetorical questions, giving in on a side issue to press forward with the main one.

Communication-3 is a joint creative process, with a different orientation and with postulates freely accepted by both sides to make the experience a stage-four experiment.

1. There is no prepared message to transmit, but some agreement to be worked out in mutual trust and self-respect.
2. The 'sender' and the 'receiver' see themselves as associates in a common undertaking, which is to devise a joint 'conclusion' that could be possibly better than what each of them could devise by themselves.

3. Communication being accepted as a creative process, they consider it normal and helpful to voice their puzzlements, their doubts, their hopes, and their fears.
4. They do not look for a 'solution' or for a firm 'conclusion' that binds them forever and a day, but for the most expedient decision that can be taken under the circumstances.
5. They postulate that developing mutual trust, self-respect, and cooperativeness is more important in the long run than putting across what one considers a valid, important, and urgent message.

Nobody communicates in the ordinary sense of the word, including the writer of this book. All we can do is to express our semantic transactions as genuinely as we know how, let the other person do likewise, and join with her or him in blending the two together as a work of art.

The art requires lots of practice. It is the art of thinking-feeling-groping together.

How to Communicate Effectively

1. Accept the other as one whom you have to take as he is, whether you like it or not. Take into account—as facts that you cannot change at the moment—his values, purposes, opinions, feelings, inasmuch as you know them at the start, and inasmuch as you will understand them to remain rigid or fluctuate in the course of the encounter.
2. Expect and invite the other to express freely her feelings, purposes, values, fears, doubts, information, interpretations, that are related to the situation in focus. Help her reveal herself as she transacts semantically, from moment to moment, within her space-time world of values.
3. Express your own semantic transactions in a similar manner, using the pronoun 'I' as the subject of your statements and making clear that all such statements are subject to elaborations and corrections in the light of whatever the encounter will develop to be.
4. Keep in a felt contact with each other, making the exchange of information and views a secondary activity, guided by a companionable feeling mood and couched in words that help enhance that friendly feeling mood.
5. Do not evaluate critically the other person's views against your own as the standard of truth and wisdom, but take the other's views as a tentative standard against which you reexamine and reevaluate your own opinions and feelings. By doing so, each of you will enrich your own range of vision and add new dimensions to your own structuring of the situation.
6. See the whole process as a dynamic cooperative encounter, not so much

for the purpose of discovering some elusive 'objective' solution to a well-defined problem, but as a joint attempt to reach a higher level of wisdom, together and singly.

7. Let each of you measure the success of the experience, not in terms of a victory for the individual views you held prior to this encounter, but in terms of the increase in mutual trust and willingness to help each other you have achieved by working together in a difficult and/or touchy situation.

On Meeting Critical Situations

There are situations in which our most cherished views, our most steadfast attitudes, and our most deeply felt emotions are challenged and threatened. There are cases when the total semantic transactor that we have become feels we have either to assert ourselves or accept a crushing defeat. To entertain the possibility of a compromise seems impossible; it would be like a shameful abdication of self-respect. There surges within us a survival call for all the resources of native resiliency and acquired skill we can muster in what appears to be a life or death emergency.

To use the analogy of heart transplants, it is like the situation of a patient who has to develop the capacity, not only to accept a foreign organ without allowing the normal process of rejection to operate, but also to make of this new heart the prime motor of a metabolism more efficient than could be expected from the habitual functioning of the organism. It calls for a high degree of self-actualization, to the point of being able to preserve the identity of the self through a transformation that threatens to destroy it.

The skill of self-mastery that this requires is like any other skill; it demands intelligent and consistent training.

Where can we safely practice that skill of self-mastery? Where can we control, at least to a safe degree, the initial disturbance that an unexpected situation creates within ourselves? Where can we learn to assimilate in our psychophysical organism ideas and attitudes that feel like foreign transplants? Or, to use a less dramatic analogy, how do we practice exercises to maintain and improve our psychological fitness as an athlete does physical fitness when preparing for a demanding performance?

From my own experience and from my observations of many people who have trained with me, I offer a suggestion that may appear almost trivial to some readers, but that has achieved significant results when followed for a few months. Here it is: *make of your learning activities*, when you listen to a lecturer, or easier still, when you read a book all by yourself, *a practice in creative learning*. Later on, when you feel you have mastered the skills of self-management in simple intellectual-affective disturbances, you may take the chance of entering with confidence clashes of opinion that may develop to become critical situations, where your emotional balance and your self-respect may be at stake.

Creative Learning

We may differentiate two types of learning. One is often called *rote learning;* the other could be called *creative learning.*

Rote learning means simply to add new information to our already acquired stock of knowledge, without changing the structure of our conceptual-affective world. It is an additive affair.

Creative learning means to reorganize our inner world of ideas and values and to start it functioning according to a different set of rules. It is not only self-enrichment or self-development; it is an attempt at self-renewal.

As examples of creative learning we may take the case of learning a new numeration system, as they do in computer programming, mastering the rules of symbolic logic, or adopting the professional outlook of a lawyer, an engineer, a physician, a priest, or a soldier. These are mostly intellectual changes, although they touch the fringe of our world of values and habits.

There is a kind of creative learning that penetrates deeper into the innards of our reactive self. It involves something that is occasionally described as a transformation, a rebirth, or a conversion, such as adopting a new philosophy of life, be it Christian Science, Zen Buddhism, or the Muslim faith. It is also the case of learning, not simply to speak a different language, but also to think in it as a native does, particularly when the new language does not belong to our familiar Indo-European group. It is also the case of training oneself in General Semantics, which means passing from the pre-relativistic system of thinking and evaluating to the intersubjective relativistic orientation of twentieth-century science. This type of learning demands a special attitude towards the learning experience itself. We have to manage it as a trip into a world of different dimensions. It involves a certain amount of risk taking, as going into orbit beyond the range of accustomed gravity.

1. We have to put ourselves and keep ourselves all through the experience in a welcoming mood toward ideas that are new and appear strange at first. We cannot criticize any single statement as it files past in its allotted place, nor judge the whole system until it has been spread under our eyes in its entirety and the joints of its structure have shown up clearly.
2. We have to reverse the direction of our quest: instead of evaluating the new system in the light of our present knowledge, we have to question our own views, particularly when they appear self-evident to us but contradict what is presented.
3. We have to resist the temptation to offer a correction or an alternative until the new ideas have been thoroughly examined with an undisturbed mind.

4. We realize that it takes time and patience before we can begin to feel at ease with a system that is new to us, or with a viewpoint that is presented from an unexpected angle and described in terms that are unfamiliar.

5. We must remind ourselves that if the essentials of a subject can be compressed into the confines of the proverbial nutshell, it is an indication that it contains little substance.

6. In human affairs there is no magical way of acquiring a new skill in a short time. Studying an atlas of anatomy does not make one a surgeon. Attending a demonstration by an expert does not give one the capacity to repeat his performance.

7. We may listen to a lecturer, take notes, and receive answers to some hasty questions of ours; or, in the case of reading a book by ourselves, we may underline a few statements that strike us as very significant. These activities are indeed a good start in the process of creative learning. But they do not go beyond the initial stage. It is like going to a first-rate nursery and buying a healthy specimen of some rare tree that we want to grow in our backyard. Our responsibility is to prepare the soil, to plant the sapling according to directions, and to take good care of it until it is firmly rooted. Even when we have to water it and feed it if we do not want it to wither and die. No nursery can guarantee the growth of a delicate plant if it is not properly cared for. No teacher and no book can guarantee the value that a new system will have for us if we fail to do our part in the joint process.

8. Our ability to manage ourselves in such a learning experience is a measure of our mental resiliency and vigor. People who have stopped learning new ways of thinking are old, whatever their age in years. People who cannot change their ways of thinking are allergic to whatever might disturb their intellectual-affective balance. If we cannot assimilate innovation when presented to us, we are not likely to produce successful innovation when situations call for it.

9. To sum up this creative or innovating aspect of learning, we may say that it means breaking the situation into parts that do not coincide with our habitual analysis, and arranging these parts in an order different from the one we are accustomed to. Creative learning that is managed consciously is a practice in the art of innovating. The art of innovating is the art of creating for ourselves and for those who will follow us a world richer than what we can imagine at our present stage of formulated experience.

When Opinions Clash

Whitehead once said: 'A clash of opinion is not a disaster; it is an opportunity.' This is a statement that sounds wise, and I accept it without reservation. The trouble is that it takes consummate skill to profit by such opportunities. Here are a few suggestions.

1. Keep ready to welcome contradictory statements as means of testing your own assumptions, conscious and unconscious, not as challenges to defend your own views, or still less as occasions to convince an opponent.

2. Keep listening until you make doubly sure that you understand what is meant. When possible ask questions to check whether you heard aright, or read over again to make sure that you interpreted correctly the statement you just read.

3. Take time to get the feel of contradictory ideas, to taste them as it were, before you spit them out. Accept the temporary discomfort you experience from their presence within your accustomed world of thoughts and values.

4. Reject only those you have taken time to taste fully. Don't be scared; none will actually poison you.

5. There may be some you will recognize you held before, or experimented with and found wanting. These you will reject without being disturbed. Your reaction to them will not be one of avoidance as if you were threatened, but one of calm recognition of a former experience.

6. Report your reaction to a contradictory statement, to yourself or to anyone else, in sentences that begin with the pronoun 'I' as the subject. For instance, instead of saying: 'This does not make sense,' or 'This is wrong,' or 'This won't do,' say something like, 'I cannot accept this at the present time,' or 'I don't share this opinion.' In other words, attach any evaluation you make—and you have the right, even the duty to make some—to your own reaction and not to the other individual or to the views. Instead of saying, 'This is hard to accept,' 'hard to understand,' 'puzzling,' you may say: 'I am puzzled when I hear you say that,' 'I feel startled when I read this statement.'

7. The statement occasionally suggested by some general semanticists, 'This does not make sense *to me*,' is half-way between 'This is wrong,' and 'I cannot accept this at the moment.' It is still an evaluation of the statement you object to, and not a description of your own semantic transaction.

8. Finally, do not attempt to demonstrate that your point of view is the only valid, right, true, or correct one! If your interlocutor says explicitly that he is interested, and if you have reasons to believe that he means it, you may then—and only then—tell him, not *why* you hold a certain opinion but *how* you happened to come to see things as you do.

9. Don't expect an immediate acceptance. Give him time to ponder over what you have just said. He needs it, too.

Communion as An Art

The pages that precede deal with the skills of communicating. They describe what to do and what not to do in order to communicate effectively and smoothly in situations of various degrees of difficulty.

It is up to you, the reader, to practice these skills until they become second nature. It is like learning to drive your car; until you do instinctively what has to be done in city traffic, where there is no time to think and no space to hesitate. Once you have mastered the skills of efficient communication, you are expected to avoid unnecessary clashes and collisions, and you can get along in verbal traffic without serious damage to yourself or to others.

Should we content ourselves with this? I don't think so. This is just a beginning, just a strict minimum. Beyond communication as smooth functioning in interpersonal relations, there is a more advanced stage in the art of relating ourselves to one another in our present world of growing nearness and interaction. This stage is more demanding, indeed, but it is much more gratifying. I call it the practice of communion as an art.

There is no end to the development of any art, and there is no limit to the enjoyment you can derive from it as a performer. Once you have mastered the skill of fingering without hesitation a complex musical phrase on the keyboard or on the strings of a violin, you are free to give expression to your understanding of the passage. You make of your performance the vehicle of feelings that become more complex and more refined as they come out again and again under the free flowing movements of your fingers. You learn to say more and more eloquently what the passage means to you, and you stimulate in your listeners an ever increasing wealth of esthetic reactions. You help them transcend their previous experience of the same passage.

If you are a composer, you achieve more original results. You create new melodic themes and you devise new orchestral combinations that bring out new structures in the world of sound and arouse new thrills of pure enjoyment in both players and listeners.

Your own enjoyment of the art and your skill as a performer or composer support each other; they react to each other in a mutual interplay; they increase in a progressive manner, and they bring your performance to higher and higher degrees of artistry. This artistry manifests itself, renews itself, and multiplies itself whenever a new occasion offers it an opportunity and a challenge.

In the course of generations people have developed arts that have increased the beauty of nature unaided. We enriched the landscape with the Parthenon, the Taj Mahal, and with the daring skyline of Manhattan. We added to the sounds of the waves on the beach and to the singing of the birds in the trees the ordered sonorities of symphonies, choirs, and military bands. We made of our need to cover our naked body the art of the couturier. We made of our need to eat the art of fine cuisine. Why not make of our need to communicate with others the art of total semantic communion enjoyed for itself and by itself?

This new art will not limit itself to an exchange of words only. It will involve all the aspects of the semantic transactions of which we are capable: bodily contact, tuning of feelings as we tune the instruments of an orchestra, blending of thoughts in contrapuntal sequences or in chords where dissonance alternates with consonance, and keeping at a common beat the basic rhythms of our innermost life processes.

The ideal milieu where this new art of total communion can be practiced and brought to high levels of performance is not the encounter group, the love-in, the weekend marathon, or the passing exchange of uninhibited feelings in a therapy session conducted in the nude. These and similar practices that have been in fashion are indications of a gradually recognized need and of an attempt to satisfy this need by breaking out of the shackles of the mores of our culture. I see them as reduced versions of the total surrender and complete intimacy of the life of a couple of lovers who commit themselves to the glorious and demanding enterprise of making the blending of their two lives the supreme achievement of the art of being fully human. Nothing stands between their bodies, minds, and souls except what they keep from their previous existence as individuals, and nothing prevents them from achieveing at all levels as full a communion as their creative capacity may devise. As they advance in the art of loving, they discover-invent forms of human harmony that transcend the most lofty experiences they have known as separate individuals.

When married life stops short of the practice of such an art, it becomes too often a frustrating experience that turns into a state of quiet desperation or ends in the disengagement of divorce.

With the practice of the art, married life may become a living art studio where small units of a new humankind create a form of maximal union prefigured generations ago in the Song of Songs and similar prophetic insights.

From this advance in the art of participating fully in a common life, let us hope that the people of tomorrow will derive unforeseen methods, of which we cannot even dream today, but which will make them capable of sharing a common fate in the conditions of closer and closer coexistence that are forced upon us.

Summary

To summarize this chapter, I have introduced the construct of participating as the primary characteristic of WIGO or what is going on, and I have introduced it as a label for the fifth stage of the epistemological profile in which this recognition is lived as a fundamental value. Participating has been going on all along, but our discursive *epistemes* eventuated in the construct of the "objective observer" and created the separation of subject and object without being aware of this as an invented value; rather, it was accepted as fact.

I made an important distinction between a stage of experience and a stage of development; the former is transient, while the latter is a relatively established way of functioning.

I also discussed the *unifying* experience as making whole what had been separated through the discursive separation of subject and object. We saw the *unifying* experience as one not limited to any particular stage of development, but characteristic of any functioning human being who moves into a state of fullness. I made a distinction between *unifying* and *participating*, with the latter being more encompassing and characteristic of the emerging phase of human development. The *unifying* experience I now limit as the full experience of stages one through four. My purpose is to show that a full experience at those stages is related and mediated by a symbolically and discursively oriented structured unconscious. A participating experience, to mark the important difference, is postulated as being lived for itself and allowed to unfold as an integral and "ordinary" aspect of human existence. New ways of differentiating within these experiences will emerge; they can be developed through one's own volition and skills, and, with relative frequency of occurrence, they can coalese into a new type of human functioning. I suggested that the human couple is presently the most accessible and expedient situation in which this can be developed as a way of life and which can eventually spread to larger and larger groups.

Finally, I offered some practices in creative communication as the basis for facilitating and inducing the environment for individuals to participate. These practices I see as a stage-four formulation, which I feel is a necessary preparation for living what I have called stage five, the semantic renewal of a humankind without "objects" as "things" or entities to which its love is attached. This is humanity unified, a fullness of life in which a higher/deeper compassion is lived, rather than the ephemeral quality of the sentimental, conditional, or parochial love we now seem to accept as our experience.

This brings to a temporary closure, the main body of practices, theorems, postulates, and models. The last chapter will offer a rough idea of some of the developments in the field of activity that this book represents. Remember, that as we embark on a new human adventure, what has been written here may seem primitive and fundamental in the not too distant future. Hopefully, many of our primary postulates will radically change as we more deeply allow the evolutionary thrust within our very selves to move us as we shape its emergence.

PART X

a growing and expanding system

General Semantics becomes the Art of Awareness, and Epistemics is the Science-Art of Innovating. Both disciplines belong to that class of human activities we call arts.

For a life of ceaseless change, we want directives that are flexible and dependable. In the past, people wrote descriptions of imaginary worlds, which they called utopias, to satisfy the emerging need for new directives. These utopias were perfect societies that were corrections or improvements of already existing conditions. In a cosmos in unexpected evolution, cultural mutation is becoming more commonplace today. We need more than utopia writing. I suggest a new science-art of utopia *designing*. It has emerged from the system invented by Alfred Korzybski to free us from the symbol shackles of Aristotelianism imbedded in our subject-predicate language. I called it *epistemics*.

CHAPTER 20

developments of
the system

The Korzybskian System and Cosmogenesis

The Korzybskian system is more easily accepted when viewed against the background of cosmogenesis. This background view is not easy to describe, but unless it is shared to some extent, many chapters of this book will be puzzling to the reader. They may seem to place too much emphasis on what is usually taken as of little importance—such as "quibbling" about the choice of words and proper mental models—and they may seem to ignore issues that are considered paramount and deserving of major concern—such as the conflict between the two cultures, the control of our lives by automated machines, or the intensification of the fight against world communism.

The view that we refer to is a parade of events, things, animals, and people that was outlined by Darwin over more than a century ago and that has been detailed by workers in many scientific fields, from geology and paleontology to political economy and developmental psychology. It is a constantly richer image of the world as a multidimensional process in evolution. A contemporary proponent of this view, Teilhard de Chardin, speaks of the cosmos as a phenomenon unfolding itself in space and in time, as a growing, expanding, and self-complexifying whole to which belong every object and living thing of which we can observe or think. Cosmogenesis (from *cosmos* meaning universe, and *genesis* meaning origin, production, creation) is his term for this all-embracing going-on. His postulates, which remind us of

Creative Evolution and the élan vital of Henri Bergson, are tacitly accepted or expressed, in different terms, in most scientific books and articles of our generation.

In this world that is continually evolving, no single element ever appears identical to a former self; every individual event is necessarily unique in space-time. This is true of every human being as well, whether "insignificant" or whether leaving a distinct mark in world history. This is true of every personal undertaking, of every human activity; each is unique and never repeats itself. Every morning we wake up a slightly different individual; every day we perform a slightly different job; every year we become a slightly different member of many overlapping communities, some small, some large, which have also become slightly different environments. We have learned to accept the fact that at the atomic and molecular level nothing stays put; solid matter is made of relentless activity that carries on with no substratum other than itself. To this notion we must add the notion of growth; and we have genesis, change-creation, and complexity increasing by self-determination in an irreversible manner.

Once we accept this view of the world, in which we see ourselves as a constituent, active, and relatively autonomous part, we have to discard any philosophy of life that fails to attune itself to cosmogenesis. Otherwise, we insert within the recesses of our deepest self a treacherous growth that tends to split us apart and lets us have no interior peace. Our semantic transactions have to be integrated in harmony with our world-wide environment, as we see it, or we shall suffer the pains of self-alienation, the tragedy of being a stranger in our own individual world.

In my estimation, a philosophy that fits well with the evolutionist view of the world is Bachelard's *Philosophy of No*, the philosophy that says "no" to its own conclusions and remains open in all directions that further thinking might take. It is a philosophy in motion, relentlessly creating not only a quantumlike series of static structures of knowledge-at-a-time but an uninterrupted restructuring process that gives ever new formulations to experience as it keeps unfolding itself in space-time.

With such a philosophy it becomes impossible to let general semantics gel into a final shape at any time and under any conditions. If the Korzybskian system is going to emerge as the typical methodology of the third conceptual revolution, it has to keep expanding, correcting itself, and inventing new formulations as months and years tick away the passage of time.

Developments and Applications

The first edition of this textbook presented an unavoidable static picture of the system of general semantics as we were then practicing it at Viewpoints Institute, Los Angeles, California. It was already different from what was taught elsewhere under the same name, including the traditional seminars organized by the original Institute founded by Korzybski and now located in Lakeville, Connecticut. It had already kept expanding and differentiating itself, as expected from a growing system (*see* Boulding's mental model No. 5, p. 214 preceding). In fact, it had moved in the academic world, in keeping with mental model No. 6, going into fields other than word usage and communication, which the term *semantics* has led many people to see as its proper location, although the qualificative *general* had been attached to it by Korzybski and his correspondent Arthur F. Bentley, for the clearly stated purpose of indicating a broader scope.

Finally it underwent a complete transformation, which was announced implicitly by Korzybski's constant usage of the term *epistemological* on his institute letterhead and by my own definition of general semantics as *up-to-date epistemology* (Chapter 2). This radical change was duly registered in the organ of the International Society for General Semantics, *ETC, A Review of General Semantics*, issue of June 1971, in an article entitled "Epistemics: A Time-binding Emergent from General Semantics."

This emergence had been prepared by a practice I followed consistently and still recommend. It is the policy of encouraging students not to limit themselves to a slavish repetition and application of the theorems offered in the textbook, but to assimilate them until they become internalized spontaneous methods, and then venture into developments of their own.

It happened occasionally in the workshops we conducted at Viewpoints Institute, and it happens also, I am sure, whenever people absorb the structure of the system and play with some of its constructs. Here are a few samples that came to my attention.

An elementary school teacher, Lee Bernstein, had barely been in contact with the notion of semantic transaction when she felt it could be represented by a different diagram, and, to her credit, "let herself" invent a different one. Personally, I like it very much, but it would have required too many changes in my text and in my illustrations to adopt it in this book. I give it here, as Figure 20.1, in the hope that someone else will assess its value and try it as in alternate version.

Instead of surrounding the organism with an environment, to which are appended two receding small frames, one for the past and one for the anticipated future, she first drew four elongated ellipses to represent (as in the original diagram) the four main clusters of our activities. She then set the ellipses on top of three concentric circles, one representing the past, one the present, and one the anticipated future—meaning that our activities spread, as it were, on these three space-time aspects of our total life, taken in its full dimensionality. This gives a pregnant unity to the whole construct, and blends space and time in a manner that powerfully suggests the space-time formulation.

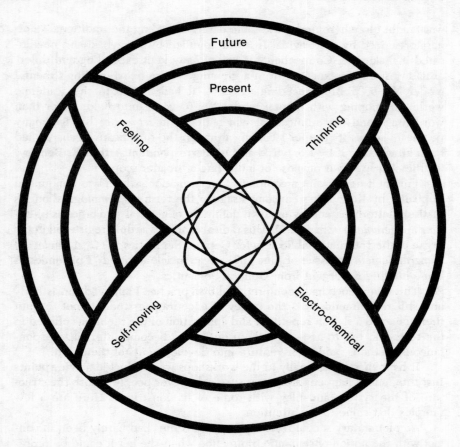

Figure 20.1. A new version of the semantic transaction diagram. It spreads the four types of activities over the three segments of time, past, present, and future, which involve their respective environments.

Another invention is the work of an engineer, Herbert Libow, and it reflects his tendency to think in mathematical terms. We were discussing Teilhard's concept of the *noösphere*, where he bids us see the earth transformed into a different planet by the presence of humans and by their activities. This can be seen as a case of the structural more, of a transformation of what belonged anteriorly to a lower order of existence and is now, by the advent of humans, raised to a higher order of dimensionality. A very simple equation condenses the whole message:

$$\text{Earth}^{\text{Humans}} = \text{Earth} + \text{Humans}$$

In words, the earth elevated to a new power (Human power) is different from the earth on which humans are simply added to other living forms.

In a paper published in the *General Semantics Bulletin*, David Bourland, Jr., tells how he happened to propose the change in English usage that he now calls "Writing in E-prime."

> The writer cannot claim credit for having made the suggestion which led to this formulation of the language E-prime. Unfortunately, he cannot name the man who did. While on a fellowship at the Institute of General Semantics in 1949, the writer saw a letter written by a man from some small town in Connecticut (Tollins?), which advanced an audacious suggestion. He recommended that we stop using the verb "to be" in any form.[1]

By E-prime Bourland means the usual English language minus the verb "to be" in any of its possible inflections. Grammatically speaking, this means giving up the use of the passive voice, much of the subjunctive mood, and some participial usages. The term E-prime comes from mathematics. If we represent the whole of the English language by the letter E, and the verb "to be" and all its inflections ("am," "was," "are," "were," etc.) by the letter e, we can write the simple equation:

$$E' \neq E - e.$$

Thus the new restricted language, E-prime, includes any noun, verb, adjective, adverb, of the regular English language, but excludes all forms of the verb "to be."

Using that language forces us to express ourselves in actional, functional, straightforward statements. It makes it practically impossible to remain in the clouds of verbalism.

For instance, instead of saying "He *is* aggressive," we will say something like this: "If I compare him to other people of similar background in similar situations, I find that he tries to impose his views more frequently—or more forcibly—than most of them do." The second statement requires more words, and we may feel that it lacks punch, but it puts the speaker back into the picture and it forces us to give the operational basis of our opinion.

With time and practice we will learn to make shorter statements in E-prime, but we will also come to realize that we must take the responsibility for what we say and do. Bourland is even willing to rewrite The Declaration of Independence in the interest of semantic clarity. In the standard text, the first sentence reads: "We hold these truths to be self-evident, that all men are created equal, that they are endowed by their Creator with certain inalienable rights, that among these are Life, Liberty, and the pursuit of Happiness." A somewhat more prosaic version in E-prime would read: "We

[1]David Bourland, Jr., "A Linguistic Note: Writing in E-Prime," in *General Semantics Bulletin*, Nos. 32 & 33, Institute of General Semantics, Lakeville, Conn., p. 113.

make the following assumptions: All citizens have equal political rights. All citizens simply by virtue of their existence have certain inalienable rights, including life, liberty, and the pursuit of happiness."[2]

Personally, I find Bourland's suggestion too sweeping. I retain two uses of the verb "to be," the "to be" of existence (the lamp is on the table) and the "to be" as an auxiliary (he is speaking).

At a conference on general semantics and creativity, sponsored jointly by the Creative Education Foundation and the Institute of General Semantics, Allen Flagg, executive director of the New York Society for General Semantics, presented three concepts of what he calls Dimensionanalysis and one of Exceptionanalysis. These concepts are: (1) Search for and Awareness of differences; (2) Search for and Awareness of Similarities; (3) Search for and Awareness of Change; and (4) Search for and Awareness of Exceptions. He writes: "I consider the above four concepts a recapitulation and summary of the General Semantics (modern scientific) methodology applied to Problem Solving."[3]

Robert Wanderer, in "The Map," the newsletter to the San Francisco Chapter of the International Society for General Semantics, announces a lecture by Norman Harrington to be given at their September 1971 regular meeting. "Norm recently retired after twenty-two years on the staff of San Quentin prison. For fifteen of those years, some of them on his own time, he taught a once-a-week class in general semantics. Some years later he pulled some of the class sign-up sheets at random and checked out the degree of success on parole history of those attending. He found a significantly higher degree of parole success for his students, particularly among those considered "poor risks" who succeeded some 50 percent better than expected. In his talk, he will use his experiences at San Quentin as the focal point for discussing ideas from general semantics and related subjects and the social questions of crime and punishment. In the semantic field, he has gone into general systems and kybernetics (that's right, a "k" and not a "c"; it's general systems applied to living organisms). He has developed a theoretical formulation that a self-regulating "semantic-communication system" such as that of the convicts and that of the prison custodial staff, will not assimilate any subsystem that it cannot control; and that even if the subsystem did get control, it would repeat the process by becoming the more general system while the former general system becomes the subsystem. Under this formulation, for example, he takes the pessimistic view that society will find it extremely difficult to improve prisons, since both the convict system and custodial system will fight change. His semantic classes, despite their proven

[2]Reprinted by permission from *Time*, The Weekly Newsmagazine; Copyright Time Inc., 1969.

[3]Allen Flagg, *Differences, Similarities, Change. General Semantics and Creative Problem Solving.* Mimeo, 1971, p. 31.

success in motivating men not to return to crime, were never fully accepted by the systems of the prison."

The pessimism of Norman Harrington brings to mind the gloomy statements Korzybski made in 1932:

> A symbolic or human class of life is very largely controlled by ignorant, hidden, often pathological, factors *beyond public control*, of which the majority are entirely ignorant. In the human symbolic class of life no one is entirely free, but all our lives are entangled in an interdependence of human relations. The dependence on those powers which are now hidden and *beyond public control*, constitutes a grave danger to all.[4]

Personally I do not share these views. I recognize that the conditions in which we live are often as Harrington and Korzybski describe them, but I do not, for all that, give up trust in the irrepressible power of the evolution of the human race. Nine years after writing his original text, Korzybski wrote at the end of his introduction to the second edition of *Science and Sanity:*

> A non-Aristotelian re-orientation is inevitable; the only problem today is when, and at what cost.[5]

We all know what he meant by a "non-aristotelian re-orientation." He had in mind what we now describe as the emergence of a new breed of human individuals, from stages two to three to stage four.

Epistemics: A Time-binding Emergent from General Semantics

At Viewpoints Institute in Los Angeles, founded by Ethel Longstreet and myself, we have kept on working on two fronts: (1) improving the methods of teaching the Korzybskian system and of applying it to personal growth; and (2) expanding and clarifying the formulations of the system itself to the point when it became a new one, broader and deeper, and including the old one as a subsystem.

The improvement of the methods of teaching the expanding system and of applying it to the process of personal growth would demand a whole treatise beyond the scope of the present textbook. It is my hope that some day their creative initiators, Ethel Longstreet, Gary David, Ada Beth Lee, Annie Muller, and Verlin Heuton will find time to put them down in writing, so as to help teachers who cannot come and learn the new skills in a first-order experience.

The development of new formulations has already made considerable advances. In 1968, the ever-recurring theme of communication was taken up and treated in a more holistic manner than usual in a minibook published by Viewpoints Institute under the title *Communication as Creative Experience*.

---

[4]Alfred Korzybski, *Science and Sanity* (Lakeville, Conn.: International Non-Aristotelian Library, 1933, 1941, 1948, 1958), p. 559.

[5]Korzybski, *Science and Sanity*, 4th edition, p. liv.

It was launched without much publicity, but we have seen its sales mounting steadily. Its Chapter 10, "Communion as An Art," which the author felt was so esoteric that he hesitated to insert it, is now often taken as the topic most suitable for a first lesson. This is taken as an indication that the cultural climate is changing: many people are looking for something beyond clever communication gimmicks. This prompted me to approve the use of that chapter, along with other material on creative communication, in this edition of the present text.

The first doctoral degree was granted in the field of Epistemics in 1975 through the Union for Experimenting Colleges and Universities' Union Graduate School. It was conferred upon Dr. Gary David who worked with me for many years at Viewpoints Institute. His thesis was a new development of what we called *participating*, and the participating stage of development, or stage five.

For the teachers who will be using *The Art of Awareness* as a textbook, there is an independent and yet closely related treatment of what we described earlier as psycho-logics (p. 46) that I do recommend strongly. They will find it in an article by Professor Melville Thistle, Carleton University, Ottawa, Canada, under the title *The Biochron*.

In the course of a full year of inquiry guided by the notions already acquired in a long study of general semantics, we gradually built, my advanced students and myself, a wide-ranging theoretical construct that eventually came out in a book, published by Harper & Row in 1971 under the rather enigmatic title of *Breeds of Men*. The publishers had added two subtitles to indicate the implications of the message, "Toward the Adulthood of Humankind," and "Post-Korzybskian General Semantics." It is a longitudinal study, along the time line of succeeding generations, of the stages of development of our Western culture from our predecessors of 400 generations ago to ourselves in this closing fraction of the twentieth century. It describes the successive appearance of four cultural breeds and the unfolding of what Julian Huxley called the psycho-social evolution, a theme that is now coming again and again in various forms, be it consciousness *I, II,* and *III* (Reich), *Future Shock* (Toffler), *The Coming of The Golden Age* (Stent), *The Images of Man* (Rosenthal), *Landmarks of Tomorrow* (Drucker), *The Pentagon of Power* (Mumford), or *The Meaning of The Twentieth Century* (Boulding).

From such broad space-time considerations, it passes on to concrete suggestions on how to use this historical scale as a measuring device to evaluate our own semantic self, that of other people, the cultural age of educational and religious institutions, the obsolescence or the up-to-dateness of statements, theories, and plans of action.

Transcending the Limitations of non-Aristotelianism

General Semantics appeared in only one of the eight large cultural families that compose humankind. Korzybski called it non-Aristotelian and attempted to avoid the pitfalls that have developed within the structure of our Indo-European, subject-predicate language. This I find a most worthy aim, and I am thankful to Korzybski for having made me aware of these pitfalls that render dangerous every field of human activity.

Living within our present condition demands that we take further steps. For me, non-Aristotelianism does not go far enough if we are to encompass conditions rather than have conditions absorb us as they now seem to do, both on the level of our personal lives and on a worldwide scale. Put in another way, as humans we must learn that "conditions" are mostly self-created abstractions, held together by our values and purposes, and appear to us to be "out there" threatening our very existence.

To encompass conditions means to grow a structurally new self that includes within its very life movement an intimacy with itself as a creative process that invents and develops the very conditions for its further evolution.

This new self must not only be a scientist, but also an artist that can tune whatever it invents, including itself, to the evolutionary thrust that envelops our planet. And, maybe most of all, this self must do all of this while dwelling in the love of its own presence, that is, bathed in an atmosphere of no "conditions."

In my capacity as a Westerner, I see myself as a member of the total human family in this day and age, when our step-by-step transformations of primitive women and men into mature individuals responsible for our own fate, demand the skill to evaluate what each of us is making of ourselves, and what others, singly or grouped in organized institutions, are making of our common heritage.

We are just a fraction of the human family, and none of our inventions, technological, political, economic, religious, or philosophical, will be accepted by the rest of the population of the planet unless it proves to be a real contribution to a better understanding of what it means to be human and to the genuine welfare of the species. The time is past when we could exploit our fellow humans and impose on them our way of life under the pretext of enlightening them or helping them out of their "ignorance." I deeply feel that the maturity of a new self includes the responsibility to make our contribution to the common weal one that reaches far and deep.

We have done so in the technological field: our satellites make instant intercontinental communication possible; we have done it in health measures: we have practically eliminated malaria and other scourges; we are on the vanguard in proclaiming human rights; we dream realistically of a world federation under some form or other.

Epistemics is in line with all these initiatives. It suggests a view of humankind that transcends the individuality of cultures. It looks for a code of values and a measurement of human growth that is not linked with any particular philosophy of life, Eastern or Western, Christian, Taoist, Buddhist, or what not.

Could we single out a common characteristic of all humans, somewhat similar to their belonging to a common genetic pool, which would give us a lead to a new philosophy of living that could incorporate and transcend the various cultures, philosophies, and religions?

I think there is one already emerging slowly out of the apparently chaotic condition of humankind. I see it consistent with the evolutionary thrust that animates the whole cosmos, including its human element. It is the development of each human individual, of each human institution, and of the whole human psycho-social living mass—or *noösphere*, as Pierre Teilhard calls it—that we are just beginning to measure, in a rough qualitative manner for the time being, along a brand new scale that covers the totality of what is significant in human history. It goes well with a notion that has become more and more acceptable, in the last hundred years or so, of seeing the human race, not as an abstract humanity with a nature that does not change, but as a living organism that grows slowly but irrespressibly toward self-aware adulthood.

To use a different analogy, we could compare the continued existence of *Homo sapiens* on the planet to a stream that started as a rivulet and gradually became a mighty river watering on its banks a variety of institutions planted and nurtured by succeeding generations. In its course the river has gone through sharp discontinuities like waterfalls that caused its waters to churn, boil, spume, and roar. In recent years we·have called these discontinuities "conceptual revolutions." In our Western world we count three major ones: one that took place about 500 years before the Christian era, one in the period that extends from A.D. 1500 to 1700, and one that is now taking place in our very much perturbed generation. All of this is the subject of the first chapter of this book. Between those major disturbances or rapid changes in the speed of the flow, such as the advent of Christianity, the birth of democratic governments following the Age of Enlightenment, the atomic age in the forties, the new industrial revolution brought about by cybernetics and automation.

According to certain widely-read authors, such as Peter F. Drucker, Lewis Mumford, Theodore Roszak, and others, we are now going through a period of total discontinuity, of an unexpected and all-pervading break in the flow of human energies to an altogether different level, to what may well be a new order of dimensionality, or, to use Korzybski's expression, a "new kind

of man." Some cultural groups have reached that stage of turmoil and transformation, some are not yet caught in it. Some institutions are still enjoying
with complacency the placid waters of some long-standing eddy that has
been turning slowly upon itself for years and centuries, as is the case in some
century-old religions; some individuals are right in the tumbling confusion of
the precipitous waterfall itself, as in the case of the generation of around
twenty years of age.

As the world becomes smaller and smaller, the various cultural groups
become more and more tightly tangled with one another, and the time is
coming when this conceptual revolution, which appeared first in our own
Western world, spreads to world affairs in politics, economics, ecological
planning, and intercommunication.

This brings about a centration and homogenization of the whole human
race, which render possible measurements that apply to practically all those
whom we used to see as partakers of an assumed "human nature." The general idea is to figure out where humankind as a whole or any segment of it
happens to be in its evolutionary growth. It is to assess its stage of development from the primitiveness of the early humans to the sophistication of the astronaut who walks on the moon, from the medicine man and his incantations
to the heart surgeon with transplants achieved through the techniques of
many advanced sciences. It is to derive, from the limited history of human
history and from the careful observation of the life of nations, institutions,
and individual humans, some scheme of thinking, some simple mental
model of what we are heading for and how we are transforming ourselves to
get there.

In my judgement, there is something we can do about it, and this is
what I propose tentatively in the science-art of epistemics. At the present
time, I see all cultures having something in common. Westerners and East-
erners, sophisticated theorists and aborigines still content with their myths,
we are all under the impression that our local view of the world and of our
place in it is *the* true picture of the universe and of ourselves. Professional
scientists call it the achievement of rigorous objective thinking; religious
fundamentalists call it a revelation from God; naïve believers in the voice of
nature expressing itself in their spontaneous gut feelings do not even suspect
that it could be otherwise. Each culture accepts its own brand of objectivity
as the only and true "real" one. It is ready to argue and demonstrate its
validity, and, in some cases, to fight to the death to bear witness to it. Look
at Vietnam, at Northern Ireland, at the Arab-Israeli clash in the Middle
East; look at the super powers, highly scientized as they claim, the U.S.S.R.
and the United States, in their defying stance of mutual deterance with
atomic weapons ready for the overkill. Religious and educational institutions
can take a different view: instead of a clashing encounter of different
philosophies they strive to convert members of the other worlds to their

creed and practice: we meet Buddhist missionaries in our streets, we send Peace Corps volunteers who introduce our technology and our way of life in "developing" countries; Western seekers of personal growth seek Tibetan or Zen training to higher levels of consciousness.

The time is past to decide who possesses objective truth and who is in error. The time is also past to attempt to combine in some sort of cultural "stew" elements that we know from experience are incompatible. Let the whole garden of human creative achievements spread itself in its glorious diversity and variegated beauty. The seeking for TRUTH has divided humankind long enough, and at a cost that we do not have to withstand any longer. Let us all join in a common attempt—guided by our most advanced sciences and skills—to innovate, to create a so far nonexistent set of formulations and values that befits the present vast movement of centration that packs all nations and institutions together on our small planet floating lonely at a speed of 65,000 miles per hour in the chilling vastness of a space filled with waves of energies we are just beginning to perceive.

bibliography

Part I

Chapters 1 and 2

Suggested Readings

BRIDGMAN, PERCY W. *The Way Things Are*. Cambridge, Mass.: Harvard University Press, 1959. "Introduction," pp. 1-15.

DRUCKER, PETER F. *Landmarks of Tomorrow*. New York: Harper & Row, 1957. "The New World View," Chap. 1, pp. 1-16.

HALL, A. RUPERT, AND MARIE BOAS HALL. *A Brief History of Science*. New York: Signet Books (New American Library), 1964.

KORZYBSKI, ALFRED. *Science and Sanity*. Lakeville, Conn.: International Non-Aristotelian Library, 1933 (1st ed.) and 1958 (4th ed.). "Preliminaries," Chap. 1, pp. 7-18; and "Introduction," Chap. 3, pp. 38-52.

LEWIN, KURT. *Dynamic Theory of Personality*. New York: McGraw-Hill, 1935. "The Conflict between Aristotelian and Galilean Modes of Thought," pp. 1-42.

RABINOWITZ, EUGENE. "Scientific Revolution: Man's New Outlook." *Bulletin of Atomic Scientists* (1963): 15-18.

THOMPSON, LAURA. *Toward a Science of Mankind*. New York: McGraw-Hill, 1961. Chaps. 5 and 6, pp. 75-105.

WHITE, LYNN JR., ed. *Frontiers of Knowledge in the Study of Man*. New York: Harper & Row, 1956. "What This Book Is About," pp. xi-xii; and "The Changing Canons of Our Culture," pp. 301-16.

WHITEHEAD, ALFRED NORTH. *Science and The Modern World.* New York: Cambridge University Press, 1933. "The Origin of Modern Science," pp. 1-24; and "Science and Philosophy," pp. 172-94.

WOLFE, DALE. "Science and Public Understanding." *Science* (1957): 179-82.

Supplementary Readings

BARNES, H. E. *An Intellectual and Cultural History of the Western World.* New York: Dover Publications, Inc., 1965.

BOULDING, K. "The Emerging Superculture." *In Values and the Future.* Edited by Blair and Resher. New York: The Free Press, 1969. Pp. 336-350.

BRIDGMAN, P. W. "The New Vision of Science." *Harper's Magazine* (1929): 444, 445, 450. Quoted in Barnes (*see above*), vol. III, pp. 1106-7.

BRILLOUIN, LEON, *Scientific Uncertainty, and Information.* New York: Academic Press, 1964.

DOBZHANSKY, THEODOSIUS. *Mankind Evolving.* New York: Bantam Books, 1970. Chap. 12, pp. 334-364.

FANON, FRANZ. *The Wretched of the Earth.* New York: Grove Press, 1968.

FEUER, LEWIS. *Einstein and the Generations of Science.* New York: Basic Books, Inc., 1974.

FOUCAULT, MICHEL. *The Archaeology of Knowledge.* New York: Pantheon Books, Inc., 1972.

———. *The Order of Things.* An Archeology of Human Sciences. New York: Pantheon Books, Inc., 1970.

HANSEN, N. R. *Patterns of Discovery.* New York: Cambridge University Press, 1958.

ILLICH, IVAN D. *Celebration of Awareness.* New York: Doubleday & Company, Inc., 1969.

JACOB, FRANCOIS. *The Logic of Life.* New York: Vintage Books, 1976. Conceptual revolutions shown through the history of heredity.

KUHN, THOMAS S. *The Structure of Scientific Revolutions.* 2d ed. Chicago: University of Chicago Press, 1970.

MEAD, MARGARET. *Culture and Commitment.* New York: Doubleday & Company, Inc., 1970.

MESAROVIC, MIHAJLO, AND PESTEL, EDUARD. *Mankind at the Turning Point.* The Second Report to the Club of Rome. New York: Signet Books, 1976.

MUMFORD, LEWIS. *The Transformations of Man.* New York: Harper & Row, 1972.

NEEDLEMAN, JACOB. *A Sense of the Cosmos.* New York: Doubleday & Company, Inc., 1975.

POPPER, KARL. *The Logic of Scientific Discovery.* New York: Basic Books, Inc., 1959.

REICH, CHARLES. *The Greening of America.* New York: Random House, Inc., 1970. New York: Bantam Books, Inc., 1971.

ROSENTHAL, BERNARD G. *The Images of Man.* New York: Basic Books, Inc., 1971.

ROSZAK, T. *The Making of a Counter Culture.* New York: Doubleday & Company, Inc., 1969.

STENT, GUNTHER S. *The Coming of the Golden Age.* New York: Doubleday & Company, Inc., 1969. Chap. 5, pp. 77-95.

Thompson, William Irwin. *Passages About Earth*. New York: Harper & Row, 1974. An exploration of the new planetary culture.

Toffler, Alvin. *Future Shock*. New York: Bantam Books, Inc., 1971.

Toynbee, Arnold. *Change and Habit*. New York: Oxford University Press, Inc., 1966.

Von Bertalanffy, Ludwig. *Robots, Men and Minds*. New York: George Braziller, Inc., 1967.

Supplementary Readings by J. Samuel Bois

Breeds of Men: Toward the Adulthood of Humankind. New York: Harper & Row, 1970.

Epistemics: The Science-Art of Innovating. San Francisco: International Society for General Semantics, 1972.

Part II

Chapter 3

Suggested Readings

Goldstein, Kurt. "The Holistic Approach." In *Human Nature*. New York: Oxford University Press, 1940. Pp. 3-33.

———. "On The Concept of The Organism as a Whole." In *The Organism*. New York: American Book Co., 1939. Pp. 213-86.

Korzybski, Alfred. "What is Man?" In *Manhood of Humanity*. 2d ed. Lakeville, Conn.: International Non-Aristotelian Library, 1950. Pp. 66-92.

Langer, Suzanne. "The Growing Center." In *Frontiers of Knowledge in The Study of Man*, edited by Lynn White. New York: Harper & Row, 1956. Pp. 257-88.

Supplementary Readings

Cantril, Hadley, ed. *The Morning Notes of Adelbert Ames, Jr.* New Brunswick, N.J.: Rutgers University Press, 1960. "Specificity of Consciousness," p. 25; "Abstracting-Symbolizing-Involving Knowns-Prognostication," pp. 30-33.

Rugg, Harold. "Felt Thought through Gestural Symbol." In *Imagination*. New York: Harper & Row, 1963. Chap. 14, pp. 263-287.

Von Vertalanffy, Ludwig. "The Image of Man in Contemporary Thought." In *General System Theory*. New York: George Braziller, Inc., 1968. Pp. 188-192.

Whyte, Lancelot L. "Au Revoir." In *Focus and Diversions*. New York: George Braziller, Inc., 1961. Chap. XV, pp. 225-235.

Supplementary Readings by J. Samuel Bois

Epistemics: The Science-Art of Innovating. San Francisco: International Society for General Semantics, 1972. Chap. 5, pp. 37-47; Chap. 13, pp. 137-145.

Explorations In Awareness. New York: Harper & Row, 1957. Chap. 7, pp. 41-50; Chap. 28, pp. 177-182.

Chapter 4

Suggested Readings

BOULDING, KENNETH. "The Image and The Truth." In *The Image*. Ann Arbor: University of Michigan Press, 1956. Pp. 164-75.

KORZYBSKI, ALFRED. *Science and Sanity*. Lakeville, Conn.: International Non-Aristotelian Library, 1933 (1st ed.) and 1958 (4th ed.). "The Organism as a whole," pp. 123-30, "General Epistemological," pp. 101-10; "Aims, Means and Consequences of a Non-Aristotelian Revision," pp. 7-18: and "A Comparison of A and non-A Standards of Evaluation," pp. 555-57.

MURPHY, GARDNER. "The Skeptical Psychologist." In *Personality: A Biosocial Approach*. New York: Basic Books, Inc., 1966. Pp. 914-27.

RAPOPORT, ANATOL. "What is Semantics?" In *Language, Meaning, and Maturity*, edited by S. I. Hayakawa. New York: Harper & Row, 1954. Pp. 3-18.

THOMAS, WILLIAM L., JR., ed. *Man's Role in Changing the Face of the Earth*. Chicago: University of Chicago Press, 1956. Summary of "Prospect," by Lewis Mumford, pp. 1141-1152, "Man's Self-Transformation," pp. 1088-1112.

VON BERTALANFFY, LUDWIG. "General Systems Theory." In *Life, Language, Law*, edited by Richard W. Taylor. Yellow Springs, O.: Antioch Press, 1957. Pp. 58-79.

Supplementary Readings by J. Samuel Bois

Explorations In Awareness. New York: Harper & Row, 1957. Chap. 6, Pp. 35-40; Chap. 8, Pp. 51-58.

Chapter 5

Suggested Readings

HEBB, D. O. *The Organization of Behavior*. New York: Wiley, 1949. "The Problem and The Line of Attack," Chap. I, pp. 1-16; "Development of the Learning Capacity," pp. 107-139.

———. *A Textbook of Psychology*. Philadelphia: Saunders, 1958. "The Nervous Systems" and "Neural Transmission," Chaps. 4 and 5.

JEFFRESS, LLOYD A., ed. *Cerebral Mechanisms in Behavior* (The Hixon Symposium). New York: Wiley, 1951. "The Problem of Serial Order in Behavior," by K. S. Lashley, pp. 112-135.

MONTAGU, ASHLEY, M. F. *On Being Human*. New York: Henry Schuman, 1950.

SOROKIN, PITIRIM A. *The Ways and Power of Love*. Boston: Beacon Press, 1954.

TOMKINS, SYLVAN. *Affect, Imagery, Consciousness*. New York: Springer, 1962. Introduction to Chap. 4, inclusive, pp. 3-149.

WHYTE, L. L. *The Next Development in Man*. London: Cresset, 1944. "The Characteristics of Man," Chap. 3, pp. 48-69.

Supplementary Readings

AMES, ADELBERT. *The Morning Notes of Adelbert Ames, Jr.*, Hadley Cantril, ed. New Brunswick, N.J.: Rutgers University Press, 1960. "Acting on value judgements," p. 35.

BERLYNE, D. E. *Aesthetics and Psychobiology.* New York: Appleton-Century-Crofts, 1971. "Emotion and Arousal," Chap. 7. A simple schematic section of the human brain clearly showing the thalamic region is displayed.

FERGUSON, MARILYN. *The Brain Revolution.* New York: Taplinger, 1973.

HARRIS, THOMAS A. *I'm OK—You're OK.* New York: Harper & Row, 1967. Chap. 1, pp. 1-15.

LANGER, SUSANNE K. *Mind: An Essay on Human Feeling.* Baltimore, Md.: The Johns Hopkins Press, 1970, Vol. 1, 1974, Vol. 2.

ORNSTEIN, ROBERT E. *The Psychology of Consciousness.* San Francisco: W. H. Freeman & Co., 1972. Chap. 1, pp. 1-13; Chap. 3, pp. 49-92.

———, ed. *The Nature of Human Consciousness.* New York: Viking Press, 1974. Part II, pp. 61-147.

PENFIELD, WILDER. *The Mystery of the Mind.* Princeton, N.J.: Princeton University Press, 1976.

RAND MCNALLY. *Atlas of the Body and Mind.* Chicago: Rand McNally & Co., 1976.

RIKLAN, MANUEL, AND LEVITA, ERIC. *Subcortical Correlates of Human Behavior.* Baltimore, Md.: The Williams and Wilkins, Co., 1969.

THOMAS, LEWIS. *The Lives of a Cell.* New York: Viking Press, 1974.

Supplementary Readings by J. Samuel Bois

Epistemics: The Science-Art of Innovating. San Francisco: International Society for General Semantics, 1972. Chap. 3, pp. 19-25.

Explorations In Awareness. New York: Harper & Row, 1957. Chap. 30, pp. 193-198.

Part III

Chapter 6

Suggested Readings

HEBB, D. O. *The Organization of Behavior.* New York: Wiley, 1949. Perception: pp. 1-59; "Relation of Early and Later Learning," pp. 109-20; "The Two Meanings of Intelligence," pp. 294-303.

NEWTON, NORMAN T. *An Approach to Design.* Reading, Mass.: Addison-Wesley, 1957. "Structure, Visual and Verbal," Chap. 2, pp. 14-29.

WEINBERG, HARRY. *Levels of Knowing and Existence.* New York: Harper & Row, 1957. Chaps. 4, 5, 6, pp. 48-144.

WERTHEIMER, MAX. *Productive Thinking.* New York: Harper & Row, 1945. "Conclusion," pp. 189-215.

WHORF, BENJAMIN L. *Language, Thought, and Reality,* edited by J. B. Carroll. New York: Wiley, 1956. "The Relation of Habitual Thought and Behavior to Language," pp. 139-59; and "Science and Linguistics," pp. 209-19.

YOUNG, J. Z. *Doubt and Certainty in Science.* New York: Oxford University Press, 1950. Fourth lecture, pp. 61-71.

ZIPF, GEORGE K. *Human Behavior and the Principle of Least Effort.* Reading, Mass.: Addison-Wesley, 1949. "Language as Sensation and Mentation," pp. 156-209.

Supplementary Readings

BATESON, GREGORY. *Steps to an Ecology of Mind.* New York: Ballantine Books, 1973. "Pathologies of Epistemology," pp. 478-487; and "Form, Substance and Difference," pp. 448-465.

BROWN, G. SPENCER. *Laws of Form.* New York: Julian Press, Inc., 1972.

CASTENADA, CARLOS. *A Separate Reality.* New York: Pocket Books, 1972.

HANSON, N. R. *Patterns of Discovery.* New York: Cambridge University Press, 1958. Pp. 4-30.

MARGENAU, HENRY. *The Nature of Physical Reality.* New York: McGraw-Hill Book Company, 1950. Pp. 54-73.

McCAY, JAMES T. *The Management of Time.* Englewood Cliffs, N.J.: Prentice-Hall, Inc., 1959. Chap. 10, pp. 71-82; Chap. 12, pp. 95-102; Chap. 13, pp. 102-111.

MURPHY, GARDNER. *Outgrowing Self-Deception.* New York: Basic Books, 1975. Preface, pp. xi-xv; Chap. 1-2, pp. 3-23; Chap. 5, pp. 46-60.

ORNSTEIN, ROBERT E. *The Psychology of Consciousness.* San Francisco: W. H. Freeman & Co., 1972. Chap. 2, pp. 15-46.

———, ed. *The Nature of Human Consciousness.* New York: Viking Press, 1974. Part III, "The Construction of 'Ordinary' Consciousness," pp. 149-210.

ZIPF, GEORGE K. *The Psycho-biology of Language.* M. I. T., 1965. Pp. 267-271.

Supplementary Readings by J. Samuel Bois

Epistemics: The Science-Art of Innovating. San Francisco: International Society for General Semantics, 1972. Pp. 135-136.

Explorations In Awareness. New York: Harper & Row, 1957. Pp. 51-69; 123-159; 131-137.

Chapter 7

Suggested Readings

KORZYBSKI, ALFRED. *Science and Sanity.* Lakeville, Conn. International Non-Aristotelian Library, 1933 (1st ed.) and 1958 (4th ed.). "On Multiordinal Terms," pp. 438-42.

Supplementary Readings

CANTRIL, HADLEY, ed. *The Morning Notes of Adelbert Ames, Jr.* New Brunswick, N.J.: Rutgers University Press, 1960. Pp. 3, 4, 5, 16, 20, and "Letter to John Dewey," p. 175.

Supplementary Readings by J. Samuel Bois

Explorations In Awareness. New York: Harper & Row, 1957. Pp. 138-159.

Part IV

Chapter 8

Suggested Readings

KELLY, GEORGE A. *The Psychology of Personal Constructs.* New York: Norton, 1955. "The Nature of Personal Constructs," Chap. 3, pp. 105-83.

KORZYBSKI, ALFRED. *Manhood of Humanity,* 2d ed. Lakeville, Conn.: International Non-Aristotelian Library, 1950. The whole book, beginning with Keyser's lecture on "Korzybski's Concept of Man," pp. 289-326.

LANGER, SUZANNE. "The Growing Center." In *Frontiers of Knowledge in the Study of Man,* edited by Lynn White, Jr. New York: Harper & Row, 1956. Chap. 16, pp. 257-86.

SIMPSON, GEORGE GAYLORD. *The Meaning of Evolution.* New Haven, Conn.: Yale University Press, 1949. "Evolution, Humanity, and Ethics," Part III, pp. 281-348.

SOROKIN, PITIRIM A. "Integralism is My Philosophy." In *This is My Philosophy,* edited by Whit Burnett. London: Allen & Unwin, 1958. Pp. 180-89.

————. *The Ways and Power of Love.* Boston: Beacon, 1954. "Mental Structure and Energies of Man," Chap. 5, pp. 83-97; "The Supraconscious in Man's Mental Structure," Chap. 6, pp. 98-114.

TEILHARD DE CHARDIN, PIERRE. *The Phenomenon of Man.* London: Collins, 1959.

————. *The Future of Man.* New York: Harper & Row, 1964.

THOMAS, WILLIAM L., ed. *Man's Role in Changing the Face of the Earth.* "Man's Self-transformation," pp. 1088-112; "The Unstable Equilibrium of Man in Nature," pp. 1113-128.

Supplementary Readings

BEADLE, G. AND BEADLE, M. *The Language of Life.* Garden City, N.Y.: Doubleday & Company, Inc., 1965. Pp. 12-13, pp. 54-56.

CANTRIL, HADLEY, ed. *The Morning Notes of Adelbert Ames, Jr.* New Brunswick: Rutgers University Press, 1960. Pp. 10, 11, 20; "The Presumptive World," pp. 41-53; "The Question," pp. 61-64.

DITFURTH, HOIMAR VON. *Children of the Universe.* New York: Atheneum, 1974.

FOUCAULT, MICHEL. *Les Mots et les Choses.* Pariss Gallimard, 1966. An English translation, entitled *The Order of Things,* was published by Pantheon in 1970.

HALL, EDWARD T. *Beyond Culture.* New York: Anchor Press/Doubleday, 1976.

JASTROW, ROBERT. *Red Giants and White Dwarfs.* New York: Signet, 1969.

LOEBL, EUGEN. *Humanomics.* New York: Random House, 1976.

McHALE, JOHN. *The Future of The Future.* New York: George Braziller, Inc., 1969.

MURPHY, GARDNER. *Human Potentialities.* New York: Basic Books, Inc., 1958. "The Creative Eras," Chap. 9, pp. 142-157.

POLANYI, MICHAEL. *Personal Knowledge.* Chicago: University of Chicago Press, 1958.

SAGAN, CARL. *The Cosmic Connection.* New York: Anchor Press/Doubleday, 1973.

SOLO, ROBERT A. *Economic Organizations & Social Systems.* Indianapolis, Ind.: The Bobbs-Merrill Co., 1967.

ZIPF, GEORGE K. *The Psycho-biology of Language.* M.I.T., 1965. "The Symbolic and The Real" and "The Degree of Reality as A Function of The Group," pp. 304-309.

Supplementary Readings by J. Samuel Bois

Breeds of Men: Toward the Adulthood of Humankind. New York: Harper & Row, 1970. Pp. 141-153; 162-171.

Epistemics: The Science-Art of Innovating. San Francisco: International Society for General Semantics, 1972. Pp. 11-18; 49-71; 113-123.

Explorations in Awareness. New York: Harper & Row, 1957. Pp. 51-63; 76-93.

Chapter 9

Suggested Readings

KORZYBSKI, ALFRED. *Science and Sanity.* Lakeville, Conn.: International Non-Aristotelian Library, 1933 (1st ed.) and 1958 (4th ed.). "On Linearity," pp. 603-14; "The Structural Aspect as Fundamental" (bottom of page 148 to end of chapter).

Supplementary Readings

CASTENADA, CARLOS. *Tales of Power.* New York: Simon & Schuster, 1974. "The Tonal and the Nagual." Part two, pp. 105-206.

WHYTE, L. L. *The Unconscious before Freud.* Garden City, N.Y.: Anchor/Doubleday, pp. 89-95.

Supplementary Readings by J. Samuel Bois

Breeds of Men: Toward the Adulthood of Humankind. New York: Harper & Row, 1970. Pp. 48-56.

Epistemics: The Science-Art of Innovating. San Francisco: The International Society for General Semantics, 1972. Pp. 27-35.

Explorations In Awareness. New York: Harper & Row, 1957. Pp. 160-176.

Part V

Chapter 10

Suggested Readings

ALLPORT, GORDON W. *Pattern and Growth in Personality.* New York: Holt, Rinehart & Winston, 1961. "The Evolving Sense of Self," Chap. 6, pp. 110-38.

GERHARD, R. W. "The Biological Basis of Imagination." In *The Creative Process.* New York: Mentor Books (New American Library), 1955. Pp. 226-51 (see Ghiselin).

GHISELIN, BREWSTER. *The Creative Process.* New York: Mentor Books (New American Library), 1955. "Introduction," pp. 11-31.

KORZYBSKI, ALFRED. *Science and Sanity.* Lakeville, Conn.: International Non-Aristotelian Library, 1933 (1st ed.) and 1958 (4th ed.). "Periods of Human Development," pp. 194-208.

POLANYI, MICHAEL. *Personal Knowledge.* Chicago: University of Chicago Press, 1958. "Dwelling In and Breaking Out," pp. 195-202; "The Rise of Man," pp. 381-405.

ROGERS, CARL L. *On Becoming A Person.* Boston: Houghton Mifflin, 1961. "A Process Conception of Psychotherapy," Chap. 7, pp. 125-159.

Rostow, W. W. *The Stages of Economic Growth.* New York: Cambridge University Press, 1960.

Watts, Alan W. *The Wisdom of Insecurity.* New York: Pantheon, 1951. "The Great Stream," Chap. 3, pp. 39-54.

Supplementary Readings

Bachelard, Gaston. *The Poetics of Reverie.* Boston: Beacon, 1969.

Bateson, Gregory. *Steps to an Ecology of Mind.* New York: Ballentine, 1972. "The Logical Categories of Learning and Communicating," pp. 278-308.

Foucault, Michel, *The Archaeology of Knowledge.* New York: Pantheon, 1974.

Gattegno, Caleb. *What We Owe Children.* New York: Avon, 1971.

Koestler, Arthur. *The Act of Creation.* New York: The MacMillan Co., 1964.

Maslow, A. H. *The Farther Reaches of Human Nature.* New York: The Viking Press, 1971. Part II: Creativeness, pp. 57-101.

Pearce. Joseph Chilton, *The Magical Child.* New York: Button, 1977.

Rosner, stanley and Abt, Lawrence E., Eds. *The Creative Experience.* New york: Delta, 1972. Interviews with creative individuals in various fields.

Stent, Gunther S. *The Coming Golden Age.* Garden City, N.Y.: Doubleday & Company, Inc., 1969. Chap. 6, pp. 97-121.

Yukawa, Hideki. *Creativity and Intuition.* New York: Kodansha International, 1973. A physicist looks at East and West.

Supplementary Readings by J. Samuel Bois

Breeds of Men: Toward the Adulthood of Humankind, New York: Harper & Row, 1970. Pp. 1-10, 31-47; 57-111.

Epistemics: The Science-Art of Innovating. San Francisco: International Society for General Semantics, 1972. Pp. 2-5, 125-159.

Explorations In Awareness. New York: Harper & Row, 1957. Pp. 94-122; 160-176.

Chapter 11

Suggested Readings

Brillouin. Leon. *Scientific Uncertainty, and Information.* New York: Academic Press, 1964.

Capra, Fritjof. *The Tao of Physics.* Berkeley: Shambhala, 1975.

Dewey, John, and Arthur F. Bentley. *Knowing and the Known.* Boston: Beacon, 1949. "Logic in the Age of Science," pp. 205-32.

Frank, Philip. "The Varieties of Reasons for the Acceptance of Scientific Theories." *Scientific Monthly,* September 1954, pp. 139-45.

Hadamard, Jacques. *The Psychology of Invention in The Mathematical Field.* New York: Dover, 1945.

James, William. *The Principles of Psychology.* New York: Holt, 1950. "The Stream of Thought," Chap. 9, pp. 224-90.

Sarton, George. *The Life of Science.* Bloomington, Ind.: Indiana University Press, 1960. "The History of Science," Chap. 3, pp. 29-58.

Schrödinger, Erwin. *Science, Theory and Man.* New York: Dover, 1957. "Is Science a Fashion of the Times?," Chap. 4, pp. 81-105; "Physical Science and the Temper of the Age," Chap. 5, pp. 106-32.

Siu, R. G. H. *The Tao of Science*. New York: Wiley, 1957. "Historical Forces Behind
    Modern Science," Chap. 2, pp. 5-10; "Why quibble about Words?," Chap. 7,
    pp. 46-56; "The Synthetic Leap," Chap. 14, pp. 135-44; "The Philosopher-
    Executive," Chap. 15, pp. 145-58.
Weinberg, Harry. *Levels of Knowing and Existence*. New York: Harper & Row, 1959.
    "Some Basic Concepts," Chap. 2, pp. 15-33; "Some Limitations of Language,"
    Chap. 3, pp. 34-47; "The Abstracting Process," Chap. 4, pp. 48-76.
Whitehead, Alfred North. *The Aims of Education*. New York: Mentor Books (New
    American Library), 1949. "Space, Time, Relativity," Chap. 10, pp. 156-66.

Supplementary Readings

Cantril, Hadley. *the Morning Notes of Adelbert Ames, Jr.* New Brunswick, N.J.:
    Rutgers University Press, 1960. "Form World," pp. 81-93.
Conant, J. B. *Science and Common Sense*. New Haven, Conn.: Yale University
    Press, 1951.
Fuller, R. Buckminster. *Synergetics*. New York: MacMillan, 1975.
Hanson, N. R. *Patterns of Discovery*. New York: Cambridge University Press, 1958.
    P. 118 f.
Hunley, Aldous. *Literature and Science*. New York: Harper & Row, 1963. Pp. 89-95.
Kelly, George A. "Man's Construction of his Alternatives." In *Clinical Psychology
    and Personality*, edited by Brendan Maher. New York: John Wiley & Sons, Inc.,
    1969. Pp. 66-93.
Kuhn, Thomas. *The Structure of Scientific Revolutions*. Chicago: University of
    Chicago Press, 1962 and 1970.
Maslow, Abraham H. *The Psychology of Science*. New York: Harper & Row, 1966.
Morgenthau, Hans J. *Scientific Man versus Power Politics*. Chicago: University of
    Chicago Press, 1947.
Needham, Joseph. *Science and Civilization in China*. New York: Cambridge Univer-
    sity Press, 1956. Vol. 2, pp. 200-201.
Ornstein, Robert E., Ed. *The Nature of Human Consciousness*. New York: Viking,
    1974. Chap. 2, 3, 4, pp. 13-40.
Polanyi, Michael. *Knowing and Being*. University of Chicago, 1969.
Russell, Bertrand. "On the Notion of Cause." In *Readings in the Philosophy of
    Science*, edited by Feigl and Brodbeck. New York: Appleton-Century-Crofts,
    1953. Pp. 387-407.
Thompson, William Irwin. *Evil and World Order*. New York: Harper & Row, 1976.
Whitehead, A. N., *Science and the Modern World*. New York: Cambridge Univer-
    sity Press, 1933. Pp. 25-26.

Supplementary Readings by J. Samuel Bois

Breeds of Men: Toward the Adulthood of Humankind. New York: Harper & Row,
    1970. Pp. 23-30.
Epistemics: The Science-Art of Innovating. San Francisco: ISGS, 1972. Pp. 91-99.
Explorations In Awareness. New York: Harper & Row, 1957. Pp. 90-93.

Part VI

Chapter 12

Suggested Readings

Boulding, Kenneth. *The Image*. Ann Arbor: University of Michigan Press, 1950. Chaps. 1, 2, 3, pp. 3-46.

Korzybski, Alfred. *Science and Sanity*. Lakeville, Conn.: International Non-Aristotelian Library, 1933 (1st ed.) and 1958 (4th ed.). "On Structure," pp. 56-65.

Linton, Ralph. *The Tree of Culture*. New York: Knopf, 1955. Uses the plant model as the guiding analogy in the study of cultural evolution.

Moore, Ruth. *The Coil of Life*. New York: Knopf, 1961. An excursion into the hidden continent of life seldom explored by the nonbiologist.

Rapoport, Anatol. "Metaphors and Models." In *Operational Philosophy*. New York: Harper & Row, 1953. Chap. 17, pp. 203-15.

Wertheimer, Max. *Productive Thinking*. New York: Harper & Row, 1945. Creative thinking as viewed by a Gestalt Psychologist.

Supplementary Readings

Bateson, Gregory. *Steps to an Ecology of Mind*. New York: Ballantine, 1972. "Problems in Cetacean and other Mammalian Communication," pp. 364-378.

Berrill, N. J. *Man's Emerging Mind*. New York: Premier, Fawcett, 1957. Pp. 51-59.

Gordon, William J. J. *Synectics*. New York: Harper & Row, 1961.

———. *The Metaphorical Way of Learning and Knowing;* edited and researched by T. Poze. Cambridge, Mass.: Porpoise Books, 1971.

Land, George T. Lock, *Grow or Die*. New York: Random House, 1973.

Pearce, Joseph Chilton. *Exploring the Crack in the Cosmic Egg*. New York: Julian Press, 1974.

Turner, Charles Hampden. *Radical Man*. Cambridge, Mass.: Schenkman Publishing Co., Inc., 1971. "The Cryptoconservatism of Technological Thinking," Chap. xi, pp. 303-347.

Supplementary Readings of J. Samuel Bois

Epistemics: The Science-Art of Innovating. San Francisco: International Society for General Semantics, 1972. Pp. 77-89.

Explorations In Awareness. New York: Harper & Row, 1957. Pp. 6-13.

Chapter 13

Suggested Readings

Kluckhohn, Clyde. *Mirror for Man*. New York: McGraw-Hill, 1949.

Linssen, Robert. *Living Zen*. New York: Grove, 1960. An introduction to Eastern philosophy for Westerners.

Thompson, Laura. *Culture in Crisis*. New York: Harper & Row, 1950. An analysis of the basic ideologies that are pressing on the Hopi culture from the outside world.

WHORF, BENJAMIN L. *Language, Thought, and Reality*. Edited by J. B. Carroll. New York: Wiley, 1956. A classic on the relations between language and thought.

Supplementary Readings

CASTANEDA, CARLOS. *The Teachings of don Juan*. New York: Ballantine Books, 1969.
———. *A Separate Reality*. New York: Simon & Schuster, 1971.
———. *Journey to Ixtlan*. New York: Simon & Schuster, 1972.
GUNNELL, JOHN G. *Political Philosophy and Time*. Middletown, Conn.: Wesleyan University Press, 1968. "Symbols and Society," pp. 3-10.
HALL, EDWARD T. *Beyond Culture*. New York: Anchor/Doubleday, 1976.

Supplementary Readings of J. Samuel Bois

Epistemics: The Science-Art of Innovating. San Francisco: ISGG. 1972. Pp. 143-145.
Exploration In Awareness. New York: Harper & Row, 1957. Pp. 14-18.

Part VII

Chapter 14

Suggested Readings

ALEXANDER, F. M. *Man's Supreme Inheritance*. "Introduction" by John Dewey. London: Methuen, 1918.
———. *The Resurrection of the Body*. New York: Delta, 1969.
DEWEY, JOHN. *Human Nature and Conduct*. New York: Modern Library (Random House), 1930. "Habits and Will," Chap. 2, pp. 24-42.
HALL, CALVIN S. AND LINDZEY GARDNER. *Theories of Personality*, New York: Wiley, 1957.
JACOBSON, EDMUND. *You Must Relax*. New York: McGraw-Hill, 1948.
KORZYBSKI, ALFRED. *Science and Sanity*. Lakeville, Conn.: International Non-Aristotelian Library, 1933 (1st ed.) and 1958 (4th ed.). "Non-Aristotelian Standards of Evaluation," pp. 555-57.
MASLOW, ABRAHAM. *Motivation and Personality*. New York: Harper & Row, 1955.
———. "Eupsychia—The Good Society." *Journal of Humanistic Psychology* (Fall 1961), pp. 1-11.
MORGAN, LOUISE. *Inside Yourself*. London: Hutchison, 1954. A popular and enthusiastic account of F. M. Alexander's work.
MURPHY, GARDNER. *Human Potentialities*. New York: Basic Books, 1958.
ROGERS, CARL L. *On Becoming A Person*. Boston: Houghton-Mifflin, 1961.
TOMKINS, SYLVAN S. *Affect, Imagery, Consciousness*, New York: Springer, 1962 (vol. I) and 1963 (vol. II).

Supplementary Readings

AMES, ADELBERT, JR. *The Morning Notes of Adelbert Ames, Jr.*, edited by Hadley Cantril, New Brunswick, N.J.: Rutgers University Press, 1960. "Experience," p. 12.

CANTRIL, HADLEY. "Sentio, Ergo Sum: Motivation Reconsidered." *General Semantics Bulletin*, Institute of General Semantics, Lakeville, Conn., no. 34, (1967).

LANGER, SUSANNE K. *Philosophical Sketches*. New York: Mentor Books, 1964. Chap. 5, pp. 75-84.

MASLOW, ABRAHAM H. *The Farther Reaches of Human Nature*. New York: The Viking Press, 1971. "Fusions of Facts and Values," Chap. 8, pp. 105-125; "Theory Z," Chap. 22, pp. 280-295; "A Theory of Metamotivation," Chap. 23, pp. 299, 340.

LIFTON, ROBERT J. *The Life of the Self*. New York: Simon & Schuster, 1976.

MURPHY, GARDNER. *Outgrowing Self-Deception*. New York: Basic Books, 1975. Chap. 6, pp. 61-83.

———. *Personality: A Biosocial Approach to Origins and Structure*. New York: Harper & Row, 1947. "The Skeptical Psychologist," Chap. 41, pp. 914-927.

SKORPEN, ERLING. "The Real Swingers." *Main Currents in Modern Thought* 23 (March-April 1967): 87-92.

TART, CHARLES. *Transpersonal Psychologies*. New York: Harper & Row, 1975. Chap. 2 contains a listing of some of the basic assumptions of Orthodox, Western Psychology as compared to the "spiritual psychologies."

WILSON, COLIN. *New Pathways in Psychology: Maslow and the Post-Freudian Revolution*. New York: Taplinger, 1972.

Supplementary Readings of J. Samuel Bois

Breeds of Men: Toward the Adulthood of Humanity. New York: Harper & Row, 1970. Pp. 3-11; 31-40.

Explorations In Awareness. New York: Harper & Row, 1957. Pp. 64-69.

Chapter 15

Suggested Readings

FROMM, ERIC. *The Art of Loving*. New York: Harper & Row, 1956.

JONES, FRANK PIERCE. "A Mechanism for Change." In *Forms and Techniques of Altruistic and Spiritual Growth* by Sorokin (*see* below). pp. 177-87.

MONTAGU, ASHLEY. *The Direction of Human Development*. New York: Harper & Row, 1955.

MUMFORD, LEWIS. *The Transformation of Man*. New York: Collier Books, 1962, pp. 175-76.

SOROKIN, PITIRIM A. *Explorations in Altruistic Love and Behavior*. Boston: Beacon, 1954.

———. *Forms and Techniques of Altruistic and Spiritual Growth*. Boston: Beacon, 1954.

———. *The Ways and Power of Love*. Boston: Beacon, 1954.

TEILHARD DE CHARDIN, PIERRE. *The Future of Man*. New York: Harper & Row, 1964. "The Grand Option," Chap. 3, pp. 37-60; "The Formation of the Noösphere," Chap. 10, pp. 155-84; "Faith in Man," Chap. 11, pp. 185-92.

WATTS, ALAN W. *Nature, Man and Woman*. New York: Mentor Books, 1958.

WHYTE, LANCELOT L. *The Next Development in Man*. New York: Mentor Books, 1949. Chap. 3, pp. 31-53.

WILLEY, BASIL. *The 17th Century Background*. New York: Anchor Doubleday, 1952, p. 79.

Supplementary Readings

Montagu, Ashley. *The Practice of Love.* Englewood Cliffs, N.J : Prentice Hall, 1975.

Needleman, Jacob. *A Sense of the Cosmos.* New York: Doubleday, 1975. Pp. 119-134.

Supplementary Readings of J. Samuel Bois

Breeds of Men: Toward the Adulthood of Humankind. New York: Harper & Row, 1970. Pp. 113-123.

Epistemics: The Science-Art of Innovating. San Francisco: International Society for General Semantics, 1972. Pp. 109-111.

Explorations In Awareness. New York: Harper & Row, 1957. Pp. 193-198.

Part VIII

Chapters 16 and 17

Suggested Readings

Perls, Frederick *et al. Gestalt Therapy.* New York: Julian Press, 1951.

Weinberg, Harry L. *Levels of Knowing and Existence.* New York: Harper & Row, 1959. "Semantic Therapy," Chap. 8, pp. 177-212.

Supplementary Readings

Castenada, Carlos. *Tales of Power.* New York: Simon & Schuster, 1974. "The Sorcerers' Explanation," part three, pp. 209-287.

Maslow, Abraham H. *The Farther Reaches of Human Nature.* New York: The Viking Press, 1971. "Synergy in The Society and The Individual," Chap. 14, pp. 199-211.

McCay, James T. *The Management of Time.* Englewood Cliffs, N.J : Prentice-Hall, 1959. "Shielding Your Energy," pp. 63-70.

Murphy, Gardner. *Outgrowing Self-Deception.* New York: Basic Books, 1975. "The Emergence of Self-Awareness," Chap. 3, pp. 24-34; "Everyday Ways of Coping With Self-Deception," Chap. 8, pp. 100-116; Chap. 10-11, pp. 132-164.

Rajneesh, Bhagwan Shree. *Meditation: The Art of Ecstacy.* New York: Harper & Row, 1976.

———. *The Book of the Secrets.* New York: Harper & Row, 1974.

Whyte, Lancelot Law. *The Unconscious Before Freud.* New York: Anchor/Doubleday, 1962. "Conscious and Unconscious," Chap. II, pp. 15-26; "The Rise of European Self-Awareness," Chap. III, pp. 27-51.

Supplementary Readings of J. Samuel Bois

Epistemics: The Science-Art of Innovating. San Francisco: International Society for General Semantics, 1972. Pp. 1-9; 77-89; 101-112.

Explorations In Awareness. New York: Harper & Row, 1957. Pp. 183-192.

Part IX

Chapters 18 and 19

Suggested Readings

BUCKE, R. M. *Cosmic Consciousness.* New York: Dutton, 1956. A classic that reached its 18th edition in 1956. Religio-mystical.

PRINCE, RAYMOND AND SAVAGE, CHARLES. "Mystical States and The Concept of Regression." *Psychedelic Review* 8 (1966): 59-81.

SCHROEDINGER, ERWIN. *What is Life?* New York: The Macmillan Co., 1945. Epilogue, pp. 87-91.

SUZUKI, D. T. *Mysticism: Christian and Buddhist.* New York: Harper & Row, 1957. Pp. 51-59.

Supplementary Readings

AUROBINDO, SRI. *The Life Divine.* Pondicherry: Sri Aurobindo Ashram, 1973. Two volumes.

———. *The Mind of Light.* New York: Dutton, 1971.

MASLOW, ABRAHAM, H. *Religions, Values, and Peak Experiences.* New York: Viking 1975 (latest printing).

MERRILL-WOLFF, FRANKLIN. *Pathways Through to Consciousness.* New York: Julian Press, 1973. A personal record of transformation in consciousness.

———. *The Philosophy of Consciousness Without an Object.* New York: Julian Press, 1973.

Supplementary Readings of J. Samuel Bois

Breeds of Men: Toward the Adulthood of Humanity. New York: Harper & Row, 1970. Pp. 112-126.

Epistemics: The Science-Art of Innovating. San Francisco: International Society for General Semantics, 1972. Pp. 161-165.

index of topics

index of
proper names